I0114190

WOMEN OF THE MAFIA

WOMEN OF THE MAFIA

Power and Influence in
the Neapolitan Camorra

Felia Allum

CORNELL UNIVERSITY PRESS   **ITHACA AND LONDON**

Copyright © 2024 by Cornell University

All rights reserved. Except for brief quotations in a review, this book, or parts thereof, must not be reproduced in any form without permission in writing from the publisher. For information, address Cornell University Press, Sage House, 512 East State Street, Ithaca, New York 14850. Visit our website at cornellpress.cornell.edu.

First published 2024 by Cornell University Press

Library of Congress Cataloging-in-Publication Data
Names: Allum, Felia, 1971– author.
Title: Women of the Mafia : power and influence in the Neapolitan Camorra / Felia Allum.
Description: Ithaca : Cornell University Press, 2024. | Includes bibliographical references and index.
Identifiers: LCCN 2023040577 (print) | LCCN 2023040578 (ebook) | ISBN 9781501774799 (hardcover) | ISBN 9781501774805 (pdf) | ISBN 9781501774812 (epub)
Subjects: LCSH: Camorra—History—20th century. | Women and the mafia—Italy—Naples. | Women—Italy—Naples—Social conditions.
Classification: LCC HV6452.4.I8 .A558 2024 (print) | LCC HV6452.4.I8 (ebook) | DDC 364.1060945/731—dc23/eng/20240110
LC record available at https://lccn.loc.gov/2023040577
LC ebook record available at https://lccn.loc.gov/2023040578

This work is dedicated to Mirabelle, Mimi, and Amadis, Ami, and their agency as they represent hope for the future.
But,
it is also in fond memory of two people who are no longer with us: antimafia prosecutor Filippo Beatrice (1959–2018), whose conversations and humanity I miss, and to my dad, Percy Allum (1933–2022), whose smile, kindness, and advice I miss too.

We cannot make sense of our stories . . . or ourselves . . . if we refuse to look at half of the picture. Or, worse, don't even notice half of it is missing.

—Natalie Haynes, *Pandora's Jar*

Io nun'sò fess ma facc'ò fess pecchè facenn' o fess' te facc fess
[I am no fool, but I play the fool, because by playing the fool, I will play you for a fool]

—Pulcinella

Contents

Preface

I now remember that it was in July 1985 that I landed in Naples for the first time at the age of fourteen. I was a curious teenager on my way to Anacapri as part of a summer language exchange to improve my basic Italian. My parents hoped that I would develop my language skills and see a bit of Italy. In time, I would do both, and more.

I should have realized back then that those couple of hours spent in Naples, transiting from the airport to the ferry port in the company of an illustrious university professor, my father's friend, were going to be the precursor to my future relationship with this big, vibrant cosmopolitan city. Naples appeared to me as contradictory, macho, virile, oppressive, threatening, daunting, lively, formidable, friendly, human, and so beautiful.

The summer of 1985 and those that followed were spent observing this friendly but foreign and alien world. I was a shy teenager in a male domain. I noticed that the Italian boys and men had power at the bar and dinner tables during heated discussions; likewise, they held forth at the beach and at parties. I failed to understand why they were allowed to talk more than the girls and women. In time, this world would become more familiar but never really mine; I was not only a foreigner but also a young woman in a changing Neapolitan environment. Even today, culturally, I remain an outsider insider seeking to study and to analyze this society as a participant observer but with my own non-Neapolitan female eyes.

I have frequently visited Naples since that summer as a girlfriend, university student, language teacher, researcher, visiting lecturer, mother, wedding guest, football supporter, concert goer, and university professor but, above all, as a white Anglo-French woman. I have gotten to know the language and the local culture well and also the city with its different districts: the center, the periphery and its diverse spaces, locations, markets, roads, squares, alleyways, motorways, parks, monuments, and churches.

My Neapolitan boyfriend became my husband. I therefore gained a Neapolitan family and a Neapolitan mother-in-law. I have continually tried to enter my husband's world but have always remained on the margins and on the outside of the hub as a foreign woman, greatly respected but kept at a distance. I still do not understand why every time I enter a fruit and vegetable shop with my husband, a few steps behind him, the *fruttivendolo*, fruit seller, addresses him as "Professore" and me simply as "Signora," without further interest in understanding who, what, and why I am! I pass as an irrelevant footnote to the man because in Naples "women's voices are not being heard [or noticed] in the public sphere."[1] This has allowed me to develop a very critical eye and a detached but interested over-view of the role of Neapolitan women in civil society, especially as I observe my sister-in-law fighting hard to have children and a career or my close girlfriends who have had to work twice as hard as their male counterparts to become full university professors.

As an English undergraduate studying politics and speaking French and Italian, I became interested in the politics and society of France and Italy. I became intrigued by the Italian mafia phenomenon and, in particular, the Neapolitan Mafia, the Camorra, the dark and dangerous underworld of the city of Naples. My father had written a book on clientelism and poli-tics in Naples during the 1950–70s but had dedicated only half a page to the Camorra.[2] His lack of attention and detailed reflection about the Camorra initially motivated me to focus my own research on this criminal subsystem, and I have since become curious and passionate about analyzing and trying to understand it better and what makes it function. However, I retained my own lens looking at the physical, socioeconomic, cultural, and political space occupied by Camorra clans.

Early in my career, I focused on trying to uncover and analyze the Camorra and its political functions and relationships during the postwar period, while quietly noting that women were systematically absent in most books, academic research, and judicial files.[3] By the time I came to study the Camorra again in 2010, this time with a specific interest in looking at its presence and activities in Europe, women were now part of the media stories, public discourse, and judi-cial investigations, although still in a very limited way.[4] The increased number of women who were now antimafia prosecutors and police officers had clearly helped to change the focus in anti-Camorra investigations.

However, we still do not really understand the agency and power relations of women in the Camorra. One female antimafia prosecutor in Naples recently offered an insight into this issue when she explained to me how she was viewed by Camorra women. She was working on a case with a male colleague. He was accosted in the courthouse by a woman whom they were prosecuting for Camorra association. She said: "*You are so great! But your female colleague is 'an utter b****h!'*"[5] This did not surprise me as it summed up succinctly the behavior and view held by women who orbit the Camorra. They do not like women investigators, because they clearly see women criminals for what they are, whereas male prosecutors still have difficulties in untangling women's apparent traditional roles and their sexual power from their real criminal and economic influence.

Another case reaffirmed this confused picture during a visit to the Naples courthouse in 2019. I walked into the big court building. There are three different entrances, one for the general public and lawyers, one for journalists, and another one for prosecutors. There are varying types of courtrooms; the different sizes and shapes are allocated according to the crimes. That day, the case I came for was taking place in Courtroom 414 on the third and last floor of the modern courthouse building. Here, the courtrooms are rather small, compared with the more official and large ones on the ground floor, with ample space for prisoners to have cells and a floor with a public gallery, where criminal trials for serious and mafia-type crimes take place. None of this was available, however, in Courtroom 414; it was simply an intimate courtroom for a minor trial, or so it seemed.

The *capitano* of the Carabinieri, who had investigated the case, was asked to come over and to explain it to me. He stated that the seven accused had been charged with being members of the Genidoni-Esposito clan ("mafia association") and for having tried to take over a new drugs and firearms market, which had cost the lives of rivals. This clan represented the latest generation of Camorra gangs: it used extreme violence to impose its power in districts where there were power vacuums. The capitano explained to me the new characteristics of these types of groups, their criminal dynamics, and how violence had come to dominate. He talked about pure brutality, lack of respect and rules, and an absence of traditional values. He concluded that "*the Camorra is dead. This clan is not Camorra.*" In a previous trial, these individuals had already been found guilty of murder. They were responsible for carrying out the *Strage delle Fontanelle*, the Massacre of the Fontanelle, in 2016, in the Sanità district (see figure I.1).[6] This was a retaliation attack where one person was killed and another injured. Everything appeared to be clear-cut and coherent in his summary of the case.

I went home and looked up the case to find that two of the accused were, in fact, women. They were the leaders of the clan and the instigators of the violent raids, particularly the mother, who had lost her husband and son in a previous attack. Labeled by the local newspaper "Mamma Camorra" (Mother Camorra), her reaction had been extreme;[7] she desired revenge at any cost for her men's' lives but also she wanted a territory.[8] Following the murders, she had suggested that if she went into the street, the rival clan would come for her because she was a woman.[9] This episode in that Naples courtroom got me thinking again: Were Camorra women small shadows or even, to use Ferrell's term, just "ghosts"?[10]

My initial hunch was that Italian investigators were still not looking for women and that they were underestimating their intelligence, skills, shrewdness, and violent streaks. I realized I was still being confronted with the masculinization of the Camorra and Italian mafias. The authorities were not giving them their due and the recognition that they deserved. This was a gender issue.[11] And maybe the roles of men had actually been conflated and exaggerated. The penny then dropped: women were invisible to them, as they have been throughout history.[12]

Another way of looking at this is to think about a photograph of organized crime. It depicts members of the criminal underworld, and the only visible clear faces and shapes are male. The men are the principal and only focus of the photograph while the women are there but their voices, faces, shapes blur into the background, into the shadows and edges of the photograph, in this way becoming invisible and hidden. This reinforces what the American criminologist Joanna Belknap noted in 2001: "I am struck by the recurring theme of women's and girls' everyday invisibility in society, in crime and in the crime-processing system. If women are represented, it is often in stereotypical, passive, and sexual images. . . . When women are made visible, it is often in stereotypical and offensive ways."[13] The same can be said for women in the Camorra as gender inequality is regularly mentioned with women portrayed in dismissive or exceptional terms.

I believe that generally, reflecting dominant social gender identities, women involved in organized crime groups (OCGs) have always been perceived by criminologists, civil society, and law enforcement agencies as "passive," "marginal," and "irrelevant," or as "victims."

Negative stereotypes have also developed around female criminals, evidenced by their being referred to as "bad girls," "tomboys," "sluts" ("skeets"), "devils," or "unruly women." With respect to the Camorra, such labels include "Camorra molls," "Camorra suffragettes," or "Camorra babes."[14] By doing this, Nagaire Naffine believes that "contemporary criminologists continue to expunge the agency of women. . . . Criminologists have failed to canvass the possibility that women may both accommodate and resist admonitions to adopt traditionally feminine characteristics and values."[15]

Indeed, these male labels and assigned traditional sex and gender identities do not help, because they distract or appease us from wanting to understand further the complexities of the issue of female criminal agency. What if, in fact, women have been present and active all the time in criminal organizations? What if, in this specific case, the gender gap was a mere illusion? As Raewyn Connell argues, "In the academic world, generations of researchers, in the teeth of the evidence their own disciplines have produced, have gone on relentlessly searching for, and writing about, psychological gender differences."[16] In other words, it could even be suggested that academics sometimes do not take the evidence into account when it is there in front of them. What if the gender differences were not so clear cut? What if, contrary to what many have argued, the glass ceiling shutting females out of the top spots in crime groups did not exist? I want to understand whether this is the case or not.

So, I asked myself whether Camorra women were present or absent, active or passive, "Madonnas" or "whores," and to what extent, if we follow the established narrative, they are both absent and passive.[17] I asked myself does the criminal organization treat them differently because of their gender. Does it block, impede, and obstruct their existence or their advancement in the crime group by default or design? Does it consciously discriminate between men and women? Is the Camorra, therefore, sexist? Or would it be an oversimplification to say this?

My approach is nuanced: by taking into account structure and agency, I try to identify and describe the Camorra's gender regime within its local context to understand the more subtle gender power dynamics at play.[18] My evidence leads me to suggest that women have criminal agency and the capabilities to act independent of the men. They can influence and shape male behavior.[19] They *can* be equal partners to their men in this criminal underworld and that the Camorra is not automatically, nor systematically, sexist.

In this interpretative study, I examine the roles of and space for women in the Camorra to try and fill in the blurred faces in the photograph where, up until now, there have been only men. I want to flesh out the missing half of the Neapolitan Underworld. In other words, I "engender" the study of the Neapolitan Camorra by looking at the women to illustrate their interactions, relationships, and engagement with Camorra members and their criminal projects and encourage all those who study mafia/organized crime to include women as part of their mainstream analysis and not as an afterthought, which tends to still be the case. But what I also end up doing is questioning our construction of gender roles and gender power dynamics in Naples and elsewhere.

Acknowledgments

This is a book that has been a long time coming, but thanks to COVID and the first lockdown in March 2020, it was written before I thought I would write it, before it was scheduled in my head! In a strange way, COVID allowed me to write about this subject, which has been part of me since I first started to focus on the Neapolitan Camorra back in the early 1990s. Finally, I had the time, as an outsider and a foreign woman researcher who has an intimate relationship with the city, to go deeper into my relationship with Naples, the Camorra, and Camorra women.

In 2017, I was awarded a Leverhulme Major Research Fellowship to study the role of women in transnational organized crime groups (TOCGs), and I thought I would include my analysis about the Neapolitan Camorra in this general comparative study. However, it soon dawned on me that this would not do justice to the question of Camorra women, especially with all the material I had collected and continued to collect. COVID closed down my ethnographic interviews for my research on TOCGs, so I settled down at home and wrote this book.

My research on organized crime and mafias continues to be a journey, not only one of the social and criminal dynamics but also one of self-discovery and self-reflection. Every time one starts a piece of research, one cannot remain neutral or indifferent. You keep your distance, but it makes you reflect about yourself. This study about women in the Camorra is very personal, because it is also about my existence as a woman in Naples, which runs parallel to the lives of everyday women of the Camorra.

I will remain forever grateful to the Leverhulme Trust for their Major Research Fellowship (2018–23), which gave me the opportunity to do so much fieldwork, collect new material, and reflect about some important questions in relation to gender, organized crime, and Italian mafias. The time it gave me to think and meet new communities, practitioners, and networks has been invaluable.

I thank my different Neapolitan communities for sharing their lives with me but also for putting up with me and my inquisitive questions. I thank them wholeheartedly for listening and reflecting with me about these complex issues. I also thank all those who fight the Camorra every day, especially the local journalists who report on the Camorra's daily activities and power; we never celebrate their hard work enough. Through their work, I discovered in particular the story of Anna Sodano, who was murdered by the Sarno clan because she no longer wanted to carry on selling drugs for them. She was good at it but she wanted out. Her only way out was to collaborate with the state, but clan members managed to intercept her and make her disappear.[20] I have often thought about her during my reflections, as life remains complicated and brutish in the Neapolitan mafia.

There are a lot of people who have contributed and continue to contribute to my research and thinking about the Camorra over the years. I thank all of them (but will no doubt forget some). First of all, I thank the local community groups I engaged with: Angelica Viola and the cooperative Orsa Maggiore in Rione Traiano; Suore Michelina, Suore Rita, and the Centro Shalom at the Torretta; Sivlia Piccirillo and the personnel of 31st Istituto Comprensivo Paolo Borsellino, Via Enrico Cosenz, Naples, for their time, care, and availability to me. Thanks to the personnel of the Italian Parliamentary Antimafia Commission in Rome, especially Francesco Comparone, and of the newspaper library, l'Emeroteca Tucci in Naples, for their material and help.

I thank the six former Camorra women who agreed to talk to me during the last fifteen years. Our encounters were unique moments for me. I have kept them anonymous (although this was not a prerequisite, and elsewhere I have written about them using their names). But here, it felt right to do it this way. During these various research projects, I have also collected "informants" (privileged observers is perhaps a better term): individuals who previously frequented a criminal space and who now have turned their back on it and shared their thoughts, experiences, and recollections with me. Teresa and Lucia were particularly kind to open up and share with me their life experiences. GP, MA, and EM have all been patient and kind to answer what might often appeared as stupid or strange questions. I thank them all. They did not have to engage with me.

Thanks also to the personnel of the different law enforcement agencies I have interacted with. Thanks to La Procura di Napoli, the prosecutor's office and all the secretariats (le cancellerie) who have had to deal with me, all the personnel from the different police forces: the Guardia di Finanza (GICO, Napoli), La Squadra Mobile (Questura di Napoli), I Carabinieri, and the DIA. Special thanks to Massimo Astrita and his team (Polizia di Stato), Mag Adolfo Angelosanto (Carabinieri), Col. Emilio Fiora (Guardia di Finanza), Col. Carmine Iuliano (Guardia di Finanza), and Col. Tommaso Solazzo. A big thank you to the antimafia prosecutors of the DDA in Naples who were so generous with their time and material with me. In particular, the antimafia prosecutors Giovanni Corona, Armando D'Altiero, Michele del Prete, Marco del Gaudio, Mariella Di Mauro, Pierpaolo Filippelli, Antonella Fratello, Ida Frongillo, Catello Maresca, and Rosa Volpa. A special thanks to the prosecutors Giovanni Melillo and Giuseppe Borrelli, who have always been more than generous with their time, material, and thoughts.

A big thank you to my colleagues Elaine Carey, Luciano Brancaccio, Alessandro Colletti, Annarita Criscitello, Ernesto Di Nito, Adalgisa Giorgio, Marisa Iorio, Giovanni Izzo, Isaia Sales, Lello Mazzacane, and Antonio Nicaso, who have looked out for me and always accommodated my requests.

I would like to thank my mother, Marie-Pierrette, for her time, support, assistance, and kindness. She is one in a million. A big thank you to my extended Neapolitan family, Piero, Margherita, Matilde, Kika, Andrea, Antonella, Chiara, and Francesco for their thoughts and sharing their everyday lives with me but also to my mother-in-law, Matilde Rajola-Pescarini who has shared her life, experiences, and memories with me over the last twenty-five years. Thanks to Adele Lauria, Julia Molinari, and Renata Spagnuolo Vigorita for their constant friendship, care, and love, and all my Neapolitan friends who over the years have allowed me to understand aspects of Naples that without them, I would not have, especially Ferdinando Calogero, Rosanna D'Amore, Alfredo De Dominicis, and Marguerita Ruopolo.

Thanks to Stasha, my Neapolitan partner, for being there and our ongoing bi/tri-cultural discussions, debates, and arguments. And my daughters, Mimi and Ami, for their encouragement, love, and joie de vivre. They are my sunshine.

Thank you to Felicity McMahon for her thorough libel read of my text and to Alessandra Diagne for her translations and transcriptions of my interviews. Thanks to Anna Mitchell for her maps and all the team at Cornell University Press, especially Jim Lance, Clare Jones, and the two anonymous reviewers for their insightful and helpful comments. All mistakes are mine and mine alone.

One last thought and thanks to Filippo Beatrice and Percy Allum—two great thinkers and inspiring and modest men whose love for Naples I hope to have done justice in these pages. Who knows what they would have made of it all. Gone but not forgotten.

Note on Translation, Interviews, and Sources

Translations

My interviews with former Camorra members now state witnesses were transcribed and translated into English by a professional translator. I translated the academic articles, books, judicial, and police material into English and got it checked where and when possible.

Anonymity

Since this text analyses what appears to be criminal behavior, I have sought to change some names and identities in order to tell their story without implying any wrongdoing. It is in no way my intention to harm the reputation or accuse individuals of criminal behavior, rather it is to tell their stories. All individuals are to be considered innocent unless otherwise indicated.

Consent

All my interviews have been conducted following the appropriate ethnical procedures.

Referencing Sources

In the bibliography are judicial and police documents that have informed my analysis but which I have not used for quotations. These show the nature and depth of the material used for the writing of this book.

Acronyms

DDA	Direzione Distrettuale Antimafia (Local Antimafia Prosecution Service)
DIA	Direzione Investigative Antimafia (Antimafia Investigation Directorate)
DNAA	Direzione Nazionale Antimafia e Antiterrorismo (Italian National Antimafia and Antiterrorism Directorate)
EU	European Union
NCA	National Crime Agency
NCO	Nuova Camorra Organizzata (New Organized Camorra led by Raffaele Cutolo)
NF	Nuova Famiglia (New Family, an anti-Cutolo alliance)
OCG	organized crime group
TOC	transnational organized crime
TOCGs	transnational organized crime groups

WOMEN OF THE MAFIA

INTRODUCTION
À la recherche des femmes

When you walk around Naples, you don't feel that you are in a unified city but rather that you are passing through many different villages, each with its own singular architecture, streets, churches, customs, identity, history, and Camorra clan. Secondigliano feels very distinct from La Sanità, the Vomero Alto very far from I Quartieri Spagnoli. But there is one constant: the presence of the Neapolitan Camorra and its women. Women in the Neapolitan Camorra are rarely "seen" and, thus, are considered by many as "irrelevant" and "marginal."[1] I have always been skeptical about this so-called invisibility and glass ceiling"/"glass elevator that is supposed to block women.[2] This is what I investigate in this book: women in the criminal world of the Camorra, and in this introductory chapter I explain the context of my analysis.

The Neapolitan Camorra is one of Italy's four homegrown and traditional, so-called men only mafias. Recently made famous by Roberto Saviano's writings, documentaries, and films, it was originally based in the city of Naples (see Figure I.1 map). Now it is present across the whole of the Campania region, with its deep historic roots, its social consensus among the local community, its hands-on economic activities (whether illegal or legal), and its access to the political establishment.[3] The Camorra is a criminal organization that is less structured and more fragmented than its Calabrian and Sicilian counterparts.[4] Today, however, the Camorra is made up of many families who are allied and work under the protection of two main and historic groups—the Secondigliano Alliance and the Mazzarella clan who control and sponsor all activities across the city; there is also the smaller Amato-Pagano group, which manages to survive within this context.[5] These two main local intergroup structures have been described as con-federations, where families have a certain amount of independence but still have to answer to the two main alliances. These crime groups retain power as effi-cient moneymaking machines with a strong cultural identity. However, Camorra women are regularly taken for granted and not considered significant players in these groups.

Naples and Campania differ from Sicily and Calabria. Neapolitan women have always had different roles and experiences compared to their Calabrian and Sicilian counterparts.[6] See, for example, the importance of Maria Lorenza Longo who founded social welfare institutions in the sixteenth century; Eleonora Pia-mentel Fonseca who was one of the leading figures of the Neapolitan Republic in eighteenth century; or Matilde Serao, a journalist and novelist of the nineteenth century who was the first woman to edit an Italian newspaper.[7] So, perhaps the local context shapes and influences criminal behavior more than we think.

However, some have argued that the existing gender inequality in Italian mafias is due to the nature of the traditional gender norms, crime group struc-tures and markets, which explains why women in the Camorra have always been considered to be more involved compared to the Sicilian Cosa Nostra and the Calabrian 'Ndrangheta. It is the loose structure of the clans and the Camorra's origin as a criminal urban phenomenon that can explain women's greater crimi-nal participation.[8] As a result, it has been argued that there are always more gaps for Neapolitan women to fill but never as independent players. They may also have benefited from a general wave of emancipation in civil society during the 1970s but always in relation to a man.[9] Again, in these explanations, it is argued that Camorra women do not have their own agency, but only become empow-ered thanks to their men and do have no autonomous power of their own. They are still depicted in distinct binary roles; they can either be good or evil, violent or passive, but this is also too polarized and does not consider women as equals. Like Hume and Wilding as well as Guiterrez Rivera and Delgado Mejia, I believe that it is necessary and fundamental to "go beyond the 'passive/agency binary'" to understand women's roles and capabilities in organized criminal groups.[10]

Another way of looking at women in the Camorra is to see them as a reserve team, or in Beatrice's phrasing, "The *camorriste* are for the clan, a kind of 'luxury reserve.' They are held on the bench until as long as possible and then, when the game becomes more difficult, in other words when the boss dies or ends up in prison, she is then able to manage the criminal affairs of the group."[11]

I had previously found some of these notions useful and convincing: first, the idea that Camorra women had become more active and visible in clans because of increased female emancipation in Neapolitan civil society.[12] And then, I was taken by Beatrice's idea of "reserve" or "B-Team" and so came to argue that

Camorra women acted as "a reserve army" because they took up leadership roles only when their men were sent to prison, but they remained linked to them.[13]

Women were also helped by the laws of harsh prison conditions (Law 41-bis) that limits the number of visitors and can make the wife the main interlocutor. According to this explanation, women were always present in the background, ready to step in to take over leadership positions when necessary, but as male substitutes only. More recently, a Camorra insider defined the wives of Camorra bosses as their "avatars" once the men were sent to prison, reinforcing the idea that women lack agency in the Camorra space and just do what their men tell them to do.[14]

Now, however, I believe that these approaches are limited and that they do not really highlight the complexities and depths of the situation; specifically, the constant presence, active involvement, and significant influence of women in the Camorra. It also continues to ignore their independent criminal agency. Furthermore, I was struck by the fact that the official police and judicial documents I was collecting were shaped by a heavy male bias that projected a traditional image of Camorra women in obedient and submissive gender roles at the margins of mainstream criminal life and organization. Camorra women have systematically been neglected by an established male narrative that gives no substance to their voices or lives and has exaggerated the importance of men.

I had never quite fully digested this crucial factor: there is a constant unconscious male filter in most police reports, judicial investigations, and newspaper articles. Men in law enforcement agencies gather data to make a case in court, to prosecute a crime rather than understand the whole picture and the power dynamics between actors. Therefore, I believe they do not see the women or pay little attention to them or their power. The clans are aware of this: for example, women from the D'Amico clan from Ponticelli would regularly pick up drug doses from other districts to sell or they would accompany male members around in cars to reduce the possible "suspicion" from law enforcement agencies who were looking on.[15] Thus, if these law enforcement agencies focus solely on the men in their reports and their trials, women become unimportant, irrelevant, and powerless. In other words, these women are systematically perceived as agency-less. This then becomes part of a master narrative that shapes the public consciousness.[16]

My new research suggests that a substantial disjunction exists between rhetoric and reality and that women in the Neapolitan Camorra are key players at all levels, even though patriarchal structures dominate civil society, culture, politics, the economy, and law enforcement agencies. Belmonte had already noted this intricate power dynamics in the 1970s when he wrote, "In Naples . . . women were not docile wives of Italian myth. . . . They did not stand by silently, a few paces behind their husbands, ready unconditionally to serve. They were not shut away from the world, in the isolated darkness of their homes. They were defiant women, ready to challenge any man's decisions if they judged them unwise."[17]

The evidence was compelling: underneath the dominant male narrative and structures, there were lots of active women participating in Camorra clans and activities during the whole of the postwar period (and even before). They were just omitted, ignored, or not considered central to the criminal act, and it seemed to me that "they were hiding in plain sight."[18] Thus, there was no sudden "pink revolution" nor feminization of the Camorra but continuity of women's involvement.

This male narrative seems at odds with Dumas's words (1854): "Cherchez la femme, pardieu, cherchez la femme!" I followed his words conscientiously and I found them! Literary and artistic references also indicate that history has had a habit of making women invisible as has happened in the academic studies on the Camorra and organized crime in general. A clear blind spot has existed around women. I am thinking of similar cases in different contexts such as, for instance, the role of Catherine Blake, the wife of artist William Blake. In the 2019 Blake exhibition at the Tate Britain in London, her role was clearly highlighted and recognized, she "was his partner in life and work, making, mixing, and applying his paint colors. . . . Catherine was central to Blake's printing and coloring processes . . . the importance of her work at his side has been neglected. . . . She carried out most elements of the design and production with her husband."[19] This illustrates my main point and underlines the existing overlap between intimate family relationships and professional activities, between domesticity and business. As these boundaries are never clear they are constantly ignored in favor of the male narrative and image.

In a similar manner, in this study, I use women's' "unacknowledged daily involvement" in Camorra clans to answer my central question: Is the Camorra sexist?[20] This question allowed me to address other important questions such as what roles do women play in the Camorra? What space do they occupy? How can their involvement be explained? What shapes their roles and their space? And are they explicitly excluded by clan members? This helped me to determine whether these women are in effect irrelevant or equal partners in crime.

But let's take a look at the story of Maria Licciardi who in some way is emblematic of all these disjunctions and contradictions. In 2000, "Italy's most wanted Mamma" made international headlines: "Godmother sends deadly message to her mafia rivals."[21] As the sister of the deceased Camorra boss, Gennaro Licciardi (also known as *A Scigna*, "Monkey"), it was alleged that, while her brothers were on the run/in prison, she was leading and managing the important Secondigliano Alliance and the Licciardi clan.[22] Referred to as *la Piccolina* ("the little Girl/

one") or *Principessa* ("the Princess"), she was described as having "exceptional intelligence, charisma, supernatural calm, the brains of a ruthless tactician. . . . She is a leader. Above all she is a woman."[23]

Former *camorrista*, Gennaro Panzuto who knew Maria personally as he was her bodyguard from time to time, described her as *"greedy and as having a superiority complex which legitimized her sense of entitlement."*[24] He goes on to explain that there was nothing feminine about her in her quest for power and that she was more masculine in her determination. Some would even suggest that she was a "mascuilino," a Neapolitan "alpha male."

In terms of her leadership style, he argues that she *"imposed her authority on clan members who were not happy about it but who accepted it out of devotion for her brother."*[25] The implication is that her leadership was successful not only because she acted as a man adopting masculine traits and values but specifically because she followed in her brother's footsteps. Indeed, from his words and those of others, there is the insinuation that she only accessed this position of supreme power as the leader of the Licciardi clan because as *"the more [male] mafiosi . . . are put away, the more their women fill the vacuum."*[26] In simple terms, she benefitted from "male delegated power."[27] Many accounts give some Camorra women power and agency, but only thanks to and through their male relations. This is a constant and recurring theme.

This portrait of Maria Licciardi, as "an exception" and merely "a male substitute," continues to perpetuate an overall public portrayal of a male-exclusive Camorra (and Italian mafias generally) where women are marginalized or submerged, rarely speak or act in public, and are nullified in public opinion. As a result, they are perceived as being kept out of major criminal activities because they are unable to make decisions or have influence. But is this reality? I wondered many times whether while she was leading the Secondigliano Alliance and directing the Licciardi clan, Maria really was an isolated, lonely female figure filling in for the men, being just "one of the boys"? Or was this a misunderstanding of the situation?

On the other hand, former Licciardi clan member and state witness Gaetano Guida gives an overview of the role of women in local public protests which provides a different perspective: *"Women,"* he argues, *"play a fundamental role, there is no doubt about it. This has always been the case in Secondigliano, in the sense that women (wives, sisters or mothers of leaders) have always had a decisional role, not a secondary role. . . . I can add that there are many activities which 'the women of Secondigliano' undertake: they take messages to prisoners, they distribute salaries to members, they manage directly illegal activities such as illegal lotto or loan sharking. In other words, they are a strength of the organization."*[28] His voice suggests a more nuanced view of the involvement of women in the Camorra, that of "normal" women who do not have "psychopathic traits in their personality set" and who may or may not be born into criminal families.[29]

Mariella Manca, a former Camorra boss, who with her husband, controlled the local drug market in her neighborhood and led the clan when he was imprisoned, explained to me that gender was unimportant when trying to unpack the internal power structures of the Camorra: "*Man or woman, to me they are the same. Nothing changes. . . . It is a person who lays down the law . . . and who is at the top* [of the clan]."[30] What she appears to be suggesting is that traditional sex and gender identities do not matter in terms of roles and responsibilities within the clan, implying that there is no clear gender stratification.

Panzuto's and Guida's different images clearly represent a contrasting view of women in the Camorra: one which, following traditional criminology, either sees women as "mini-men" with male-conferred forms of agency ("bad girls" born into criminal families) or sexual objects looking for social mobility through marriage with a powerful mafia boss to then become traditional homemakers, mothers, and educators. And a contrasting one, which gives women their individual voices, their own criminal agency, and free will to happily cohabit with and in Camorra clans. This contradiction and disjunction between narratives intrigued me, as I have always been interested in understanding real people, their behavior, and activities and not how they are perceived, in particular, by the mainstream media, popular fiction, and civil society.

So, I challenged myself: I would seek out the voices of women who orbited, lived, and navigated in the Camorra space to listen to their personal stories and firsthand accounts as Siebert, Ingrasci, and Dino had done for the Calabrian 'Ndrangheta and the Sicilian Cosa Nostra.[31] I would listen to their words about gender and traditional power dynamics as well as their descriptions of other women who cohabit with the Camorra on a daily basis. This entailed me spending time in the city observing the Camorra world, and interviewing and listening to women talk about their lives and experiences. To tell all the stories that I have collected, and to protect myself and the protagonists, I decided to change the women's names or give their accounts anonymously.[32] In some of the accounts, I decided to omit some personal details and specific anecdotes that could lead to recognition, and I wanted to avoid further problems, including libel.

The criminal world is, after all, hidden, dark, and dangerous, and I realize that my analysis in many places goes beyond the usual judicial and police discourse ("guilty" or "not guilty" of specific crimes) as I seek to develop a more sociological picture of female participation and involvement. Caution is required.

Between 2011 and 2023, I was able to talk to six former Camorra women (*pentite* or *collaboratrice di giustizia*, in English, "state witnesses") whose interviews together with new judicial sentences, police reports, archival work, ethnographic interviews, and participant observations informed my analysis and left me with some strong emotions. Their names have been changed here to let their words speak; each had their own story to tell. Rita Longo, Giorgia Verde, Mariella Manca, Laura Letto, Francesca Francetti, and Angela Giallo had become state witnesses and shared their personal journeys with me: Rita, Giorgia, Mariella as wives and partners; Laura as a daughter; Francesca as a mistress; and Angela as a small-time drug dealer from the rough suburbs.

The main recurring theme in our conversations was that there was more to female criminal involvement than caught the eye, even though some female clan members could not recognize nor articulate this themselves. The words of a female clan member of the D'Amico clan underlined the innate sexism that exists in Neapolitan society, in particular her use of the words "*even though*" and "*only*": "even though *we are only women, we are in charge of the clan, we are in charge of organized crime.*"[33] I soon came to realize that there was general tendency (not only in Italy) of seeing any women involved/close to OCGs as victims and never protagonists in their own right.

Reflecting about women in Camorra groups, Francesca elucidated, "*I don't see them at all as victims. . . . There are women who want to be men.*"[34] Mariella explained the real difference: Women "*are smarter and they have a broader view. . . . If a woman wants something, she gets it.*"[35] And Angela, underlined the delicate wife-husband dynamic, where women always assume a strong role as a wife:

> *You know what your husband is doing. And, you know that today or tomorrow your husband will go to jail, where he will stay for a long time. You have to do what he does. . . . These were the women who, when their partner or husband got arrested, immediately rushed in. Why? Because she has always been there. But she stood still and would say nothing to let her man speak. And, when her man is gone, the woman comes forth . . . because often, men discuss things with their wives: 'What do you think? What do we need to do? What about that?' A woman who is with a boss. . .. always knows everything about her husband. Always, always, always. Even when her husband kills, she knows because she has to know.*[36]

Francesca confirmed this obvious but unacknowledged complicity between *camorristi* and their partners: "*I would see everything. I am no fool. I knew what they were planning at that moment, what they were doing. . . . I knew everything . . . I was aware of everything.*"[37]

Talking about their experiences, the women raised several pertinent gender issues: what is gender stratification? Is there a gender gap? Also to be unpacked were issues of visible power versus invisible power, criminal roles versus criminal spaces, patriarchy versus matriarchy, masculinity versus femininity, individual versus collective, and the victimhood-subjecthood-perpetrators-offenders continuum? Is culture more important than market rationale? Moreover, the more I analyzed the new judicial investigations, the more I interviewed police officers, antimafia prosecutors, social workers, students, church organizations, the more I had to rethink the question of sexism in the Camorra as this new material provided me with enough evidence to reevaluate the role of women.

Therefore, what I set out to do in this book is to write a gendered historiographic account of the modern Camorra and its internal gender dynamics through the biographical stories of women in order to illustrate their influence, power, and importance. What I end up showing is that Neapolitan civil society constructs its idea of gender identity roles in the Camorra while the Camorra itself appears to attach less importance to these traditional roles.

But we must be very careful not to fall into the paradoxical trap that Italian mafias have set for us: on the one hand, as they do not want us to understand the role of women, they play games with us, pretending to exclude or to ignore them. Yet, on the other hand, on closer, more meticulous, inspection, women appear at the heart of the mafia space, business, and activities whether their men are in prison or not; they are not just the "porter, . . . butler, . . . cleaning lady, [or] food suppliers."[38] What comes to the fore is the key role of women in these interconnected human relations and that boundaries are fluid. Indeed, "in setting out their stories as biographies and as accounts of relationships," I hope to show how they are not an irrelevant "footnote to the lives of men" but central to the Camorra.[39] I focus on the women who have been systematically neglected and marginalized and listen to and recount their personal narratives and experiences.

This book is organized to reflect my focus on women and my use of gender as a lens of analysis. What follows is a "her story" position of Camorra women.[40] I follow Scott's approach of analyzing women as historical figures, to "give value to an experience that had been ignored (and hence devalued) and to insist on female agency in the making of history."[41] In this way, I depart "from conventional history and offer[s] a new narrative."[42]

In chapter 1, I present my methodological choices—including my grounded theory approach—while in chapter 2, I analyze the stories and experiences of five women involved with the Camorra from the 1950s through the 1980s to demonstrate the continuity with modern Camorra women. Chapter 3 provides an overview of Camorra women and discussion about them in the "gray zone"; those women who exist in the Camorra Space without having set roles but who are associates, enablers, and facilitators. Chapter 4 explains the Camorra's cultural value system [Camorra culture], in terms of the ideology and tenets in which Camorra women live and act. Chapters 5 to 7 examine the different roles

of women through specific case studies to underline how women are foot soldiers, middle managers, and leaders; they have their own agency which may be
negotiated, but is theirs nevertheless.

In chapter 8, I challenge some of the persistent perceptions we have of these
women that may explain why they are incorrectly written off as irrelevant
"*footnote*[s]."[43] In my conclusion, I reflect on Camorra women and how some
of them have chosen between light and darkness, between love and fear in the
space they live in. The picture that emerges from my research may not be clear cut
enough, not incisive enough, not a crisp enough black-and-white photograph,
but it is a collage with different shades of gray and sometimes colorful passages.
So be it.

For the rest of this chapter, I define the context and actors in this story: Naples
and Campana, the Neapolitan Camorra, Camorra women, and Camorra Space.

Naples and Campania

When I write about Naples, I often forget the importance of its context, what
has been called its "microspace": its physical location and geographical space
and how it is impossible to refer to the Camorra without discussing Naples and
Campania. It is often forgotten that context, space, and location are key to the
Camorra's features as it is for all OCGs. Thus, a very brief overview of Naples and
Campania to provide a background to the existence of the Camorra is helpful.

It has rightly been argued that there is not simply one Camorra, but many
Camorras.[44] There are many different Camorras because of where these groups
develop and take root; the Naples city Camorra is fundamentally different to the
Camorras from the province and places like Casal di Principe or Vallo di Lauro.
The economic, social, cultural, and political features of a context are reflected in
the Camorra's local makeup and manifestation.

Campania is a region in southern Italy. Naples is its capital. Naples is no
different from other big port metropolises; it suffers from the same socioeconomic hardships as cities such as Marseille and Liverpool. Naples and its met-
ropolitan area have an estimated population of more than three million people
and cover an area of more than a thousand square kilometers, making it one
of the most overpopulated cities in Italy.[45] It is a big cosmopolitan metropolis
with rich and well-to-do districts, Posillipo, Chiaia and Mergellina, but also
harbors harsh suburbs and slums such as Scampia, Secondigliano and Ponticelli (see Figure I.1 map).

Naples has always been an important city in Europe, culturally, socially, and
politically. Historically, it was the capital of the Kingdom of the Two Sicilies

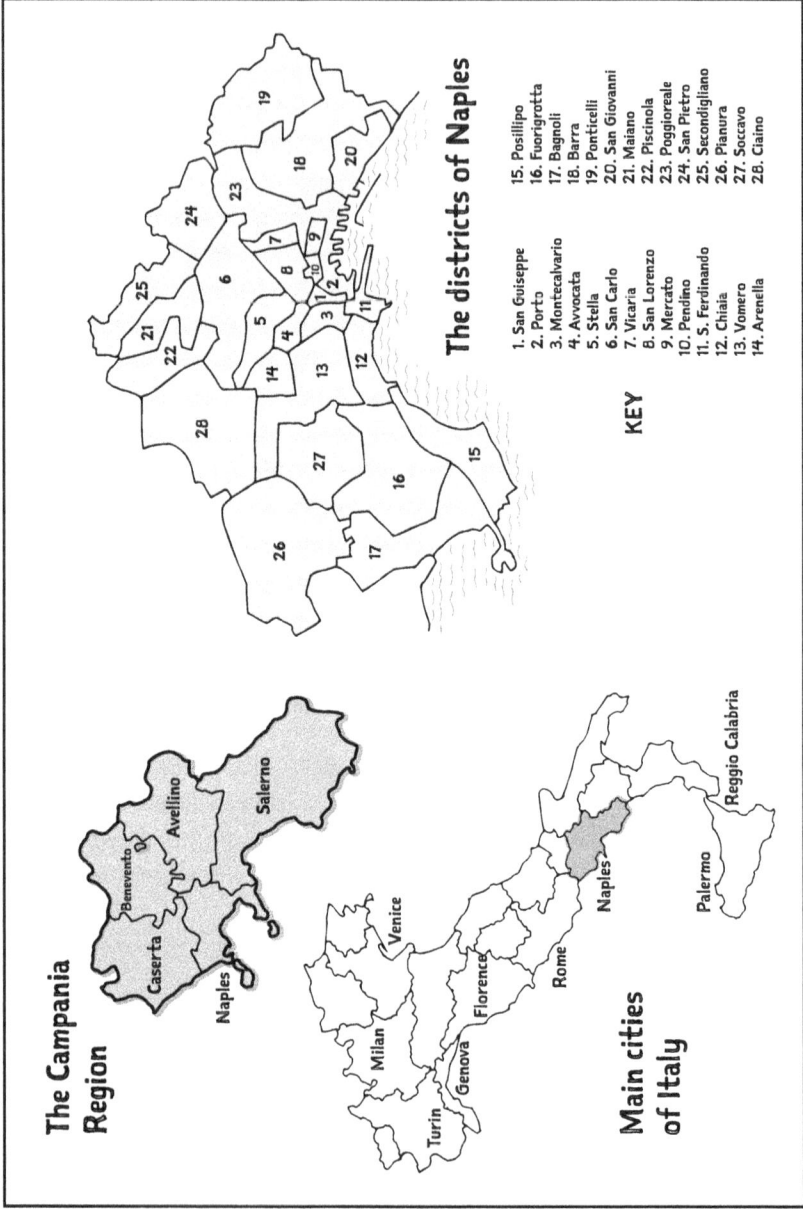

The Campania Region

Benevento
Caserta
Avellino
Salerno
Naples

Main cities of Italy

Turin
Milan
Venice
Genova
Florence
Rome
Naples
Palermo
Reggio Calabria

The districts of Naples

KEY

1. San Guiseppe
2. Porto
3. Montecalvario
4. Avvocata
5. Stella
6. San Carlo
7. Vicaria
8. San Lorenzo
9. Mercato
10. Pendino
11. S. Ferdinando
12. Chiaia
13. Vomero
14. Arenella
15. Posillipo
16. Fuorigrotta
17. Bagnoli
18. Barra
19. Ponticelli
20. San Giovanni
21. Maiano
22. Piscinola
23. Poggioreale
24. San Pietro
25. Secondigliano
26. Pianura
27. Soccavo
28. Ciaino

FIGURE I.1. Naples and Campania

(1817–61) and the second largest European city after Paris during the seventeenth century. The region has been ruled by various foreign powers (Spanish, Austrian, and French), which may explain the Neapolitans' indifference toward central government. The architecture and buildings of the city reflect its once royal status with fortified walls, beautiful piazzas, tall and palatial buildings with the noble upper floors and the low-level flats, *bassi*, for the poorer classes. Its history continues to impose a significant influence over the city today. Since Unification in 1861, Naples has never regained its once special status of a grand European city, although since 2010, tourism has picked up and made it a favorite holiday destination. It is a city full of pockets of economic inequality but also luxury.

During World War II, Naples was occupied by the Germans and was bombarded by both the Allies and Germans. It was liberated by the Americans; their presence would have an impact on the city and its underworld. In terms of financial investment and planning, this region has been economically neglected by the central government compared to the industrial north. However, the Democrazia Cristiana (DC, Christian Democrat) governments invested heavily in the Cassa del Mezzogiorno (a special investment fund for southern Italy). This was supposed to rebuild and to relaunch the economy in the South. But this money was poorly managed and often given to the friends of politicians through clientelistic practices. Although many of the national politicians who funneled state money to their friends were originally from the region, this perverse political nepotism reinforced a resentment toward Rome.[46]

Economically, Naples has been described as "a pre-industrial society" since its capacity to industrialize was never fully developed.[47] In the city center, many diverse small industries, such as artisans, flourished. In 2005, the main economic activities in the Province of Naples were public services (30.7 percent), manufacturing (18 percent), commerce (14 percent), construction (9.5 percent), transport (8.2 percent), financial services (7.4 percent) and agriculture (5.1 percent).[48] Many of the poor and working-class have lived off the "casual" and "informal" economy, where semilegal and illegal activities blur boundaries so they can put food on their table. We must not forget the specificity of Neapolitan identity and culture: "Naples is a complex and contractionary city. Its population is heterogeneous, and its landscape is fragmented. Although aware of this, and in spite of it, Neapolitans frequently express a strong sense of identity and recognize themselves as members of a collectivity which shares a number of characteristics."[49]

In particular, the importance of its language (specifically, the Neapolitan dialect), food, theater, and song are noted. Sophia Loren, who encapsulates what being Neapolitan means, recently explained, "Naples is so strong, so vital. It's about music and dance. Books and books of history."[50] Naples has a unique local cultural identity linked to its historic past and its own dialect, Neapolitan, which is quite different from Italian. Neapolitan is its own language, a mixture of French and Spanish, which fosters the "us versus them" mentality once again. Neapolitan food is also important, not only for the distinct local dishes but also for the social occasions of giving, pooling, sharing, and distributing food.[51] We must not forget the role of the Catholic church. In Naples, there are roughly a thousand churches and millions of statues of Madonnas or saints in the streets. Although not necessarily regularly practiced by the younger generation, Catholicism still structures and marks the lives of many Neapolitans.

In short, the Neapolitan context, with its macrostructural factors, is characterized by sharp economic, social, and political contrasts between the poor and the rich. Its citizens have a strong sense of cultural identity. They are very traditional in their way of life and outlook, following formal Catholic ceremonies and Saints' days without regularly attending church. They have a skepticism toward central government and have endured clientelism and corrupt malpractices by local government officials and politicians. Poor and badly managed investment in the South have produced great poverty and a casual and black economy that gives many people a living while unemployment remains high. Naples and Campania are specific places that have some unique traits, a sense of identity, and history, while having features that they share with other metropolises.

The Postwar Neapolitan Camorra in Context

A word about the nature and history of the Camorra to highlight how the local context influences and shapes its structure, behavior, and activities. "Organized crime" and "mafias" are challenging terms to define and study. Indeed, as Rahman et al. suggest, "Organized crime (OC) is a somewhat nebulous concept that is hotly debated by criminologists."[52] For me, there are two simple ways of conceptualizing these labels: (1) organized crime as a general umbrella term under which there are different specific forms of crime groups such as mafias, criminal enterprises or gangs; organized crime is a genus and mafias are a species of organized crime;[53] or (2) there is a continuum; at one end, we find gangs, which are disorganized, ad hoc, and temporary, and at the other, mafias, which are organized, permanent, and interested in politics.[54] OCGs are in the middle of the continuum.

Initially, in the eighteenth century, mafias did not function "as anti-state but as a state-within-a-state, substituting itself for the state in functions such as the maintenance of public order, the use of force, economic regulations and the administration of justice wherever public institutions are weak or absent."[55]

Over time, as both the state and markets developed and innovated, mafia groups adapted to these changes and modified their priorities and activities. For example, from extortion rackets to drug importation and distribution. So, as Jamieson points out, "the Mafia, therefore, is not a product of economic underdevelopment but is a parasite that draws its strength from and aggravates the inadequacies of the parent body [the state]—in Borsellino's words, 'not the price of poverty, but the cost of distrust.'"[56] I would argue that today's mafias (and OCGs) exist because of a combination of all these social structural factors—distrust, but also neoliberal values that produce poverty, lack of opportunities, education, and violence. In clearer terms, the nature of the state is crucial but so also is the local context (culture, economic activities, and political structures) that the state produces and interacts with, producing and explaining criminal behavior.

The Neapolitan Camorra is one such mafia-type criminal organization. It has been a constant presence in the Campania region during the postwar period. Initially less organized, today it has become a notable force and threat. It has been defined in various ways, but generally it is the label given to mafia criminal families, clans, and groups active across the Campania region in Italy. Sales defines the Camorra as "an informal group of criminal clans with similar behavior" or, more precisely, as "a mafia which can be defined as a criminal association interested in social, economic and political power."[57]

These definitions are different from those of the scholars who argue that mafias "are a specific type of formal organization," to be precise, purely an economic organization that "sells protection and services" because the state is missing.[58] While these approaches have some value in terms of explaining some of the business rationale of these criminal structures, especially when these groups' activities were mainly extortion, they fail to acknowledge the power these groups seek to impose on their territory, on citizens' daily lives, and on local political-economic activities as well as the role of women. Power is key.

Brancaccio while also using an economic-focused definition still sees power as one of its main aims. He highlights violence as one of the Camorra's main features to obtain power: the Camorra is a phenomenon of the violent government of markets. It has three main features:

1. Family, as the place of education and reproduction of the group
2. Violence, as a systematic instrument of imposition on social spaces and markets
3. Business, as a means of multiplying resources and power[59]

Unlike the Sicilian Mafia, there is not one coherent criminal structure but many. For example, Camorra groups and families we focus on in this study are not the same type of formation; clans are large aggregates of family groups whereas groups and families differ: "While the average lifespan of a group is relatively short, elements providing continuity over time are ensured by criminal families with larger dimensions, who in the most successful cases can give life to true dynasties that remain in power four or five generations."[60] Many of the historic Camorra families have been a permanent fixture in the Neapolitan underworld during the postwar period while the looser Camorra groups reflect changes in civil society, global markets, and the local context. They "are highly sensitive to variations in markets and in general to the conditions of their context."[61]

One of the defining features of Camorra groups, and that which can differentiate them from other criminal groups, is that Camorra groups reinforce their power, territory, and longevity when they manage to take control of a section of a legal/illegal market.[62] Other criminal groups, which don't quite manage to get this type of foothold in a market, can quickly disappear.

The Direzione Investigative Antimafia (Antimafia Investigation Directorate, DIA) (2019–20) uses another useful definition which underlines the multitude of groups, clans, and different formations linked to the territory:

> The main feature of the Camorra System is the persistence of a sort of overlap of levels where at the higher level, there are the families with a real consolidated criminal history. . . next Camorra cartels embedded in social, public, and economic fabric and at the lower level, smaller groups, less structured organizationally and strategically, that seek to control illegal activities across small areas of the territory.[63]

Another vital feature of Camorra clans is its interconnection with the local context. What remains key to understanding the Camorra is its territory of origin, its specific local urban or rural context, as this produces the spatial criminal stratification and explains the coexistence of the variety of different criminal formations and activities. In Campania, there are three local geographic and historic contexts that translate into three very different types of criminal formations, and which form a hierarchy of the Camorra:

1. In the city, a Camorra elite (Mazzarella clan and Secondigliano Alliance), and minor clans and families with a criminal/illegal tradition
2. In the outskirts and periphery of the city, Camorra groups interested in drug dealing
3. In the provinces of Naples and Caserta, clans involved in illegal and legal economy including links with local politics[64]

Some would suggest that the roles of women differ according to these different criminal formations; we will consider this in this study as I will look at a range of different formations across Campania.

So, in short, for this study, I adopt a simple definition of the Camorra because questions of definitions are for other studies: the Camorra is a criminal association whose members use violence to control civil society (citizens), the local economy (economic activities), and political institutions (political decisions) to achieve their main aims and objectives: power and money. While in Naples and Campania, the Camorra is a criminal association, the more it moves away from Naples, the more it becomes businesslike, legitimate, and more "liquid."[65]

A quick overview of Camorra history in the postwar era might be helpful to understand not only the local context, but also the criminal opportunities that appeared in Naples and in Campania at that time. In contrast to the Calabrian 'Ndrangheta and the Sicilian Cosa Nostra, context and history are essential in "setting the phenomenon of the Camorra within a historic frame . . . [in which] one can observe a very wide range of cases, which differ by their organizational structures, sectors of activity, forms of leadership, patterns of emergence, symbolic references and relations with the ruling class and the institutional rule of the state."[66]

The Camorra's criminal activities during the postwar period can be identified in five important stages which overlap over time:

1. 1945–60: agricultural mediators
2. 1955–70: smuggling of cigarettes
3. 1970–: drug trafficking and distribution
4. 1982–: public contracts, earthquake reconstruction, waste management and health services
5. 1990–: counterfeit activities, clothes, electronic goods

Drugs was the one business that allowed the Camorra to transform itself into a modern criminal group with access to huge sums of money it could invest in the legal economy (for example, businesses and public contracts). Angela Giallo, a former drug dealer, explained to me that "*drugs is big business. . . . If you take drugs away, you destroy the criminal underworld because they all line their pockets with drugs. Drugs is everything.*"[67] Today, all clans are involved in drugs, whether importing them directly into Europe or reselling them on the street. In terms of organizational structures, four main forms evolved:

1. *guappi,* individuals with allies
2. smugglers, individuals/ small groups with allies
3. clans, units based on families and blood ties
4. alliances, umbrella alliances such as the Alfieri Confederation, Nuova Famiglia (NF), Nuova Camorra Organizzata (NCO), and the Casalesi Confederation[68]

Different Camorra clans reemerged after the Second World War, evolving from individual guappi during the 1940s and 1950s. Guappi were strong individuals who were involved in both legal and illegal activities. They mediated between farmers in the province and customers at Naples market, making a profit from these transactions. They also delved into illegal trafficking, such as selling petrol and cigarettes. Between 1955 and 1970, smugglers (*contrabbandieri*) appeared interested in cigarettes as contraband and went on to become drug traffickers. From the mid-1970s, smugglers became organized into clans based on blood ties. These groups then diversified their activities from drugs and extortion into counterfeit goods and shifted into the political arena. The 1980 Irpinia earthquake proved to be a fundamental event that enabled many groups to move into politics to access public contracts and funds.

One last point is the Camorra's economic footprint, which must not be neglected. Former Naples chief antimafia prosecutor Melillo recently noted how the three main Mafias resemble three different economic systems, three different points of the economic development of a company: Cosa Nostra works as a Fordist system, the 'Ndrangheta as a holding company, and the Camorra as an international network.[69] In this way, the Camorra is flexible, adaptable, with many contacts, which makes it even more dangerous.

It is also worth noting that the different roles that exist in Camorra clans may differ from other mafias in terms of being less clear cut, more overlapping, and multidimensional. In a traditional Camorra clan, the following actors are present, bottom up (see figures 3.1 and 3.2):

1. Associates, "enablers" or "facilitators" (outsiders)
2. Foot soldiers, who undertake criminal activities
3. Managers, who coordinate certain individuals and tasks
4. Leadership group, usually from one blood family

Throughout this study, I will investigate to see if women ever take on these roles, and if so, how they behave.

Camorra Women

By "Camorra women," I first mean women who are involved in criminal clans with camorristi and who have specific crime-related jobs. Then, there are other women who participate in legal activities related to the Camorra whose tacit complicity and closeness to camorristi also makes them Camorra women. Their defining features can be one of the following: complicit involvement, tacit presence, or complete awareness. In other words, I refer to all women who knowingly engage or accept Camorra activities (illegal or legal) and whose behavior, directly or indirectly, advances the criminal organization and reinforces its power. It is worth saying that at times, it may not be easy to identify these women and untangle their participation. Sometimes, the situation and, consequently, the nature of their influence and power can become blurred.

Defining Camorra women in this loose way can be considered controversial because there are no boundaries between those who are recognized members, loyal sympathizers, or blood relatives, and those who are not members of the organization but who are still in some way involved. As we know, there is no official affiliation ritual as with the Sicilian Mafia. It has been suggested that if we do not adopt a fixed definition of membership "it would be surprising not to find roles for women in what seems to encompass the whole of society."[70] However, this *is* the point; women's participation in the Camorra can be subtle, flexible, and complex, not set in stone and overt. Even just being present and having passive behavior can be a form of adherence and acceptance of the Camorra's power and projects: tacit presence-complicity. Arguing that Camorra membership and involvement can be rationally defined is dismissive of the overlapping blood ties, economic households, social relationships, and cultural values which coexist and intersect between family, clan members, and activities in the public and private spheres where they live:

> The only way to reach the conclusion that women have acquired pivotal roles in the mafia is to minimize the importance of membership by adopting an extrinsic perspective and identify the boundary of the underground group with that of the network that becomes apparent through judicial investigations. . . . No social scientist should confuse membership into a club, or even a cult with the connections of all those that help run it . . . no matter how essential those connections are to the life of the members of the club.[71]

This approach is slightly reductionist when looking at the intricate picture of Camorra women's involvement, almost considering women as second-rate citizens. The argument that a mafia is similar to an exclusive (gentlemen-only) club with specific membership rights and those who run it, porters, cleaners, and caterers, cannot be considered members because they have not paid up, is to miss the point. If we look at this in another way: members of an exclusive club also have extensive membership benefits, some even have a membership plus one benefit, this means that members can bring a guest, a guest who does as they wish. This gentlemen-only club perspective also neglects the culturally subtle bonds and intricacies including the importance and relevance of cultural codes that are intertwined with the mafia, and how difficult it is to untangle features such as formal and informal membership, formal and informal participation, formal and informal presence.[72]

Membership and signing up to being a member to be included in Camorra activities will vary; there is no unique pathway into a clan. Women are not necessarily fully paid-up members of the Camorra system all of the time, but they can be active in helping the clan against the state and in helping the clan to survive in difficult times. It could be argued that one of the main ways women become involved is through the family context compared to men who become involved not necessarily through the family context but through the social setting, in other words, the street and friendship groups.

Evidence suggests that female relatives of a clan member can automatically be considered a member without having to opt in or to opt out actively and openly. Their membership and participation become blurred with blood ties, complicating our understanding of their actual involvement. There are also some women who tacitly accept the (criminal) situation (and money) while others who will openly distance and remove themselves from the Camorra space and clan. They will walk away, while others will stay. All know and understand the situation. With this in mind and for this study, I have decided to see and define "Camorra women" in the following ways:

1. Women related to Camorra members through birth or marriage (blood/kinship ties define their involvement).
2. Women who are employed by the Camorra in criminal activities (money, survival, lifestyle, and power defines their involvement within the system).
3. Women who are sympathetic to Camorra activities (who help the Camorra directly or indirectly), especially as front names in money laundering and recycling operations. These women can be professionals.

As we shall see, not all Camorra women are the same and there can be some small differences according to their family, districts of origin, class, education, and crime groups. For example, women in the Casalesi Confederation in Casal di Principe (Caserta) are different from women in the Graziano clan from Vallo di Lauro in the Avellinese (see figure I.1) or the suburb clans such as the Pesce clan from Pianura or women in the Ponticelli clans—the D'Amico clan or the Pazzignane clan.[73] Rita Longo underlined this difference when she made clear that she was regularly treated differently by other Camorra wives because she was from Naples and not from the Casal di Principe: *They felt superior.*[74] However, while their detailed stories as women might differ, there are often similar recurring themes and life choices including female agency, masculine power, and criminal power.

Camorra Space

When one studies the criminality that exists in towns and cities, it soon becomes apparent that different types of criminals coexist in a so-called underworld. Yet this domain is more than an underworld; it is a physical territory where criminals impose their rules and behavior on local communities. They project their desire for power and control to create a criminal space where local criminals and their activities coexist. In some towns, this space is chaotic and shared by many where not one criminal group manages to predominate over others. In other places like Campania, it becomes the Camorra space as Camorra members inhabit and dominate this criminal space and seek to make it their own by projecting their criminal markets and projects on the territory.

To be clear, Camorra clans and families operate in a cultural, social, economic, and physical context which they project and create in the streets, villages, towns, and cities across Campania. This is a criminal space that they transform into their own Camorra space. Territory and territoriality mean power for the Camorra because it provides clan members with markets, customers, money, protection, and public contracts (to mention but a few), which is why understanding what the "Camorra space" is and where women are located within this space is useful.

For this study, the notion of Camorra space does not correspond to that of place or territory, because not all place or territory are Camorra space, not all urban districts, neighborhoods, or streets are under Camorra control. This space can be very fluid, with some districts having more Camorra space than others, often depending on who is in prison and who is out and about in the territory. A place "should be viewed as [a] specific location, as a wider territory"; it is the wider local social, cultural, economic, and political context that is different from space.[75] Indeed, "people's identities are created through defining themselves in relation to places."[76] This is crucial as cultural identity and place are intertwined, especially in the Neapolitan context.

Camorra families, clans, and members therefore inhabit what I call the Camorra space, which exists in different places, across districts and provinces in Naples and Campania and even, in some foreign locations.[77] The Camorra space expands across the public sphere of civil society, where much of the Camorra's activities take place, to the private sphere, and in particular, to the family and household. The public local space is a "physical and social landscape . . . imbued with meaning in everyday place-bound social practices and emerges through processes that operate over varying spatial and temporal scales."[78] It is these different social spaces in civil society that the Camorra seeks to inhabit in the city center; it is the historic narrow alleyways whereas in the outskirts, it is the neighborhoods of public housing, which become "a Camorra fortress" and a no-go area.[79]

Historically, this urban terrain has emerged in parallel with the development of the Camorra's power in the city. Slowly and using mafia methods, clans have established this urban space that is their territory. They have put down roots, they control and protect it, using violence, threats, and intimidation: depending on which clan predominates, the local territory is not a fixed space, but continuously a negotiated, disputed, or contested space. The Camorra space can be defined as the clan's distinct urban territory, these are the "local urban spaces" and "distressed urban neighborhoods" the clan wants to control, and which clan members constantly patrol and protect.[80] Let us not forget that a clan without territory is nothing.[81]

But I want to be more specific. I identify the Camorra space as the spatial dynamics of public outdoor spaces in Naples, where the cultural, social, political, and economic meet in local streets, piazzas, alleys, café terraces, neighborhoods, and districts where most of the Camorra's criminal activities and business are played out. In this space, camorristi, citizens, businesspeople, police, lawyers, politicians cohabit, meet and live, and it is vital for the Camorra to dominate this arena in any way it can. This physical space is unique to every district in Naples and contributes to a street culture that camorristi create and belong to.

The street, the *vicolo*, is the central place where camorristi earn their capital that reinforces their power. And, interestingly, this space is usually considered to be a male-dominated space, where only young men roam and affirm their masculinity.[82] Writing about gangs in the UK, Bakkali argued that the street was "still a space where women operate and form a central part of the culture despite this tending to be only reluctantly recognized among male participants."[83] The same is true for women in the Camorra. The Camorra space is not only an economic space, but it is also a human, cultural, and social space; it becomes an outdoor theater, albeit it at times a dangerous one where capital is earned. It is the space where clans impose their power over the local population using many different symbols, tools, strategies, and techniques. From cultural symbols (such as religious statues to recall the dead as heroes and martyrs) to putting up CCTV cameras in the streets as a form of security to monitor its territory and detect the arrival of the police or rivals, the clan defends its Camorra space and territorial boundaries. At times it can even become a question of life or death.

To exist, the clan must control the local community within its Camorra space; the Camorra space is the power the clan imposes on the community but when the clan is weak so is its Camorra space. To establish a strong Camorra space, the clan can use different violent, terrorist, and combat war techniques to impose its power. The use of *stese,* shooting in the air by young clan members, usually driving around on mopeds in a rival's district, is a good example of physical control of the territory. One clan will seek to violate and provoke another clan in their Camorra space. This has great symbolic value for the local community as each clan seeks to have more credibility, respect, territory, and control than rival clans. This provocation also forces the disrespected clan to retaliate in order not to lose power and reputation among the onlooking citizens and clan members. The clan can also use more subtler tools to project and protect its Camorra space. For example, it can organize big public symbolic gestures in the street as a form of territorial control. The use of firework displays is one. Often, clan members use firework displays openly in the street or piazzas to communicate significant moments in the clan's life or give messages to local rivals and the neighborhood: for example, the success of the clan's hit squad, the release of a boss from prison, and/or the arrival of an important drug shipment.[84]

Connected to this outdoor space, I believe the Camorra space extends into physical indoor spaces because clans no longer respect private spaces of citizens and in some instances, go beyond the front door to impose their rules on the daily lives and living arrangements of their members and others. The use of Palazzo Fienga by the Gionta Clan in Torre Annunziata is a telling example. This historic building had many different flats giving on to the public staircase and the courtyard, all of which were used by the clan as open-air meeting and discussion rooms where women contributed with coffee and advice. The Nuvoletta clan from Marano quite literally closed off a public road on a hill outside of the town and established the clan's headquarters there making it a dead-end and no-go area for citizens.[85] Other Camorra clans, such as those in Pianura or the Spanish Quarter, install CCTV cameras in the streets to monitor the coming and goings and to all effects, transform a public space into a no-go area and the streets into a Camorra fortress. In this way, they inhabit not only the houses and the roads but also the surrounding open countryside.

Another more recent example of the clans trying to control and takeover the public space is the inauguration of murals. Clans already had a tradition of installing minichapels dedicated to religious figures as well as murdered members in very public spaces such as busy main roads or roundabouts in the suburbs. These are religious ornaments but also public tributes by the clan to their fallen members, a way of normalizing their criminality in the local community and imposing their rules and their mentality on others. Recently, local Neapolitan antimafia associations have been using street art as a form of civil resistance to the Camorra's takeover of public spaces.[86] In response to this, clans have been fighting back and putting up murals that celebrate young men close to the clan who has been murdered. In this way, these young men are transformed into martyrs in the Camorra space for all to see and bow to. It is easy to understand why the street and the Camorra space is identified as "a male space" because it is the location where violence, threats, beatings, deals, and social gatherings usually take place.

But the Camorra space is more than just the public sphere. It is also the private sphere where we find the "irrelevant" women. The Camorra space is the clan's projected power onto the public outdoor space in civil society where public governance takes place, but it also exists in the private indoor space. These spaces overlap and merge and spatial dynamics become crucial to the clan and its internal power dynamics. Women, are at the center of all of these spaces, out in the streets and indoors, but in particular we find them at the center of the household in the private sphere. Some women are oppressed in these spaces, but there are also women who empower themselves here. It is here that they gain their power and can contest the existing patriarchy to dominate and have an influence. It is these women I study in this book.

In the next chapter, I present the theoretical lens and the methodology I use to study and analyze the role of women in the Camorra. It has meant going beyond the already sociologically rich but biased judicial and police investigations and collecting as much varied material as possible, including oral stories, testimonies, interviews, discussions, and observations as well as archives. I have ultimately tried to put Camorra women's words at the center of my analysis so I can unpack the notions of gender and power in relation to who is in charge in the Camorra and ask whether the Camorra is fundamentally sexist.

LISTENING TO WOMEN'S VOICES

Naples has been my field site and one of my homes for the last twenty-five years. This relationship has made my work on the city fascinating, frustrating, and challenging, because, as a result of these circumstances, I have a dual personality, a participant who is never neutral and always unconsciously an observer. Indeed, in Naples I am involved in a continuous ethnography observing different relationships, interactions, boundaries, practices, identities, and situations both in the street and at home. Using my eyes and my sensibility, I collect observational data that contextualizes my archival, judicial, and interview material.

In this chapter, I explain the mixed-method methodology I use to study women in the Camorra and in Naples. An example of this is the observation I did in September 2020 on Piazza Carolina. Piazza Carolina is a small but busy piazza in the center of Naples with a taxi rank, shops, a few bars, a newspaper stand, some public benches, and a few young trees. It is to be found next to the majestic royal Piazza Plebiscito and runs parallel to the busy shopping street of Via Chiaia, in the territory of the Elia clan. I carried out five day/night (twenty-four hour) observations there to get a good sense of the territory and of the spatiality of women in this specific district to help me capture some moments of Neapolitan life and identify daily routines in public spaces. Young men on their mopeds tended to hang out in the early hours of the morning, while older men were more prevalent between 8:00 a.m. and 10:00 a.m. Women congregate there during the afternoon, but in particular, between 4:00 p.m. and 6:30 p.m. when they would gather to talk and let their children play together.[1] I also noted some women on their own who would sit on the benches at random times during the day, contemplating life. The piazza in general was a male space in the morning and early hours whereas it became a female space all afternoon.[2] It is not a narrow patriarchal space in itself, but a shared space in which different social and generational activities took place that highlighted a gender division.

Some Theoretical Considerations

The Piazza Carolina gender division clearly corresponds to the gender inequalities that seem to exist in Neapolitan civil society: supposedly gentle, caring women as traditional mothers involved in domestic tasks, strong men as mobile, active, and self-confident workers engaging in business in the public sphere. To understand the subordination of women and their "difference" compared to men, we have to focus on the notion of patriarchy.

Patriarchy is often presented as a blanket term, with fixed and solid structures across cultures, societies, and institutions, all having the same characteristics and impact. Coward argues that patriarchal relations can be defined either as "the oppression of all women by all men (what is often also referred to as sexism), or a particular kind of kinship structure, or finally a residual ideology of male dominance."[3] But she concludes more specifically that "the population appears to enter voluntarily into the [patriarchal] structures and ideologies, which are actually enforced, because the sexual identities of men and women are constructed as leading logically to this structure."[4] As a consequence, if we define patriarchy as a system based on constructed sexual identities, we can better understand the organization of today's society based on the subordination of women. Thus, constructed sexual identities produce gender differences and gender socialization that create patriarchy based on the subordination and exploitation of women.

Patriarchal structures change from location to location and are not the same across societies, classes, countries, or continents; they have different manifestations. Moreover, it has been noted that patriarchy has not always been the dominant system and that the development of patriarchal structures coincided with the establishment of capitalism. Capitalism is a system that continues to oppress and exploit not only the workers but also women.[5] However, ancient societies were different, they were much more based on matriarchal structures where women played a central role as both providers and carers, but this later changed when new forms of society developed.[6] The overlap of different economic systems explains why patriarchal and matriarchal structures must not be seen as settled or absolute as is often asserted about Naples.

Today, we live in a constructed "gendered society" with gendered spaces: in Naples, the public and private spheres are distinctly "gendered."[7] However, this is often not acknowledged as a place to look for an explanation in terms of gender dynamics in mafia groups because no clear distinction between the public and private spheres is made. Gendered criminal activities in the Camorra don't exist apart perhaps from the violent commandos. Even then, women do order murders and violence, meticulously organizing every aspect. These public and private gendered spheres, although often presented as one and the same thing, confuse our understanding. They are seen as overlapping spaces in which men are dominant and women are relegated to the sidelines, but this is an oversimplification. The main Italian macrostructure is essentially a classic patriarchy and, in many areas, but not in a systematic way, very misogynistic. The situation is more subtle where there are many negotiated spaces, including the Neapolitan underworld.

In general, as I have already mentioned in the introduction, the main studies that focus on women in mafias and criminal organizations rarely acknowledge the basic gender inequalities or examine the power relations that exist for women in the public and private spheres. They look for theories that pay little attention to gender per se. They appear as gender neutral or gender blind approaches with "genderless" theories which in fact concentrate on men because "the study of criminology over the past 240 years has in large part been a study about male offending, about crime problems generated by males, studied by males and explained and responded to be males."[8]

So far, studies on the roles of women in organized crime groups (OCGs) have been based on the "family/gender role division. . . .. or/specific structures of particular crime organizations" where women are seen as having limited roles.[9] Then "the emancipation of women both in society in general as well within criminal groups" was given as an explanation for the more visible and emerging role of women.[10] In this vein, Varese writes, "In sum, mafias grew out of structurally sexist societies and institutions and are themselves slow to change."[11] Thus, women "cannot acquire independent positions of leadership."[12] He asks, "Why [do] women continue to be formally excluded."[13]

My material—and my grounded theory approach of first collecting data and then finding a theory—led me elsewhere, to explain the "apparent" domination of men over women, who even when they were active were said to be *only* under the orders of their menfolk.[14] From my evidence, I do not think that women's roles are limited or irrelevant; it is just that we are asking the wrong questions and looking in the wrong direction. The role of women is more subtle, their power more nuanced, with lots of complexities of when and how it works. Their criminal existence lies outside of the male defined traditional categories, boundaries, and definitions of crime that we find in much of the literature.

I believe that we must study and consider the public and private spheres as separate gendered spaces and see how they relate to each other within the general context of a Neapolitan patriarchal society to explain Camorra women's partici-pation. In other words, after much reflection, a simple and enduring framework of structure versus agency inspired by Giddens appeared helpful to unpack wom-en's involvement in the material I had collected as it recognized women's agency and capabilities within the Neapolitan structure.[15] I could focus on women's agency in the Camorra's local gender regime.

I looked at the intricate gender interplay in civil society to find contradic-tions and tensions about women's roles in crime groups. I believe that a closer look at how gender is constructed in each society could be vital to understand how women are considered, treated, and behave in both the public and private spheres as these may be very different. But this is beyond the scope of this study. The construction of gender is the power developed by the state over its citizens in terms of "the control over the bodies of their subjects."[16] Throughout time and history, it is the state that has created, constructed, and perpetuated notions and expectations of manhood, womanhood, and personhood in civil society. It is the state—made up of men—that has regulated and regulates women's lives and bodies.

To understand the roles of women in criminal groups requires us to acknowl-edge the construction of gender in Neapolitan civil society and to see how it plays out in both the public and private spheres, either as an obstacle or as an advantage in this local gender order. Gender "is multi-dimensional; it is not just about identity, or just about work, or just about power, or just about sexuality, but all of these things at once."[17]

The question of gender and mafias/organized crime in general, therefore, is multifaceted. It is first a political question about how gender is constructed in a specific country through time. Not all countries construct gender in the same way, which may explain differences in gender dynamics in criminal groups. Sec-ond, it is a sociological question about how this power plays out: do genders have the same power and influence in crime groups in the public and private spheres, or does a disjuncture exist?[18] And last, it is a criminological question about why and how genders become involved in crime. Do women have different criminal skills than men or not? Does civil society create these differences according to their construction of traditional gender sexualities and identities?

In the case of postwar Italy, it is both the state, as it emerged after the Second World War, and the long-established patriarchal Catholic Church that have had a significant role in shaping and determining the construction of gender and the role of women in society. See, for example, the timing and debates about the referendums on divorce and abortion during the 1970s and 1980s, when the state sought to impose itself on women and their bodies. These kinds of public actions and debates have all contributed to establishing a male-centric Italian society and an image of Italian women and how they are perceived and treated in modern Italy. Although Italian feminist movements in the 1970s sought to change Italy, gender inequality is still rife. Women must still fight to attain equal rights in the public sphere, and the state can still intervene against women's better wishes. The position, role, and space of women in the private sphere is not considered, and if it is, it is always and only in relation to men, not as women with their own agency, their own capacity, and power.

As a result of this delicate balance of variables and gender patterns, I found a disjuncture between the role of Italian and Camorra women in the public and private spheres. The Neapolitan public sphere can be defined as predominately a "masculine" society in which "men are supposed to be assertive, tough, and focused on material success and women are supposed to be more modest, tender, and concerned with quality of life.[19] This public sphere is a male and heteronormative dominated space, a classical patriarchy, where older men predominate over everyone, including young men. It must be said that women are still fighting for gender equality in Naples.

However, in the household and family, the situation is rather different as the patriarchy does not transfer perfectly. What I found was the female space that Anne Parsons had already identified during the 1960s: in Naples, "the father who lacks power in the home is able to find male companionship outside it [the Camorra]. His absence from home in turn increases the power of women and perpetuates the matrifocal system. . . . The fact remains that masculine power and prestige are based to a far greater extent on activities in a male extrafamilial world than on an authority role within the family."[20] Neapolitan women's position in the household is thus not necessarily dictated by their economic status but by their blood ties and their important social capital (love, help, attention, emotions, sexual relations), which they use to engage with the existing patriarchy.

The Neapolitan household is the female realm where an informal and unrecognized matriarchy reigns: there are maybe women who are oppressed in the home, but I am focusing on those who manage to carve out a space for themselves. These women dominate the household, which gives them status and respect. They are carers, homemakers, providers, organizers, and deciders. In addition to female domesticity, women become central for social, emotional, economic, and cultural activities for the core and extended family in the public sphere. Inspired by Bourdieu's (1985) notion of economic, cultural, and social capital, Nicaso and Danese identified different forms of capital in the criminal underworld: "human capital" (individual skills, knowledge, and experience), "cultural capital" ("shared values of insider group"), and "social capital" (bonding and bridging).[21] Examples of these forms of capital are being proactive, organized, business minded, and having a clear overview of the criminal and judicial situations. I believe that women collect these in the household and use these different forms of capital as survival or self-interest strategies that empower them to have agency and challenge possible gender inequalities in the home and beyond.

As mothers, sisters, daughters, and daughters-in-laws, they bargain and negotiate with the macropatriarchy; they develop their own agency, which challenges structures that could block them to become powerful players. These women are not passive. They engage with the patriarchy in an active way; they are not lost, oppressed, subservient, or subordinate to men and, to use Kandiyoti's concept of "patriarchal bargains," they forge their own agency through "strategies and coping mechanisms."[22] They adapt, they learn, they act, they survive, they live, they enjoy in the Camorra.

Therefore, I found that Camorra women in the household bargained and negotiated with patriarchy, and this gave them capital, power, and space to have their own agency in the family. This capital makes them resilient and resourceful and contributes to establishing their female influence, role, and power independent of men. Ultimately, it produces their agency, which can translate into criminal power in the Camorra. In some instances, this can make women equal to their male counterparts.

This does not necessarily produce a collegial sisterhood; if anything, women who contest the patriarchy become more important players, reenforcing the existing male structures and the criminal power that they endorse. Consequently, women in the clan can be seen as equal partners and not as second-rate citizens, but because they remain in the private sphere, they are treated as invisible, hidden, and irrelevant.

In brief, I adopted a general gender lens to analyze Camorra women through stories about their lives. I use a structure versus agency approach to unpack the notions of agency, power, and power relations to examine whether they are active, passive, subordinate, or independent. And I use this as my analytical lens, my pair of glasses to tell the stories of women in the Camorra who are so often forgotten, ignored, or dismissed as unimportant and irrelevant.

This reminded me, of course, of Marx's concept of "invisible labor"; Neapolitan women provide "invisible labor" to the Camorra, vital "invisible labor" and are a workforce that stem from their position in the household in the private sphere, and which, many would argue, is gendered because women only carry out lowly jobs such as selling drugs and counterfeit cigarettes.

Although in this study I concentrate on the importance of women by using a gender lens, I think it is necessary to stress that no single factor, but rather a combination of intersecting factors, can explain the role of women in criminal organizations.[23] This crisscross of factors, such as gender, class, religion, nationality, and race/ethnicity, intersectionality, all matter equally to explain Camorra women as multidimensional actors with various layers of complicity (what Chesney-Lind and Pasko identify as "multiple marginality").[24] Within this intersectional framework, I zoom in and specifically use gender as the main anchor to discuss and analyze the role of women in the Neapolitan Camorra.[25]

A Methodological Reflection

The complex nature of researching organized crime is, at times, never fully appreciated.[26] The difficulty involved trying to study its intricate, sometimes impenetrable complexities are never clearly articulated. Indeed, "organized crime probably rates as one of the most difficult areas on which to collect data. . . . [because of] its covert nature and high-risk activities."[27] The latter make it a particularly challenging because "it can be costly, time-consuming, potentially risky, and present ethical barriers."[28] Traditionally, organized crime has been studied by analyzing secondary data (newspaper articles, official reports from the United Nations and Europol, judicial material, and police reports, among others) with some important ethnographic studies of local communities that have also contributed to our understanding of organized crime activities.[29] Today, there is also a lot of quantitative analysis as well as the use of social network analysis to explain and analyze varying forms of OCGs and activities.[30]

Over the last twenty years, I have developed a specific mixed methods–qualitative approach that has become a very personal methodology for me: it combines ethnographic interaction and interviews with participants about their lives with a more traditional analysis of secondary sources to triangulate findings and versions of events.[31] What I do in this methodology, is always try to get as close as possible to this illegal phenomenon and listen to those involved in order to build up a picture that I can then analyze. In this way, doing research and visiting the field site is a never-ending journey of discovery, especially about ethnography, and myself, as it is "as much part of a self-educational process as it is the collection of data."[32] To this, I add the caveat that "doubt is [also] a wonderful research method,"[33] even though it might not be a good idea to admit this. The concepts of "doubt" and "subjectivity" have always been part of my methodological thinking process, always questioning everything from as many different perspectives and angles as possible as well as my own. This entails accepting the idea that "the research process is never neutral" and that "a research project cannot be entirely value-free."[34]

With this in mind, my methodology is not an autobiographic or autoethnographic account but rather a "personal human reflexivity" that I have developed with Naples when researching organized crime and the Camorra there.

I "ruminat[e] on the ways in which [our] my own aspirations, characters, values, philosophies, experiences, belief systems, political commitments and social identities have shaped the research."[35] Therefore, my research methods are expansive and intense and they favor depth over breath.[36] I am aware that my research identity toward Naples is double, interconnected, and overlapping. I am both an insider and an outsider. An insider, I have enjoyed living a Neapolitan life, following its routines, rhythms, and religious festivals, full cultural immersion (even having "cultural clashes" from time to time). As an outsider and an international researcher analyzing and studying a social and criminal phenomenon, I realize that having this dual identity with a dual lens means that this research is a continuous learning process and a cultural and emotional voyage that is fairly unique but which I hope to share here and elsewhere.

My mixed-methods approach has always had a strong qualitative focus. This was a reaction to the fact that analyzing purely secondary sources or state-produced data was never enough to study criminal organizations. As Windle and Silke have argued, these types of sources "could be the prolongation and dissemination of unchecked folklore regarding organized crime" and the employment of "politically motivated" and "constantly shifting conceptions of which activities are to be included as organized crime."[37] However, some organized crime scholars are skeptical about the nature of qualitative methods and their value; they argue that they produce fragmented and dispersed snapshots based on "anecdotal evidence." Indeed, "many scholars minimize or decry qualitative findings as 'unscientific' and 'ungeneralizable.'"[38] In this way, they dismiss the contribution made by qualitative methods and do not see how these can be "informative, richer, and offer enhanced understandings."[39] Such methods focus on meanings and traits, defining characteristics of events, people, interaction, settings, and cultures compared to quantitative modalities. It is about doing deep research.

Quantitative approaches on the other hand, concentrate on numbers, statistics, and numerical descriptions, have a more scientific approach with respect to social science and use specific definitions, concepts, and variables, which they make operative. Critics often also misunderstand what qualitative methods seek to achieve; both approaches have different objectives and benefits. If I had tried to study this phenomenon using only quantitative methods, it would have been nearly impossible because of the limited material available. I encountered a similar challenge with my study of the Camorra in Europe.[40] Qualitative methods allowed me to ask the "what, how, when and where of a thing—its essence and ambience"—rather than the amount of the measure that is being analyzed.[41] Ultimately, the fundamental difference is that the qualitative methods approach "centralizes and places primary value on complete understandings, and how people (the social aspect of our discipline) understand, experience, and operate within milieus that are dynamic, and social in their foundation and structure."[42]

Thus, I believe that mixed methods for analyzing criminal organizations is an efficient way of capturing many of their different layers and aspects. Since 1992, the resources that I have collected have been basic, traditional newspaper articles and extensive judicial investigations and sentences with in-depth ethnographic interviews. This time, it soon became clear to me that this material was not enough and that it would not get me far in terms of analyzing the specific role of women, in particular. To do this, it was important for me to move beyond the Italian law enforcement data because it was only focused on proving specific crimes and not the nature of women's involvement nor the nature of their power. Indeed, I kept coming back to the words of Daly and Chesney-Lind: "To understand crimes by women, it is important to get your 'hands dirty' and to plunge more deeply into the social world of girls and women."[43]

During 2018–23 and the time away from university teaching, I had the opportunity to go back and take a closer look at my existing material (including my interviews with former camorristi) and now collect new data to unpack and listen to the stories of real women in the Neapolitan Camorra. But first of all, I had to decide which women to focus on in my case studies.

My first challenge was to identify Camorra women and their clans and to elaborate a list, from which I would collect and analyze my data. In particular, I used law enforcement maps produced by the Legione Carabinieri di Napoli during the 1980 and 1990s and the DIA in their latest biannual reports.[44] For example, in a 1988 Carabinieri document of clans in the province of Naples, forty-four clans were identified with clan members named; only seven women from three different clans were recognized. Because of my contacts with Naples and Caserta, I specifically concentrated on clans in the regions of Naples city, Naples's province, and Caserta. I also looked at Avellino. I did not analyze the clans in Benevento and Salerno. I examined all clans since the 1980s, and the main traditional clans that have been very resilient over the last thirty years and where few women were identified. There are about fifteen to twenty-five traditional clans that were established during the 1970s and that still exist today. They can be defined as the Camorra elite. Special attention was paid to these.

My second step was to use newspaper articles and judicial and police documents to add new clans to my list where there were women present in Campania between 1980 and 2023. I could then map them out to check for geographical representation and spread across the region. From these documents, the majority of the clans had active women. I selected and studied twenty-five clans in depth. Once all the clans and women were identified, I used the purposive sampling method to select the stories of women because this "technique [is] widely used in qualitative research for the identification and selection of information-rich cases for the most effective use of limited resources."[45] I then used typical case sampling that allowed me to use my already established knowledge of different women and their Camorra clans and how their stories were emblematic, in terms of recurring pathways into crime, types of crime families, education, values, choices, activities, and power relations.

I then zoomed in on them and started collecting as much raw material as I could to reconstruct their lives and criminal careers. I was interested in the gritty detail of their existence, choices, and actions. I amassed the basic judicial resources, court material, transcripts, and interrogations. I undertook an in-depth narrative analysis of the different police and judicial files to reconstruct their stories from this primary data.[46]

Since this was insufficient material, and because I accept the limitations and over-reliance on judicial and police files that are solely interested in prosecutions, I then added to these resources. The sociologist Pizzini-Gambetta recognizes the difficulty of collecting material on Italian mafias but argues that it "does not justify methodological shortcuts and the supine adoption of the judicial perspective."[47] For me, judicial material has always been the starting point and not the end point of my curiosity and my research. Newspaper articles usually highlight specific cases of interest, which I then followed up by seeking out the judicial and police material; this could be quite time consuming.

I then wanted to complement this judicial material and utilize as many and varied perspectives as possible. This meant identifying potential privileged observers who knew these women directly or who were aware of them. I therefore decided to use semistructured interviews with antimafia prosecutors and police officers who knew the territory, the clans, their activities, and the women I was interested in. In addition to seeking specific details of women's lives, which may have been discarded in the judicial documents, it was important for me to triangulate all my material and to avoid a monolithic approach, using the same kind of material from a single institution. This has enabled me to collect general material on the Camorra in the postwar period and then to find the different women so that I could focus on them. In each clan, there are the stories of the clan's women, if you read attentively.

My case studies are the stories about, or the reconstruction of, Camorra women's lives that I collated. I decided to concentrate on Naples city, Caserta, and Avellino (see figure I.1) as specific contexts and traced the clans that included women from the 1980s. I collected and analyzed as much new information as possible, legal documents, police reports, trial transcripts, witness testimonies, in-depth semistructured interviews with judges and police officers, and more important, my conversations with former Camorra women, in order to be able to assemble their narratives, their clans, activities, and main events into what can also be called "a sociobiography."[48] Overall, there are many similarities in the women's stories. Some of the narratives may be more limited than others because of the sparse material, but I have tirelessly tried to piece together as much different information as possible.

In order not to perceive these life-focused accounts as static, it is important to see stories as dialectical and synthetic processes that evolve as Campbell explained: "I had to put it in the context of the long trajectory of the past. We are who we are today because of the cumulative events which have shaped us into these people. The past is expressed in the choices that we make today, just as those choices will constrain the future that has yet to arrive."[49] I tell the tales of Camorra women's lives either through their own words or the words of those who observe them in order to explain their criminal careers, to show how active they have been, and their power relations in the clans: "The telling of life stories, whether to others or self alone, is treated as an important, shaping event in social and psychological processes, yet the life stories themselves are considered to be developed in, and the outcomes of, the course of these and other life events."[50]

I have decided to tell these stories, these biographical tales, with a special focus on the notion of "agency," to highlight these women's relationship with their menfolk. In each story, I underline the agency and the criminal agency that women have. I use the word *agency* to indicate "the capacity, condition, or state of acting or of exerting power independently," not being influenced by men when making decisions about how to act and also undertake/influence criminal acts.[51] Connected to agency are the notions of "power" and "power relations," which will also be included in my analysis.[52] Power can be exercised overtly, covertly, verbally, nonverbally, interpersonally, and intersubjectively. Interlinked with power, are concepts such as influence, rule, authority, domination, control, and force, which may also form part of our stories.

I use the case studies of specific women's lives to show through their biographies and relationships their unique agency and their intricate power relations with their men.[53] In some instances, I have been able to present an insider's perspective, a firsthand account using their words from interview material as well as judicial investigations. Where this is not possible, I have reconstructed their stories using other firsthand accounts, testimonies, judicial material, conversations, and interviews to capture this very subjective space, that is, that of women and their experiences within the Camorra context.

Focusing on these women's words and subjective worldview, I want to show their agency and how they see and live the Camorra, in this way highlighting their stories, agency and criminal agency but also their difficulties, contradictions, and incoherencies. So, I tell the stories of Camorra women, and as Haynes argued for her Greek women: "Their stories should be read, seen, heard in all their difficult, messy, murderous detail. They aren't simple, because nothing interesting is simple."[54]

I have been able to combine this ethnographic strategy[55] with the more traditional approaches of analyzing judicial files and police reports since this material "alone is not sufficient to capture the complexity and diversity of OC's groups' organizations and markets."[56] Since September 2018, I supplemented my data extensively with qualitative ethnographic observations collected during my regular visits to Naples with the latest judicial sentences and reports, and new sets of in-depth interviews with key informants and privileged observers, as I believed that "the way we understand as opposed to know a phenomenon is to vicariously experience its lived reality—to sense what it would be like to be that other person, to see the world through his or her eyes."[57] But, as Campbell has stated,

> The trouble is that if this is the goal, the only route is to talk to the people you want to understand. And that takes time, a determination to give up one's own perspective in favor of someone else's, and a messy involvement in the social and emotional demands that accompany a relationship between researcher and subject.[58]

Indeed, listening to insiders' accounts in their words, experiences, and worldview, either those of state witnesses or those of people in the local community is a central part of my work. In this study, it became vital for me to listen to former Camorra women's firsthand accounts as well as those of other female protagonists to capture their stories and understand their lives through their words: for example, understanding what former drug dealer, Angela Giallo means when she says; "*I saw myself as a monster, I saw myself as a bad woman. . . . I was with people who were monsters. . . . Only later, I became the devil.*"[59]

To give some validity and verification to the stories collected and facts that I assembled, I systematically tried to double check and triangulate them while being aware that one objective truth does not exist.[60] If anything, all facts and stories amassed were constantly evolving and changing in meaning, narrative, and symbolic representation. Indeed, it is my role as a researcher to understand the cultural landscapes that the official documents were written in and which formed the context of the interviews that I collected so that I could identify patterns and trends. At times, there was also only one source that I tried to double check but which I had to accept because of the value the information bought to the overall picture. This happened in only a few cases.

During this "methodological puzzle," the use of qualitative methods meant that I became both a detective and a kind of artist.[61] I became a detective by trying to map out the presence of Camorra women in the different clans across

Campania over time and space using my previous knowledge and understanding of the context. I became a kind of artist because I used the "bricolage" approach. By "bricolage," I used whatever materials I could access because I wanted to move beyond the obvious and analyze the multifaceted reality in front of me. As Kincheloe argues, "Bricoleurs move into the domain of complexity" because "the domains of the physical, the social, the cultural, the psychological, and the educational consist of the interplay of a wide variety of entities—thus, the complexity and the need for multiple ways of seeing [is] advocated by bricoleurs."[62] In other words, "bri-coleurs work to avoid pronouncements of final truth" because of the complexity and flexibility that is the world around us.[63] In research terms, this meant "drawing on theory from any discipline, using a combination of data-gathering methods and analytical techniques, and taking a similarly eclectic approach to the presentation and dissemination of research."[64]

Although I had collected judicial court cases and police reports over the years (1993–2018), this activity became more intense between 2018 and 2023. During that period, I consulted and read more than 150 judicial/police documents, and pre-COVID, 2018–19, I spent on and off four months in Naples looking for the women. Since 2021, this has started up again. The judicial and police material has always served as a starting point for further elaboration and investigations, to which I then sought to add other relevant information from alternative sources (in-depth interviews, newspaper articles, and immersion, among others). In this way, I built up my knowledge of information so that the case studies I chose were based on a variety of sources comprising differing information, making them rich and robust case studies. It is critical to note that for the stories relating to some of the more invisible women, such as foot soldiers and associates, there may have been less information accessible, which is a clear limitation, but I have done my utmost to supplement all cases studies as much as I could.

To be able to discuss the situation from the postwar period to the present day, I have also had to do some historical archive work in order to put together a histographic reconstruction of the roles of women in Camorra clans in the postwar period. I accessed four very different archives: (1) my personal archive of judicial documents (1992–2023 with more than three hundred judicial/police documents/reports), (2) the Naples newspaper archive, L' Emeroteca Tucci; (3) the archive of avvocato Gennaro Pecoraro (criminal law office, studio legale) based in Naples; and (4) the archive of the Carabinieri of Naples Province (although not as much as I would have wanted).[65]

Since 1993 I have collected many different judicial investigations which I have archived: this includes both investigations and police reports on specific clans and historic cases (1940–2023). In addition, I spent time in the Emeroteca Tucci in Naples reading and collecting newspaper articles for this research period 1940–2020s. I accessed the historical archive of the avv. Dott. Gennaro Pecoraro. He was a prominent criminal defense lawyer working in Naples during the 1950–1990s. Many of his clients were accused of Camorra membership and he dealt with some important cases, including the Pupetta Maresca case in 1955. I was lucky enough to interview him in 1997 (which I recorded on tape for my PhD research) and more recently, his son gave me copies of some of his Maresca trial documents which were very useful. I also accessed some files from the Commandante del Nucleo Investigativo del Comando Provinciale dei Carabinieri di Napoli (the Carabinieri Investigative Unit of the Province of Naples). In their archive, they have files on different investigations and court hearings from the postwar period which interested me.

Interviews have formed an essential part of my research approach as "a window" into someone's life and views; this is important to capture context and moments as well as more general information.[66] To do this, I used face-to-face interviews to access information from the different protagonists on the Camorra scene, engaging with the following groups:

1. Law enforcement, judges and police officers
2. Local community, social cooperatives and other community organizations
3. Former criminals, whether under protection or not

For law enforcement agents (judges and police officers) I used semistructured interviews as the basis of formal interviews but for my interviews with civil society and former Camorra women, I used specific ethnographic interviews, which allowed me to engage, build trust, and have a meaningful rapport with my interlocutors. With the former Camorra women, I utilized ethnographic and life story interviews, but more as "a conversation" and using "women talk" as suggested by Heyl.[67]

To achieve all this, I reached out to the various networks that I have built up over the years. These networks are built on trust and mutual respect and include the prosecutors from the DDA (Direzione Distrettuale Antimafia) in Naples and different local police forces, Guardia di Finanza, Polizia di Stato, and Carabinieri. I used semistructured interviews with law enforcement agencies in order to understand the context and their thinking; I also tended to go back for follow-up interviews. Some were recorded but usually, I took notes. I have carried out more than twenty semistructured and conversational interviews. I interviewed and spoke with antimafia prosecutors from the local DDA in Naples, prosecutors from the DNAA (Direzione Nazionale Antimafia e Antiterrorismo) in Rome, and other informed judges.[68] I had discussions with police officers from La Polizia di Stato, La Guardia di Finanza, I Carabinieri, and the DIA, in Naples.

Additionally, I interviewed representatives from civil society, Catholic associations, and former Camorra women, or women who have been involved in or close to Camorra clans. To capture the differences between districts, I sought to contact outreach charitable organizations across the city: Rione Traiano, southwest of the city center; and La Torretta-Mergellina, districts on the waterfront of the city, in order to engage in conversations with them about women in Naples and the Camorra. Gaining access to these groups and finding reliable gatekeepers took a bit of time but once they were found, I was able to engage. I have been in regular conversations with key workers from the NGO L'Orsa Maggiore, a social cooperative, that runs a "Mum and baby" group, Spazio Mamme, based in Rione Traiano; and nuns from il Centro Shalom, an after-school club located in La Torretta in central Naples.[69] The discussions that I had with these two associations informed a lot of my thinking.[70] I also visited a middle school near Naples Central railway station.[71] In these three spaces, I organized focus groups and discussions with children (aged eleven to twelve and thirteen to fourteen years) and women about what the Camorra means for them and how they see Camorra women.

For a long time, I have been interested in the insider's perspective of organized crime, so I was keen to capture women's voices in this regard. Interviewing protagonists was a key part of this project. This has not been easy, and again, gaining access to reliable gatekeepers has been a real challenge whether in the local community, police forces, or the judiciary, but all worthwhile.

Between 2010 and 2013 and again between 2018 and 2019, I had the opportunity to undertake semistructured ethnographic interviews with six former Camorra women, "collaboratrice di giustizia" or "pentite" (state witnesses) from very different clans from across the region.[72] These are previous Camorra women who are now state witnesses living under the protection of the Italian state. The interviews organized by the Italian Nuclei Operativi di Protezione (Police of the State Witness Protection Program) took place under strict security conditions and so are of exceptional value. The majority were born into noncriminal families but are representative of different types of Camorras with a diverse range of roles and tasks.[73] I requested to speak with these women to collect stories about their lives and to spend a bit of time with them.[74] Some accepted, others refused. The plurality of their voices and the kaleidoscope of their accounts, nevertheless, drew quite a coherent picture of the Camorra and women's involvement with recurring themes such as agency, power, respect, family, criminal values, money, and children.

There are still relatively few Camorra women state witnesses: in 2018, there were 1,189 state witness in total, of which 504 were from the Camorra of which 17 were women.[75] The Camorra represents 42 percent of total state witnesses and women were 3 percent of these. I interviewed 35–40 percent of these women (6 of 17).

Interviewing these women was very different from the "open interviews and unplanned conversations" that Siegel undertook with members of the Russian mafia in Amsterdam. Her interviews were "based on daily contact with 12 to 14 informants and their families, weekly meetings with 38 Russian-speaking legal immigrants, 14 illegal immigrants, and interviews with officials from various relevant institutions and organizations."[76] In my case, my interviewees already knew what I wanted to talk about and so there was no need to approach the topic of crime, the Camorra, and their involvement sensitively, since everything was out in the open. These moments proved to be quite intimate, intense, and thought provoking. As women we compared notes, thoughts, and lives.

I was aware that they were telling me *their* truth, but this is what I was interested in, the missing bits of the story. I believe that I gained more from interviewing directly key players than from reading other people's interpretation of their words. I traveled to various locations to undertake these semistructured interviews. On average, dialogue with these principal actors took three hours; they were real immersion moments for me. I spent this time, with them on the other side of the table, reflecting about their past lives and their future hopes. This was time listening, time just in their company in Rome, Naples, Turin, and Bologna in order to understand their complicated existence yesterday, today, and tomorrow. I have learned so much from them.

By talking to me, they were able to convey their female insider's perspective and to force me to think about some of my sexist stereotypes around the role of women in mafia groups. At times, they recounted very personal situations and experiences, but the more I met with them, what became obvious to me was that up until now, we had really ignored their voices and their experiences. Or, to put it another way, we were not capturing their full active role within the criminal organization and how fundamental these women were to the success of its operations and its longevity.

Interviews are very often criticized as a research method for collecting data because those interviewed present their truth and not the truth. Windle and Silke explain that they are "an expensive method" where there is "a risk of the interviewer being biased and it is not clear the truthfulness and validity of the accounts." But, they also have great potential: they "are a flexible method" where the researcher controls the process and there is a good response rate.[77]

Indeed, interviewees do not explain reality as it is, they do not present the truth, but they offer us their personal insight into a specific context and reality from their point of view. The researcher needs to acknowledge and consider that they can often explain poorly, lie, distort facts because language and events are not "objective" but are articulated through their biases and experiences. I believe that I have systematically evaluated the question of interviewee bias and have taken this into account. To make sure that I captured what was not said as well as what was said, I recorded all my interviews, then transcribed and translated them. I then undertook a systematic discourse analysis of their interviews, looking for concepts, explanations, and images to answer my questions. I regularly went back to the audio and written interviews. This allowed me to identify patterns, reactions, and trends around topics such as family, childhood, Camorra membership, activities, and violence for example.

In addition to these discussions, I also spent time in different districts where Neapolitan women and girls congregated and spent time there, having different encounters. During my fieldwork, I also, by chance, came across various women whose lives had been deeply marked by the Camorra. I sought to interview them and continued to have conversations with them to understand their involvement with the Camorra.[78] Moreover, I also struck up some stimulating and in-depth conversations with two men from different districts of Naples whose lives had been deeply shaped by the Camorra.[79] Both GP's and MA's visions, opinions, and views were helpful and illuminating. In particular, their specific male insight and perspective were helpful as I developed my thoughts and thinking. Conversations with EM, a former member of the Calabrian 'Ndrangheta, has also provided a comparative context to my thinking around the Camorra as a criminal organization and also to Neapolitan women and their involvement.[80]

Various criticisms and limitations have been developed vis-à-vis interviewing criminals and former criminals. There are two main issues that may be problematic: first, some researchers have suggested that "trying to get closer to informants," means "identifying with them." And, linked to this also is the need to protect your informers/interviewees.[81] Protection of my sources has always been a priority for me in any research project, so much so that on some occasions I have not used information in order not to betray the trust I had with my interlocutor. Others have also suggested that "the reliability and validity of the data obtained through interviews with 'organized criminals' can be questionable."[82]

Moreover, interviews are "peculiar situation[s]" and I needed to be aware that an interview is a "complex situation that calls for different modes of inference at different moments."[83] In other words, interviews are landscapes of cultural, social, and political meaning, and they "tell us something about how people make sense of their world well beyond the interview situation."[84] So, I needed to be aware of how interviewees talked in different contexts, using diverse cultural and symbolic representations and narratives. I did not accept what they said as a given, but studied, questioned, and engaged with their words, acknowledging that interviews are indeed "cultural landscapes."[85]

I would argue that the benefit of interviews, and in particular interviewing former *camorriste*, Camorra women, and criminals outweighs the possible disadvantages. In particular, the interviewing process helps to "tear down the walls of misconception." This is very pertinent, because in this study interviews have indeed allowed for a 360-degree analysis of the different levels and roles of Camorra women. In other words, included for the first time here is a female perspective rather than accept a narrow male point of view as the one and only valid framework.[86]

As a foreign researcher, observation and immersion have been instrumental methods for me to gain access to the communities that I was interested in understanding. These methods are not perfect. Windle and Silke have noted that "the primary weakness of participant observation is that as a case study, it tends not to be generalizable or replicable . . . immersion in the field and humanization of participants can weaken researcher's objectivity . . . and the presence of the researcher can change the situation being observed."[87]

Nevertheless, they are the only way to get a real and genuine insight into these communities. Observing a context was key for me to get a good understanding of a setting. I was now able to spend more quality time in Naples to engage with the community and to establish a trusted relationship that would allow me to follow various groups over four years. As already explained, I also visited a middle school, an afterschool club, and a mum-toddlers club to build up a relationship with these different groups of people to follow during the fellowship and to have discussions with them about the role of women in Neapolitan civil society and the Camorra as well as discussions with specific focused groups.[88] I engaged, observed, and related with these local community groups, nuns, women, lawyers, and teachers. I spent time observing and talking with these communities, talking to the women, children, and men about Naples, mafias, and women. In some cases, this became monthly discussions about how things were going or whether any unusual events had occurred.[89] I also spent time in the courthouse to attend different Camorra trials. I then went back to the research notes I had taken over the years of studying of the Camorra; these are reflections, thoughts, and notes taken on previous fieldwork.

I did not do as much immersion into the local community as I would have wanted. COVID in March 2020 haltered my regular visits to Naples, but I carried on as I could (including undertaking interviews via zoom/skype). By immersion, I mean being close to the locations, districts, and communities that I was interested in. I adopted the creative research method of "flaneur" which entailed me walking around Naples and living "sensorial experiences" in relation to the space, architecture, and time of the city. According to Lenz Kothe "the city is produced as a place through these aspects of flânerie, making each walk part of the flâneur's creative practice within the city. Even if a flâneur did not seek to make anything concrete out of their strolls about the city, the historical and cultural characters were created out of that wandering."[90]

These meanderings have been essential for me to relate to the city and to the different locations that I studied, such as visiting the cemetery in Marano di Napoli, the covered market in Mergellina, or Piazzetta Mondragone. "Mindful walking" was a useful practice that allowed me to engage with the context, people, and space that I wished to understand and to observe. I spent a lot of time wandering through the different districts of Naples to get a feel for the different locations, from Scampia to Ponticelli to the Vomero and Marano. I also accompanied the Police Flying Squad (La Squadra d'Unità d'Intervento) on different occasions, touring Naples and its different districts by day and night in order to get a firsthand view of the territory—Barra, Soccavo, San Giovanni, and La Sanità (see figure I.1) for example.

All studies on organized crime have limitations and my studies are no exception. Four traditional limitations come to mind: first, the nature of the subject matter. Because of the hidden and secretive nature of OCGs, it becomes difficult to study them fully and transparently. As women in OCGs are even less visible, this complicates their study and examination even further. In addition, finding material that can help put together a detailed and clear picture of organized crime is challenging at best; therefore, I decided to collect the voices of Camorra women and those who study them to then triangulate them with other data and material to put together the most coherent picture of this phenomenon.

Second, the difficulty in accessing material and what is actually available and recorded. The different types of documents analyzed may offer different qualities of material (police and judicial documents versus newspaper articles), which means that some aspects of the analysis may be more reliable or thorough than others. In addition, there may exist an unconscious gender bias in the collection of data and elaboration of material. In relation to organized crime this is clearly the case but also in relation to mafias. Often police and judicial material are collected and written by men, which means that there is an inbuilt male bias. This may or may not be acknowledged.

Third, generalizability. Will the analysis and themes that emerge from my case studies be generalizable? This is a legitimate question. I believe that that depth versus breath is also valid here. In other words, I have selected specific case studies which I believe, from the many case studies I have looked at, have a generalizable value but also the added value of detail and depth which is rarely possible with other methods.

Lastly, I acknowledge once again that the analysis presented in this study is not neutral nor objective but written by a subjective, white European middle-class woman who brings her own experience and biases to what she has seen, discussed, and heard. To suggest that these kinds of studies can be neutral and impartial and produce a universal truth is to not understand the essence of academic studies. This is not *the* history of women in the Camorra. It is *a* history of women in the Camorra.

WOMEN AND THE EMERGING POSTWAR CAMORRA

Alfredo Maisto and Lucky Luciano, two notorious criminals who marked the Neapolitan underworld during the immediate postwar period, had three women close to them: Alfredo's wife Concetta Sequino; his sister Emilia Maisto; and Igea Lissoni, a Milanese ballerina, who was Luciano's wife.[1] They were never fully appreciated for their potential influence on these men and their criminal strategies. Perhaps they had some bearing, perhaps none; what is obvious is that they are rarely mentioned in the history books because there is such sparse interest and information about them. This is a major problem looking back now, as it has produced over the years a gendered history of the Camorra based on men by men. A closer look suggests a more balanced picture of gendered involvement.

In this chapter, I discuss the criminal landscape pre-1982 to show that women were more active than is suggested and that they were more than just irrelevant. I have selected five case studies of women involved with camorristi, who lived between the 1950s and 1980s, to illustrate the continuity between these women's roles, actions, values, and behavior, and those carried out by women more recently. I selected them because they represent different contexts: two from the Province of Naples and three from the city.

In this way, I place my analysis of modern Camorra women into a historical context to challenge the dominant concepts, so far developed, of "emancipation," "pink tsunami," "pinkification" or "sexual"-"gender" revolution which have recently taken place in the Camorra underworld. With respect to my research methodology, since I am looking at historic cases since the 1940s, the analysis becomes more difficult because relevant documents may no longer exist. My stories here were determined by the availability of the material. With these limited resources, I ask whether or not these women were just "an army of subordinates," "lackeys," or "vassals" prior to 1982?

Women in the Camorra during the Postwar Period

Women have been a constant presence in Camorra activities, regardless of the changing criminal markets or organizational structures. Already, in 1862, Marc Monnier, one of the first to write about the Camorra, highlighted the importance of women in clans and activities, even though subsequently, his comments appear to have largely been forgotten. He noted that women were violent members of the Camorra, although he seems somewhat surprised by this:

> This Camorra is represented by a woman: yes, a woman! She has fire in her eyes and a knife in her pocket. She is in charge. Not one argument takes place without her getting involved, not one fight takes place without her jumping into the middle of it with her arms out. She runs her little business in her home, she uses what she finds, oversees the negotiations, taxes the suppliers, imposes her rights over everything: the others know it and keep quiet because they are scared.[2]

In addition, in the first comprehensive study of the Camorra in English published in 1996, the author explains in a footnote why he uses the masculine pronoun "he" to refer to camorristi arguing that it is "deliberate" and that

> while female activity with Camorra gangs certainly exists at a higher level than within the Mafia, there are, apart from Raffaele Cutolo's sister Rosetta and Pupetta Maresca, no significant examples of women becoming major gang leaders; indeed, both these women's "criminal careers" were probably mapped out by their brother and husband/lover, respectively.[3]

More recently still, Saviano also reinforced this female-on-male dependence: "The typical image of the Camorra woman is of a female who does nothing but echo the pain and will of her men—her brothers, husband, and sons." He then stressed that a change had taken place: "But it's not like that. The transformation of the Camorra in recent years has also meant a metamorphosis of the women's role."[4]

Personally, I contest these notions and the idea that a "transformation" or "metamorphosis" has taken place because I believe that Italian mafia women have always been a constant influence over their male counterparts as a Sicilian journalist explained in 1994: "Their lives run parallel to those of their men."[5] In Naples, the lives of women living with camorristi are so interconnected that they are fundamentally part of the Camorra's modern history.

From the evidence I collected, women have always been part of emerging Camorra clans in the postwar period, not as male dependents but both as leaders and foot soldiers. Let us not forget that the historian, Gribaudi, has argued that women in Naples have always been part of the Neapolitan illegal economy, saying that "if you talk to the people who run local businesses, they'll tell you women are in charge of the Camorra families' finances. They're very conscious of it, it's a tradition in this city."[6] She sees women as playing a significant role in the illegal informal Neapolitan economy: women using their soft powers and interpersonal skills in the local community to look after the illegal lottery and loansharking. These women together are an army of women that are considered peripheral to the daily criminal activities of the Camorra.[7] But, as Gribaudi highlights, there are "strong women" who navigate the Camorra and who have taken on important roles and tasks, if we are curious enough to look.[8] The image of women as a vast army undertaking small-time criminal activities to survive and not being fully active and immersed in the Camorra is only half of the picture and has been an image projected by local male police officers and businessmen, willing or unwillingly, for most of the postwar period.

Already in 1985, the journalist Giancarlo Siani, drawing attention to the fact that women were involved in less soft and more hands-on criminal activities, such as smuggling of cigarettes during the 1970s and 1980s, noted that

> in the files of the Carabinieri the names of certain individuals who became "famous" in those years appeared. Pasqual Marano, alias "*O' Nonno*," ["Granddad"] believed to be the "historic leader" of the activities of contraband cigarettes together with Francesca Gallo, more famously known as "Donna Pereta," who was considered to be the mother of all the youngsters who became involved in this [contraband] activity.[9]

The case of Donna Pereta reinforces my hypothesis that she was well respected by the local criminal community (in particular, the up-and-coming ambitious young criminals), fully involved in smuggling of cigarettes, and according to *Carabinieri* documents, she was fully involved in other illegal activities such as producing fake documents.

It is important to note that between 1948 to 1982, women are regularly mentioned in the local newspapers, in particular in *Il Mattino*: for example, Marisa Romeo and Rachele Somma (on November 15, 1948); Vincenza De Meglio (on September 21, 1947); Antonella Gallo and Agiovanni Guagio (on March 28,

1948); Concetta Muccardo (on November 15, 1957); and Anna Biondi (on January 21, 1956).[10] All these references arise in connection with cigarette smuggling and scams.

An Overview of the Situation Pre-1982

It is difficult to understand the true nature of the involvement of women in Camorra activities in the immediate postwar period from the 1950s to 1980s, because it was only in September 1982 that the crime of "mafia membership" was formally and officially recognized by law. The Rognoni-La Torre Act, law 646/82, established that a crime was committed by individuals when they were believed to belong to "a mafia-type association'" (416 bis law). The mere fact of belonging to a mafia group was a crime because of the groups' power to intimidate and impose itself on others. Prior to this legislation, the mafia and male *mafiosi* were not identified as such. This made our analysis of Camorra women during the 1950–80s particularly challenging.[11]

Because more than half a century has passed since the 1950s and 1960s, it has been complicated to collect material and study Camorra women from that historical period. Most documents—judicial sentences, trial transcripts, or police reports—have been destroyed, lost, or are inaccessible today, added to which many of the key protagonists are no longer here to tell their story.[12] Those judicial files, police reports, and newspaper articles that exist and that I was able to access recount events and give a clear timeline. I have spent time reading these in order to reconstruct life stories and specific incidences.[13] However, since many of these articles were written by male journalists, Camorra women were rarely seen or noted. The newspapers are full of film stars or tragic *faits divers*, generating news where crime is rarely linked to women.

Second, because women were ignored or underreported at this time, history has forgotten their active and nuanced presence, erasing them altogether from history books, a form of historic amnesia takes place. Male historians narrate history based on documents they access, often those that adopt only a top-down approach, and have tended to write women out of their reconstructions because of preconceived bias. Indeed, many of their historical accounts have been written retrospectively and continue to omit women, often perpetuating traditional and negative stereotypes, errors, misunderstandings, and misinterpretations.

As a result, mafia experts and journalists reading these histories have unquestionably represented mafia organizations as "gender exclusive" with clear gender stratification. Male historians and journalists also naturally project their own values, norms, and prejudices into their interpretations of historical situations.

In other words, unconsciously, they privilege and propagate a male point of view onto a historical male account. Without questioning it, we accept a male-written history of the Neapolitan Camorra that is presented as gender neutral, when in fact it is a loaded male interpretation of events and roles, a double bias embedded in historical narrative. We could ask whether it is a sexist or even misogynist interpretation of facts in which women are reduced to a very limited, passive, and powerless role. A rereading of life stories and events giving space and a voice to the women may show that things were, in fact, quite different.

Third, there can be a disconnection between reality, newspaper accounts, and historical texts that produce a confused and sexist reading of the situation. For example, the involvement of Anna Mazza in Camorra activities remains unclear. She died in April 2017 at the age of eighty. She was the wife of Gennaro Moccia, a boss from Afragola who was murdered by rivals in 1977 and the mother of the Moccia siblings who made up the Moccia clan during the 1980s. On the one hand, we have the media's portrayal of her as a passive domesticated wife and mother, defined in relation to her husband: the "Widow Moccia" (in Italian, *Vedova Moccia*), or the "Camorra Widow" (*Vedova della Camorra*), or the "Black Widow," (*Vedova Nera*).[14] Like many other journalists, Capezzuto describes her as "the Black Widow of the Camorra," (*la Vedova Nera della Camorra*), which offers a vulnerable and fragile image of *La Zia,* or "Auntie," as she liked to be called.[15] She cultivated this image by wearing black everyday of her life after her husband's murder like a good loyal widow should. This rational decision reinforced her traditional gender role as an obedient and loving wife as she mourned her husband and showed him eternal devotion and respect for the rest of her days.

On the other hand, we have the explanations of various state witnesses from her clan, who described a more forceful, alert, and active person. Clan members called her *La Signora*, showing her the upmost respect, but this yet again refers to her position in relation to her husband. She was the "Mrs" to a Camorra boss and therefore, inherited his social capital, reputation, and respect, or did she? The state witness Rocco D'Angelo explained that she was "*very reserved and did not deal with [ordinary] members* [in other words, foot soldiers]," preferring instead to use go-betweens, so-called *consiglieri*.[16] He goes on to say that "*she manages the clan*" and it is clear that the "*Signora Mazza is the most cunning of them all.*"[17] D'Angelo continues, noting that "*they go and speak with the [leaders] and with La Signora to decide things* [including murders]."[18] One pentita recalls how her brothers became involved with the Moccia clan: one of her brothers worked for *La Signora* (including delivering death orders to clan members). She explains how she was very demanding and precise in her loan sharking business, even ordering one of her other brothers to leave the region because he was not behaving properly.[19]

Finally, I believe that in the postwar period all four Italian mafias have adopted a clear "branding" strategy of how they want to be perceived in the public sphere. The evidence indicates how one of the aspects of this patriarchal strategy is to be a man-only institution and a gender exclusive organization and brand. Women have always been dismissed by camorristi and mafiosi as "irrelevant" and not capable of doing the job, of not being up to it, of not being violent enough, of not being intelligent enough, of not being discreet enough, and of not having the appropriate capacities and skills to belong to a clan. Indeed, I believe Italian mafias cultivate and project this specific virile image to their communities, civil society at large, law enforcement agencies, and judges. They play to the established gendered identities. They promote this traditional macho public relations image to reinforce their power and the status quo. But, if we look beyond this simplistic and basic image, we may find that it is clearly only a show for the outside world, a way of manipulating and controlling the public sphere. Women are there, useful, participant, and willing, but to display this to the outside world would be to underline a possible weakness. Clan leaders keep women under the radar by consistently and intentionally dismissing them as irrelevant, incapable, backwards, and stupid to preserve their own image and power.

In conclusion, during the postwar period, the rhetoric of Italian mafias has been to state and to behave as though women of all ages were incapable of being involved in criminal activities. As a result, the outside world and civil society has ignored their role, falling into the mafia's trap and public relations stunt. It is only now that we are giving women their dues and understanding their contribution and what they are really worth.

Women and the Camorra since the 1950s

In the immediate postwar era, we find women in two different criminal situations: (1) ordinary women who work in the illegal economy in their street level flats, *il basso*, and (2) women close or related to emerging camorristi. Women in the illegal economy were either ordinary women trying to make ends meet and were regarded as not being involved in criminality or there were women who participated directly in organizing emerging Camorra activities (such as smuggling of cigarettes or money laundering). Either way, the nature of their involvement is neglected and not considered criminal.

Then, there were women close to the emerging Camorra context and well-known camorristi. A number of women have been systematically used as examples to suggest that Camorra women, compared to Cosa Nostra and the 'Ndrangheta, have always been more active in the postwar period. It could be argued that these are always the same well-cited women who have become "token examples" and thus, too obvious. These women include Anna Mazza from Afragola and Rosetta Cutolo from Ottaviano; the former was the wife of Gennaro Moccia and the latter the sister of Raffaele Cutolo. A lot has been written about them.[20] They both emerged as being heavily involved in criminal activities once their men became a lesser force. Anna Mazza gained prominence after her husband was murdered in 1977; Rosetta Cutolo was believed to have led Nuova Camorra Organizzata (NCO) troupes during the 1980s when her brother was incarcerated from 1981 onward. These observations meant that it was automatically deduced that the women filled a vacuum and only took that space and were respected because of their relationship to the men.

On the contrary, I have analyzed five examples of women involved with their men in Camorra activities who did not become a major force once their men had withdrawn from the criminal scene. I looked for women who might be less obvious but whose stories might be helpful in terms of understanding their criminal agency. I have sought to show that they are not inferior, but rather, respected individuals who have their own social capital, influence, and power.

These are the well-cited Assunta "Pupetta" Maresca from Castellamare di Stabia and Maria Orlando from Marano (both from the hinterland) and Gemma Sacco from Forcella and Angelica and Maria Zaza, from Santa Lucia (these latter three being from the Naples city center). We can illustrate this by listening to the famous story of Pupetta Maresca who died on December 29, 2021, at the age of eighty-six.

Partners or Bystanders?

Compared to the Sicilian Mafia, the Neapolitan Camorra took a bit of time to reorganize in the immediate postwar period to become the business efficient groups they are today. In the hinterland, initially it was individuals and small groups that started to undertake basic illegal activities such as cow stealing, petrol smuggling, price fixing, and cigarettes and drug smuggling and dealing.[21]

During the 1950s, Pasquale Simonetti from Nola was considered a lone criminal, a so-called *guappo,* but in fact he had many associates, including his wife. Assunta Maresca was born in January 1935 in Castellamare di Stabia, a town in the bay of Naples. Her father, Alberto, was a renowned smuggler, and her uncle, Vincenzo Castellano, went to prison for seven years for having killed his brother Gerardo.[22] Hers was a well-respected family with a criminal reputation, known as the *Lampetiello* for their ability to take out their knives to defend themselves in a lightning flash.[23] But it would appear that they never developed into a full modern recognized Camorra clan.

"Pupetta," meaning "pretty girl" or "little doll," was the nickname given to Assunta. It was a kind and affectionate word to describe her striking beauty. The name stuck with her ever since. Even in old age, well into her eighties, she had good looks and charisma as well as determination.[24] Because of these attributes, Pupetta was a mafia icon and popular reference in Neapolitan and Italian culture since the 1950s, as well as an inspiration to fictional authors of novels, films, and television series. One example, Franco Rosi's 1958 film, *La Sfida*, is based on her life story. Indeed, in any mafia movie or story where there is a woman, the characters have been inspired by Pupetta's narrative.[25] Despite this, her full agency as a camorrista has never been fully appreciated or emphasized as much as it merits. A Ministry of the Interior document on "Women in Italian Mafias" in 1996 noted that *"Pupetta is cold, lucid and in certain ways, diabolical,"* although this report has never been officially cited.[26] Indeed, in the collective imagination, it has always been the softer and more feminine image of her that has predominated, when in fact there is so much more to Pupetta. She not only had beauty and charisma, but also a streak of evil and determination.

Assunta was one of five, together with two brothers and two sisters. She was the second child and first daughter of Alberto and Doralinda. Her mother owned a grocery shop in Castellamare di Stabia and distributed milk locally, but on occasion, she was also party to receiving stolen goods.[27] Her father was already involved in criminal activities while Assunta was growing up; this impacted on her home life, upbringing, and education. She grew up in a world where criminal values and criminality were the norm. For example, it was suggested that she wounded a classmate at school, who dropped her allegations once she left hospital because she had been intimidated by Pupetta.[28] A judicial document noted that it was because of her traditional education based on criminal values that *"she was not an emancipated woman."*[29]

On Christmas Eve 1954, when Pascalone e' Nola, or Big Pascal from Nola, an-up-and-coming local guappo, an important criminal, came out of prison, he rushed to Pupetta's house in Castellamare.[30] Pascalone, a tall and burly bloke who towered over everyone, came from nearby Palma Campania, a town in the hinterland of Naples. He courted Pupetta and swept her off her feet. He was a traditional and charismatic criminal who respected values, hierarchy, and rules in a changing environment. He started out doing small-time crimes that were initially part of a survival strategy, or *l'arte di arrangersi*, but soon had become involved in more profitable and violent businesses, such as the contraband of cigarettes, petrol, food, and drugs.

Pascalone's criminal career is emblematic of many *guappi*, or bosses, of the same era. He was both ambitious and power hungry. His brazen behavior meant that he upset people. During the 1940s, he, together with some of his friends-turned-associates such as Antonio Esposito, another guappo, had started importing contraband cigarettes from Sicily. He went to prison in 1953 for shooting another guappo rival or what was recorded as the "attempted murder" of Alfredo Maisto. When he was released at Christmas 1954, after having served two years of his sentence, he became *Presidente dei prezzi* in Corso Novara where he mediated-fixed prices between the farmers and the market sellers in Naples, while taking a hefty cut for himself, making many dangerous enemies.[31] Indeed, Antonio Esposito fell out with Pascalone and a profound rivalry emerged, not only around illegal deeds but also because of their cigarette smuggling activities. However, a year later in July 1955 at Pascalone's wedding, Esposito was nevertheless his best man, although many tensions remained.[32]

This setting represented a perfect environment for violent individuals who wanted to make a name for themselves and money fast. Market mediation was never really portrayed as a Camorra-type activity because it was described as being undertaken solely by individuals. This is an unfair historic representation. I would argue that during this period, there were many groups active across the region. It is the big personalities, such as Alfredo Maisto or Antonio Esposito, who are remembered. In other words, although these men, including Pascalone, were presented as lone guappi, they were in fact all surrounded by a group of foot soldiers and associates. Pascalone had a personal chauffeur, a group of associates including henchmen and investors, and his wife, Pupetta, who all supported and participated in his criminal activities.

In April 1955, at the age of nineteen, Pupetta married Pascalone in a big, brash wedding attended by many local criminals and politicians. One month after his wedding, on May 5, 1955, Pascalone was shot in broad daylight in Corso Novara, the main marketplace in Naples. This murder was carried out by one of Esposito's associates, a sidekick named Carlo Gaetano Orlando.[33] This was a public act of violence and belligerence, the punishment of a rival which was full of symbolic value for a criminal underworld competing for emerging markets. At the time, Pascalone's murder was reported as a local "règlement de comptes," score settling between emerging bosses. Essentially, Esposito wanted to get rid of his former business partner, Pascalone, who, once out of prison, had started to challenge his supremacy.[34] An alternative explanation is recorded as,

> She made it clear that when her husband came out of prison (1–2 months before the wedding) Esposito's activities were in full flow, in the sense that he continued to "offload cigarettes." Simonetti's regained freedom was not appreciated by Esposito who was taking a % from the others involved and careful who should complain. Once he [Esposito] tried to do the same with her husband, and this is when the problems started.[35]

This was the backdrop to Pupetta's appearance in the criminal underworld. She is often portrayed as a young and vulnerable woman who did things out of passion and without thinking of the consequences, but this was not the case at all. She was decisive, independent, and loved her husband dearly.[36] Judicial documents highlight that she was a well-informed wife, not a passive bystander. She was not only Pascalone's wife, but his partner and friend. She listened to him and was fully aware of what her husband was involved in. One description stated that "*she recalls how her husband often confided in her at home.*"[37] When he was dying in hospital, he wanted to speak to no one except to his wife. It was reported that Pascalone asked his friend "*to call his wife to whom he would tell everything.*"[38]

Pupetta explained that "*before her husband died, he had confided in her that it had been Esposito who had ordered his murder, but he had at the same time forced her to swear not to tell anyone out of fear that she could have come to harm as a result.*"[39]

After Pascalone's death, Pupetta asked the police for help to investigate and find the culprits of the crime, but soon felt let down by them. Throughout her life, Maresca has had a strong sense of self-identity and how she should act. Indeed, she never did what was expected of her. After her husband's murder, her family and in particular her older brother, Vincenzo, saw a golden opportunity to make money from this tragic event and wanted to blackmail Antonio Esposito, who had tacitly accepted responsibility for the murder, for what he had done. It was stated that "*Pascalone's blood could have produced a solid profit.*"[40] However, Pupetta "*logically rebelled. She had a fiery and wild temperament, she was still profoundly and emotionally attached to her husband's memory and . . . any possible transaction linked to this, was for her an unspeakable and intolerable outrage.*"[41]

She did not passively accept her family's criminal project, nor for that matter, the police's apathy, and indifference. She acted according to her sense of self and showed great loyalty to her husband and her own ideas about what was right and wrong. Here, she demonstrated her own agency in a hostile environment. So, as the police had ignored her request, she took matters into her own hands to avenge her husband's murder. Heavily pregnant, she drove from Castellamare di Stabia to Naples with her teenage brother and killed Antonio Esposito.[42] Pupetta went on the run for a couple of months but eventually gave herself up. She vindicated her husband and accomplished her vendetta; she had defended herself and her husband's honor. This murder is often described as a "*passionate murder*" and a "*crime of honor and love,*" one conducted by feelings, emotions, and sentiments, not devious, but full of violent revenge. The judges concluded that her crime was in her blood and her education: "*To this end, she followed a traditional code of crime and the Maresca family also belonged to a terrible criminal tradition, that which respects the value of 'vendetta' and believes in the notion of vendetta.*"[43]

Her actions have always been presented as an act of personal vendetta by a bitter and twisted widow. In typical criminal tradition, "*the crime belongs exclusively to Assunta Maresca who presents in the event involved an occasional and impulsive character, the unmistakable footprint of passion and pain."*[44]

At the time, her actions were systematically interpreted by journalists and today by mafia experts as the act of a lone woman eaten up by revenge, but who valued the concept of vendetta because of her criminal education. She wanted vengeance and nothing else.

In a recent interview, Pupetta recounts these events, but there is no mention of *vendetta*, nor revenge but rather, *legittima difesa* (self-defense):

> *When my situation happened, I had already denounced this person at least ten times to the police. When I went into the Questura in Naples, he already knew everything so much so that he would come and threaten me at my parents. Then I met him. He came towards me with a big gun, I also carried a small gun in my handbag because he had started to threaten me. When he came near me, he wanted to open the car door so that his killers could kill me. In that situation, what should I have done? I defended myself, nothing more nothing less. He shot me 12 times, I shot him 6 with my small gun.*[45]

She concludes that her *"error was to have killed."*

Before the trial in 1959, a journalist-judicial narrative was already constructed around Orlando, the supposed murderer of her husband and Pupetta herself, reporting that *"in Naples, the press has already imposed on the judges a constructed narrative that Orlando was the 'sinister hired assassin' and "Pupetta" Maresca was the avenger of her destroyed love*).*"[46]

She was never recognized as having her own agency and a role in Pascalone's criminal activities.[47] She was merely seen as having *"a boisterous and fiery character,"* and her actions were always very emotive as *"she was profoundly attached to the memory of her husband."*[48] On the contrary, however, Avvocato Pecoraro suggests that her revenge was for Pascalone's group and not for herself. Things may be slightly more nuanced because ultimately, Antonio Esposito remained a problem and obstacle for Simonetti's associates.[49]

The context of Camorra tensions between different young guappi and their associates has been completely ignored in mafia history books describing the postwar period, yet this might be more helpful in understanding Pupetta's premeditated reaction. The only point that has been underlined about the Camorra at this time is that Pascalone e' Nola and Antonio Esposito represented two different forms of emerging Camorra. On the one hand, Pascalone was typical of the older, more traditional Camorra; on the other hand, Antonio Esposito reflected the new modern, entrepreneurial Camorra.[50] Pupetta's role within Pascalone's Camorra context was never really touched on, but a closer look at her court case files shows traces of a developing Camorra context that she was aware of. One document recalls that "*Assunta Maresca and her collaborators knew all of this [Camorra dynamics] because they had a clear idea of the situation in Corso Novara and of Antonio Esposito and his associates*'" thinking and projects.[51]

She was therefore not an ignorant bystander but an interested participant because she had an equal relationship with her husband, even if for the public she remained solely defined in relation to him, a token woman. Nonetheless, she was anything but that; she was a woman of consequence with experience and knowledge. Throughout her life, she had a voice and was outspoken but ignored and marginalized. In May 1959, Assunta was sentenced to eighteen years in prison for manslaughter. Her son, Pascalone Jr., was born in prison in January 1956 and was brought up by her family outside jail. In the end, she only served thirteen years and came out of prison in 1971.

This was not the end of her Camorra life. In 1973, she met Umberto Ammaturo, a young emerging drug trafficker in the Naples Tribunal. They fell in love, and she became his partner. Umberto Ammaturo and Pupetta were equals in their criminal careers as the Naples Camorra scene started to explode during the 1970s–1980s, although this was never really acknowledged.[52] One of her relatives recalls how initially, she was a little cold toward her, and she saw her as "*detached.*" She describes Pupetta as "*a determined woman. A woman who knows what she is doing, for sure. Of great intelligence, yes. A woman who knows what she's doing.*"[53]

During this period, she remained overshadowed by her partner, but documents show that she was no bystander in Ammaturo's activities or his in hers. She moved to Fuorigrotta, his home district, and opened clothes shops, one there, and another one in the city center. In 1980, it is suggested that Felice Malventi, a well-known and respected man of honor, and the father-in-law of Ammaturo's older brother Antonio, in some way insulted or offended Pupetta in her shop in Fuorigrotta: this was not left to lie and Malventi was shot and punished while in his car with his lover.

Another event that marked a change in Pupetta's life was the murder in March 1981 of Aldo Semerari, a criminologist-psychiatrist, who acted as an expert witness for different Camorra clans and groups. Semerari was murdered and horrifically dismembered after a meeting with Ammaturo. He had helped Ammaturo escape prison by stating that he was "*insane,*" but the problem was that he also helped some of Ammaturo's bitterest rivals, a fact that bothered Ammaturo immensely. It is believed that this is why he was murdered. "He had betrayed Ammaturo, and he knew too much. . . . Ammaturo was accused of this awful crime and later admitted it."[54] It was suggested that Pupetta was involved because "*Pupetta Maresca is always well informed on all of Ammaturo's business activities and decisions.*"[55] Indeed, it would appear that she *"knows much more than she is letting on."*[56]

In November 1981, she was accused together with Ammaturo and her younger brother of murdering a member of Raffaele Cutolo's NCO because of turf wars and drug interests and threatening his family to keep quiet: *"According to the women* [the mother of the victim] *in relation to the threats received and other factors, those who had ordered the murder were these three* [CM, Pupetta Maresca and UA]." Pupetta and Ammaturo were both described as *"important members of the underworld and not only members of the local one."*[57]

In essence, she continuously defended her family throughout her life, whether it was her husband, her son, her brother, or partner in question. In February 1982, she held a press conference to speak directly with rival and NCO boss, Raffaele Cutolo, in order to threaten him in the middle of a Camorra war and to warn him off her family. She stated that "I am speaking for myself and for my relatives. If Cutolo touches someone from my family, I will murder without pity/ women and children. . . . And also say that I am not scared of killers and when they want to find me, they know where I am."[58]

While Pupetta served time for the Semerari murder while Ammaturo fled to Latin America alone. He was arrested in 1993 and on his return to Italy, he became an important state witness acknowledging many of his crimes. Pupetta remained in Italy and withdrew from the Camorra front line.

Reconstructing Assunta Maresca's story has been a challenge because of the notorious level of omertà that surrounds her. Additionally, she was systematically misportrayed by judges and journalists as a passionate and desperate young widow or a headstrong middle-aged woman, not a woman with her own agency. In the life story I have managed to put together, clear criminal agency appears. Her early involvement with Pascalone and the emerging Camorra context shows that she was active and not passive. Pupetta made decisions of her own accord without being forced, manipulated, or instructed by a man. She was always her own woman and a player in her own right.[59]

Historically, she was attributed with little capacity to determine her own agency and destiny. She was never presented as a woman with her own independent criminal prestige and agenda, and her own *aurora*, power and thinking. She was always mentioned in relation to the men she was involved with and consistently reduced to her gender by the men who encountered her. This falls short of reality: it is an unfair reflection and ultimately a sexist one, because she was not just an extension of her father, brothers, husband, or her partner; she was far more. Since she was never associated with a strong, stable Camorra clan, she was never considered a modern important player but an inconsistent and weak figure.[60] In actual fact, she did represent the true essence of a Camorra woman, silent maybe, but fully cognizant and intelligent enough to know when to withdraw from mainstream criminal activity to protect herself.

Our second example is that of Maria Orlando (1914–2008). She was a strong matriarch at the center of a large extended Camorra family and yet nonexistent in history books. She had lots of capital, which has been rarely recognized. Again, the Nuvoletta clan was an important clan from the 1970s onward, in particular because of its links with Sicilian mafiosi but also because of its capacity to invest its illegal profits. This clan was versatile, modern, and forward thinking; today it is less compact and efficient as in its heyday. The matriarch, Maria Orlando, mother of the two most powerful leaders, Lorenzo, and Angelo Nuvoletta, is intriguing. She was born in 1914 into a large family from Marano di Napoli, north of Naples. She died in 2008 at the age of ninety-four. She was one of six siblings, and married Giovanni Nuvoletta in the early 1930s at the age of sixteen to seventeen years.[61] She had six children and her sons, Ciro, Lorenzo, Gaetano, and Angelo, eventually led the Nuvoletta clan during the 1970s and became members of Cosa Nostra. Her older brother, Angelo, was the communist mayor of the town during the 1950s and the father of Carlo Gaetano Orlando, the presumed killer of Pupetta Maresca's husband.[62]

Maria lived most of her life between Marano and Villaricca. Today, Marano has become a suburb of Naples, but back in the postwar period it was still very much part of the countryside and rural. From the 1970s, Maria lived in her sons' compound, Poggio Vallesana, an estate and group of houses on the hill outside of Marano, which was their fortress when they became a significant Camorra clan.

Marano became synonymous with Camorra thanks to her sons and their criminal, commercial, and political activities.[63] They were very business orientated and learned quickly from other Sicilian Mafia bosses who were banished to the region, as well as from emerging bosses, such as Antonio Bardellino.[64] They were focused and power driven regardless of whether they sought economic or political contacts. Relatives were removed if they did not fit in with their plans. For example, they did not protect the Maisto brothers who were related to them. Enrico Maisto was married to one of their cousins, the daughter of Maria's brother Antonio Orlando, and he was sacrificed for business; Maria was there.[65]

She appears at various points in official police reports and in particular, in a Milan police report that was monitoring telephone conversations. They identified hers as of the telephone numbers that the Sicilian boss, Luciano Leggio, was in contact with. The document noted that "*during the surveillance of telephones, they were able to identify that the suspect Leggio, contacted Nuvoletta and his associates through telephone numbers registered to Maria Orlando, Azienda Agricola Avicola, via Allenuova Marano (NA), mother of the Nuvoletta and registered to Nuvoletta Lorenzo, via S. Maria a Cubito, Marano 12/A, Marano (NA)."*[66]

Indeed,

> the company, that is registered under the name of Lorenzo's mother, Maria Orlando, provides agricultural products and chickens to the military base in Caserta and the majority of their contracts are for public institutions. Some questions are being asked if the head of services of the military base asked the Carabinieri to check whether the company from Marano had all its paperwork in order to be a recognized supplier. On the 7th of September 1982, the Carabinieri eliminated any doubt and gave approval because M. Orlando "in public is well respected and has a good social and commercial reputation.[67]

No one mentions her relationship with her son Lorenzo, the Camorra boss; his contacts with Cosa Nostra; his criminal activities; and the visits of certain well-known Sicilian mafiosi to Poggio Vallesana, the estate where she lived with her family.[68] She is never given her true role in the clan, and when she appears it is to put investigators off the scent. She is buried in Marano Cemetery next to her husband and sons.

Collaborators or Onlookers?

Here I wish to reflect about two modern Camorra city clans where women were present as these criminal groups emerged during the immediate postwar period. The Giuliano clan became notorious at the beginning of the 1980s as part of the NF alliance to counter Raffaele Cutolo and his criminal project, the NCO. But, Gemma Sacco, mother of the Giuliano brothers who led the clan, had her own criminal story.

Gemma Sacco was born in 1932 in Cassino (Lazio region) and lived the best part of her life in Forcella, a central district of Naples. Her parents moved to Forcella from Cassino, where they originated from, after it was badly bombed. When her parents decided to go back after the war, Gemma elected to stay in Naples where she lived with her husband, Pio Vittorio Giuliano. He started out as a *contrabandiere*, a smuggler, in the streets of Forcella, selling anything that was needed in order to make ends meet and to put food on the table for his large family.[69] Her eldest son Nunzio Giuliano recalls that "my grandparents respected her decision but were sad because they were concerned about leaving their daughter in such a poor degraded neighborhood."[70]

Gemma bought up her eleven children.[71] Nunzio explains, "I was born in 1948, my parents lived in hardship: they did not have a house, nor a job and did not even have the opportunity to provide food for me."[72]

The siblings went on to become the Giuliano clan during the 1990s. One description states that "[the Giuliano clan] are the sons, cousins of the bosses of

Forcella who were [brothers] Pio Vittorio, Salvatore, and Guglielmo during the late 1940s and early 1950s. But this second generation [that of the 1990s . . .] is no longer content with the profits of stolen goods and the sale of 'bionde' cigarettes to the locals."[73]

There are contradictory descriptions of Pio Vittorio. On the one hand, he was seen as "the patriarch of Forcella" who remained outside ("external") to organized crime activities.[74] According to another view, we could consider him "a noncriminal" or "non malavitoso." On the other hand, a more tangible picture is possible, in that, together with his brothers, he took control of criminal activities. "The black-market flourishes especially in Forcella, the ghetto behind Via Duomo and offers refuge and omertà to anyone. It is there that the Giuliano brothers rule: Pio Vittorio, Guglielmo, and Salvatore. It is under their guidance that the activities in the casbah take place and under the directives of Pio Vittorio in particular, that the successful traffic of contraband cigarettes takes place."[75]

Gemma is often forgotten as she died early at the age of forty-three in 1975 of a heart weakness, leaving three children under the age of sixteen.[76] There are some small traces of her that suggest that she was a willing participant in her husband's illicit activities. One report describes that "the emerging criminal [Pio Vittorio] had married Gemma Sacco who always helped him in his illegal activities."[77] As a young mother, she was involved in the selling of American cigarettes on street corners. Indeed, after having been on the run, she was arrested in 1956 at the age of twenty-four for dealing and selling smuggled cigarettes. Her name appears in the 1956 "Rubrica delle Persone Ricercati," which is the list of wanted criminals.[78] She was arrested and also had to pay a fine.[79] She fits in well with the notion an "army of women" who worked in the illegal economy during the postwar period to survive and put food on the table. I would argue that this illicit economy is not separate from the emerging Camorra groups of the beginning of the 1970s, and that Gemma was fully involved.

Like many other Neapolitan mothers, Gemma had a protective instinct. Figurato and Marola commented that "people remember that Gemma Sacco, wife of O' Padrino, Pio Vittorio Giuliano, would flick out a knife whenever someone dared say something bad about her children."[80]

She was the true matriarch of the family-clan but was never really acknowledged as such. Clare Longrigg, who attended a Giuliano wedding in the mid-1990s, only mentioned the patriarch, Gemma's husband, not Gemma, saying that "We join his father-in-law, Pio Vittorio, a man with pale blue eyes and a pale blue shirt, with strands of hair dyed purple slicked across his big bald head. A kindly man with a broad smile, Pio Vittorio is the patriarch of the Giuliano family, father of Luigi, 'the king,' Ciro, 'the baron,' and Carmine, 'the lion.'"[81] Gemma Sacco is an emblematic case study because she represents many women from the city center during the immediate postwar period, and yet her role as an emerging Camorra woman is omitted and her presence remains quasi-invisible and forgotten.

One of the best-known Neapolitan camorristi found in organized crime history books is Michele Zaza. Born in 1945 and the youngest of six children, he was always supported by strong women: in particular, his sisters and aunt. Also known as "Mad Mike" or in Italian, *Michele O' Pazzo*, or "the King of Naples" (*Le Roi de Naples*).[82] He became a criminal heavyweight in the Naples underworld in 1971. He is often portrayed as a lone criminal and a solitary cigarette smuggler, but he was a well-connected emerging criminal and by the end of the 1970s he had contacts across different international underworlds.[83] He was well supported and had many close criminal allies, including his brother; his father-in-law; his nephews, Nunzio Barbarossa and Nunzio Guida; and other strategic allies such as Antonio Bardellino.[84] More important, he was also surrounded by a tight female network that constantly supported and assisted him throughout his criminal career, but in books on the Neapolitan Camorra their presence is rarely mentioned.

Zaza married in 1974. His wife was described by *Il Mattino* in 1984 as "the daughter of the owner of one of the most beautiful boutiques in the world and a modern languages graduate from the Sorbonne, Paris. Michele Zaza is very linked to the concept of 'family' believing that everything that is feminine in his home must not be harmed."[85]

During a 1983 Rome police drug squad investigation into the different mafia networks in Palermo, Naples, Rome, and Milan, all the wives and partners of the criminals were put under surveillance. The Rome police noted "*in this investigation, the role of women in this association has been analyzed. The wives and daughters of certain Camorristi have been denounced because the investigations have proved their direct participation in the activities of their husbands. . . . The women of the Sicilians have never emerged during the telephone taps if only because of their natural position in their homes.*"[86]

In the early 1980s, they tried to seize his wife's house in one of the most residential roads of Naples because they believed that she was one of Zaza's front names. The police report read that,

> *according to documents, it would appear that his wife cannot be considered a member of a Camorra association. The unique element against her is the fact that she is the owner of a villa and a flat in Naples, in Via Petrarca, which are at her husband's disposal. It appears indeed, unequivocal that she appears to have allowed herself to be presented as the owner of the properties cited, in virtue of being married to Zaza, who has a stronger*

personality, but this does not mean that she is a member of a criminal organization.[87]

However, the nature of the relationship between spouses was not investigated further to understand the power relations: Michele was the husband, and his wife was apparently a traditional wife.

When Zaza moved to France, the French authorities sought to have a better understanding of his setup. When he was condemned for his involvement in an international smuggling ring, the French courts did not find her guilty of being involved in her husband's French criminal activities: *"Zaza's wife was found 'not guilty of Mafia association.'"*[88] But they did try to qualify her traditional role more precisely, concluding that she was *"a loyal wife"* and that *"she confirmed that her husband had never told her about his activities,"* although the French court found that she *"respected all the rules of her husband's life."*[89] In other words, she was close to her husband. In the files from the Questura of Rome it was remarked that *"one clear example of this is when she was transiting via the French capital [Paris] when she was told of her husband's heart attack and instead of going to his bedside continued her journey as imposed by her husband and this behavior proves without a shadow of a doubt the importance and priority of the economic interests over health questions for the Zaza group."*[90]

Another important female figure in Zaza's circle was his oldest sister, Maria. She was referred to as *"the one among all the relatives who has/had the most concerns for her brother."*[91] Referred to as "Maria *La Zitella*," or Maria, the Spinster, she openly admitted to seeing herself as Zaza's second mother, given the significant age difference. She was seventeen years older and immensely protective toward him. She *"was in real terms, his mother"* (*di fatto sua madre*) and her unmarried status added to this role.[92] It was reported that *"it was she who paid his bail money, it was she who visited him in prison, it was she who helped him as best she could."*[93] As a result of this behavior, she was often accused of *"being a member of her brother's Camorra association,"* but did this mean she was actually a member? We just do not know.

Maria always cared for Zaza and actively participated in managing his day-to-day criminal affairs. When Michele became ill in 1983 in Paris, Maria, insisted that Michele's wife fly back to Naples. This interplay was commented on by the Questura of Rome who stated that *"Maria Zaza insists that her sister-in-law returns home but as we have clearly demonstrated she is fully aware of her husband's commitment and illegal activities in Los Angeles, especially as she participates in their economic aspect which she needs to deal with before returning to Italy [and her ill husband]."*[94]

On one occasion, it was noted that Maria informed *"those in Los Angeles, not to worry about what was happening in Italy and asked her . . . to get Zaza's medical files . . . because these files would show he was abroad.*"[95] On another occasion, she asked her niece to produce an invoice *"that would justify the possession of a valuable watch which Michele was wearing when he was arrested."*[96]

In addition to these routine activities, Maria also appears to have been a traditional front name for some of her brother's financial assets and property investments in Rome; records from the Rome Questura state that *"the role of Zaza Maria is important for the management of Zaza's economic assets, at least in Rome."*[97]

After careful analysis, the evidence suggests that she systematically helped her baby brother. It was seen that *"she [does] provide her brother with 'assistance' money from her inheritance and other sources."*[98] The judicial authorities argued that she could not be a member of Michele's clan as the evidence *"allows us to understand that Maria Zaza does not really fully understand her brother's activities."*[99] Furthermore, Maria was *"believed not to be socially dangerous because her involvement in her brother's life and activities were believed by the judges to be due to 'family solidarity.'"*[100] Yet, at the same time, she helped her brother alter identification documents. The following description was reported by the police that *"he would have taken out the thing [photo] to put his which his sister [Maria] would have given or sent him."*[101]

So, was she so innocent and passive? Maria seems to have been complicit with Michele. She was always very careful about how to behave, as she knew she was being observed and listened to by police. The latter documented that *"during the conversation she warned her interlocutor that her telephones were being taped by both Italian and American police."*[102] She even used specialized coded language to put police off the scent. It was recorded that *"in a conversation between Maria Zaza . . . it becomes clear that the word "roba" [stuff] certainly means heroin."*[103]

Moreover, she was informed of important business in Los Angeles when a relative had received *"a parcel containing 93 kg of plates (1/4 of stuff) and that this parcel was received by their relative."*[104] This shows that she had a complete understanding of the context within which she was operating; she did not appear to have been a submissive player but a willing and helpful participant in an international criminal network.

Officially, the Italian judiciary never found Michele Zaza's female relatives guilty of Camorra association. Judges argued that they were merely showing *"human and family solidarity not during the most important criminal moments [of his life] but only when he was in basic need."*[105] I would beg to differ. These judges were all men, and they undervalued the fact that women were part of Zaza's decisions, strategies, and choices. They were active and took collective decisions; these women were not irrelevant subordinates but respected partners and intellectual equals.

A Hidden Presence with "Invisible Labor"?

This chapter has highlighted various women who were present and active in the Camorra underworld from the 1940s onward. I have sought to show that regardless of the limited historical sources and the predominant male biases of their storytellers, these women did have their own agency and were involved in criminal activities.[106] They were not just representatives of their men or simply submitting to them.

Some might challenge my analysis by arguing that these women were "exceptions" and "outliers" and apart from them, there were no women active in the Camorra. But we must remember that the Camorra was developing, and there were still few investigative tools to see what was actually going on, let alone to investigate the women. But women were there if we take a closer look. They were involved not only in the illegal economy as a reliable labor force in the form of street vendors, selling smuggled cigarettes (*bionde*) and illegal petrol in the city center, but later selling drugs in the alley ways and piazzas. They were also there in relation to the emerging Camorra bosses of the 1980s, by their sides, present and involved in shaping the development of the Camorra. Camorristi are visible and active in the public sphere as they and civil society perpetuate the patriarchal padre-padrone model of the Camorra underworld, neglecting the presence and activities of women. However, as I have shown it would be naïve to suggest that women were not present, involved, aware, consulted, and participant in the criminal activities of their male relatives. But we can also see their autonomy of action and independent ideas within these stories.

WOMEN IN THE CAMORRA SPACE

In or out? Joining a mafia is not as clear cut as previously believed. It is a much more problematic issue. In this chapter, I discuss and give an overview of Camorra women before looking at those who orbit this criminal world without necessarily being fully involved or paid: those women who navigate the gray zone ambiguously where boundaries are fluid.

Although some mafias, such as the Sicilian Cosa Nostra and the Calabrian 'Ndrangheta, have had specific rules about joining, with an official and recognized affiliation ritual, the Neapolitan Camorra has not had this. Moreover, the recent explanations of Emanuele Mancuso, former member of the Calabrian Mancuso *cosca*, about joining a mafia proves that mafia membership is not standard for all members, not even in the 'Ndrangheta: "*I was a member of the 'Ndrangheta by birth/family/blood ties*," he states. He is very clear: "*I was never baptized.*"[1] Therefore, he never underwent an official initiation ritual because he was the son and nephew of the bosses. This highlights the flexible membership boundaries that exist for even the most organized mafias. This shows how reductionist it is to use narrow definitions of membership for all mafias. In fact, I think it can even distort our understanding of Italian mafia membership and the role of women.

To be a member of a mafia means what exactly? What responsibilities, tasks, and duties does membership entail? Does everybody understand them in the same way? Do they create loyalty, obligations, and commitment? Do you have to be active and present? Does it imply criminal acts? When we take a closer look at Camorra women, we tend to focus solely on possible formal, legalistic, and traditional clan roles, and when no clearly defined role is identified, we simply conclude that they have no role nor autonomy and are therefore marginal players without criminal agency.

But the reality is much more complex than this simple reading. Lines between "formal" and "real" participation in the Camorra underworld are blurred and this needs to be noted. Formal participation means participation that is recognized by both the clan and the local community, but more importantly, by law enforcement agencies and which can be proven in a court of law. In Naples, this is the visible face of the Camorra, which means that the Camorra tends to be seen as exclusively "male" and "macho." As was made clear to me recently, police officers investigate a crime by a clan, not the power and influence of the women in the clan and how it relates to the crime.

But there is another invisible dimension to Camorra participation which is the real informal, substantive, and essential form, often taken for granted and not acknowledged for its true worth. This form of real participation is female, it is undertaken by women but is not seen. For example, listening to women's accounts of their life stories in Camorra clans, it soon becomes clear that they themselves often do not recognize the nature of their own participation, power, and influence. Rita Longo repeatedly explained, "*I didn't participate in anything, meetings with members, businessmen, or politicians. My role was to be the mother of the children. I don't feel involved in this thing. I'm passive . . . I couldn't make decisions because I was a nobody to take decisions. . .. I was passive. I was at home, and I would earn money. They would bring money to me. . . . I didn't mind it because in the end, I was living there. Full stop, end of story, I didn't take decisions.*"[2] And yet. . . .[3]

From the Family to the Clan

If we adopt traditional concepts such as hierarchy, violence, and respect to study mafias, their members and structures, we will continue only to see the men as we have constructed gender for men to belong to these so-called criminal male spaces. Women, on the other hand, supposedly do not frequent these spaces and are absent. This does not mean that women are less important or irrelevant; it is just that we continue not to see them there because we are using terms that automatically exclude them.

If we adopt a more holistic approach, with more general concepts, which takes into account the whole criminal landscape and also the overlapping legitimate context, it allows us to capture the public and private spheres, including households. If we understand the household dynamics, then we see different actors and power dynamics at play. We find women in roles at all levels, including leadership and advising roles, but they mostly play a subtle role in "governance," first in the family, then in the clan with their "coordination and bargaining, in place of issuing commands."[4]

In other words, if we look at concepts such as influential power, coordination, and bargaining action, then we see the women. If we can unpack this influence and governance in human interactions then this helps us to identify the work, the responsibilities, and the power of the women as this is what they do there. Their power spreads discreetly influencing individuals, families, and clans, first in the household, then in the criminal structures. In this way, women are present and visible. A Neapolitan woman's central position in her family and her role in the household can explain her power in the crime family and beyond. This can be seen as a useful characteristic to investigate further. For example, during a recent investigation in 2022 into a city center clan, the mother of the boss was arrested as she was considered to have been the leader of the clan for the last fifteen years but once her son was back out of prison, she withdrew so he could manage the activities once again. This is not to say that she did not do an efficient job or nor that she was not powerful.[5]

We should note that there may be possible differences in the nature of the involvement of women between those working in the city clans, those who live in the province and those in the Caserta region, and also between the clans whose main activity is drug dealing and those who have the propensity to launder money and invest in the legitimate economy. It appears that women from lower socioeconomic backgrounds access power and violence more easily in city clans compared, perhaps, to the more entrepreneurial groups in the province where women are more involved as front names of companies and properties. I believe that the local context can explain these criminal differences but the equality in the distribution of roles remains the same: the women fulfill the same roles as men and occupy a respected place in the Camorra space and system. This gender similarity of roles is generally underrated and systematically ignored as the traditional gender expectations are reinforced.

A Snapshot of Women in the Camorra Space

It has been suggested that Italian mafias have difficulty existing outside of Italy because their cultural value system, based on trust, would not be recognized outside their natural environment.[6] This argument can also be extended to the wives/partners of mafiosi. In other words, it could be suggested that Camorra women can only be Neapolitan or from Campania because only they understand the cultural

codes, meanings, values, and norms of the Neapolitan-Italian language and culture. Thus, for a Camorra boss to be successful and resilient, having a Neapolitan/
Campanian wife/partner would be of paramount importance because they must
understand and trust each other. This is not true; reality suggests otherwise.

Although it is true that most Camorra women are local Neapolitans, not
all are. There are some women from other regions of Italy. Some come from
the south, Sicily in particular, while others come from the north near Brescia.
There are also some foreign women who married camorristi, and there are more
than we think: we find important Camorra bosses with wives and partners from
France, Tunisia, Ecuador, Austria, and even the United Kingdom. Being foreign
does mean that these women have a different cultural perspective and approach
to life, but they still managed to get on with Neapolitan men and perhaps accept
their way of life, but it may also be easier for them as they can just walk away
when things become too much because they are not completely immersed in the
local Neapolitan and Camorra culture.

Indeed, one young East European woman who got involved with a charismatic traditional boss and had a child with him did not hesitate to leave Naples
and return home when the time was right for her and her child, leaving the father
in Italy. She had a strong sense of identity and purpose, so much so that she spoke
to her child in her native language although she was sneered at by the other
women of the clan for doing so. They looked on and considered her strange and
self-important.[7]

Many women move to be with their husbands and partners; rarely, does the
man move to the wife/partner's district. From this point of view, women are
very mobile; they change district, region, and country for their men and their
activities. For example, women have moved from different parts of town, from La
Torretta near the sea to the Vomero district on the hill, but also from the Vomero
alto district to the Casertano as well as from Naples's city center to Mondragone
(see figure I.1).

When leaders and foot soldiers of the Amato-Pagano clan left for Spain en
masse in 2003 because of an ongoing feud with the Di Lauro clan, the wives
and children went too.[8] It has been suggested that a group of twenty members
and their families moved to Barcelona. This can be interpreted as a way for the
women to provide their men with domestic stability. The same was the case for
Michele Zaza in France and Gennaro Panzuto in the United Kingdom. Some can
afford to take their wives and kids, but this is not the case for all.[9]

Many who have gone on the run abroad have gone alone and have found
foreign lovers while their wives remained at home: a boss from Marano, found
himself a Brazilian lover in Spain with whom he had a child, while a boss hiding in Germany, found himself a German girlfriend.[10] Years earlier in the 1980s,

Vincenzo De Falco had had a French lover in the south of France where he spent his time on the run and returned regularly, as did Mario Iovine, arrested at Sollies Pont near Toulon.[11]

There are some cases of men moving across districts in Naples, but they move and then find lovers, whereas women move for love. There is the example of a boss who moved from Pianura to Ponticelli after problems with rivals and who found a new partner there. Thus, as with the 'Ndrangheta, Camorra women no longer have to be automatically local, but it clearly helps a couple if they have the same language and cultural norms and values.[12]

Nicknames

Nicknames are a substitute or alternative for a name. They vary from kinship terms, affectionate-pet terms, or honorific titles but most importantly they underline an intimacy between individuals of a group. Nicknames in criminal organizations are key not only for the internal dynamics of a group and their bonding but they can also be helpful for those investigating the membership of an underground network.[13] In the Camorra, the use of nicknames indicates a special status, a rapport and intimacy between individuals which without the bonds of attachment and obligation would not be clear. They are not street names to be used by all but special names to be used by those who belong to the same group or community.

It could be argued that nicknames can be negative and quasi-insulting, creating a barrier and tension between individuals, but for the Camorra this does not seem to be the case. In the Camorra, nicknames are often given to members when they are young and making a name for themselves.[14] In this way, they confer on individuals a sense of belonging and a cultural identity, but also an intimacy within the group. They create an "us versus them" feeling, an insider versus outsiders dynamic, and a closeness and connection within the Camorra family, which is important. Usually, they are not very original, but they underline the importance of the group culture. Nicknames are very common, almost systematic, for men, and women are not excluded from this and are very much included in this identify-building custom, this creation of a sense of belonging.

Most of the time, traditional nicknames for Camorra women are simply a diminutive of their name: Annunziata becomes "Nunzia"; Carmela, "Lina"; Giuseppina, "Pina"; Renata, "Rene"; and Anna, "Nannina" or "Annarella." But they also have the function of acknowledging the clan hierarchy. They underline the existing kinship positions: "Zi," or "Auntie," places you clearly and is a particular favorite as it confers both respect and positionality in the clan. The wives and mothers of important Camorra bosses are also given nicknames that confer on them their owed respect and their top status. The partner of one top boss was called "la cummara" (the companion), by members while Mariella was called "Zia" (Auntie).

Then, there are some nicknames that refer to the people you work with, such as "La Vecchia di Pasqualino," "Pasquale's old lady." Perhaps less flattering but nonetheless picturesque: nicknames are based on physical appearance, for example, "Nase e' cane," "dog's nose"; "Annarella a' secca," "thin Anna,"; "A piccerella," "the small one,"; "O Bionda," "the blonde one,"; "O Ciccia," "the fat one,"; "A' Corta," "the short one,"; "Bassotta," "the short one"; and "Teresa a corta," "Teresa, shorty,"; "Maria Rosaria 'a ceccata,'" "the blind one." They are also often based on resemblance to other things, a "cipolla," "onion"; "Patanella," "small potato"; "o 'passilona," "black olives"; and "la mohicana," "Mohican." They can also be based on where you come from, "A' Polacca," "the Pole" and "A' Romana," "the Roman one." In short, the use of nicknames for women indicates their presence, their familiarity, and role within the Camorra clan. Perhaps, some clans give more nicknames to women than others, but nevertheless whether the use of nicknames is common or not, women are included in this crucial bonding exercise.

Jobs

In many mafia films, women are portrayed as only enjoying the benefits from the dirty money of their men. From the evidence I collected, very few women actually purely enjoyed the money and wasted it. Those who are not born into the Camorra logic aspire to having a luxurious lifestyle. Camorra women, in fact, are hardworking and continuously involved in money-making activities, not only to survive for the lower classes but also to enjoy a lifestyle. I would even say that they do like money but are also aware of the necessity of making money and keeping the money flowing in. From this perspective, women are proactive. The popular image of women only interested in the glamorous lifestyle is largely based on distorted stereotypes. In the real Camorra world, women are proactive, functional, and fully participant in the money-making processes.

It is interesting to note what jobs Camorra women accept. Very few are only engaged in domesticity and living off the clan's ill-gotten gains. In the different judicial and police documents, two simple categories appear. Firstly, women who see, define, and portray themselves as "housewives." These women stay at home and look after the house as well as the children and family. They do not have any regular official income from elsewhere. The Italian legal term used to describe them is often *nullafacente*, that is, "someone who does not work." Women in this category can be the wife of the boss or a simple foot solider; they have no official recognized job but do work full time for the clan. For example, a female member of a city clan defines herself as "*a housewife*" to her young daughter, while selling drugs on the street. Another example is that of the wives of top city bosses who had no official jobs, but they spent their time going around shopkeepers and businesses collecting racket money for the clan.[15] There are many such examples of women who formally appear as homemakers doing nothing else, but this is in parallel to their illegal activities, which is their real, main, and hidden line of work.

In the second category, some women have official jobs. There are three subcategories. First, women who have jobs in their own right. A member of the Belforte clan worked as a porter, or *concierge*, in a primary school as well as being the owner-manager of a television/telephone/electro-domestic goods shop.[16] Some have been schoolteachers while others managed hairdressing salons, a grocery shop (*Market piu*), or worked in a jewelry shop in the city center. Another young woman worked in a shop during the day and was a dance teacher in her own dance school at night, whereas another member worked as a cleaner, while a woman from the Beneduce clan worked in a funeral parlor.[17]

Second, some women have jobs that are linked to the clan's legitimate activities and companies. They officially work for some legal Camorra-related companies, such as shops or businesses that may be a front for the clan, and in this way, they become the front names or cover names of legitimate companies hiding illegal Camorra money. Many of these front names and companies tend to be in the hospitality industry. The jobs of the wives of many top bosses varied: from managing a farmhouse bed and breakfast (that produced wine), to managing a food company, from working in a local pizzeria, to owning and working in an ice cream parlor or from a photo shop to managing a tanning center or an underwear shop. All businesses in the legitimate economy.

Third, the clan forces state institutions or businesses to give jobs to their members/associates. For instance, an important city clan was able to place some of its close female members to work in the Hospital of San Giovanni Bosco in Naples. The relative of one clan member worked in the hospital while she also sold drugs for the clan.[18] A high-ranking member of a Camorra clan from the Casertano region tried to get a woman a job at a beauty parlor by demanding it from its owner, while bosses of the clan from Mondragone also sought jobs for their close women friends in hospitals or beauty parlors.

Women's Positions and Roles in the Camorra Space

Women in mafias have long been portrayed as either enjoying the money, status, and lifestyle because of their position in the family ("women are perceived to be the beneficiaries of the criminal lifestyle, not participants in it")—or absent or invisible in terms of not having recognized formal criminal roles.[19] This follows the great tradition of mainstream criminology that has always appeared to be less interested in female behavior and which as a result has given women less criminal agency. For example, the gang literature sees women as "secondary," "ancillary," "auxiliaries," "associates," or "background roles."[20] The white-collar criminal literature has "also paid relatively little attention" to women.[21]

Both poverty and wealth are motivators for becoming involved in OCGs. Vincenzo Ruggiero explains that "the deficit paradigm" (a deficit of wealth, socialization, opportunities, love) can help to explain how and why people become involved in criminal activities to survive.[22] But he also stresses that greed for wealth can explain possible motives for organized crime involvement. This could be called "the profit paradigm," the capitalist desire to make money, always more money, and attain a lifestyle of luxury and riches.

Many of the life journeys of the Camorra women that I interviewed and analyzed can be explained using these paradigms. Life choices and decisions because of a deficit in something (family, love, identity, support), or a desire for money. But, within this, what is more imperative to recognize is that women can and do assert their own criminal agency. However, this theoretically has not been elaborated very much. Women are never theoretically considered equals or capable of having their own agency while involved in traditional criminal activities. For example, when writing about Camorra women, Zaccaria suggests that they don't exist quite in the same universe as the men but in "un mondo di mezzo," "a world in the middle," a continuum that spans from female boss to a witness of crime.[23] This is a space where they can move and exist in and out of the confines of the Camorra. Siebert, on the other hand, argues, that women in the Sicilian Mafia are excluded from this private space: "The exclusion of women seems a fundamental element in the cohesion of the group. . . . By this exclusion the mafia imaginary produces a feminine and sanctions feminine roles on which to found an instrumental use of family relationships which in turn becomes a functional part of mafia criminal activity itself."[24] She believes that mafias are antiwomen, an "exclusive" group of men that functionally manipulate women to favor the clan and its activities; in other words, women are excluded and complicit but still do not have their independent criminal agency.[25]

On the contrary, I believe that for Camorra women this is not the case. Women can inhabit the Camorra space and can have equal influence there: they participate and are fully integrated into the clan, performing similar roles to male camorristi thanks to the power they have accumulated in the household. They are not necessarily coercively controlled or subjugated, thus they are not victims or downtrodden souls. There are women who are, but I am interested in all those women who have developed their own agency, who use their own capacities to make good and bad choices, good and bad decisions, independently of men, women who knowingly associate, act, and help the criminal group. This point was repeatedly made to me by the women whom I interviewed: they noted that women were treated differently, as though they were lesser beings, not by the clan but by the authorities. They had their own agency, but often it was taken away from them by the outside world, not by the criminal community.

The question of women's' "positionality" and "spatiality" in relation to female agency in the Camorra remains an intriguing one for me because roles, positions, and space in the clan have repeatedly been considered separate and autonomous of each other. Active women live in the clan and in the Camorra space, yet officially they play no formal role in Camorra clans, are not involved in their criminal activities, and have no presence or knowledge of the Camorra space. Dino argues that "mafia women experience a *triple absence* (1999): as women in general, as women in the South and as Mafia women."[26] The evidence I collected suggests otherwise: women in the private sphere do have roles and do exist in the Camorra space. In this private sphere, they challenge the "masculine ideology" and patriarchal structures to have agency that does not necessarily go against the clan dynamics; if anything it reinforces it.[27]

It is generally suggested that women's involvement in the Camorra is fundamentally linked to a male relative (father, brother, boyfriend) and that they *only* get involved if there is a male connection. This suggests maybe a distorted way of looking at the question of recruitment, as there are also numerous cases in which women/girls, whether the daughter of a camorrista or a group of mixed friends including girls, help the recruitment of young men into the clan. These cases are rarely documented.

There are usually two main recruitment routes and ways into the Camorra for women/girls: (1) relatives/family context (insiders) or (2) rational (economic) decisions (outsiders). Family values and ties can manifest themselves in a variety of ways: for example, during the 1980s and 1990s a whole group of young men became involved in crime in order to revenge their brothers' murders by the Camorra group, the NCO. As a reaction, they set up their own Camorra clans and anti-NCO alliance. There are similar examples for women: the murder of Laura's brother precipitated her participation into her father's emerging clan.

Because the family belongs to the private sphere, the importance of women and their involvement in this space is underestimated. Dino discusses "the 'exclusion' of women from Mafia environments," which she links to "the overall situation of marginalization" of Italian women in the public sphere ("spheres of power, management and law"); women "are relegated to the private domain" where they become invisible.[28]

Women can exist in patriarchal spaces and be subjugated to a male dominant culture but still have their own agency. I noted that the overarching Neapolitan patriarchal context structured the private and public spheres, but in the family and household, I found women who had their own criminal agency and could make decisions independently; they "bargained patriarchy" in these "negotiated spaces."[29] The relationships, plans, and strategies were not only male; women decided together with them, whether formally or informally. The blood and crime family overlap and interconnect, creating blurred lines and fluid boundaries when it comes to roles, decisions, and positions in the family and in the clan. Thus, women's power is established in the household and transfers into the clan. The family of origin gives women various types and amounts of capital, which they can use as they wish—carry on in crime and become an active member, ignore the importance of their capital, pretend they don't understand it and become a tacit accomplice, or reject their capital all together and walk away.

Insider women are not dismissed as stupid or ignorant, and their position in the family empowers them to have a role if they wish. Not all women in crime families are involved, but their presence does portray a form of silent acceptance. Many of these women contribute to the clan knowingly and willingly to make the clan stronger and more efficient. Women exist in the Camorra space, and they take on roles, they make decisions, they have an influence and can be equal partners, all on their terms and with their own agency because of their position in the family and their blood ties. The clan does not automatically or systematically discriminate against them in the crime family. They can be found undertaking all roles in the Camorra and more important, they inhabit the Camorra space, negotiating, engaging, and at times, dominating it.

To be clear, in a traditional Camorra clan, the following actors are present:

1. Leader or leadership group (usually from one blood family)
2. Managers/advisers/lieutenants (who coordinate certain individuals and tasks)
3. Foot soldiers (who undertake different activities: violent acts or selling of goods)
4. Associates, enablers, or facilitators (the so-called gray zone: white-collar outsiders who help the clan in various professional ways) (see figure 3.1)
5. Familial associates (not officially in the clan but who support, help, and assist without a direct salary) (see figure 3.2)

I have identified women active at all these levels where their gender does not handicap them. In addition to looking at participatory roles in which female agency is expressed, why not also consider the role of women who are present while not actively participating in the space inhabited by the Camorra? As we

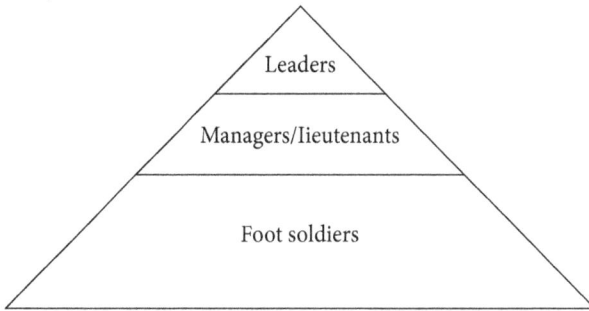

FIGURE 3.1. Structure of a Camorra clan

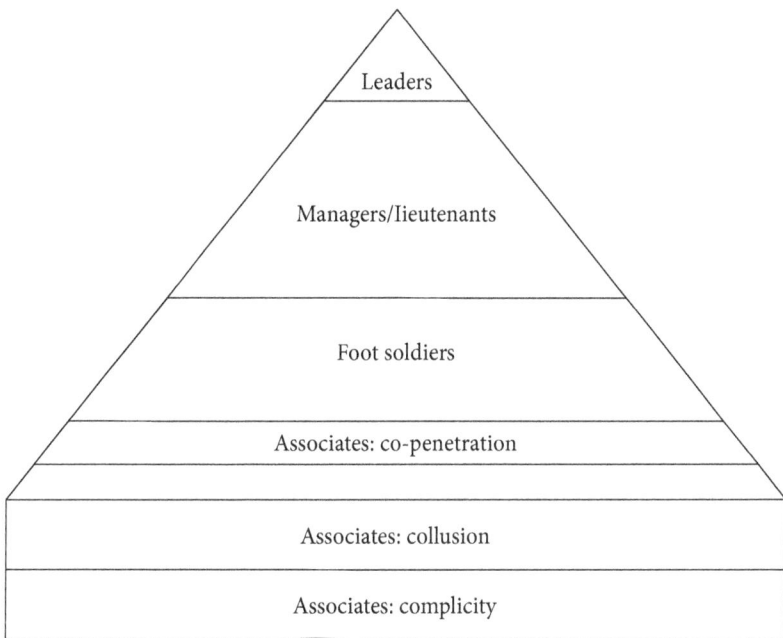

FIGURE 3.2. The Camorra's gray zone

have said, the Camorra space is not a male-only space. It is a vast urban space, with neighborhoods and streets but also flats and social housing estates populated by women. In this space, beyond the family, women have real influence; they are constantly present in *i vicoli*, the narrow streets, of Forcella, in the abandoned historic buildings of Torre Annunziata, or the high-rise flats in Ponticelli; they are in the streets, at the windows, in the piazzas, in the parks, at the cafes. They are a presence, eyes and ears, but also they have opinions and ideas. They are not neutral and indifferent bystanders. I believe that roles and space can overlap to produce influential Camorra women, women with gravitas, powerful women. Indeed, women not only have central roles in the criminal family and clan but also occupy a fundamental space in the Camorra; both aspects combined together do not make them marginal and agencyless. These women through their presence and participation can shape and determine criminal behavior in Naples.

There are also women outsiders who become involved in the Camorra without having any direct family link. These women tend to be found in the outer circles of Camorra activities and perhaps even in the gray zone as business associates. Nevertheless, they are there, ready to act or give a helping hand in the legitimate economy and civil society.

In the next few chapters, I investigate women in the Camorra by recounting their life stories to explore if they take on these active roles in the Camorra space and analyze the nature of their power to show that they are not only secondary and remote figures. The stories are determined by the availability of the material. This is why in this chapter I discuss outsider women who form part of the so-called gray zone and define them as "Camorra associates" as they orbit the Camorra, at times in an ambiguous way. These women can be professional or business enablers or facilitators as well as enthusiastic supporters. The defining element is that they do not receive a regular salary or assistance from the clan. The complex notion of "real" active participation will become clearer in the different life stories of foot soldiers, managers, and leaders in the following chapters.

The Gray Zone

Mafias need managers and foot soldiers, but they also need outside complicity for their activities to survive and ultimately flourish in the legitimate economy and civil society. Falcone argued that mafias exist not only because of their members, but also because of those who support them from the outside, in the gray zone.[30] Pardo explains that "ordinary people operate in the 'grey area' . . . between 'legality' and 'illegality' without becoming or considering themselves 'real criminals.'"[31] This is key because it suggests that the gray zone is composed of a heterogeneous group of professionals as well as of ordinary people.

The gray zone is usually made up of white-collar professionals who are not formally paid-up members but whose expertise, support, assistance, and advice to mafia groups guarantee their economic, social, and political existence and survival. They receive benefits in return for their services. Nicaso and Danesi argue that "like any corporation, every Mafia family has 'associates' with whom business is carried out, even though they are not members of the specific clan. Associates are lawyers or public officials who are hired as go-betweens between the family and mainstream society, allowing the crime family to gain access to legitimate sectors of society."[32]

These actors are formerly outsiders, but their assistance and expertise are essential in supporting and legitimizing the clans in their business activities and strategies in politics, civil society, and the economy. They provide support from the noncriminal (professional and business) sectors of society. By engaging with the Camorra, these outsiders legitimize its existence, helping it become more normalized and legitimate actors. But there is another layer of associates who are not usually considered. These are informal, familial associates, friends and relatives who help out without being paid.

There are different ways that we can frame and define mafia associates (or helpers and supporters). Italian law has adopted a clear and narrow judicial approach, which it uses to differentiate those who may not be fully paid-up members of a criminal organization but who, nevertheless, provide support and help for the Camorra's criminal project. This support can come in all kinds of different shapes, sizes, and forms. The important thing is the ability to recognize it, as in many contexts it is not clear cut.

These individuals in Italian law are defined as providing mafia-type associations with "outside external help" ("concorso esterno in associazione di tipo mafioso"). In other words, they are not insiders, but as outsiders they provide help and expertise to further the clan's criminal projects. It has been argued that individuals from the legal and illegal worlds have a lot to learn from each other: "Apprentice criminals pass from one status to another in the legitimate opportunity system and as they do so, develop a set of relationships with members of the legitimate world."[33] Indeed, changes in society and the local and international economy encourage these relationships to flourish:

> Contemporary developments in criminal networks signal the establishment of dirty economies and fuzzy business careers, that is to say, the expansion of grey areas of business where overlaps between white-collar crime and clear-cut kinds of conventional organized crime are found. The nature and operations of these economies are to be understood within the context in which the licit, semi-licit, and overtly illicit economies are constantly developing points of contact, common interests, and strategies. Together, they form bad business. Dirty economies consist of encounters which add to the respective "cultural, social and symbolic capital" possessed by criminals and entrepreneurs, who interlock their practices to become market leaders and old challengers.[34]

The British National Crime Agency (NCA), on the other hand, adopts a narrower classification and defines these type of facilitators as "professional enablers." They see enablers mainly as professionals who facilitate the activities of organized criminal groups: "They are key to a wide range of *economic crime*."[35] In particular, they contribute to the legitimization of criminal finances by providing access to money laundering services, banking, accounting, and legal worlds.[36] Whereas the Italian approach includes any kind of person who can provide potential external assistance, including doctors and nurses, "the Anglo-Saxon literature . . . concentrates chiefly on the role of financial and legal service providers such as lawyers, notaries, accountants, tax consultants, tax specialists and real estate agents."[37]

The Italian definition of "enablers" is wider in terms of help and assistance. We are not referring to *just* economic or legal assistance, but also logistical, material, and emotional support. This concept has been added to the Italian mafia association Law 416 bis. According to this law, this external contribution can take different forms. It can be:

1. Occasional and individual help
2. Functional help
3. Casual help that reinforces/consolidates association
4. Anyone who in general is aware they are helping

This is a legalistic approach, which seeks to capture those outsiders whose assistance to the Camorra is more nuanced, blurred, and gray. Police officers and judges can monitor the nature of this help, but this is not always clearly recorded in legal reports and for our purpose can be somewhat limited. Indeed, we must not forget that judges seek to put together a case to prosecute these individuals who are so fundamental to the clan's activities and existence but whose relationship is ambiguous, ambivalent, and not clearly defined.

In this chapter, I am interested in a wider sociological understanding of the notion of "associate," or what Pizzini-Gambetta defines as "all those that help run it [the clan]" but who are not paid-up members.[38] They are facilitators and enablers who act in a way that benefits the clan. They are a crucial part of this solid support system but exist at various levels and in different manifestations which are not purely economic or political but also a form of social and welfare assistance.

Complicit-Collusion-Co-penetration

As we have seen, the concept of the mafia's gray zone is still not fully developed in the literature. This is perhaps because it remains difficult to study in depth. It is, after all, an invisible relationship that remains on the margins of mafia associations. I believe that Sciarrone adopted a useful approach that developed these relationships and concepts.[39] He considers enablers and the gray zone not as people but as "a physical space," "a meeting ground" between different types of relationships and logic that motivate individuals to have links and contacts with criminal clans. I believe that this idea of "space" is a good starting point, because it conceptualizes this gray space/zone as being a multidimensional crisscrossing social space and not just a fixed economic exchange.

Sciarrone correlates (1) the type of relationship with (2) the logic that motivates individuals into that relationship.[40] He identifies three possible types of relationships between associates and mafiosi:

1. Complicity: an economic exchange between specific actors
2. Collusion: an agreement to undertake business together, a continued exchange
3. Co-penetration: helping out because of a developed sense of belonging and identification with the clan (nonfamily members) (see figure 3.2)

A good example of this last scenario is the case of BC, a businessman who worked with the leadership of the Secondigliano Alliance in the counterfeit sector.[41] He used the expression *noi* ("we") as in "we the clan," which indicated his strong sense of loyalty and showed that he did not consider himself an outsider."[42] His support and behavior was that of a full-time member.

I use Sciarrone's framework to analyze women in the Camorra's gray zone as I came across women associates who had roles that were not purely economic.[43] They belonged to the complicit and collusion categories because they were complete outsiders with no kinship ties to clan members. In exchange for their support, they would receive material things such as gifts and money.

In the co-penetration category, most women were related to the clan members. We can call them "familial associates." This is very different to men, for

TABLE 3.1 The relationships of the gray zone

RATIONALE	NATURE OF RELATIONSHIP	TYPE OF RELATIONSHIP
Functional	One-off economic exchange	= *Complicity*
Co-participation	Permanent common business deals	= *Collusion*
Belonging/self ID	Long-term stable organic relations	= *Co-penetration*
NEW		
Belonging/self ID	Long-term stable organic relations	= *Blood ties–*
		co-penetration

Source: Rocco Sciarrone, "Mafie, relazioni e affari nell'area grigia," in *Alleanza nell'Ombra: Mafie ed economie locali in Sicilia e nel Mezzogiorno*, ed. Sciarrone (Roma: Donzelli Editore, 2011), 36–37.

whom it is possible to begin as an outsider then become an insider through a co-penetrative relationship and strong self-identification with the clan.

Rarely are there women who are complete outsiders with co-penetration. These women relatives are insiders because of their kinship links, and they naturally provide support and are expected to give full obedience to the clan without necessarily being fully paid-up members. It is this aspect that confuses matters as it could be argued that they are exploited by the men. These women are neither paid foot soldiers nor managers, but their kinship determines an instant co-penetrative role of constant support. They are to all effects "used" by clan members because of their blood ties where love and loyalty to relatives are natural and spontaneous, and they are outsiders because this is not their paid work.

But this is a thin line because their blood ties produce natural social capital and reputation even if they are not paid systematically. Out of family loyalty, they enable, facilitate, and support the clan's interest and benefit from this. They are not outsiders as such because they identify with the clan, but because they don't have systematic salaries, they cannot be defined as purely members. Their help is innate because it is familial, and it becomes natural to develop a sense of belonging and self-identification with the clan. To reject this kind of role may require courage, determination, and an awareness of risk.

Complicity

The act of complicity is defined by Sciarrone as occurring when an associate engages with a clan in a functional way.[44] There is a rational exchange between a camorrista and another, which is purely based on a utilitarian exchange. There are no emotional or kinship attachments involved; it is solely an economic exchange and tends to be a one-off act but can be more regular if necessary. These were professional women who were identified to help clan members and who, it was believed, were above suspicion. Why would they become involved? Perhaps because they were in financial difficulty or perhaps because they thought it could help their career.

We can illustrate this with the case of Sara. She was a paramedic nurse working in a prison in northeast Italy. She was approached by the relatives of a clan boss who was incarcerated in the hospital ward of the prison. Why? Because she was the nurse who looked after him and administrated his pills. She was seen as caring and "*always close*" to the boss in his everyday care. She was identified and considered "*ideal*" by the clan to act as their go-between with the boss inside the prison. To do this, they provided her with a mobile phone (registered under someone else's name) for her to call them with updated information about his health condition.

In return for paying the boss *"special attention,"* she was offered 2,000–2,500 euros. She explained why she became involved with the clan and did what they requested: she needed the money as *"she had messed up* [financially]," *"sono inguaiata"* ["I am in trouble"].[45] She did what they asked of her and more. For example, when some clan members from the South came to visit their relative, she offered to put them up in her home for the night, but they preferred to go to the hotel as there were three of them.[46] This example highlights that it was not purely a financial exchange, and that Sara had started to befriend the camorristi's relatives and feel close to the clan.

A completely different example is that of Zara. She was a young lawyer working in central Italy and was a member of the legal team that defended a powerful Camorra family. She was actively involved in sorting out a variety of legal and logistical issues. What would she do? She would meet with the boss's partner in a layby of the motorway to keep her up to date on emerging judicial matters and issues because she had different criminal clients. In particular, when one of her clients decided to collaborate with the state as this could threaten the boss's children, she warned them.[47] Her other main tasks were to take the boss's messages in and out of prison and give them to a specific lieutenant on the outside. She also received instructions from the boss's partner and financially looked after one of the boss's cellmates as requested. In return she received many presents.[48] Although she communicated with relatives, she was often employed to bypass the family and partner to guarantee the boss an independent channel of communication. Zara was employed by the clan because they believed that, as a female lawyer, she would not attract attention, although the Carabinieri did eventually understand what she was up to. It is not clear here why Zara got involved. She was not in financial need but may have enjoyed the attention of clan members, the presents she was given and the thrill of engaging with dangerous criminals.

Another example is that of Kim. She seemed to be a world away from the Camorra's underworld as a civil servant. And yet, it is alleged that she was approached by some businessmen connected to various clans and she was able to get them to promise her money, a car, and a job for a friend in exchange for access to the public tendering process for food outlets in various Neapolitan hospitals. She allowed them to try and manipulate the tendering process. Her behavior demonstrates clear complicity in a functional exchange where she sought to get what she wanted. There appears to be no moral issue for her as she understood what she was doing.[49]

In this category, we should find the more formal, professional, and functional exchanges and relationships between clan members and complicit women. But this does not appear to be the case. What we find is that women are identified for their professional jobs in society and then a more human and endearing rapport develops. It could be argued that these women are cruelly exploited by the clan because they appear "vulnerable," as they are often in financial difficulty or seeking some form of career progression. But this professionally complicit gray level is not purely an exploitative relationship; these women know what they want and know what they need from the exchange and can also develop an emotionally rewarding attachment.

Collusion

The notion of colluded-corrupt women is different from that of complicit women in the sense that these women are more involved financially without necessarily being fully aware of the criminal details, or if they are aware, they ignore the possible criminal implications. Women here seemed to be co-opted or used for their gender and position in society and not necessarily fixated on getting some financial reward or maybe they are. These women tend not to be related to core Camorra members, although they could be related to some more peripheral members. Their importance is the role and position they have in legitimate society as professionals; in other words, they are considered "clean," and this is their value to the clan. They are far away enough from the clan to be useful to it in the legitimate economy and world. For these women, it may be money but it can be also other forms of attachments or relationships they gain by helping the clan.

For instance, Giulietta. She was the daughter of a businessman who was close to a powerful clan. Previously, her father had made his money from construction companies and real estate agents in partnership with some shady businessmen who orbited around various clans in the north of the city. First, these businessmen were involved with the established clan and later, after a violent war, moved on to the more successful modern clan. Giulietta's father soon got dragged in.

In 2013, in her early twenties, Giulietta officially opened an ice cream parlor. By all accounts, she did not actually run the business or ever turn up to work there. It is suggested that the business belonged to the local boss and was set up using illegal drug money for money laundering. Her involvement appears to have been purely formal. She was a front name, a name on paper, as all decisions and money came from the clan. She made no business decisions, and the business bank account was accessible to clan associates. Even her brother was unaware of who to serve when he was working there; for example, it was necessary to clarify whether the nieces and grandchildren of the boss had to pay for their ice creams.[50] The boss's daughter underlined this when she was once overheard saying that "*she was the owner*" and Giulietta was just a "*wooden name.*"[51]

Giulietta was a classic case of collusion because it was a sustained relationship without being one in which she identified with the clan. Her parents perhaps did, but she did not. The business provided money for her and her family but above all facilitated the business activities of the clan.

Another good example is that of Elisa. Elisa's relative was married to an important Camorra member. He was not only a killer but also managed to develop a substantial economic portfolio thanks to his drug trafficking and loan sharking activities.[52] Elisa became part of the outer layer of associates in the gray zone. As the camorrista was in prison and needed to recycle his dirty money into the legal economy, Elisa and her husband stepped up. She was given 260,000 euros in cash in various installments to invest in two businesses that became very popular: "*People pass and say. . .. 'But it is the nicest place in the shopping center.' People pass by and say: 'What a lovely place.' This is a really satisfying feeling.*"[53] This money went directly toward buying two businesses. In this way, the couple became active front names as they were the official owners and managers.

Elisa was fully involved. She not only followed the ownership paperwork with the solicitor but also worked long hours and employed extra staff when necessary: they made "*enormous sacrifices to manage* [these] *two bars*" but were fully aware of what they were doing because the illegal cash was used to pay for the businesses and all the extras.[54] They also had to deal with clan members who expected freebies because they knew who was behind the business. Indeed, at different times, the camorrista showed his frustration when talking about these business ventures because, as a condemned camorrista, he realized he could not be directly involved; he even complained, "*Did we invest. . .. to give food* [a job] *to your relative?*"[55]

Let us turn to the case of Fabrizia. She was the wife of an accountant who was close to a clan. Fabrizia and her husband "owned" a shop that she managed in the periphery of Naples. Once the clan decided to sell it, she became involved in making sure that the sale went through; she oversaw the whole process with the new owners and solicitor. She played the part when it was clear that it was other individuals who controlled and managed the situation. She formally participated in the sale and exchange of contracts but knew that she was not the person making the decisions nor were the people she was dealing with. It was another professional, close to the boss who was making the final decisions.[56]

On the other hand, we have Susanna. She managed a restaurant for the clan without being an official member. The clan helped her to open her own restaurant: it gave her the initial start-up funds to set up the business and even closed off public street space to lure customers. They agreed that she would give them 50 percent of her profits and was allowed to pocket the rest. She went beyond her restaurant related activities and engaged in other criminal activities such as hiding firearms for the clan and loan sharking if there was a need.[57]

A clear outsider, Letizia was not related to any members of the clan nor was she a formal member. But she became fully involved in the clan's logistical organization in the 2000s. For example, she provided a safe haven for fugitives and members who needed to meet or disappear; she put her third floor flat at the clan's disposal.[58] In return for her services, she was paid 400–500 euros per month. Moreover, the boss's car was formally registered under the name of her husband, who was considered "*a good person*."[59]

Co-penetration: Relatives or Outsiders?

This mixed category corresponds to two overlapping groups: (1) women relatives, who on the one hand, are not paid a regular salary but whose familial links imply natural criminal knowledge and loyalty ("familial associates"); and (2) women who are not related but who develop criminal sympathy with clan members. Stepping away from helping relatives and the clan can create tension, violence, and serious repercussions. An ambivalent relationship develops in terms of knowing and doing. For example, some wives did not hesitate to act as money couriers; they would take the illegal cash and put it into their bank accounts. One of the wives of a businessman-camorrista from an important clan was brought cash (made from illegal activities) by another associate and she took it directly to her bank branch. So, no one suspected where the money came from.[60]

Invisible Family Insiders

Family ties impose organic relations with the clan, and this develops a sense of self-identification and belonging. The majority of women in this category are female relatives although there are also unrelated women, but the central point is that they are not paid for their services. They do it out of a sense of identification with the clan and loyalty to its values. Delia and Beatrice, for example, were the wife and daughter respectively of the banker of a clan during the 2000s.[61] These women were considered as "*emblematic*" of women's co-penetrative relationship, where family membership automatically overlaps with illegal projects and entails criminal loyalty and identity. But they were not paid-up members. Their relationship to the male camorrista produced duties, commitment, and loyalties toward the clan without formal links.

Delia was fully aware of and involved in her husband's criminal discussions and decisions. When he did the clan's accounts, she helped with the calculations, took notes, gave advice, and remembered all the different detailed transactions. In addition, she made her house available for clan members and was paid to hide their firearms but had no regular salary. Her behavior indicates full identification with the clan, as she did everything she could to protect its interests. Her daughter, who was married to another clan member, also showed total criminal solidarity toward the clan despite not being salaried. Although, they benefitted economically as they were reimbursed for their services, they went beyond doing small and marginal jobs. They demonstrated an active interest and loyalty in the clan. Their identification with the clan can be seen through their preoccupations when members were arrested and how they adapted their behavior to the clan's new circumstance. This was not only a job to them but a way of life and value system they totally respected.

Logistical support is also fundamental for clans. Barbara provided logistical support and surveillance assistance to the local clan of which her brother was a violent member. Her father helped, but she was very active of her own accord. She supported the clan by helping fugitives to avoid arrest, especially when the local police were monitoring the local districts and countryside by car patrol.[62] If a clan member was arrested, she would try and obstruct the police's work. Once she was asked to quickly remove a truck from an address so that the police could not confiscate it for their investigation.[63] She was not a paid member, but her actions showed she completely identified with the clan, its members, and its fate out of loyalty.

Claudia was the former wife of a Camorra boss, and her daughter became a camorrista. As her husband was a womanizer, she left him with her daughter. She did not participate directly in his emerging clan or his criminal activities as much as his partner or his new Brazilian girlfriend. However, she did not completely break ties with him: she agreed to having her name used as a front name for one of his initial legitimate business ventures.

A pentito from her husband's clan explained her situation in further details:

> From what I know she had no operative role in the clan. She was aware of all the activities of the clan but did not participate directly. She was only his front name both in the management of slot machines and for his bank accounts (both through the post and bank) because as I have previously said, the boss does not appear in the first person—he held no property or bank account in his name. He used her for the companies, she was only a front name and did not participate directly in criminal activities.[64]

For her role, she was paid 350 euros a week. This example shows how, once you are in the family, it becomes difficult to completely detach yourself from it.

Paolina was the younger sister of a member of a violent Camorra inner circle. Her brother was an active killer and was arrested after having been on the run for six months.[65] She participated in his group by making herself available whenever clan members asked for help. Indeed, she attended summit meetings, but it was her logistical support that was essential. In particular, she dealt with the logistical management of fugitives to help them avoid arrest and was very good at managing their sleeping arrangements and finding the most appropriate flats for them to stay in.

Another specific task she undertook was to give the all-clear to clan members before an assassination (a hit). She would check the roads and local districts before the killers took to the streets to murder their target: "*she would go around the neighborhood to find the victim and tell PS when he could act and murder.*"[66] She was considered very trustworthy, and the group of fugitives counted on her totally.

There are many other such cases of co-penetrative women. Federica was the sister and wife of traditional clan members of a clan just outside Naples. Although she had no official criminal record, she was fully involved supporting the clan at an organizational level. She efficiently organized summit meetings at her house, which was next door to the boss's, and relayed messages between members.[67]

Carlo was Tommasina's father. He was as a businessman-camorrista in the building sector from the outskirts of Naples who was close to an important boss. Carlo had a relatively successful business career, in part because of the confidence and trust the boss had in him to invest a lot of his dirty money in his building projects, particularly in Spain. Carlo also got other clans to invest in his building projects.[68]

Tommasina's legitimate business assets were used by the clan and her dad, in particular her construction company set up in the early 2000s. The company managed various building projects in Spain (in the provinces of Barcelona and Tarragona) and had an office in one of the small coastal towns.[69] It was suggested that the money invested in these Spanish building projects (including holiday flats) were the direct profits of the clan's drug trafficking activities. Tommasina was not only a front name but also had regular conversations with clan members. A former member recalls how she "*was not only a front name because we* [clan members] *often had contact with her and she discussed the issues and problems I raised with her.*"[70] In other words, she was well informed and up to date on internal clan business; she knew what was going on while her company in Spain enabled the clan to invest in real estate and this was important for the clan.[71]

Another example is that of Antonella and her husband. Her father was very close to a powerful Camorra network. She extensively assisted her dad, who was fully involved in counterfeit business activities. She lived in Switzerland and sent and received money via money transfers (and Western Union) from different members of the counterfeit scam. She was instrumental in facilitating the movement of money among the different actors and could not have done this unknowingly.[72] This overlap of family loyalty and criminal assistance is especially extensive among women. They may not benefit from a regular salary, but they do enjoy the social capital and reputation of their clan member relatives. They are the invisible insiders.

Outsiders Inside

We also find outsiders who are unrelated to Camorra families but who develop an affinity to camorristi. They have no blood ties but have a genuine friendship, loyalty, and allegiance with camorristi that explains their continued support. For example, Vincenza was close to an important drug clan. She supported the clan in a very simple way: she lent her private space, her flat, to the clan. Her flat became a firearms depot, a safe store for clan members where they kept their artillery: Beretta 3 guns, revolvers, machine guns, and cartridges as well as cash. On one occasion, 35,000 euros in cash were found there.[73] As there was no systematic financial salary, it could be argued that she did this because she identified with the local clan. She was not forced or intimidated to do this but did so out of her own free will and friendship with clan members.

Leonella is another example of a co-penetration relationship but hers is more refined, where financial considerations and friendship intertwine. She was a close friend of SB, one of the main members of an established city clan. The Contini clan formed part of the Secondigliano Alliance and was very active in Rome but also in the center of Naples (San Carlo Arena, Sanità, Forcella, Maddalena, and Vasto districts).[74] He was involved in the financial development of the Contini's clan's activities. Leonella had "*a great friendship*" with him as "*he was like a brother*" to her.[75] Indeed, there was a lot of socializing: their families often dined and traveled together. Together with her husband, Leonella involved all her family in her business activities, which served as a channel for the investment of the clan's dirty profits into the legal economy.

Systematically, all through their business career, they interlinked their activities with those of SB, who would protect them when and where necessary. They started out selling clothes in shops in the city center, which were paid by credit and which she would be paid for two-three months later.[76] In particular, they sold the label "FC," which was managed by the clan, and which gave them the monopoly over access to certain factory supplies. In 2000, they opened a bar-pub together in a piazza near the main train station which Leonella managed. Again, SB acted as her guardian if any local issues and threats emerged; he would resolve them and protect her. She would utter his name if she was challenged. This she did on many occasions to show that she had solid Camorra contacts who would look after her but also when different payments and issues got out of hand.[77] Leonella and her husband provided him with a direct channel into the legal economy. They acted as his legal front name, but their friendship meant that it was not purely an economic and functional exchange as it became more than this. For this reason, it becomes clear that Leonella identifies with her guardian and the clan. The personal relationships women have with camorristi can determine the nature of a woman's involvement.

Eloise was the personal assistant and secretary of one of the businessmen involved in the Secondigliano Alliance counterfeit business.[78] Her boss was fully immersed in the business and criminal activities of the Alliance; he went as far as helping the boss go on the run by procuring him a passport. She carried out her job as a PA, but by doing this she thoroughly engaged in the criminal organization of the counterfeit business. She knew what she was involved in and what she was doing, but we could suggest that she was only doing her job. Her behavior appears to be that of a co-complicit.

Susie's involvement with the Camorra was more complicated and messier: she was a businesswoman who moved in Camorra circles and whose activities were semilegal and even illegal. She was an important link in the Camorra network of a city clan's economic reinvestment strategy: her clothes business existed in what has been labeled "the parallel world."[79] Together with another dubious businessman (who was also putting his business activities at the disposal of the clan) she connected the illegal world to the legal one. She bought bulk counterfeit clothes, sold them door to door and to her vast network of contacts (including the wives of prisoners) through legal companies with front names. Indeed, one of her close collaborators and friends was Celia, who worked with her and whose name officially appeared on the bank accounts that Camorra members managed. Susie was the lover of a drug trafficker from a city clan and because of this, she felt protected in everything she did. The way she behaved was not only that of collusion, but of a more complicit nature. She worked regularly with other businessmen connected to the Camorra and even used the Camorra's coded language and names when referring to specific bosses, clearly demonstrating an intimacy and familiarity with that world.

Blurred Lines, Blurred Worlds

In this chapter, I have sought to show that, outside of the Camorra space in civil society and the economy, women support their relatives and friends. In the public sphere, women professionals help functionally or formally, and they let their sentiments show. In the economic realm, on the other hand, women lend their names but remain rather distant and indifferent to Camorra activities. In the private sphere of the Neapolitan family, where there can be fluid and limited misogyny, women are respected and help out their relatives out of loyalty and friendship. Consequently, it is relatively easy and natural for these women to provide a supportive hand, to lend an ear, and give good advice without necessarily being paid or fully involved in the clan's criminal strategies or plans. All in all, the nature of support of the women in the gray zone is blurred and ambiguous but it is there and available.

WOMEN AND THE CAMORRA'S CULTURAL VALUE SYSTEM

In this chapter, I elaborate on the Camorra's cultural value system that I have identified over the last twenty years.[1] By grasping the Camorra's precise value system, analyzing its language, its words, its expressions, its tone, its codes, its nuances, and the ways both camorristi men and women think, I hope to gain a greater understanding of their worldview. These values are both positive and negative, legal and illegal, but are often neglected because the importance of culture as a key aspect of OCGs has been serially downgraded despite the fact that it is fundamental. By undertaking an in-depth analysis of trial transcripts, pentiti interrogations, and interviews (1980–2023), I have been able to identify some of the core values, norms, and recurring meanings that emerge from these accounts, and which form the basic Camorra cultural value system.

Like all social groups, the Camorra has an internal cultural value system or culture-subculture, which I also call an "ideology" or "mentality," that defines it and is crucial to its existence and survival.[2] Reuter and Paoli also suggest that mafias elaborate a "cultural apparatus," which allows them to "generate an enduring commitment to the organization and a sense of family and belonging."[3] However, they explain that mafias develop more formal and visible tools as part of this apparatus such as initiation rituals, a written set of norms, penalties, which may explain why they do not consider the Camorra a mafia. The point here is that the Camorra and the other mafias do have formal and visible cultural apparatuses. They have important criminal values that develop and are very similar to traditional values. They are fluid, multidimensional, and quasi-invisible, but they dictate and shape Camorra behavior.

By "cultural value system," I mean a "set of common beliefs and attitudes" that a group shares that is distinct from the dominant, "parent culture," which in our case here is the Neapolitan culture.[4] Camorristi use, manipulate, and transform these existing cultural values (traditions, customs, norms, and beliefs) into their own cultural value system to create a sense of Camorra identity and belonging, as part of an extended social self. These values are transformed by camorristi, including women, on a daily basis into resources that shape criminal behavior so much that they often influence outsiders. As Signora Teresa, the wife of a former boss, noted, *"When you hang out with these people, you become another person."*[5]

For the Camorra system to flourish as a criminal entity, it needs to be protected and insulated by collective values that reinforce its identity, existence, and reputation. It has developed within traditional Neapolitan culture, which, while not being criminal itself, has core values that can be easily manipulated to facilitate criminal activities. Camorristi follow these core values and implement them as resources so that they become rules of behavior for the local community and clan. As women dominate the private sphere in the local community, they play a key role in maintaining and upholding this cultural value system and, in particular, when they educate and socialize children. A good example of this is when, in November 2017, there was an incident on the pretty Mergellina waterfront involving an off-duty police officer. He was returning from a wedding with his family and stopped to get an ice cream from Da Ciro, a renowned ice cream parlor on the Lungomare. A moped was blocking his car, so he asked nicely for the owner to move. At this point, the owner and his friends start to threaten and punch the police officer. The owner of the moped was encouraged by his girlfriend who shouted, *"Kill him, kill him, he's a cop!"* The girlfriend was none other than the daughter of a boss and the moped owner was the son of a clan associate.[6]

One of these core values is the family, the central unit because it is based on a traditional male-female, husband-wife relationship that have been transformed into the solid foundation of the criminal clan. The couple is not only an intimate family relationship but a functional criminal partnership as Brancaccio explains: "The family is one of the cornerstones of Camorra power."[7] Mariella Manca articulates this clearly when she argues that *"if a man becomes a camorrista, it is because there is a great woman behind him. If you are a camorrista and you don't have a woman to lean on, you're a nobody."*[8] In other words, in the majority of cases, women who become involved with camorristi know what they are doing: *"I knew what I was doing and what could happen. . . . You do things . . . and you don't even realize what you are doing."*[9] It becomes normal behavior. This aspect is pivotal in our analysis because the influence of women in this traditional Neapolitan partnership has always been underplayed when explaining the Camorra.

The Camorra's Cultural Value System

The Camorra's cultural value system (also Camorra culture/subculture) is a fluid system based on core Neapolitan cultural values, such as loyalty, omertà, power, love, and violence that are used as resources in criminal strategies and evolve and develop over time.[10] The existence of a strong local identity in Naples, aptly called *la napoletanità*,[11] interconnects with organized crime blurring the lines between the criminal world and civil society: "The clear-cut distinctions between good and bad, between what is normal and what is pathological, represent an over-simplification of reality. The impossibility of drawing a line between "us" and "them" . . . means that there can be a natural . . . transition from the world of legality to the criminal world."[12]

In other words, I would argue that some traditional core values from Neapolitan civil society have, over time, been appropriated by criminal families to become a stable cultural value system that camorristi exploit to impose their power and rules on the local community. These values have been interpreted, adopted, and manipulated by criminal clans who have transformed them into everyday resources.

Camorra women identify very strongly with this Camorra cultural value system. Angela suggested that "*respect, the code of silence* [omertà] *and never to betray*" were Camorra values,[13] while Francesca explains "*Camorra wives think that omertà* [law of silence], *money . . . are values.*"[14] This system becomes ingrained in them at different stages of their lives; some are born into it, some identify with it or marry into it, while others learn and get used to it. Rita Longo who did not identify as a Camorra-born woman, argued that her children were contaminated and influenced by their father's family, commenting that "*they have that blood. It's impossible to make them change.*"[15] She also highlights other values, which lead us to reflect on the double standards and "double morality" women accept and enact.[16] In particular, she reflects, "*I don't call it hypocrisy, but selfishness. Selfishness because they* [the men] *only think of themselves*" not only in terms of their lifestyles, their criminal activities, but also their sexual adventures.[17]

Women live these core values with their many contradictions but remain staunch defenders of them. Ultimately, they embody this value system by their own very existence, sometimes even more than the men. This can be seen by the way women try to convince male relatives not to become state witnesses. For example, one clan member from the Gionta clan was publicly warned by his mother in court not to do this. This was her way to "silence" him and to impose omertà. During a busy hearing, she made a public statement for all to hear, including other clan members who might have been having similar ideas "*Think of us: if you are a man, make a decision and kill yourself right away, do not make us all suffer. . . . From now on, it is up to you, you chose this life, either you carry on as before or you find a solution by killing yourself.*"[18]

The mistress of another boss refused to follow him into the state witness protection program, preferring not to collaborate with the state. In another instance, Amalia Stolder, the wife of a Camorra boss, refused to follow her husband, Carmine Giuliano, and forced him to backtrack and interrupt his collaboration with the state and stop providing important testimonies.[19] These were two clear symbolic acts by Camorra women, full of meaning, that they were not prepared to follow their men in breaking with the Camorra system. Their public lack of approval shows how far they were willing to go to defend this criminal value system.

What are the main cultural values that form the foundation of the Camorra's cultural value system? There are four core supervalues:

1. The family: mothers, children, education, love, sex, lovers, and trust
2. Power: a sense of order, justice, freedom, right/wrong, control, and omertà
3. Money: the importance of money, spending it and prestige
4. Violence: punishment, justice, revenge, and pleasure

They are glued together by the notion of "trust," which reinforces them, but which can also quickly be transformed into betrayal. Francesca explained that camorristi *experience betrayal with anxiety.*"[20] Trust, and being able to count on someone, being able to rely on them totally and know that they will look out for you is key to Camorra and criminal behavior. It is naturally found in the family/kinship/blood ties context and initially explains why the family is so important to the Camorra.

The Neapolitan Family

"The elementary unit of social life in Naples is the family," concludes Belmonte.[21] This remains the case. Its importance "is explained by its centrality in strategies designed to help individuals and groups survive, or perhaps prosper. But, in addition, the family provides the emotional context within which people experience their most important and intimate emotional relationships."[22] It becomes essential, not only as an economic unit, but also as a social and cultural space: "The family is an integral part of social and political processes and is integral to issues of power, authority, and economic rationality."[23] The family unit is fundamental in all Neapolitan social classes, proletariat, middle class, or aristocratic. It is important to note that those who dominate the family become key players.

For a long time, southern Italian society has been described as "a patriarchal society," but this is far from the truth. Anne Cornelisen declares "the society of southern Italy to be organized on a matriarchal and not, as is commonly supposed, a patriarchal pattern."[24] Anne Parsons in her study of the Neapolitan proletariat also wrote, "I would conclude that the basic family form for the Neapolitan subproletariat is strongly matrifocal, sometimes becoming the pure matricidal family in which paternity is only a biological and not a social fact, but more often retaining in an intermediate position in which, within the family, the father's role is minimized."[25] She makes clear that "even though a pattern of clear-cut maternal authority is not widespread, there are strong tendencies in that direction within the Neapolitan family."[26] From my evidence, I would say that even today Neapolitan families are more matrilineal, matriarchal, matrilocal, and matricentric.

Some, however, disagree. Belmonte believes that it is the men who rule: "*The women in southern* Italy are powerful only in the sense that they perform 'powerfully' the innumerate tasks and chores which men and children set for them. Women as wives are extolled, and women as mothers are deified, but women as women do not count for much in southern Italy. Mothers teach domesticity and toughness to their daughters. They teach aggression, predation, and phallic pride to their sons."[27]

Although women are present, he insists that "the power of the male, and the idea of the power adhering to things male, continues to suffuse a culture whose masters have always been sons and lovers and likewise tyrants first, and only secondly, husbands and fathers."[28] He continues that a woman's "proper place is in the home."[29]

So, although families may appear to be a patriarchy where men rule exclusively, I believe that the Neapolitan reality is more nuanced. Today, men decide mainly and superficially in the formal, official, and visible public space. Men appear to rule and dominate; macho masculine values exist and are respected. Indeed, this public sphere can be identified as "antiwomen," a sphere that excludes women or at the least, obstructs their existence. In this space, men act as *padre-padrone*, or "father-boss," figures; they are the center of attention, dictating patriarchal rules and giving orders but this is more formal than real. Women have effective but invisible power in the public sphere.

Moreover, behind the front doors of the private sphere, female power is more extensive and embedded, although this is not a generally accepted idea. In this private space, women decide, lay down the law, manage, and advise because as Parson's work has suggested there is "a greater respect for the mother than for the father."[30] Pardo explains,

> Mothers, sisters, wives, fiancées, even daughters and sisters-in-law are important protagonists of ordinary life. . . . Women are experienced

repositories of information and managers of certain areas of gossip and of both discursive and confrontational language. They are mediators *par excellence* in the household, the kin group, and the neighborhood. They start or mediate quarrels and crises, are often key figures in business competition, and in cooperation among relatives and sometimes friends or neighbors . . . and may have power as links via marriage to locally powerful persons. . . . In short, they may upset crucial social relations just as they may be instrumental in strengthening them.[31]

In the intimate Neapolitan private sphere of the family, we have a matriarchy, a matriarchal space where "motherhood is the dominant idea," which is interlinked with the Neapolitan identity and self.[32] Some argue that women cannot have influence or a role in the household if they do not contribute economically but this is not the case. Neapolitan women are strong-willed, intelligent, and efficient and understand how to navigate this sphere. The mother is the center of the family and is the center for her sons', husband's, and brothers' lives at all levels but it's not only mothers. Wives, daughters, sisters-in-law, and aunts have another role. They are equally important, but the men, sons, come first in the eyes of their mothers, and this translates into the structure and activities of the criminal clan.

The family unit has always been presented as central to the structure of the Sicilian Cosa Nostra and Calabrian 'Ndrangheta.[33] Family, we are told, explains everything, but less so for the Neapolitan Camorra. For the Camorra, the family has always been seen as less important because clans continuously make fluid and flexible alliances, forever changing when it is necessary to survive, even betraying relatives.[34] But this now seems quite reductionist as the family is a fundamental core Camorra value and resource.[35]

In the postwar period, clans have transformed their blood family into a strong value, which acts as a cement to keep the collective criminal unit together. Even Raffaele Cutolo's NCO in the 1980s had his close relatives involved, his sister and son. Carmine Alfieri's federation was made up of clans, but they were all family based, for example, the Moccia clan, the Galasso clan, and the Cesarano clan, among others where mothers were always present as a supportive blanket.[36]

Today, we can see that the family is a Camorra value, not only as a self-help instrument but also as an efficient organizational business unit with its own set of values. Rita argues that "*it's all about the family*."[37] She goes on, "*When they* [the camorristi] *need, they always talk with the person who's closest to them. They never talk with the foot soldiers, because they can betray them, but not the wife, not the kids, not the brother, not the sister and not even the mother can betray them. They need the family*."[38] It is ultimately based on trust, love, and loyalty.

The Camorra family unit has, in the postwar period, developed a dual and overlapping criminal function:

1. It is a safe and reliable physical and cultural space where blood relatives are looked after, fed, protected, and educated. It is a safety net, a self-help unit where very positive values emanate.

This overlaps with and extends into:

2. A criminal organizational structure that provides clear and efficient rules on how to behave, how to do business and make money. These functions have now become a strong value of the family, based on respect for blood ties at all costs. Brancaccio explains, "Camorra clans operate like extended family businesses: wide alliances based on kinship, interwoven with economic activities and often connected through strategies involving marriages with other violent families of the same rank or a lower one."[39]

These values extend and exist in the Camorra space, the physical space and territory that the Camorra seeks to control.

It is in the private sphere, this physical and cultural space, where we find many values that are linked and which reinforce the role of the blood family, values such as self-help, support, duty, loyalty, devotion, love, caring, defensiveness, and protectiveness. To ignore the importance of the traditional family value is to fail to understand the Camorra, but also the values family produces, in particular, the power of mothers and wives and the values they promote.

Traditionally, Neapolitan mothers play a special role within the family unit as educators. The presence of family members, the home environment, and emotional setting are essential in the growing up, development, socialization, and education of an individual. Mothers play a key role in the lives of their children, in the daily lives of their male sons. "*La mamma è sempre la mamma*" is a powerful and insightful statement that explains how present mothers are in the lives of their sons, even after they get married and start a family of their own. Van Dijk et al. confirm that the family is a place where important criminal socialization takes place, especially with a parent organized crime offender (and even endorser); they argue the "children of organized crime offenders are extremely high risk of intergenerational continuity of crime."[40] Parents', and in particular mothers', behavior influences and shapes their children's criminal activities whether they offend or, as I believe, endorse the Camorra's cultural value system.[41]

Giorgia Verde was very explicit about her mother-in-law's influence on her son, saying, "*I hold her responsible.*"[42] Camorra mothers (and mothers-in-law) tend to be strong and visible matriarchs who support their sons, husbands, and brothers by providing emotional, financial, functional, and physical assistance.

They do this to protect their families, share their criminal projects, and look out for them. Often, they are authoritarian, dictate the rules and acceptable behavior within the family in the private space. Fundamentally, they act as a safety net for the family; without her, the clan is weaker. Mothers love, educate, support, and promote values; they are supportive, helpful, loyal, and protective. In every Camorra family, there is a matriarch. Giorgia argues that mothers are crucial, because their support and approval is what drives the men on. Without it, the men are less able and potentially disorientated: "*His mother had the same ideas* [as him]. . . . *It is normal that if you have your mum's approval, you carry on. . . . His mother was complicit with him.*"[43]

Mothers provide constant material and emotional support for their camorristi sons in their daily criminal activities. One clan member asks, "*Did you go to my mum's* [to get the money/advice]?"[44] On another occasion, the mother of a clan member "*allowed us to cut up the drugs in her house.*"[45] The mother of the leaders of a clan from the northern suburbs was actively involved in her children's drug-selling business. She lived close to them and participated fully in their drug-selling operations, bagging up and selling: "'*How much stuff is there left?*' '*I will ask mum*' was the reply of one of the leaders."[46] This shows that she "*manages the merchandise of the family, in other words, the drugs that are sold in her house.*"[47]

More recently, in 2020, the wife and mother of an emerging Camorra boss from Ponticelli, has been considered a key organizer in her son's clan and its violent strategy, especially in its recent conflicts with rival clans over the distribution of funds for members in prison. Arrested in 2018 for hiding firearms in her house, a telephone intercept revealed her involvement in the new violent Camorra war: since she had "*come out of prison, everything has gone mad.*" She was more influential than appeared.[48]

Another way mothers demonstrate their constant support is with monthly prison visits. Camorra mothers, young or old, from the city or the province, follow this ritual and travel to visit their men. They visit with or without wives or partners. All even take the long and costly journey to faraway prisons in the north of Italy. The mother of one boss who visited her son in prison with other relatives, worried about his diet and eating habits while the mother of a boss from the Casertano visited her sons in prison regularly and was present at discussions on clan activities and criminal strategies when they were discussed in prison.[49] The mother of a small-time boss knew everything about her son's criminal activities. She was very honest in her analysis of the situation and critical of him and his behavior toward his own daughter.[50] Rita Longo describes what happened when she visited her partner in prison: "*I went and visited him two or three times in jail and she* [the mother-in-law] *would always come with* [me]. . . . *More often than not, she visited because she was his mother. . . . She knew everything because she was his mother . . . for most of the time, he spent his life at his mother's.*"[51]

She believes that her mother-in-law managed the criminal situation, especially when the men were in prison, saying that "*she was the one holding the situation together. She was the regent, let's say . . . she was managing everything.*"[52] These visits are an act of duty, love, and obedience but also proof of loyalty and complicity in Camorra activities because, during these visits, everything is openly discussed, although in code, including business and murders.

This maternal duty can also translate into other supportive acts; they become their son's representative and lawyer. If a mother has to choose between loyalty to the clan or to their son, they often speak out and without fear in favor of their son. They are openly critical of other clan members. They seek to resolve conflicts with the clan on behalf of their sons and they plead their cause when the son might be out of sorts with the clan.

So, while the sons are in prison, mothers can act as go-betweens with the clan. They transmit or refer news and favors between prison and clan members, as many wives also do. Elisabetta did not hesitate to become the intermediary between her son in prison and the clan to pacify the situation between them.[53] Angela did not hesitate to ask the local clan to give her son a job as soon as he came out of prison,[54] and in another clan, in the province of Caserta, "*the mother and wife of Tommy went to speak with the female boss and managed to get Tommy back in the clan. The boss had great respect for Tommy's mother.*"[55]

Mothers will also go to great lengths to sort out their son's mess and involvement in crimes. For example, in 2011, the mother of one clan member from an up-and-coming clan, asked someone to burn a specific moped because there were traces of her son's DNA on it, which could have implicated in the murder of a rival boss, and she wanted to avoid this at all costs and protect him.[56]

Even financially, they seek to protect their son's interests. When the son has no wife or next of kin and is in prison, it is the mother who manages their salary. For example, Giacomo explains how his salary was delivered to his mother's house when he was in prison without any other family knowing.[57] There are even examples of mothers taking on their son's criminal jobs or covering for them while they are in prison so that they can keep their position in the clan and avoid being replaced. Angela, for example, looked after her son's job until he came out of prison.[58]

Mothers educate and socialize their children into the Camorra's cultural value system and hence their resources. Mariella Manca argues that "*what matters is education because if a person wants to grow up differently, if they want to take a different path from the family* [they can. But] *they are rotten themselves if they take this path. But if the values are there.*"[59] This education is a form of indoctrination, teaching them and socializing them to appreciate the Camorra's cultural core values such as violence, power, and money.

This shapes children's way of thinking and their attitudes, which influences their world view. These women are proactive and positive about the criminal Camorra system, which also lacks respect for the state, laws, and law enforcement agencies. Angela argues that "*if the son of a boss from the underworld goes to school and he has already beaten up the teacher, blackmailed the teacher, that's already the underworld. They grow up that way.*"[60] Mothers play a very special role in this educational, socialization, and training process as they have a special bond with their sons and children. Recently, the mother of a young murdered camorrista together with her husband set up an altar in the courtyard of their flat where his ashes were laid as well as a statute of her son's face, to celebrate his life and her maternal love but also perhaps to reinforce his reputation and status.

Giovanni Messina, a former Camorra member, explained to me, "*They* [the children] *are born and grow up with this mentality. They die with that mentality. There is no choice there. A child, perhaps, is not responsible for where he is born but then, he will become responsible. It is a forced choice.*"[61] Giorgia Verde developed this further: "*That's the mentality. If you go to the root of these people living for the system, living for the street, that's the mentality. They do it because they like it . . . because they grew up with that idea, that mentality, that being the wife of a camorrista, the wife of a boss is a good thing.*"[62]

In other words, a socioeconomic context, together with a normalized criminal mentality such as the Camorra's cultural value system, can help explain the vital roles mothers play in facilitating this situation.

It is rare to find a camorrista without children because children represent so much, that is, virility and possible new members. In Naples, Camorra families tend to be quite extensive, maybe less now than in the 1950s. Camorra women have children and bring them into a specific world, one of violence, death, money, and often prison visits. Having children demonstrates a man's virility and is an important act of power. The youngest and more recent generation of camorristi, who emerged at seventeen to twenty years of age, are all already fathers. For example, Emanuele Sibilio, also known as ES17, who died at the age of nineteen, was the father of two children while many of the young leaders of the Giuliano clan from Forcella or the Amato clans from Melito were also fathers of one or two children before getting to their twenties.[63] Often, the women knowingly accept bringing children into a world of uncertainty, death, violence, and prison visits, accepting the likelihood that they might have to bring up their children on their own.

The Camorra world children are born into has already been decided for them and it is hard for them to get out of it because of the family context and economic situation. For example, one of the managers of a drug piazza in a smart central district, a mother, took her young daughters with her wherever she went to do business. When she was cutting up drug doses in her living room or on her moped to sell to her buyers, the children were always present. One of the children, an eight-year-old, even asked her mother's accomplice: "*Uncle, do you like this job* [of making up cocaine doses]?"[64]

The same dynamics can be seen in a clan from Ponticelli. The boss was a mother of six children. Her children were always in the middle of the planning of criminal activities that took place in her living room.[65] She allocated her oldest his own piazza.[66] Thus, unscrupulous mothers co-opt their young children into their criminal activities. It is very difficult for the children to walk away from their roots because they know no different; they do not necessarily know what is right and what is wrong but are just being educated by their loving parents or relatives.

It is also important to note that there are some women married to camorristi who consciously or unconsciously keep their children out of the Camorra space and its cultural value system. There are a few examples of women who stay aloof from their husband's activities, either not wanting to know or being kept in the dark by their partner. The overall Camorra context can be difficult to counter and mothers in this situation can be a lonely voice, a real exception.

For example, when Rita Longo decided to collaborate with the state in the early 2000s and asked her daughter to follow her. Her daughter replied, "*You are now dead for me.*"[67] In another district, when the daughter of a powerful boss understood that her father wanted to collaborate with the state and take all his family with him into the state protection program, she decided to do otherwise. She took her younger brother away from her mother in order to try and sabotage the whole operation. She even threatened her mother: "*I am not giving you my brother back. Dad must decide to no longer collaborate with the state so we can all be good together again.*"[68]

She continues and confronts her mother: "*Mum, if you want, dad will change his mind, if you want, dad will change his mind.*"[69] Her father responds by saying, "*Does she know that they can kill her husband?*" but no, she only wanted to block her father's desire to leave the Camorra.[70] Girls appear to have particular difficulty in detaching themselves from the Camorra's value system. However, there are other examples of young men who have managed to remove themselves from the Camorra underworld, as was the case of Maldresto, who was related to the Presiteri clan, an ally of the De Lauro clan.[71] Thanks to his mother, he went on to have a successful singing career and even appeared at the annual San Remo Music festival.

The boss Raffaele Cutolo's criminal organization, the NCO, was not based on blood ties but he did portray himself as the father figure for his numerous and loyal members, "the lost souls" of Naples who found a way out through crime.[72] In many clans, however, we do find "Mamma Camorra," "Camorra mother" fig- ures, women who act as mothers to the young and inexperienced members. They don't necessarily have to be leaders of the clan such as Nunzia D'Amico, but they do mentor, encourage, and cajole the new young recruits at the start of their Camorra careers. This is a crucial role in an organization that needs young recruits, from inside and outside the blood family, to keep it going, energetic, and vibrant.

Recently, journalists have once again drawn attention to the involvement of minors in Camorra activities and violence, the so-called baby gangs described by Saviano and of even younger children.[73] But this is not a new phenomenon: we must remember that we have examples from the past where there have already been minors involved in Camorra-related activities. For example, Ciro Maresca was thirteen years old and Luigi Moccia, fourteen, when their sister and mother involved them in violent vendettas.[74]

Clans have always recruited younger family members, when necessary, as under eighteen-year-olds are not prosecutable and remain below the police radar. If we take a closer look, there is a whole army of minors, present and active. They occupy both important leadership positions and are hard-working foot soldiers, trying to get promoted up the ranks. There are also those who try to impose themselves, whether related to Camorra members or not. The son of Angela who was only ten years of age was violent and threatened citizens and other clan mem- bers in the local district much to their anger.[75] Gianpietro was an active member of the clan involved in violent activities and attempted murder and was only seventeen. Another well-known example, that of ES17, started his criminal career when he was only a minor, and although he went to a youth offenders' center, he still carried on with his criminal activities when he came out.[76] He was still a minor when he led his full-on attack on rival Camorra clans to gain supremacy. Youngsters from other clans such as the Giuliano or Amato-Pagano clans also started their criminal careers young. Hence, the label "baby gangs." These are all male examples, but there are also some girls who as the girlfriends in the back- ground or as minors attracted by the buzz of the criminal activities and lure of easy money rarely get picked up by police investigations.

Wives, and in particular wives from non-Camorra families, might be lower down in the family Camorra hierarchy compared to their mothers and mothers- in-law, but rarely are they absent. Although some wives appear unaware or indif- ferent to the clan business, they cannot be. Their passivity in the Camorra space demonstrates a form of continuous support, devotion, loyalty, duty, and love, even being indifferent because they are not denouncing or rejecting the Camorra system or distancing themselves from it. They accept it by being there, even if not actively participating in clan business. Women do decide the type of life they want, who they marry, and ultimately, their future. They have free will about whether to be fully involved or accepting to be indifferent. If there are situations where women are trapped in a marriage, they can seek to walk away. But often they don't.

Emblematic of many wives, we have a case where the wives of a couple of brothers in prison for mafia-related crimes spent a huge amount of energy, time, and money on their husbands while the men served time in prison for Camorra association. First, they provided constant psychological support and advice. These spouses visited their husbands regularly in prison across Italy, the prisons being usually located in the north or in the south of Italy, which constitutes important journeys. These visits were both financially expensive and psychologically tiring, but essential for a camorrista's reputation and well-being. Between 2011 and 2016, it was calculated that they spent 9,000 euros purely on travel and prison visits. Wives constantly provide advice. Men listen to them and appreciate their input, whether it is business decisions or legal advice. Mariella explained that because she was the only one who could really read Italian properly, she was able to follow the judicial and police investigations to see how much evidence they had against her husband and his clan.[77]

Second, they provide financial support. Access to money for prisoners was extremely important as it meant they could buy goods/services while in prison, but also increased their prestige and power. It was calculated that in those five years, more than 20,000 euros were sent to their husbands in prison, roughly more than 5,500 euros per man. Last, they organized and sent with great attention and love every month "goodies" parcels to their men in prison.[78] At times, of course, they had to choose between their husband's needs and those of their children: "*Are you saying that it is more important that they* [the children] *go to the seaside, than you come to visit me here* [in prison]?"[79] asked a camorrista to his wife on a prison visit.

As mothers, they normally choose their children over their husband, saying "*I have two children, they have got the right to go to the seaside* [on holiday]."[80] This caused tensions between the couple, whereby the woman is only doing her best, that is, "*I do what I can*" but the men in prison alone are not objective toward their wives and this can result in jealousy, bitterness, and nastiness.[81] Women outside prison are free of their husband's control and can act as they wish, even if the clan, at times, tries to exert control over them. Women have more freedom than is believed if they are intelligent enough to manage it.

Women are generally very supportive, demonstrating a clear unconditional sense of duty, loyalty, and devotion to their spouses and blood relatives. A clear example of this is when, in 2016, a female minor accused a boss of sexual attention and abuse. Once his wife found out, she did not ask her husband to explain but marched down to the girl's family home, insulted the family calling her husband to come down, which he did, and started to shoot at the girl's home, surrounded by loyal clan members.[82]

Love in its different forms is important in the Camorra, although often presented as less significant in front of omnipotent violence. I would argue that though it is a key value, it is not only love for a person that motivates Camorra women, but for a lifestyle and what that lifestyle represents. Here the love of the lifestyle is love for the Camorra system and its main cultural values: money and power.

Growing up in a Camorra family naturally means that you frequent like-minded people and eventually, end up with a camorrista, which is not unusual. It is very natural for girls born into Camorra families to find young men who embrace the Camorra. Indeed, there are many examples of Camorra intermarriages which everyone approves of, but also marriages that were not forced but based on love and respect. In the Casalesi Confederation, the wife of the boss arranged marriages: "*She arranges marriages with whoever is convenient to her.*"[83] On one occasion, she warned a young woman away from her son because "*she didn't measure up to him*" and didn't come from a reputable Camorra family.[84]

Some young women are completely ignorant of their partner's criminal life but when they become aware of the situation, they are very loyal and believe in love, even though they know that they may have to face many challenges alone: heartache, loneliness, betrayal, and death. Some young women believe in a naïve way that their love can change their man: "*There is also the 'red cross nurse' syndrome because they* [young women] *think they can change them* [young camorristi]. *But, in the end, they are the ones to change . . . but my point is—if you're a girl, a woman, before putting yourself in such a situation . . . either, you kind of like it, because if I know that a person . . . is a camorrista . . . no, I try not to fall in love* [with him]. *I don't know, I would do something to avoid this situation.*"[85]

Some young girls can also become the gateway for young men into the clan. In other words, young men fall in love with girls from criminal families and enter the Camorra this way. This was the case for Renato. His was not from a criminal family, his father was a butcher, but his girlfriend belonged to a criminal family, and after he fell out with his family, he got involved in drug dealing with his mother-in-law. He was far from his district and abandoned by his family. Soon enough he was "scouted" by a local clan that needed new members after recent mass arrests. To mark the beginning of his new official life as a camorrista in the clan, he even set up a new account on social media, with a new name and quasi new identity. He became a regular clan member and one of the clan's killers and would do anything for the leaders of the clan, even being badly injured during an attack. In this case, it was his involvement and love for a young woman that changed his life and marked his future criminal career.

Women show unconditional love, faith, trust, and loyalty, knowing that they have not chosen an easy path and can even be betrayed. There are many examples of women who follow their love, whatever they do, even if undertaking illegal activities. One Neapolitan thirteen-year-old echoed this when she explained that she would even break the law to follow her boyfriend, because "*love is love.*"[86]

Girlfriends become wives and accompany their young men on a criminal life journey. Mariella believes that "*it's normal for a woman to always end up* [involved]. *That's the path of any woman married to a camorrista.*"[87] They are partners and share the glory and the hardship. Nunzia D'Amico's children frequented the clan as the clan operated from her flat and so it was not surprising that her children got boyfriends/girlfriends from the clan. Laura explains how she fell for one of her dad's lieutenants.[88] The girlfriend of a young emerging leader wrote him a text message when he went on the run, saying, "*My love, I beg you, tell me what is going on? Your behavior is worrying me. I love you.*"[89] Some women are in for the long haul: Michelina was the long-term girlfriend and partner of an established boss. When he went on the run in the early 2000s, she also disappeared overnight. She was only seventeen, and when he was arrested fifteen years later, she was there by his side, now aged thirty-two, in a dressing gown. She had followed him fully aware of who he was and what kind of life she was going to lead.

Sabina was the long-term partner of a boss for eighteen years. She was devoted to her man even though he had a younger lover, a Brazilian woman. She did everything he asked of her, collecting money from her loan sharking clients, and intimidating the relatives of possible new state witnesses.[90] She even moved to live in a town that was closer to the prison where he was held so she could see him from outside the gates and wave. Her love was total; she writes in a letter to her partner:

> As regards the comings and goings, my love, I would stay with you all day, but you angrily send me away. So, I think that you no longer like me, and I leave. But, my dear love, I am only pretending to leave. I move from where you can see me, but I stay to look at your empty window . . .
>
> 1. Since I have been here, I write to you every day.
> 2. Can you understand how important it is for me to write to you.
> 3. I stay under the prison window all day even if you send me away if you don't return and don't show yourself.
> 4. My day in town is only worthwhile when I am under your prison window, otherwise I stay at home.[91]

Mariella Manca loved her husband, an up-and-coming boss. They were a strong criminal team, but when he went to prison, she was left to organize the clan. Alone, she fell in love with a sailor from a local town. It was not so much him she loved, but she loved the idea of being in love.[92] She loved him and believed in him until he lured her into a trap so she could be punished by her husband's family, who saw her promiscuous behavior as inappropriate and outrageous. They beat her, threatened her, and even took her home and daughter away. She escaped by becoming a state witness.

Some wives have demonstrated true loyalty, not to the Camorra but to their husbands and their choices. Some have broken free from the Camorra's cultural value system and its space to follow their husbands in their difficult decisions. The behavior of Sara, wife of an important boss, shows the love, devotion, and dedication to her husband, not the camorrista. In 2009, her husband, wanted to become a state witness, and Sara became the target of the local community for being the main reason why he wanted to collaborate with the state.[93] As this took some time to organize, the whole clan and district reacted by threatening and putting pressure on her, as she was trying to protect her man at all costs, even if she was threatened by her own children.[94] She managed to be strong and resist these attacks when others would have given in.

Within the traditional Neapolitan family, there are quite a few taboos, social customs, or norms that are avoided, not mentioned, and even ignored. Two obvious taboos about sexual behavior here are: (1) homosexuality-transgenderness and (2) mistresses/lovers. Homosexuality and trans still remain relatively taboo subjects and are problematic for traditional Camorra clans, although the Camorra is more "gender fluid" and accepting of different sexualities.[95] Gribaudi noted that there are a good number of declared lesbians in the Camorra compared to other mafias.[96] But even the Camorra is accepting up to a point. The story of Giovanna Arrivoli highlights these complex issues. Giovanna was not scared of being open about wanting to transit to being a man. However, her transgender sexuality challenged the traditional Camorra status quo. Giovanna was born a woman but wanted to be a man and transitioned to become Giovanni. She was not scared of any repercussions; she showed great strength of character, just wanting to be herself as a man and a clan member. They challenged the clan's thinking, but probably because they knew too much they were executed as a result. The local newspaper commented, "*She was killed as a man because the Camorra has a way of killing women and a way of killing men. And Giovanna was killed as though she was a man.*"[97]

Although Giovanni's story ended badly, there are other more positive stories such as that of the son of a boss from Torre Annunziata who transited and became a woman without being too bothered by their father or his clan at the time. Years later, their father, a lifer in Rebibbia Prison in Rome, has reconciled himself with his daughter and accepts their choices.

Having a mistress is accepted but formally shunned. Indeed, for a man to have a mistress reinforces his worth and self-confidence; for a Camorra member to have a mistress means that his sexual power and prowess reinforces his criminal power. It is a taboo subject but over the years has become an accepted norm, that like in society, married clan members have mistresses. As we have seen, wives are fundamental to a boss, his criminal project, and clan; mistresses provide another level of support and assistance, which can be very useful.

The love Camorra women have is not only translated into passion and loyalty, but also into illegal behavior; they can become involved in criminal activities for love. One boss left his traditional family and started to collaborate with the state to be with his lover. He met her at his sister-in-law's house and there was an instant feeling. She moved into a flat he rented for her and participated actively in a murder plot as the support team. When he started to collaborate with judges, he avoided talking about her and her participation, but she told them the whole truth that she was involved in organizing the hideaway as well as accompanying the killers.

The story of Francesca is also a tender love story that upset traditional values as she became the boss's mistress when she fell in love with this married man who was an emerging camorrista. "*I found this guy fascinating,*" she explains.[98] He already had a young wife and child but when they met it was love, real love. She did whatever he asked of her, even criminal activities (hiding firearms, getting money to members, looking after drugs). But she always actively sought to take him away from his clan and its illegal activities, especially when she had a son with him. Since she was not from a Camorra family, she was freer, and when he eventually got arrested, she was able to convince him to collaborate with the state to have a solid future together.

The importance of mistresses can also be seen by the number of Camorra bosses arrested by the police on their way to their amorous encounter. One leader of the Casalesi clan was arrested in 2004 in Krosmo in Poland on his way to meet his young Romanian lover.[99] On another occasion, it was the boss's mistress who disappeared before being arrested by the police: she disappeared in 1992 as the police issued an arrest warrant for her and looked for her in her flat. They clearly thought she could have useful information for them.

Camorra wives suffer at the hands of their husbands when they have mistresses but somehow it is the collective good of the clan that must predominate over individual worries. For the Camorra wife, it is a form of humiliation in the community but as it is not formally recognized, she remains the wife with the power. Indeed, sometimes, some mistresses can get so jealous and upset that they can get their lover arrested by the police, as was the case in 2011, when the mistress of a boss from Pozzuoli informed the police on what he was up to and got him into serious trouble.[100] But all in all, the case of the wife and mistress working side by side for the clan is the ideal set up for any camorrista: in 2019, both the wife and mistress of a boss from Torre del Greco were accused of being involved in collecting extortion money from local businesses.[101]

Power

Power is another core cultural value in the Camorra and a vital aspect of the Camorra's self-identity, which also becomes a vital resource in daily life. Often Camorra women are fascinated and attached to this concept of "power," even if it is challenging to define and refine. Power as defined Merriam-Webster is "the possession of control, authority, or influence over others."[102] Having power, possessing power, and being powerful in the Camorra is very multidimensional, while the feeling of being powerful gives a thrill and a buzz to many women.

In this study, power and being empowered can mean: (1) having criminal power, (2) having economic power, and (3) having sexual power over others within the Camorra space. It may be the power of men over women, men over men, or of women over men and women over women. These three concepts are all interlinked and overlap, but the essence of power and control over others in some shape or form is essential for Camorra women. This power does not have to be openly visible but can also be imperceptible. This invisible female power to influence and shape male behavior is a form of power that appears less obvious to many, but that may well reflect true female Camorra power more accurately. Camorra women are not empowered by their relationship with men but by their position and status in the family.

How do Camorra women articulate the notion of power? Giorgia defines it in traditional terms: "power" is "*telling people what to do; power is when you instill fear into others, for example, 'they respected him* [the boss] *because they feared him.'*"[103] This is fear-based respect and is not based on charisma or admiration. Laura on the other hand, believes that power is "*money and always becoming more powerful*" thanks to it.[104] She links being powerful to having money, which in turn, produces basic respect from clan members. She argues "*For me, there has to be respect and maybe women have this role in the clan*" to be respected by all.[105] Francesca also links power to money but this time, in terms of accessing *la bella vita,* "the good life." Having luxury goods and money makes women feel powerful and superior in the local community:

> *They have a sense of superiority. It is in their personality; they like to be superior . . . but then they get fascinated by "power." They're women who love to be at the center of attention. I love that too, but my husband has to put me at the center of attention. For them it's the power. They are blinded by it. They want to win.*[106]

It has previously been argued that mafia women only access power because of their relationship with powerful men and that they only benefit from "temporary delegated power" and have no actual power for themselves. The opposite could also be argued. The daughter of an influential boss, for example, was interested in power and in placing her husband in a leadership role in her father's clan. So much so that she sought to remove her mother from an influential position in the clan so that, as a result, she and her husband could become the most powerful couple, not her mother who was her father's representative. This highlights that often men have just as much to gain from their association and marriage with Camorra women as the other way around. In this particular case, power flowed from the boss's daughter to her husband, and he became someone, thanks to her. Once he divorced, it could be argued that he lost his position in the clan and all criminal credibility. Another good example is the case of the three sisters married to the top bosses of the Secondigliano Alliance. It could be suggested that they are key because they are at the center of various blood ties and kinship relationships that connect the three criminal clans and the larger alliances altogether. Thus, the blood family extends to reinforce the criminal family and its alliances, and women are crucial to this dynamic.

The power-family relationship is complex and needs to be further unpacked. We have two different dynamics here: on the one hand, the women who are born into criminal families and who are aware of their status, power, and role. They are the "insiders": they are educated and socialized into the crime system with these core values. And, on the other, women outsiders who may be attracted to the criminal power of men. They are "outsiders" but learn and believe in these core values, maybe more than those born with them, because they want to show how much they believe in these cultural values and system. It is this second group of women, the so-called power-hungry women, who journalists tend to focus on.

But this is an oversimplification as there are different power dynamics and tensions at play: for example, there are women who are forced into marriage with camorristi for the greater criminal project and pressurized by keen parents; there are women born into criminal families who carry on with the criminality and believe in it; there are women who marry into camorra families and who either become criminalized, passive, or who walk away. Some women marry camorristi but pretend that they don't understand what their men do. This can also be considered a form of complicity and knowing one's place. In all these instances, apart from the cases of forced marriage, women are very willing and aware of the part they have to play in the local community, which includes an understanding of their status, reputation, and power as part of a Camorra family. Women's initial power comes from being a member of a crime family and their domesticity, but this is soon transformed into real-informal power and agency to act and to undertake criminal activities. Their power is not only due to their relationship to a man but to the way they decide to act. There are also many examples of men who become powerful camorra players because their sisters marry important camorristi, but this is considered an unimportant detail. We focus on the women being subordinate, full stop.

Other more ambitious women want power for themselves and see power as "masculine." Nunzia D'Amico's sense of being a woman and a good camorrista was linked to her understanding of male power: "*I told him I am a woman but only on the outside because inside I feel like a man, I did not allow him to speak anymore. . . . I am no one's girl and have never been someone's girl.*"[107] She saw and articulated the gender difference while at the same time undermining its importance. In other words, for her, only men are strong, but as a woman, she also considered herself strong, stating, "*We are the Camorra now, now it is worse, now, there are the women.*"[108] She was also powerful and violent: "*He mustn't even dare to try and do anything . . . I am coming, I will show him.*"[109] This behavior would confirm the theory that women are only accepted as criminals if they take on masculine values and behavior. Nunzia and many other women from Ponticelli were very feminine and lived their femininity to the full not only in the way they dressed, the way they looked after themselves, the way they seduced men, but also because they had children.

In sum, some women are attracted by power, while others just have power for who they are and what their family represents. I believe that when discussing "power" in the mafia, we always use black-and-white male terms of reference to frame our analysis; terms such as control, violence, decision making, and money. And yet, power in mafias is much more nuanced and subtle; it is not simply patriarchal power, flowing from all men in the public sphere. In the private sphere, women are powerful players who have power in the Camorra. They don't become empowered because of some external event but already have power because of their position in the family.

Money

Money is at the heart of the Camorra's criminal activities. Money is the Camorra's bloodline: "*It is always about the money . . . it is always money that motivates you to do all of this.*"[110] It becomes a value and a way of behaving; wanting money at all cost breeds reputation, power, and prestige but it can also promote violence, arrogance, underhanded behavior, ferocity, brutality, cruelty, foul play, and fearlessness. Indeed, Laura admits that "*when you start to have so much money, your values change.*"[111] Mariella goes further: "*Financially a camorrista wants for nothing. As I told you, it is always about money. Beyond respect, you feel omnipotent because you are respected and if you go down the street, if you go into a shop, it is always about money. You have everything you want.*"[112]

Women often manage the finances of the clan when needed because they are perceived as being more careful with the money. Perhaps, they save and are more careful or it is a way of avoiding the money going into the hands of rivals. I am interested here to discuss the intimate relationship Camorra women have with money, not their work relationship with it or their ability to manage it for the clan.

We need to distinguish between two different main relationships:

1. Money for mere survival or the need for food to be put on the table so all can eat, the famous art of *l'arrangarsi*, the art of making do.
2. Money to pay for a lifestyle and luxury goods, in particular, at the leadership level, which also produces reputation, power, and prestige. Women are attracted by this money, which ultimately needs to be put back in the economy and women are good at that.

It is easy to forget that many people get involved in Camorra activities because there is no other source of income. Francesca explains the necessity to make money to survive: "*There are women selling drugs. It's wrong. But they do it to eat . . . it's not at all justifiable, of course, but it's true that maybe they do it because they need to eat . . . although, what I say is that if you need to eat, you can always go and clean toilets. But maybe they don't do it because they are ignorant.*"[113]

Laura highlights how money is at the base of everything in the Camorra: "*The priority is to have money, so to get money you need to continue illegal activities because everyone constantly wanted money for lawyers and others.*"[114] She goes on, "*As I have said, money for me was important because our clan made a lot of money and then, it used violence to make more . . . because money is never enough . . . but always for money.*"[115]

Camorra money brings women either a salary or a hand that feeds them while others get a regular sum of money every month, without having to work as the wife, daughter, or mother of a Camorra member.[116] What is clear is that these women are not ignorant or innocent about the true origin of the money, even if they choose not to understand: *"It's obvious, right?"* where the money comes from.[117] Signora Teresa explains how having money helps to have a good and secure life: *"Yes, there was money and even a lot of it because, in that period, every system [clan] earned a lot. The bosses had it good. They had houses! No, no, you would see a lot of money. For a period of time, we had a somewhat comfortable life."*[118]

Then, her husband was arrested and got a life sentence. The clan helped with expenses but when she decided to break off from the clan, she found herself in a precarious position, in constant debt with poor mental health. Poverty is always around the corner.

There is also the so-called bella vita, the "good life": *"That's the first thing, it is the money."*[119] Money brings the lifestyle but also respect in the family and a reputation in the local community. This can act as a key motivator for becoming involved in criminal activities. *"There are many types of women. . . . If we're talking about women who are still with their husbands after so many years, in my opinion it's because they like this life. I'm sorry to say because we are women. They like the lifestyle. . . . I think they are fascinated by the life. . . . to be honest, it's called the 'bella vita.' Everything is easy."*[120]

Camorra women are coquettes and fascinated by the luxurious goods money brings. They also are attracted to the joys of plastic surgery to embellish one's body—lips, checks, breasts. Whether young or old, rich or poor, all Camorra women are now investing in plastic surgery. One just has to look at their images on social media. One Camorra woman *"always wears Louis Vuitton, has certain [fabulous] suits, Ferragamo decolté,"* while another *"was wearing a jacket worth 1000 euros."*[121] Indeed, it was said that the wife of an important boss, *"shared her husband's luxury lifestyle."* It was once suggested that during a visit to London, they spent their ten-day stay in the Ritz.[122] Laura reflects about what money means to her, saying, *"In time, I liked it because we made so much money, so it was good for me. . . . I liked it because I was well off."*[123] She develops further: *"It changed my life because I was well off and spoilt. In the end, it spoils you. It is like, I don't know, a drug. You take drugs and you take up that habit."*[124]

Not only does money allow access to luxurious items, but it also provides a high quality of life, even though it is a life that moves between life and death. Mariella exclaimed *"They gave me everything. . . . I was attracted to this thing . . . I was attracted by the different lifestyle."*[125] It is fascinating to note that many Camorra women leaders and those related to important bosses have personal assistants, chauffeurs, and even bodyguards. Maria Licciardi had her own chauffeur, and the wife of a boss from the northern districts had her own personal assistant, Mario, who organized her diary; accompanied her to visit the lawyer or prison if and when necessary. He also organized family events such as parties.[126] The sisters of some prominent bosses also had an assistant chauffeur who accompanied them on prison visits or to see the lawyers.[127] This is quite emblematic of Camorra women leaders.

Children of camorristi also love easy money and famous brands. Stefania said she "*loved wearing branded clothes* [Hogan, Fay] *so much so that I recall that she would go to Naples to do some shopping and would buy very expensive clothes (Louis Vuitton, Fendi). Obviously, she did not have a job that would allow her to buy these things.*"[128] For her eighteenth birthday, she "*told her uncle that she would like a FIAT 500* [2,000 euros from each brother and her father and her uncle would provide the difference]."[129]

The daughter of another boss believed that she had a special status because of her surname, deserved special treatment and recognition, and became resentful because she didn't get enough money.[130] Camorra women can overdo it to the point of excess, even though they do not have a regular job. So, when a wife complained, "*I need to pay the bills, I need to prepare for Christmas, I need to buy presents,*" the harsh answer that came back from her husband was "*buy less! Because you buy three times more than what everyone else buys.*"[131] Moreover, many of the women from the Casalesi confederation would go shopping, whether for clothes or food, and expect not to pay.[132] They also expected to have regular holidays, both a winter/ski holiday and a beach holiday. One wife would take her three kids to the Val d'Aosta ski resort to ski while her husband was on the run.[133] The leadership of the Secondigliano Alliance spent their month of August in the south of France while the Amato-Pagano clan members spent their holidays in Spain in Malaga, and another clan member spent his holiday in Porto Cervo, Sardinia, spending 20,000 euros on hotel bills.[134] All this when the women did not work, but it was the lifestyle they expected.

Here is the contradiction. Often, Camorra women do not work but still expect a high-quality lifestyle from Camorra activities. This creates tensions and misunderstandings among relatives and clan members.[135] The wife of one of the top bosses of a clan in the suburbs expected to receive money from the clan's different activities because of her status as the wife of a leader, even though she never worked. Another woman left her camorrista partner but still expected to get paid a salary by the clan.[136]

In one clan, the wives of the leaders constantly complained about their financial situation although none of them had a regular job and yet received a monthly allowance from the clan. While their husbands were in prison, they received 2,500 euros a month, and when they were free, they were always looked after by the boss, their relative who "*always wanted them to have good standard of living . . . a good 'tenore di vita.'*"[137] He had a soft spot for one of them: *"They have had to pay her journey and everything else for the last three years,"* and this created tensions and made others jealous: *"They have never paid anything for me."*[138] Maybe this was because she was not a local girl.

Money creates tensions and rivalries because members are treated differently and are given varying sums of money, which is perceived as *"unfair."* From there, hatred, resentment, and bitterness slowly develop until it explodes: *"The problem is always money, money. Then you want to leapfrog people who are bigger than you, when you can't really do that."*[139] Thus, it is right to conclude that while money is the Camorra's ultimate aim and objective, it is also a core value that plays a vital role in the mentality and thinking of Camorra women, whether it is to put food on the table for their hungry family or to live a luxurious life with only the best cars, clothes, shoes, holidays, and houses and decoration. Money matters.

Violence

Women give life. They look after life, but they are also involved in taking life. Violence is fully part of the Camorra value system, a continuous presence both in the private and public spheres, because camorristi seek to control "the territory" all for themselves by whatever means necessary.[140] In other words, *"If you are in the Camorra, you have to be violent,"* and *"violence is automatic."*[141] This applies both to men and women, highlighting the fact that in the Camorra, contrary to public perception (the existing narratives being that Camorra men are constructed as masculine and Camorra women as feminine) violence is not gendered. One frequent image that comes to mind in relation to ungendered violence is when the police come to arrest the men, women rebel and seek to block them, often becoming violent toward the police: women lack respect for the state and lash out becoming violent. For example, when police came and tried to arrest Alba Rossi, she insulted them and resisted them.[142]

Mafia women have for a long time enjoyed an untainted image of being traditional women in Catholic Italy, innocent, loving homemakers and carers, blissfully ignorant of more complex criminal issues. More important, women are supposedly incapable of violence usually because violence is "naturally" associated with masculinity and because they demonstrate "an alarming degree of incompetence."[143] This does not reflect reality: women are capable of inciting violence and of committing violent acts. The D'Amico sisters from Ponticelli were described as *"scary, really scary"* because *"they wanted to shoot, they wanted to kill"* and *"because they hurt you so bad as to put you into a coma."*[144]

In relation to this perceived "masculine" violence, it is worth noting that women become fascinated with violence and guns because they represent for them so-called masculinity.[145] One girlfriend, when seeing her boyfriend's gun exclaimed: "*I want one, my love, I want one with my name written on it.*"[146] Another young woman in the D'Amico clan showed off a newly purchased gun. She said euphorically: "*I bought myself a 38* [38 caliber revolver, long barrel]. *A long barrel, that is a monster of a gun . . . it's a beauty!*"[147] A female manager from Torre del Greco also had the reputation of being "*good with a gun.*"[148] During a shoot-out in the street, the wife of a boss in Barra was heard shouting, "Shoot the b*****!" while Anna Terraccino, a boss of the Quartieri Spagnoli, never hesitated to use violence and guns to gain respect from the local community, but most important, to challenge male rivals.[149]

Women use the language of violence, this so-called masculine value, to impose their ideas, their presence, and their strategies on the clan and local communities. It is striking to note that with this acceptance and full ownership of violence often comes a cold heartedness, a lack of emotion or empathy which does not belong only to men. Women, perhaps to survive in the street or in the clan, also demonstrate these traits. They are just as hard as men. The women from the D'Amico clan systematically showed this: for example, when the women from the D'Amico clan armed with baseball bats wanted to beat up a woman whose husband belonged to a rival clan, she only managed to escape by walking across a balcony,[150] or on another occasion when the wife of a boss wanted to force a female tenant to move out of a flat (a kind of "forced expulsion" by the clan) so that her daughter could have it, she publicly slapped her in the face and intimidated her forcing her finally to leave.[151]

Women don't have to be caring or soft and display full empathy, but can be hard and emotionless. A mature woman boss, who herself was not violent, did not hold back when she heard the description of an act of violence; she "*continued to laugh,*" showing no empathy toward the victims and being rather indifferent to other people's safety, hurt, or pain.[152] Another Camorra woman boss from the district of Ponticelli showed no emotion either when her clan accidently killed an innocent bystander: they accidentally murdered a nineteen-year-old who was caught in the crossfire in a bar and all she could say was: "*Now the damage is now . . . it is what it is*"; in other words, let us move on and the death of an innocent victim is not a big deal, illustrating her violent nature.[153]

In a slightly different context, there are also many examples of women who accept the violence dished out against their loved ones and don't seem to care or be particularly bothered or emotionally touched. They don't give the impression that life is scary, and they accept the cruelty of everyday violence that clan members enact. For example, in a clan from Barra, the husband of a female clan member was murdered by her brothers in November 1991. Her husband was a member of their clan but was murdered by his brothers-in-law with his wife's full knowledge and perhaps consent. They felt justified in their use of violence and she accepted their violence because there was a valid reason: "[The] *unhappy marriage . . . the continuous and violent arguments between the two, his anger toward this wife being guilty of agreeing to her brother's requests who continuously asked her to do things for them, in particular, the transport of firearms and drugs.*"[154]

The disappearance and murder of Gino in 1993 also shows female indifference and contempt. Gino was a nineteen-year-old who, it was believed, seduced and behaved in an inappropriate way with the young daughters of an important city Camorra family. Even though he was considered an up-and-coming camorrista with criminal potential, he was punished for his arrogant behavior and dangerous liaisons. Both the daughters and mother of the Camorra family knew how he was horrifically beaten, violently murdered, and callously dumped at sea in the bay of Naples, but they never openly spoke about it and even denied it to the mother who was mourning her son's death.[155] The true dynamics and motives of the murder were only revealed seventeen years later thanks to telephone intercepts and state witness statements. And these women formed an essential part of the wall of omertà around this case, even when his mother and sister came asking for news.

Female violence in the Camorra is therefore multifaceted. We can see that it is used and manifests itself in three different ways: (1) as a form of vendetta, (2) to resolve clan-related issues, and (3) to resolve personal issues. Violence is a value and in turn a resource used continuously by Camorra women to enact or incite acts of revenge or vendetta. This was the case for Maria Licciardi, as the boss, Luigi Giuliano explains: she *"has always been the 'Mother of the Camorra,' especially after the murder of her brother, it was indeed from that moment onward that her criminal charisma practically exploded. When her brother* [Gennaro] *was murdered, she demanded that we as leaders help her to 'revenge' her brother's murder . . . she was hungry for revenge . . . after this event, she embraced me and said, 'I now live only to revenge my brother's death.'"*[156]

Maria was the one who expressed and behaved in such a way that showed her drive and determination, compared to her sisters, to use violence in a desire for vendetta thus becoming a determined bloodthirsty camorrista who wanted *"a life for a life."*[157] Illustrating this recurring theme in Camorra activities, we have the case of one of the leaders of a clan east of Naples. One of her associates recalls,

> One day I went to her house. I saw a framed photograph of her father who I knew had been murdered. I kissed the photo and as a reaction to this gesture, she started to cry. At that point, she told me that she was waiting for the release of a camorrista . . . to avenge her father's murder. She told

me that, on top of other things, she wanted to murder him with her own hands. In response, I asked her why she wanted to 'butcher' him and she answered saying that she wanted to kill him because he had shot her dad.[158]

These are many similar stories.

Camorra women frequently use physical and verbal violence as part of their everyday clan business. The same Maria Licciardi faced with a situation whereby her brother, the leader of her clan, had been publicly insulted in a Naples's courthouse by Assunta Sarno, the wife of boss Giuseppe Misso of the rival Misso clan (Sarno allegedly told Licciardi's boss, "Go back to eating bananas on your tree"), instigated an awful act of violence. She informed the clan that this insult was not only an act of disrespect toward the leader but also a serious challenge to the clan's authority that had to be punished. Assunta was returning from one of her husband's trials in Florence on March 11, 1992, when her car and that of her associates were blocked along the motorway by two other cars. Assunta was shot and died instantly with some of the other passengers. It has been suggested that Maria Licciardi was the brain behind this deadly ambush undertaken in defense of her clan.

In another case, we find an internal clan dispute resolved by a female leader using violence. During a heated discussion with one of the clan's killers who accused her and her husband of not showing him enough respect and recognition, she defended her clan: "*Out of the blue, [she] took a candelabra from the table and hit him around the head*" thus causing his death.[159]

Women can use other forms of indirect violence, and even forms of psychological torture. For example, the D'Amico clan wanted revenge against Angela when she decided to collaborate with the state in 2014. This time they would not do it through direct acts of violence but through emotional pressure: "*The truth is they wanted to destroy me; to destroy me they wanted to get to my son because when they want to destroy someone, they will target the person who is dearest to you.*"[160] So, they sent her photographs of her fifteen-year-old son, who having abandoned her and the state witness protection program, returned to selling drugs for the clan in her old piazza. A clear message from the clan, a form of cruel vendetta, worse than violence, to underline the fact that that he had returned to the clan and crime, abandoning her forever.

Violence is also used to defend one's livelihood but also indirectly, the clan's business activities. At the higher level, Camorra women can delegate violence to their hitmen or resort to intimidation to avoid police interventions. Nunzia D'Amico regularly took decisions to initiate violent acts or even declare wars against rival clans to spell out who was boss. For instance, to maintain law and order in her own clan, she would not hesitate to punish clan members who did not behave or show enough respect. And, when the rival clan in 2016 started to impinge on her clan's territory, she was very proactive in leading the charge against them while her male associates were rather noncommittal. She stated, "*Here, we decide, not them* [the rival clan]. *Go and sort them out!* [be violent!]"[161] In 2015, the wife of a boss from the Pesce clan violently beat up in public a clan member who was completely lacking respect toward her and her leadership. Another example is that of Chiaretta Manzi who in 2002 in Vallo di Lauro together with her daughter-in-law, Alba, took part in a violent shoot-out in broad daylight against women from the rival clan.[162]

Whereas Nunzia D'Amico was clearly identified as a leader, some of the wives of renown bosses who were supposedly merely extensions of their husbands, adopted similar violent behavior to protect their clan by using threats with verbal and physical abuse. On many occasions, these acts of intimidation were initiated by the women who took the lead, without male involvement. Their menacing acts were not instructed by their men but rather were driven by their criminal instinct of survival for their family and the clan.

Women ultimately threaten anyone who poses a threat to the clan's existence and impose l'omertà, the law of silence, on everyone and everything: "*The code of silence is about what you're doing, supporting your principles and your things. . . . If you have it, you have it. If you don't have it, you don't. Following the code of silence is something that you have to feel.*"[163] A good example of this is when, in 1999, seeing that rumors were rife that the local boss's son was one of the killers of a rival clan member, his wife and mother-in-law all went to visit the victim's widow. They went to her house and aggressively shouted at her and her brother that the son's boss had nothing to do with the murder and that she should not help investigators.[164]

Mafia women have all shown themselves to become particularly active when it is a question of protecting the clan against new possible state witnesses; in other words, when camorristi decide to talk and collaborate with the state in exchange for a new life. In certain instances, these revelations can put the future of a Camorra clan in peril and these potential "rats" must be silenced at all costs because omertà is crucial to keep power and control. Laura bullied and intimidated a relative when she wanted to become a pentita, with a continuous program of intimidation: "*I would like to make clear that my wife was threatened by her cousin* [Laura] *who told her to tell me to shut up, otherwise, even if they were blood-related, those who would have got the worse of it would not be those in prison but those outside* [in other words, her]."[165]

Maria Licciardi waited for the wife of a clan member who was having doubts about his loyalty to the clan outside the hospital and, using threats, she managed to get her to force her husband to drop his intention to collaborate with the state: "*Maria blocked PS's wife outside of the hospital—the Monaldi—and was very threatening. She told her that her husband should not collaborate with the state.*"[166]

Another example is when an important boss was starting to feel uneasy about being in prison and thinking about collaborating with the state in May 2015. The women, his sisters, and sisters-in-law, got him to reason about this and not to do it because his decision would have forced them to go out and work.[167] So, the women sought to convince him to change his mind and they succeeded. One of his sisters-in-law warned him: "*You are intelligent, very intelligent, be calm and everything will be resolved! You know what you have to do, be serene!*"[168]

There are indeed many examples of women who go out of their way to stop possible clan members collaborating with the state because they have too much to lose. Women freely use intimidation, threats, and violence, even if they don't carry them out themselves, they can be the brains behind such violence. They have the ideas and intention to do harm to others while the men are the muscle and carry out the harm.

Brute violence is probably more present in the lower ranks where the army of women foot soldiers use violence daily in order to survive. One such was Angela, a low-level drug dealer, who used violence when she needed to make a point to her customers. Another, Nanna, was given the job by the Contini clan to "*beat up the women*" who had not followed the clan's rules.[169] Another still, Emilia, in similar circumstances, offered to sort out some women who "*had to be beaten up. She not only offered her availability to do so but also said that she would get Angela to help her.*"[170]

Finally, while remaining firmly grounded in the Camorra space, some women will use violence to sort out their own personal disputes. They feel entitled to act violently without having to justify what they do, since violence is the everyday language in the Camorra space. For example, the daughter of a boss, beat up an acquaintance, "*I believe for personal reasons.*"[171] They use violence in their everyday life to resolve their own whims and personal disputes.

In the case of the murder of one of the leaders of the Mazzarella clan in 2011, although there might have been some clan-related and criminal tensions, the main motivation for his death seems to have been a very strong personal element: two female relatives collaborated in his murder after he targeted and bothered them. He was the nephew of the bosses in that his mother was their sister. While the main top leaders were in prison, he directed and led the clan with his own personal style, and he ruffled feathers. His style and way of doing things clearly upset some clan members. In particular, he had a gripe against one of his cousins and took it out on the cousin's wife who was living in the local district. He decided to reduce her allocated monthly salary and threatened to take it away altogether because of her husband's lavish lifestyle. This feeling grew into frustration and resentment, and so, when another leader came out of prison she helped and facilitated his murder. He was murdered in her flat and she "*got the silencer and latex gloves to use in the crime and it was she who threw them away in the rubbish bin.*"[172] The women cleaned up the traces of blood to be found in the staircase and landing as well as giving false information to the investigators who soon arrived on the scene. Women know everything: the sister of the victim a few days later when things had calmed down met with the two women who had been involved in the murder and attacked them.[173]

Last but not least, women act on love-related revenge. For example, Chiara, who falsely suggested to her lover, a respected boss, that a man she knew was "*bothering her*" ("*la importunava*") when in fact this man was a former boyfriend and she wanted to get rid of him. She got him murdered by the clan.[174] On another occasion, she became infatuated with a young female hairdresser whom she befriended. When she refused her advances, together with her brothers and associates, she kidnapped, drugged, and raped her continuously for a month. Her behavior shows utter contempt, violence, and hatred toward other human beings.[175] The young woman managed to survive this awful ordeal. She did not go to the police but told her boyfriend. Chiara and her accomplices started to target and harass him. As a result, he lost his job and was murdered one night in January 1995 on his way home.

In another example, full of symbolism and significance, the wife of a boss ordered a murder when she found out that her husband was having an affair; not only did he have a mistress, but he also had a child with her. The boss had had a relationship with this woman before his marriage. This bothered his wife so much that she ordered the murder of his lover in October 1991. The judiciary believe that it was she who had ordered the murder and the husband who had physically carried it out because "*all of the Marcianise district knew that he had had a daughter with her* [his mistress] *and for this, she* [his wife] *had lost all credibility in front of the other women of the clan.*"[176] The wife of the boss ordered this murder because she had been disrespected and had to impose her power and regain her standing in the community.

The Importance of the Camorra's Cultural Value System

To understand the roles of women in the Camorra, I believe that the local context cannot be ignored or underestimated, including the cultural values. Context is key to unpack how criminal organizations behave, how markets evolve, and how individuals think: in a word, their culture. We often neglect the cultural value system of criminal organizations to our detriment and neglect systematically the way members think, behave, and act. When studying and analyzing criminal groups, its cultural dimension, its value system, must always be considered, especially when we look at the role of women.

In this chapter, I have sought to give a flavor of the Camorra's cultural value system, which exists in the Camorra space. I have discussed it using Camorra women's words, and the four core values which I have identified and on which I believe the Camorra's cultural value system is established. By discussing these values, I showed how women fully endorse and live by them. These values are transformed into rules and resources that become human capital, intelligently used by women. In sum, this cultural value system is central in explaining women roles in the Camorra.

HARD-WORKING FOOT SOLDIERS

In this chapter, I discuss the involvement and agency of women foot soldiers and show that clans have different relationships with them.[1] Foot soldiers are the foundation of all mafias. Without them these organizations would not survive, because it is a question of power in numbers. The more foot soldiers that belong to a clan, the more powerful the clan is. A 1990 Carabinieri document lists the names of clan members, and the more powerful clans were those with an army of members, that is, low-ranking members who do the day-to-day hard graft. This is why recruitment is vital in and outside of the family. Foot soldiers are the Camorra's violent street army, the day-to-day eyes, ears, and body of the clan in the Camorra space, in its territory, streets, and piazzas, ready to intimidate those who do not respect the Camorra's rules and requests. These hard-working foot soldiers remain the recognizable face of the clan in the street—the reference point to go to, if need be.

In popular culture, we have images of these foot soldiers as rash, brutal, hot-headed, streetwise young men belonging to male-exclusive clans. For example, in the TV series *Gomorrah* and the documentary *ES17*, the action, behavior, and violence are hypermasculine: it belongs to boys and men.[2] Women exist but in very specific roles as girlfriends, wives, or mistresses, in very familiar spaces: inside the home, inside their flats, at the window of the basso that gives onto the street. Even in the documentary *Robinù* the older women are mothers, drug dealers, or prostitutes and the younger women are infatuated by the image of the older, charismatic Camorra bosses and their easy wealth.[3] According to this narrative, the women are "extras" to the Camorra action and are rarely alluded to as foot soldiers.

In the postwar period, women were referred to as being fully involved in the Neapolitan black economy as a survival strategy but separate from Camorra activities.[4] I would argue that the development of the black economy was in parallel to the development of Camorra clans and that there soon existed an overlap between the simple ad hoc black economy (dealing in American products, petrol, etc.) and the more organized black economy of smuggled cigarettes and then drugs that soon came under the control of the emerging clans. This more sophisticated level of the black economy became the bedrock of the modern Camorra, and since the 1980s, it is managed by the bulk of the Camorra army, the foot soldiers who are predominately female. This army of women of all ages have more need to become involved because they often have children and need to make ends meet, so finding a job in the clan becomes essential to their financial survival. Once involved, women participate in other activities to earn money but also because they identify with the clan and its collective identity and project. Indeed, some of these women do more than drug dealing, and they need to be recognized as having a concrete role. Although the majority may not partake directly in squads of killers and violent retribution (although there are some who do), they are very much complicit to these actions and not separate and innocent from them. Women are fully participant and immersed; they not only have the same responsibilities as men but occupy a significant and special space in the street, in the Camorra space.

When I interviewed Angela Giallo, a local drug dealer from the suburbs, she showed good knowledge of her main criminal market: "*The business is bigger, it's stronger if you deal in cocaine, if you deal in weed, these are the markets. The big business is drugs. . . . If you take drugs away, you take the underworld away because they all line their pockets with drugs. Everything is drugs. If you need to buy drugs, all you must do is wait with 2 grs of cocaine and you can then buy shoes, Vuitton handbag, everything.*" However, she recognized her culpability: "*I committed crimes, I might have done it unconsciously, or even in good faith or even because I was naïve. However, I did it.*"[5] She understood the full pervasive nature of the clan and its leaders: "*Let's say if you want to leave* [the clan and its criminal activities] *right? You can't. It's like a cage and you can't leave.*"[6] Ultimately, "*They own you,*" and "*it's a miserable life. A shitty life. A dead-end life.*"[7]

One of the defining features of Camorra women foot soldiers is that they are paid a salary by the clan for specific tasks and jobs. If arrested, their family is financially looked after by the clan. Not only does the clan act as an employer but also as a kind of trade union, looking after its members by providing welfare benefits. It can be seen as a positive aspect but also as a controlling factor, but kinship ties can sometimes blur this relationship. Basically, what emerges is that these women, who occupy space both in the public sphere (in the street and piazzas) and in the private sphere (family units) are very resourceful, with their own initiative and agency.

Women as Camorra Foot Soldiers

We don't often talk about the fact that women are also simple Camorra foot soldiers. We ignore the fact that they are often fully paid-up members, employees, troopers, workers, staff, and personnel of the Camorra. But, as with any membership, the roles and tasks of foot soldiers are not always clear cut—they can be fluid, changeable, and adaptable. So, it can be quite difficult to qualify and quantify them precisely.

Because women are not considered, theirs is seen as trivial work, yet as I said, they are the backbone of the organization, even if their presence in the street is often easily denigrated, disregarded, and dismissed. Some of them do simple things like selling drugs from their window, a parking space or specific piazza but they usually do more by just being present in that space. In other words, their presence in the Camorra space occupies the territory and thus plays an essential policing role for the clan.

Having said this, I have identified two levels of foot soldiers:

1. Traditional foot soldiers
2. Specialized foot soldiers

They are both important for what they bring to the clan, although a hierarchy appears because of the business tasks and responsibilities involved. Blood ties and family relationships may also underpin these roles and blur some of the relationships and dynamics. But generally, traditional foot soldiers multitask and, as a consequence, have more criminal responsibility and freedom of action. Specialized foot soldiers often only deal in one sector: drugs, extortion, or loan sharking. There are many examples of women who are both traditional and more specialized foot soldiers. Within these roles, they demonstrate a street intelligence, an awareness of the criminal dynamics, and strategic business thinking that makes them essential to the organization.

Traditional Camorra Women Foot Soldiers

At this level, there are many women, young and old, but why do they join? There are many different reasons why as individuals they join the Camorra. Three main explanations can be highlighted: (1) they are born into a Camorra family or are sentimentally involved with a member, (2) they are seeking revenge for the murder of a relative and (3) they are actively recruited because of the skills they have previously demonstrated.[8]

Foot soldiers are the crucial operational level of the clan, the foundations at the bottom in the street, holding everything together. They carry out the orders coming from above by distributing salaries, transporting drug supplies, hiding firearms, and preparing hits. They do not make any independent decisions for the clan, though they can take their own initiatives to make money on the side and in some cases, decide to branch off to organize their own clan if they have the necessary skills. Generally, however, they act for the clan collective, taking risks and providing all the hard work in return for a salary and, if they are arrested, they are looked after by the clan and have their lawyer paid for while their family receives a monthly payment.

Traditional foot soldiers are individual members who do a variety of jobs and are paid from the common clan account. Their tasks are fluid, flexible, and adaptable. These can vary from lookouts to selling and collecting drugs or demanding extortion money. They may also be involved in violence and murders, especially if they like guns and are good at handing out beatings. As not all foot soldiers are good at violence, not all become killers or a member of the hit squad. Laura Letto suggests that women don't need to be violent because they are more intelligent: there are not many women killers but there are a lot of women who not only help in the detailed preparation for violent hits but can also be the instigators and those who encourage the group to put words into action.[9]

The stories recounted here are of traditional women foot soldiers who prove to be all-rounders, constantly multitasking, and they are very efficient at it. The Caldarelli clan was a compact family clan based in the Mercato district of Naples.[10] It was an ally of the bigger Mazzarella-Misso cartel and was considered small in terms of membership compared to its allies and other clans.[11] It had useful contacts in various sectors and existed in one of the city's busy districts. This made it efficient in various criminal markets, such as illegal drugs and counterfeit goods as well as extortion rackets from local businesses (bars, restaurants, and shops). In order to be cost effective, the clan boss needed to be able to count on dependable employees. Like many of its counterparts, the clan employed women, and even young minors to undertake vital support work rather than violent actions.

Sofia and Giulia were two such typical foot soldiers paid by the clan. Both in their forties, they were not related to the leadership, so they acted as employees but always with the best interests of the clan in mind and were always proactive and thinking ahead. Sofia was the mother of two adult sons and a daughter.

When her husband was arrested in the late 1990s, she decided to reach out to the boss to find work for herself to put food on the table. She did this off her own initiative by herself for herself but also to continue helping the clan. She worked with her daughter and received 300,000 lire (the equivalent of 150 euros) as a weekly salary. Their work consisted of *fare la mollette* in jargon "to hang up pegs," which meant that the clan could use their house as a deposit for drugs and sell from there.[12]

Multitasking is the key feature of Camorra foot soldiers, especially for women. Giulia and her family were also all involved in the clan's other activities. She made up doses of drugs in her home and sold them for the clan, but also did other, more important jobs for them. Firstly, she looked after younger minor clan members. This protected the clan. This meant that when a young clan member got into trouble and was on the run from the police, she would identify where he was, pick him up, and keep him safe by hiding him in a secure location. Second, she looked after the public relations for the clan and its public affairs with the local community when necessary. On one occasion, for example, she bought a watch that the clan wanted to give a police officer as a token of gratitude for his services to the clan.[13] These foot soldiers undertake whatever jobs were necessary to make sure that the clan is efficient, both in terms of its criminal activities as well as its general survival strategy. They were low-ranking soldiers but were hard working and occupied an important place in the Camorra space.

Another example is that of a clan located in the center of Naples. During the 1980–1990s, it was a powerful family clan led by three siblings. It was only in the late 2000s that one of the brothers was released from prison and sought to regain control over the local district by becoming involved in counterfeit goods, drugs, extortion, and vote exchange. To do this, he relied heavily on women relatives who were respected members of the local community. Here, there was a clear overlap between foot soldiers' responsibilities and tight family members positions, because trust, loyalty, and understanding were key to the leader's reestablishment of his power base in the local territory as well as his success.

Many of his female relatives were involved in his various criminal activities, and he counted on his intimate family network to relaunch his criminal career. Out of ninety-three people arrested in 2013, eighteen of them were women and they all undertook important jobs for the day-to-day running of the clan. They were not managers but workers doing the basics. His female network worked hard for the clan. His wife was present and active in the Camorra space, moving discretely around the district, supplying drugs to the various piazzas in the district as well as passing on her husband's orders to the local drug dealers. She managed the profits from drug deals that went into the general kitty, she looked after the money and hid it in secure locations to prevent it from being confiscated if the police visited.

His daughter was also fully aware of her father's criminal activities and was complicit in them. She was involved in drug dealing and tried to develop this activity further to increase the clan's profits. One relative made her house available to the boss as a safehouse so he could use it to do business: either for clan meetings or even to make up drug doses for the piazzas. Another woman was the clan's accountant. Her specific and difficult job was to calculate and oversee the clan's finances and distribute salaries to members every month. Close friends also assisted: *Mammina* ("sweet, dear, lovely mummy") acted as his general eyes and ears in the local district, monitoring everyone. She inhabited the Camorra space as his private messenger, constantly reporting back to him; she was his go-between, giving orders to clan members on his behalf. In this way, she was his representative in the public sphere and was paid 300 euros a month for her work. There was another woman whose *sole* task was to act as an intermediary, as the go-between between the leader and his clan members. She could be defined as a loyal and reliable foot soldier but one that had a special status because of her exclusive relationship with the boss.

It was not only the leader's female relatives who undertook foot soldiers' tasks and who formed the basic support for the leader. It was also the wives and family members of other male foot soldiers: Ella collaborated with her husband in the management of drug trafficking. They looked after the local supply and demand aspects of their zone as well as acting as couriers to collect drugs from a clan based outside of Naples for their drug piazzas. Chiaretta managed a drug piazza with her husband for the clan as a partnership, and Gloria was involved in the counterfeit business (supply and selling) for the clan.

Whereas in the Caldarelli clan, traditional female foot soldiers employed their soft skills and did not use violence or intimidation, this was not the case in the D'Amico clan.[14] The boss, Nunzia D'Amico, often used and incited violence to encourage punitive acts and impose her rule across the local territory. These acts of violence were indifferently carried out by male or female foot soldiers although some clans preferred to use women to punish other women.[15]

The D'Amico clan was a very violent clan whose violence was as much male as female. The district of Ponticelli with its overcrowded social housing, poor public transport links, high unemployment, and bad facilities, may well explain this specific characteristic. The D'Amico clan was a small clan active in Parco Conocal, a housing estate in Ponticelli in the suburbs of Naples. This Camorra clan had a vast army of female foot soldiers (traditional and specialized) who were involved in various activities at different levels of the organizational structure in its territory, in its Camorra space. These women were the backbone of the operations. As traditional women foot soldiers, they were not mono-functional in their tasks, as some were involved in more than one sector, depending on their experience and contacts. For example, some women's tasks ranged from involvement in selling and transporting drugs from one location to another or being a lookout.

Alice and Fortuna were traditional foot soldiers while also being related to the leaders: Alice was related to the leaders and Fortuna was married to one. They are representative of many women who are connected to the emerging male clan leaders but who develop their own criminal activities and space. Their capital comes from their crime family but also from their own charisma and capabilities. They did not have standard managerial roles but did some of the invisible hard work, in part because of the clan's relatively small size but also to make sure that operations were efficient. Because of her blood ties, Alice enjoyed a certain amount of respect to be able to organize and impose her activities. She took over an existing and profitable scam in the Conocal housing estate where every resident of the social housing flats would have to pay 7 euros a week to have their flats cleaned by the D'Amico cleaning service. This service was imposed on all residents of the estate; they had no choice but to pay and to accept to have their flats cleaned. Although Fortuna was close to the leaders, she did not manage the clan's operations but did take on a very active and practical role by running and managing small-scale operations in the streets including the many drug piazzas in the small housing estate of Parco Conocal.[16]

This clan also had very young female foot soldiers whose job was to be the clan's general gofers. Adrianna, a minor, was such an odd job person: she took orders directly from leaders and managers, and did whatever Nunzia D'Amico, the boss, told her to do. She collected money from the clan's different extortion rackets, carried messages between clan members, was the go-between with the drug couriers coming to provide supplies, and collected letters from corrupt prison officials to give them to clan members. She was trusted and would undertake even more delicate tasks. For example, she was the mediator when one of the women in the clan was in contact with a local doctor to get a doctor's certificate, to avoid direct contact between both interlocutors. One of the clan's female managers shouted to her, "*I gave you an order*," confirming her job as the clan's general lackey.[17]

In another clan, based in the eastern suburbs of Naples, women undertook the day-to-day drug activities. This clan was a large family-based clan that organized an extensive network of members. Because it recruited locally from the poorer districts, we do not see relatives of the leaders at the lower level as industrious foot soldiers but as managers coordinating activities with the foot soldiers.

Two respected clan members, Federico and Giulio, oversaw the general drug operations of the clan. They were the gatekeepers and interlocutors with the higher leadership level. They communicated and liaised with one of the clan leaders, Luciano. Adele was the daughter of Giulio. He was a member of the clan who not only organized drug piazzas but also accompanied members to the dentist, organized prison visits, and more. Adele lived with her young daughter, as well as her brother and her mother. Giulio arranged jobs for his two children— looking after heroin and cocaine for the clan as well as transporting illegal goods. Adele was particularly valuable to the clan because, as a woman she would not draw attention to herself and so could do a lot of jobs for them. She *"was used in virtue of the fact that she is a woman, without a criminal record and therefore it is easier for her not to be stopped by the police added to which she looks after her four-year-old daughter, this places her even more above suspicion."*[18]

Although officially unemployed, Adele was involved in various small-time illegal activities, and she highlights the varied roles of a foot solider. She had three specific jobs: (1) holding cocaine and heroin at home; (2) acting as a mediator between members and delivering messages/instructions (giving *l'ambasciata*); and (3) acting as a lookout for the clan (shouting the code word "Michele" if a police car approached).[19] Her flat was used as a general drug deposit for the clan as she was constantly on call for members who organized the drug piazzas. She often used coded language because it was important not to talk openly about activities over the phone.

There are several other similar stories. Carolina being such an example. She was the mother of four boys who were heavily involved in selling and distributing heroin in the local district. They were a drug selling subgroup of the clan. Carolina was fundamental to the running of her family drug business as she was the general organizer of the whole business, the one who had the telephone conversations and decided who to send down to the piazza to work. Indeed, it was she who directed the activities of all her relatives, giving out clear instructions about the assignments of who should be selling in the streets.

Marisa's story is emblematic as it illustrates the status of foot soldiers in the clan and how the clan looks after its members. She was seventeen when she had a daughter. Her daughter went on to marry Paolo whose family worked for the local clan. In her police interview, she didn't give too much away: *"I accepted to do what certain people whom I didn't know asked me to do, in other words, to prepare drug doses for them. I do not know the channels through which the heroin was bought or sold."*[20] Her involvement in the clan was identified by the fact that the Sarno clan, once she was arrested for dealing, offered her assistance, under what has often been called "the welfare system of the clan."[21]

In return for their hard work and loyalty, Marisa was given help in three ways: (1) legal support during and after her arrest; (2) money; and (3) the use of both a car and a driver to visit relatives in prison. Ida was given the same special treatment and benefits as Marisa. She was well looked after by the clan because "*she kept the drugs for the clan* [in her house]."[22]

Specialized Foot Soldiers

Specialized foot soldiers are a subcategory made up of members recruited into the clan initially for one specific job, that of selling drugs in small piazzas where customers can drive in and pick up their stuff. These individuals are paid from their own drug profits and not the general kitty even though their actions benefit the clan's interests and strategies. Members from these fluid subgroups are less often directly related to core clan members and can be defined as the lower level of foot soldiers in the clan hierarchy: "*When you deal, you are always under some-one.*"[23] Compared to traditional members, these members are different because they officially have less autonomy, although in reality they do what they want on the side to survive (such as setting up their own drug deals with their own customers).[24]

This subgroup is often overlooked but it represents the mass army of members (the labor force, *la manodopera*) who do the dangerous frontline work and run the risk of being arrested daily as they sell drugs or face potential rivals. For example, in one housing estate, it was estimated that that there were fourteen drug piazzas in that compact space and each piazza required two to three people to run.[25] These foot soldiers are the lumpenproletariat of the criminal clans (on zero contract hours), exploited by them for money and profit and owing them nothing. However, it is worth noting that over time, some of these subgroups can gain more confidence and independence and try and buy drugs from different clans, which may cause tension with their clan and possible violent acts.

The Army of Drug Dealers

It is continuously argued that women who deal only do this; they do nothing else and therefore cannot be involved with the clan or clan specialized foot soldiers. Francesca explained, "*There are women who sell drugs. It's wrong. But they do it to eat. . . . It's not at all justifiable, of course, but it's true that maybe they do it because they need to eat.*"[26] And this needing to eat also becomes a form of complicity and guaranteed employment that often they cannot find elsewhere.

Whereas in the suburbs of Naples, the specialized foot soldiers tend to work in public spaces, in the city center they can also sell their drugs from home (from a flat, or basso). Ferdinando and Lorenzo for example were two local camorristi who had carved out a drug's market for themselves in this busy criminal space. They were allies of a larger clan who protected them. But, as this clan had been in great turmoil since 2005 with many arrests and rival groups attacking them, it had left an extensive vacuum in the local drug market that independent groups could fill. These smaller drug selling groups developed their own drug piazzas from home and acquired a certain degree of autonomy. Although this was a very precarious and dangerous position, they could be seen as specialized foot soldiers because they lived within the same criminal space as the clans and brought their supplies exclusively from them.

Vittoria was part of this drug dealing subteam that was built around a family nucleus: herself, her husband and his brother, his wife, and an associate, Diego. Together, they managed and organized a small cocaine piazza in the city center. When the men were out of prison, Vittoria worked closely with them. When they were arrested, she decided to continue to manage their drug piazza, with the collaboration of their associate Diego, to make sure that it continued to be efficient and profitable and most important, that it not fall into the hands of a rival clan. Diego would sell during the day and she at night, but after a while, she decided that it was best for her to manage the business alone without Diego. This was an important decision that highlights her complete independence from him and her male relatives. She broke away from the so-called patriarchal constraint that should not have allowed her to do this. So much so, that her sister-in-law believed that she was taking massive risks and would end up in prison: "*Aunty Vittoria wants to go to prison.*"[27]

Angela Giallo, a Specialized Foot Solider

Now, I would like to tell the story of Angela, one of the army of drug pushers who keeps the Camorra going. She was very lucid about her criminal life and journey, in and out of the Camorra. Up until my interview with her, I had interviewed women higher up in the clan hierarchy. She was a petite woman, dressed in joggers but with sad eyes, a sorrowful expression and tattooed eyebrows. Younger than me, she had lived a thousand more lives just to survive. Her heart-rendering account was hard to listen to and which I felt was representative of so many other young women in housing estates across Italy and across Europe.

Angela was a nobody and yet fundamental to the running of the clan's local drug piazzas. She was a drug seller/dealer for a clan in the suburbs of Naples between 2007 and 2014: "*She had a low-level job. She only did drug dealing but worked on one of the most important piazzas in the housing estate.*"[28] She was one of the foot soldiers of the army of drug dealers. Her specialty was selling drugs at all times of day and was considered very good at it. But, although fully involved with the leaders and other core clan members, she always remained at the periphery of the Camorra clan.

Angela's story appears emblematic of the lower levels of Camorra clans. She was not a decision maker but an instruction taker, although a lot of this became blurred when she made decisions about her own life. She was born into a relatively poor family in the Vomero district. Her mother married young, but her parents were never involved in crime. They had eleven children. She explains, "*We were not a wealthy family . . . we had nothing, but we were happy.*"[29] She lived in the street and carried out the day-to-day business of selling drugs to fill the clan's common fund.

Her mother was "*a hard worker*" but fell ill and could no longer cope with all her children.[30] The five youngest children were put into an orphanage run by nuns. The oldest siblings stayed home while the minors were taken into care. Angela spent ten years in the orphanage, where she "*lived the life of a* [typical] *teenager although she went to bed at 09:30 pm as imposed by the nuns!*"[31] At a certain point, she and her two sisters were offered the opportunity to move back home but they declined, preferring to stay at the orphanage. Every Saturday and Sunday, Angela's mother would visit her daughters to spend the day with them. On Saturday afternoons, she would take Angela to visit her older brother who was doing time for robbery at the local youth offending institute (Nisida in Procida). Angela suffered greatly at being separated from her mother: "*I wasn't happy because I missed my mum.*"[32] Consequently, this was not a good time for her. She describes her childhood as "*ugly*" and "*hard*" and "*even though there were no bars, the orphanage was like a prison.*"[33]

There she met her future husband, a young small-time criminal. He took a liking to her. At the age of seventeen, she became pregnant with his child. She went home to her mother's house in a housing estate in Ponticelli, where she also had a second child. The children were looked after by her mother-in-law who reported her to social services. Social services organized for her to go and live with her children in special accommodation. She spent two years there and was able to save up enough money to rent a flat. She found a small flat in the district of San Giovanni a Teduccio, a district south of Naples, but her time there became a nightmare. She and her flatmate became the prey of the local clan. They targeted her to transform her flat into a local drug factory where they cut up, sold doses, and controlled the district. She became involved without intending to: "*I participated because I was there. I saw things. I saw weapons, I saw what they were doing.*"[34]

But the situation got to be too much for Angela, and pregnant again, she returned to her mum's flat at the Conocal housing estate with her two young children. In the estate, she was in a desperate situation: her husband in prison, two young children, an overcrowded flat (her sister and brothers were also living there), a baby on the way and no money coming in. "*I had nothing, not even nappies and I said, 'What can I do? What should I do?'* She met a woman member of the D'Amico clan in 2007, who offered her "a job" and real money. Gaia managed many different piazzas on the estate. She "*presented herself* [to Angela] *as a very good person, the underworld gives you their heart.*"[35]

The job she offered Angela was to sell drugs for the D'Amico clan in the piazza under her house: "*I started dealing first, and then my sister.*" Initially, they promised her 10 euros per sale then at the end of the day only gave her 50 euros when she had made 10,000 euros. She soon understood that the D'Amico clan controlled everything and that it was everyone for oneself: "*I used to sell weed and hash for them* [in the Conocal housing estate], *the market was theirs. . . . If she said it was 'X,' it was 'X.'*" But Angela learned to put money away for herself without getting caught. She recalls: "*I never slipped up with them. I was trusted.*"[36] So, she soon adapted and learned that to make money for herself, she had to be more switched on than they were. She would run her own business on the side, especially as their weed was of poor quality ("*like water*"). But she knew what she was doing: "*My market was strong. It was the strongest in Ponticelli. It was making more money than . . . You won't even imagine.*"[37] With pride, she remarked, "*My trouble was. . . . that I was good at selling. I was selling a lot.*"[38]

There are many women like Angela who are foot soldiers at this lower level in the drug sector; in fact, all clans that sell drugs rely on this female workforce. But there are also men, as it is a workforce based on kinship structures. Angela would deal together with her sister and brother-in-law in the Conocal housing estate, but to appease the warring clans they would pay them both a percentage. The clan saw them as their workers, but they were intelligent enough to keep everyone happy and not be targeted.

Angela did not consider herself as a full member; she was just doing her "*job.*" She then realized that her actions proved her membership and that eventually "*you start dealing with bigger things and you can't back down.*"[39] Though on reflection she had difficulty acknowledging the agency of Camorra women, she accepted that women are strong. Take her description of Fortuna, the wife of a leader, for example. To Angela, Fortuna is "*more than a woman. She wanted to act more like a man than a woman. In fact, she even walks like a man. She's a man when she walks. She keeps guns in her bag.*"[40]

She describes how she sees herself: "*I saw myself as a bad woman. . . . I was a monster . . . because I was with people who were monsters. And, many times, I told myself: 'Hopefully, they'll arrest me tonight. So, I'll put an end to it.' But I knew that even if they arrested me, once I was out, I would go back there, because it's a circle that you don't . . . when you go in, you can't leave.*"[41] Angela's account also highlights the dangers of being a specialized foot soldier on the clan's periphery and in its lower ranks: these soldiers are the ones who occupy the street, the dangerous space where clans do business, with all that it entails.

Women More than Just Foot Soldiers

As we have seen in this chapter, women go beyond just "making do" and working in the black economy. Does it mean that they are not members of the Camorra?[42] I would argue that it is the relationship between the illegal economy and the Camorra clans that we need to focus on. In the immediate postwar period, the Camorra was a limited and emerging force while the illegal economy was flourishing. So, to survive, women were on the frontline of the illegal economy and very visible while the Camorra was trying to develop its criminal activities discretely.

As the clans developed during the 1950s and 1960s and took control of the illegal economy, women joined in this process: women who worked in the black economy to survive started to work for clans when they started to control the illegal economy (in the smuggling of cigarettes for example). Women were not separate from the Camorra's control of the illegal economy but were its army of workers in the 1970s as they are still today.

Women come to form an essential part of the Camorra's workforce either out of necessity, survival, or thrill. It is true that often the women featured in this chapter were not in direct contact with the general leadership of the clan, but I think I have demonstrated that they did work with midlevel managers, depending on how big the clan was. Women are available, active, and understand how to do business; they "*do their job*."[43] This in turn develops in them a sense of identity and belonging to the clan which they are willing to defend. In Parco Conocal in this small compact housing estate, for example, there were both women and men foot soldiers, some were paid, others not, some were involved in violence, others were not. Both took initiatives, sometimes independently, but women were not male substitutes. They had their own piazzas, their own contacts, and they demonstrated a strategic understanding of their criminal markets and the internal dynamics of the clan and members.

EFFICIENT MANAGERS

To run a clan efficiently requires a good team. Camorra bosses count on a few middle managers or lieutenants who do not make decisions but who can give out and relay their instructions to the foot soldiers. Very few clans do not have managers as these are particularly instrumental and vital for the survival of the clan, in particular when a boss is arrested.

Managers can be either male or female; they are nearly always blood relatives because kinship, trust, and loyalty are essential. To avoid losing power to young and ambitious rivals, it has been argued that female relatives step in at short notice as a kind of "reserve army" on standby,[1] or as in football, men and women are part of the same football team, with women on the bench, ready to take to the field when needed.[2] Women can do this since they inhabit the same space as their men and, more important, because they have been collaborating and helping their men all along.

The wife of one of the leaders of a small inner-city clan became his trusted representative and lieutenant when he was arrested in 2015 as she had always closely followed his activities. The first impression she gave was that she did "*nothing without first asking her husband*" as some clan members suggested.[3] She also explains during a telephone conversation: "*I am scared because he* [her husband] *can tell me that I am a no one to take decisions.*"[4] But, in reality, her behavior was much more complex: "*She carried on acting in the first person because she did not trust* [the men foot soldiers]. . . . *She felt like a man, and she needed to manage directly the drug piazza and its suppliers like a man, and she needed, however, to always 'be in the middle'* [of everything]."[5]

The same pattern appears for Camilla, the wife of a high-ranking member of a powerful clan. When her husband was sent to prison, she became his "*ambassador*,"[6] dealing with loan sharking matters, his drug markets, and even the latest clan gossip. Indeed, she was extremely proud of the fact that other male clan members treated her as they would have regarded her husband, with full respect.[7] Not all wives in this clan were fully involved like her because the top boss had so many loyal managers and foot soldiers. Because of this, she did not need to become his close lieutenant. His wife was his wife and felt that she was respected by all clan members because of her special status as the boss's wife. She was proud to tell people this. Because of her special status, she was given carte blanche to start up her own business which would help the clan to launder its money. In particular, she set up a business in the hospitality sector using clan money and sought to impose her products on local outlets.

In general, evidence suggests that wives tend to become efficient managers, filling the shoes of their husbands whether in prison or abroad. For a long time, it has been argued that the wives of the major Camorra groups, cartels, or alliances only enjoyed the lifestyle and the money which the criminal activities produced, that is, they only enjoyed the proceeds of crime. I would argue that this assessment is unfair. In recent examples, the wives of established bosses looked after the local criminal activities by intimidating citizens who were not paying the clan their due sum.[8] In other words, we often have traditional stereotypes about women's roles and behavior that rarely reflect reality.

In this chapter, I recount some of the experiences of these efficient, reliable, and trustworthy female managers to try and rectify this traditional view.

Middle Managers or Lieutenants

Camorra women are sometimes described as *vicarie*, deputies or second in command, which means that they are the representatives of the male leaders and therefore, middle managers who oversee the workforce. Whereas the leader is proactive in having a clear strategy, a specific criminal vision, and in making decisions for the clan, the manager implements the leader's decisions, playing a discreet role. Numerous women are content with the simple and less visible management positions, but some can evolve into leaders because of their strong personality and power-hungry desires.

When camorristi are imprisoned, it is said that suddenly women become visible. I would suggest that they are always there in partnership with their menfolk. Needing no training and ready to move horizontally from the private to the public sphere, from the domestic context to the criminal one, these women do not take over the reins of the clan so much as continue while their men are in prison. But, when forced to be on their own, they need to act more openly to defend the clan from younger ambitious Turks who may want to take over the clan and its livelihood. In many clans, in a crisis situation, women "appear" in a way that was not necessarily evident previously so as to enable the clan to function in the new situation. This "new management" appears when the clan becomes unstable after police arrests or violent internal conflicts. Prior to such events, women managers continuously advised leaders without being visible. In this way, they become essential to the survival of the clan. Italian law enforcement cannot see women as essential actors because they are focused on the crimes and not on the power of the different actors. One could even say that because Italian law enforcement agents often have a misogynist bias and consider women incapable of criminality, they have been able to undertake these crucial managerial roles with impunity. I was able to document this thanks to several interesting case studies, including the story of Alessia Torbia, which demonstrates how women are good, intuitive, and reliable managers. She shows respect for her menfolk, but this does not mean subordination. She shows forward thinking, criminal awareness, and independence of mind when necessary.

Responsive Manager

Alessia Torbia encapsulates the perfect model of the Camorra manager because she prioritized the collective good of the clan over her own needs and always seemed to put the clan's interest before hers while remaining in the background. Growing up in the Camorra space, she had the necessary know-how and skills but never sought to become a leader in her own right, preferring to stay in a lower managerial role.

She was born in Naples in the 1980s into the Camorra underworld. At the age of sixteen, she married the son of another Camorra boss and her marriage came to be considered as a classic example of mafia intermarriage, whereby two clans were joined together in a criminal alliance through one matrimonial union: "Her pregnancy turned a teen romance into a peace bond, uniting two Camorra families who have been at war intermittently for over a decade."[9] This was also described as an "*excellent marriage*" since it "*sealed a pact of power between dominant Neapolitan city Camorra families.*"[10]

Until 2009, her criminal role seemed to be relatively quiet and obscure. She was under the judicial and police radar but busy in the Camorra sphere. A close associate remarked: "*She always wanted to be a boss. I called her 'Pupetta Maresca.*'"[11] Instead of taking on an active leadership role, she fitted the traditional mafia wife position and acted as her husband's spokesperson but without seeking her own independence or autonomy. She could have easily done so because of her family connections and criminal status, and yet she did not. She remained a manager and deputy and acted as the representative and assistant of her father-in-law.

Since the early 2000s when the male leadership was arrested, she systematically implemented their instructions. She passed on their orders to clan members about regular business: "*I emphasize that those orders are and were given by her husband either verbally or through written notes. Alessia then gave these instructions to Gennaro (for certain sectors) or to Fabrizio, both of whom immediately implemented them.*"[12] There were also more precise orders to shoot people: "*This assault was decided by Alessia's husband, and the order was given during a prison visit.*"[13]

She had a direct line of communication with her father-in-law inside and outside of prison. She became his messenger and assistant. On one occasion, her uncle asked her to fix a problem relating to certain shops who were managed by his friends and that were being extorted by her husband's clan:

> *This time I spoke directly with my niece about the issue of extortions being imposed by their clan on all shops, stalls, and street sellers in [. . .] and other districts. This time, Piero asked me to intervene to avoid paying the extortion racket; after having asked Luigi and having found out that he did not manage them but that they were the boss's orders, I asked my niece if she could ask him and we got a result in the sense that he agreed to exempt Piero [and] . . . his shops . . . to no longer pay extortion money. Piero went to the boss's house to thank him after my suggestion.*[14]

In addition to these tasks, she naturally claimed another responsibility, that of defending the clan. She took it on herself to act as an enforcer and intimidator to protect the clan, its activities, and its members. She often subtly dealt with the possible reactions of discontented members or locals, preempting them and looking out for the clan's interests and those of her loved ones.

She was involved in two internal disputes where the leaders sought to cleanse the clan and eliminate potential emerging threats. The first one involved the murder of a lieutenant of her husband, Andrea, in 1999. After his murder, together with her mother, she showed her own initiative as a manager: she visited Andrea's family and threatened them in order to make sure that they did not help the police in their investigations, imposing total omertà. Andrea's partner explained, "*The two women continued to shout at me, repeating that Alessia's husband was not involved, and I answered that I had never said such a thing and that I had never pronounced his name as responsible for the murder.*"[15]

In 2005, we find a similar example of her agency. The right-hand man of her father-in-law, a loyal and bright member and partner of one of her relatives, was murdered by the clan because members felt threatened by his possible plans to expand his activities and power base. A few days before his murder, Alessia went to see her aunt and signaled in usual threatening coded language that there was a problem, that they were in danger and that he might be killed. This unprompted intervention by Alessia shows how deeply involved she was in the protection of her husband's clan with no regards to her blood family.

In both cases, her active role was never really appreciated by the judiciary or the police: she "*has no criminal record. She is young . . . the difference with her mother is that no other forms of criminal behavior have appeared, other than* [those] *which are contested here, and it is her relationship with her relatives which can influence the serious nature of these crimes and her personality.*"[16]

She did have a strong connection with the Camorra, some of her actions indicate that she had her own agency and did not act purely on the delegation of power for her husband or father-in-law. She did behave in a traditional way (respecting men's positions and never challenging their power) but rising above the mundane role of the boss's wife interested in money, luxury goods and lifestyle, she demonstrates her capacity to represent the clan's interests and, in a way, her role as the unacknowledged clan's backbone, going beyond the responsibility of a mere manager. In 2009, she was arrested for her involvement in the clan and served a ten-year sentence. She was released in the late 2010s.

Precise and Quick-Witted Managers

Bianca and Emma Cupetta were the oldest and youngest sisters of ten siblings, who together with their in-laws formed a clan in the suburbs that emerged during the 1980s. This clan was located in the periphery to the east of Naples.[17] It was heavily involved in a range of criminal activities, encompassing extortion, drugs, and firearms. All five sisters were engaged in the clan's activities: for example, from 1989 onward, an older sister, Enza, managed the clan's loan sharking business as well as the profits of her brothers. But it was Bianca and Emma who, in particular, became the spokespersons for their brothers and their efficient managers. They managed the clan's illegal activities, substituting for the brothers when necessary (especially when they were in prison) and visiting them in prison to discuss clan business. It was believed that Emma's role in the clan was underestimated by the authorities and the clan made the most of her young age. Below the police radar, she acted as she wished.[18]

This clan developed during the mid-1980s after several attacks against one of the emerging bosses. Although this was a so-called traditional male-dominated clan, the different sisters were given responsibilities for various illegal sectors because, as the judges have explained, this clan adopted the "sea urchin" model whereby all family members are involved in every criminal activity. All sisters were given space to become competent managers in these illegal sectors and enjoyed a certain amount of autonomy. They also looked after the distribution of salaries to wives of clan members. But, they always referred back to their brothers, the leaders in prison. In the material I collected I noticed Bianca and Emma because they were particularly outspoken, resilient, savvy, and forceful managers. But there were also other women in the clan who if they were not happy with the men's decisions, rebelled and established a sort of "women's committee" to pressure their husbands and the boss to change their minds.[19]

During the 1990s, Bianca had her own specific sector of loan sharking, providing advice to her brothers as well as dealing in other illegal activities in the district. It is believed that she became vital to the clan when the brothers were arrested in 2005 as she regularly visited them in prison to get instructions for clan members. Additionally, she managed the clan finances, especially the paying of clan members and lawyers' fees. From 2003 onward, Emma managed a drug piazza with her husband in Corso Sirena, but also oversaw many of the clan's activities and members. Not only did she work her drug piazza successfully, she also participated in clan-related murders. She played her role fully to entrap victims who trusted her as was the case for the attempted murder of Stefano. On this occasion in 2005, she invited to her house Stefano, a clan member who was becoming too self-important. The excuse was that he should collect his bonus from her, as the clan had made a considerable profit from a drug deal. Stefano "*fell into the trap*"; after all he was only being invited to the boss's sister's house, so there could be no possible danger.[20] There he was met by one of the bosses and one of his killers who together were unable to finish the job and kill him. Emma was fully involved in the planning and organization of this murder plot, and we must note that she also lashed out at Stefano with full force, contributing to his death.

Some former members of the clan described her as the true *reggente del clan*, "the queen of the clan," and her power obviously upset rivals as can be seen by the number of bullet markings on the outside wall of her house. Others underline the importance of the sisters by explaining how "*they always had the last word*."[21] It is clear that these sisters worked in full unison with their brothers. On many occasions, they would threaten clan members by stating that they would refer information back to their brothers in prison. These threats were used by the women as an efficient tool to affirm their power and respect regardless of whether they actually reported back to their bothers. They were clever enough to use all the necessary instruments and tools to increase their respect, influence, and power with clan members.

Resourceful and Autonomous Managers

In another district of Naples, two other young women have had an impact on their clan, as enlightened managers. Mati Maletta and Aurora Crussi were two sisters-in-law belonging to a small city clan. Mati was the youngest sister of the three bosses and Aurora was married to one of them. The clan was very small, family structured, and managed four drug piazzas in their territory, two small districts that are located along the waterfront and up the hill, Mount Echia to Monte di Dio, behind the elegant Chiaia district and Via Toledo. These neighborhoods are not visible because they hide behind Piazza Plebiscito and Via Chiaia. They are made up of small *vicoli*, zig zagging across the two districts. They were traditionally linked to cigarette smuggling activities, today it is drugs.

Clan members do not hesitate to fight off rival clans who seek to take over their drug piazzas, as was the case in September 2018, when they organized a shoot-out in Piazza Trieste e Trento against members of the rival clan from the Spanish Quarters. The latter was starting to grow in influence and threaten its territory and wanted to take over one of its drug piazzas. This clan reigned in these two small adjacent districts where its main business was hashish, heroin, and cocaine selling, but it was also involved in the extortion of local businesses, using firearms to intimidate when necessary. In particular, clan members regularly undertook stese, or shooting in the air, in their territory in order to show who was in control and to gain respect from the local community.

The leaders of the clan were brothers. The two sisters-in-law were present in the clan, not seen as managers but merely as temporary replacements, substituting for their imprisoned husbands. Aurora worked with her husband when he was free. When he was imprisoned, she carried on with her activities, organizing, overseeing, and managing drugs and extortions. Again, like other clans, she employed minors, using her teenage children as well as her husband's associates. Mati was also a very dynamic and good manager. She lived in the upper territory, in Via Solitaria and Supportico d'Astuti, which comprised narrow streets and alleys that were harder for the police to monitor. She had a solid group of associates who worked for her and who supported her activities, including her daughters, in-laws, friends, and their friends, a total of six associates, including minors.

Between 2015 and 2018, Mati and her associates concentrated on the drug business. She was perhaps given the freedom to do this because she was the daughter of the boss but maybe also because she was bright and focused. She proved highly efficient organizing the women to sell drugs from their houses, i bassi, and the whole process of bagging up the product and its distribution to customers.

The episode that highlighted the fact that Mati was not just a passive manager of a drug piazza took place in July 2015. At this time, the clan was led by her older brothers Paolo and Luca and their sons. On the night of July 3, a group of men went to Mati's house to intimidate and threaten her because she refused to pay the leadership a percentage and, in particular, her nephew's demand of an increased weekly tax on her drug business. This demand would have meant an increase of 300 euros a week for them which she felt was totally unjustified. Here, the male leadership wanted to take more profits away from her and her associates while not applying the same policy to other piazzas. Indeed, some piazza managers benefited from preferential treatment. Mati's refusal to pay provoked a series of violent acts of retaliation. For example, one of her close associates even had her moped burnt and her house shot at. But Mati resisted. She "*took up arms*" and did not hesitate to challenge the male leaders: she was never going to pay the increased tax, no way.[22] The leadership eventually backed down.

Aurora and Mati proved that they were their own people. They did not follow the rules laid down by the male leaders when it did not work for them. Mati was a good example of a drug manager who did what she was told for the good of the clan. However, when she disagreed and thought that things were unfair, she stood up for herself and her associates against the leadership, her relatives, even if this provoked violence and put them in potential danger. She did not hesitate to do what was right for her, not the clan, when she felt that they were not thinking of her, and so she acted in her own self-interests against the collective good. This demonstrates that these female middle managers had their own independent agency and criminal strategy.

Careful but Strategic Manager

Anita Lea was not born into a criminal family, but to survive she became a clan member. Born in the early 1970s, between 2009 and 2014 she became an efficient and reliable manager of a clan from just outside Naples, so efficient that some even considered her to be the leader of the clan.

Between 2003 and 2009, as a low-level, specialized foot soldier, she was just selling drugs for this local clan and frequenting with its members but was not really involved in other criminal activities. She was often arrested for possessing and supplying illegal substances. The turning point came in 2009, when another local clan murdered her father as a form of provocation and disrespect. This awoke a sense of revenge, vendetta, within her, especially as she was bringing up small children.[23]

This event motivated her to become more actively involved in the clan. Thus, she quickly became a crucial member of the clan as she was considered hard working and reliable. Initially, she sold drugs and protected the clan's territory by chasing people whom she did not trust and whom she felt were too close to rival clans. She soon gained considerable criminal prestige and became more and more involved as a resourceful manager.

Her main job was to manage key criminal activities: selling drugs (such as cocaine), managing drug piazzas in Ercolano, and keeping the clan's accounts in a notebook, the *libro maestro,* which she prepared and worked on, in her kitchen where she also hid the clan's firearms.[24] As she became more active, she got family members involved too, including her brother, his wife, and her daughter and became a mentor to many of the younger emerging male leaders. She was considered to be a real and proper Camorra woman because she had ambition, know-how, and was selfless for the clan. We are told that even when she was under house arrest, she defied the conditions of the house arrest by meeting clan members and organizing activities, which she was forbidden to do. Arrested in 2012, she became a state witness in 2017, but refused to be interviewed by me.

Dynamic and Meticulous Manager

I was able to interview Laura Letto in 2012 in Naples and therefore I can tell her story in more detail. Born in 1977, she was the daughter of a boss whose clan was based in Santa Maria Capua Vetere. Her family was not an established traditional Camorra clan. They were hard-working fishmongers, who owned their own shop, an occupation passed from father to son.

Laura and her younger brother, Alessandro, grew up in a broken home. Her parents separated when she was ten as her father was a ladies' man and perpetually collected lovers which destroyed his marriage and disillusioned his children. Her father had *"a strong and rigid personality,"* a *"padre padrone"* type, and moved in with Martina, who became his partner. Alessandro went to live with his father while Laura stayed with her mother. After that, her life was quite normal, quasi banal, until she was twenty. Alessandro and his father started to develop a semi-legal slot machine business with his new partner's brother.

Then suddenly, Alessandro was murdered by members of the Casalesi clan in a night club as he sought to defend one of his girlfriends who was being bothered by one of their members. Laura recalls, "[The other guy] *probably could not return home, having been beaten up . . . because he would have lost respect and become a no one.*"[25] Laura pinpoints this event as key to her life: "*The death of Alessandro is the moment in which our lives changed . . . certain decisions were made.*"[26] It was after this fatal event that this family became a small but active clan in the Marcinese region; the clan covered the towns of San Prisco, Capua, San Tammaro, Casagiove, Casapulla, Limatola, Castel Morrone, Curti, and Caserta in the early 2000s. This clan became close to a larger and more powerful clan as Laura's father was a cousin of its leader.

At that time, Laura had finished school and started studying law at university, but her father asked her to join him. He had decided to seek revenge for his son's murder and needed more help and competent members. He realized that Laura would be a useful accomplice in his project. She says that Alessandro's murder transformed her father into a revenge-hungry individual who was willing to do anything to avenge his son's death, including becoming a *camorrista* and the boss of his own clan.

Initially, her father only wanted retribution and he dragged all his relatives with him. In particular, he approached his cousins who were camorristi from the Marcinese region and then his only daughter, Laura. She soon became a fully paid-up member and was asked to manage the finance of the new emerging clan's slot machine business: she explained, "*At the beginning, I didn't know what to do . . . I never liked maths or accounting but then all of a sudden you are in the middle of it because the woman is the one who is less involved in violence. . . . Everyone thinks . . . all the clans think that the wives can be front names for companies or bank accounts or similar because the state does not look at the wives, daughters, aunts . . . but then in time, they eventually get there.*"[27]

In particular, it was Laura who organized every aspect of the slot machines business. "*I managed the economic sector/slot machines specifically. Although they went to buy a slot machine, I had to tell them to go . . . in other words, I imposed myself. I imposed myself in the area I looked after . . . they listened to me. I had this 'power' over them at least for this activity* [Andrea, an emerging lieutenant who supported her dad, the boss, commanded the violent sectors]."[28]

In 2005, a new law was introduced that changed the rules and regulation of the slot machine sector, but Laura found ways to play the system: "*She knew how to use the 'black machine' to fix the machines. . . . She was fully aware of how to clone the machines. I want to be clear that whenever her dad was absent, it was she who commanded and gave orders to the group* [together with Andrea]."[29]

She imposed a hundred slot machines on different bars in the Marcinese region and fixed all of them. She explained to me.

> When it became illegal, I looked after the illegal. I fixed the slot machines because as I repeat, they [other members of the clan] didn't know how to use them. It was explained to me how to modify the cards . . . because we would send them every month the total they had made from the slot

> *machines. Therefore, I fixed the incoming and outgoing amounts. They* [the bars] *would have 1,000 euros and we would take the 20,000 that had been played. We took everything.*[30]

She had clear plans to develop her own slot machine business:

> *I no longer had the legal slot machine business because they had confiscated everything in one day . . . I repeat that women think. I was thinking of turning my slot machine business into a legal business because it was no longer a question of power. I would have got close to the Casalesi clan* [for my business]. *I had also thought about doing this . . . I knew where to go and who to speak with. Maybe they would not have engaged with a woman, but I would have talked about paying them and I would have invested* [in] *the slot machines.*[31]

In relation to other activities and in particular loan sharking, when her father was away or in prison, she dealt with the finances: she prepared the money that had to be lent to customers, and acted as the intermediary receiving money from clients which was then handed over to her father or to the bank when he was away because he "*traveled a lot because he had many lovers, in his absence, it was* [his partner] *and his daughter . . . who took the money to the bank.*"[32]

In all of this, she explains that she never used violent means because she was a woman and considered herself a businesswoman. But a *pentito*, has a different account "*I would like to add that my wife was threatened by her cousin* [Laura] *. . . who told her to shut up because if she talked, although they had the same blood, she would have got the worst of it and not the people in prison.*"[33]

He described Laura's role:

> *From the start, she managed the slot machine* [video games, etc.] *business* [allocate money, catalogue machines]. *She was informed of all movements of machines from bar to bar to profits made. She decided and identified where the new machines should go. She was involved in the cloning of cards for slot machines and in the reinvestment of profits from illegal activities through financial operations and buying real estate. She was also the one, together with her mother, who had the clan's bank accounts and it was her who would visit the bank to get cash. When the men were not around, she would see the loan sharking clients.*[34]

He insists that this clan started to put pressure on him and his partner, and that it was Laura herself who violently threatened and intimidated them. In particular, she wanted him to accuse himself of crimes in order to clear her father's name as he had become rather depressed and suicidal in prison and had asked his foot soldiers to lighten his load by not accusing him systematically.[35]

Laura acknowledged in our interview that she had flourished in the criminal underworld because as a woman she was "*colder* [and] *more calculating*" more able to keep ahead of the game in terms of both her rivals and the police and excel at being an efficient and successful manager.[36] She proved her sense of initiative and independent thinking when eleven members of her clan were arrested. She orchestrated their response: she wrote up their false testimonies saying that they were not there and therefore, not guilty. Each member had to sign the document before presenting it to court.

In 2010, she was arrested and again in 2011, before becoming a state witness in late 2011. We have seen that she was not born into a Camorra family, but that events in her youth meant that she had a career in her father's new clan, not as an ordinary foot soldier but due to her education and intelligence as the manager of the main legal and illegal activities of the clan. As he saw himself a padre-padrone whom all women should follow, it might appear that the formally traditional patriarchal model defined the clan, but informally, we must acknowledge that she implemented her own ways and methods in her Camorra activities and strategies. She was very much her own person and although loyal to her father, she made decisions initially for the clan but then for her own self-interests and survival. She articulated the intelligence of Camorra women: she was proactive when necessary and had her own criminal strategies while listening also to her father. Maybe she was more than a manager, but she proved that women are never passive.

Hidden but Reliable and Competent Managers

Women Camorra managers are often hidden in the background. But they are very versatile and, as we have seen, undertake a variety of important tasks (not all at the same time necessarily) similar to their male counterparts:

1. Take orders and instructions from leaders to pass on to foot soldiers and others
2. Coordinate and implement instructions from the leaders
3. Manage and organize members and business sectors or, in other words, multitask
4. Look after clan finances by managing the clan's kitty, calculating members' salaries, distributing them, and dealing with lawyers, among other chores
5. Train new members and give advice
6. Provide pastoral care for members

Managers occupy a central space in the Camorra as they are the link and the connection between the lower strata of the clan (foot soldiers) and the top level (leaders). They constantly communicate and exchange instructions with him/her, and exclusive access to the boss gives them unique status, respect, and immense power with the possibility to replace or to substitute for the boss one day. They also enjoy the freedom to occupy and move in all spaces. It is probably the complexity of the managers' role and their overall presence in the clan that gives them respect and great criminal prestige regardless of gender. However, it is important to note that women are particularly efficient and good at managing.

In the extensive sources I collected I found that there is a recurring theme that needs to be strongly acknowledged: women are very reliable, resourceful, and efficient Camorra managers. They tend to remain loyal to their leaders and their strategies based on a kind of "delegation of power," but in the majority of cases, as we have seen because of their position in the family and their personalities, they also go beyond and show independent and strategic criminal thinking and their own agency. They are not mere male substitutes because they do more than just follow passively instructions; they implement their own actions and strategies when they believe it is necessary and for the good of the clan.

STRATEGIC AND INTELLIGENT LEADERS

A common theme in my conversations with all the former Camorra women I spoke to was that women are powerful, strong, and capable of making decisions and of ordering violent murders, and therefore, of being efficient leaders.[1] Laura, for example, clearly articulates the idea that men think they make decisions and lead a clan, but that in fact women are just as capable and perhaps even wiser: "*Women think a lot. . . . And they are the ones who take the decisions: I thought with my head, I no longer followed my dad's instructions.*"[2] Mariella affirms, "*My husband and I were like that, we were equal . . . we always thought in the same way*" when they were both free. But when he was arrested, clan members "*respected me because I was his wife and at the same time, when he was arrested, I took over the situation.*"[3] In clear terms, she became the boss, and "*for me it was normal. I even liked what I was doing.*"[4]

In this chapter, I show how women can be leaders in their own right, not just as secondary figures, or beneficiaries of their relationships with men. I emphasize that thanks to their central role in the family and household, they can be independent and make autonomous decisions in their clan without being influenced continuously or directed by their menfolk as robots. I establish that they have their own criminal agency, space, and power. Former national antimafia prosecutor, Franco Roberti, argued this precise point in a Rai documentary: "Initially women were in the shade, and then often they came out into the open, out of the shade. They played an important 'replacement' role substituting for the men when they could no longer lead the organization. Often, this 'replacement' role became a leadership role, no longer purely a replacement role but a fully independent and autonomous one."[5]

The key elements that I am using to define leadership in a Camorra woman is criminal agency and

1. Having an ability to make independent criminal decisions and not taking orders from others
2. Having her own vision for the clan and being listened to
3. Having the respect and necessary charisma to regroup clan members so that they follow her
4. Using her house as the clan headquarters

To document this, I analyze the life stories of six women who have come to the forefront of the Neapolitan criminal underworld since the 1980s with their own agency and personalities. I selected them from the many stories that I had because their specific accounts allow for generalization and the unpacking of recurring themes (such as family, strategic thinking, influence, power, decision-making, shared visions, invisibility, and the true nature of female involvement). In particular, their life stories encapsulate for me issues, trends, and patterns that are not unique or exceptional, but which are common to many of the other Camorra women I came across. In retelling their stories, I emphasize their power of agency as well as their ability to dictate power relations in the clan, showing that they were not dominated by the men. From the evidence collected, I can show how active they were in their life choices but also the different forms of capital they gather, which makes them strategic players.[6]

Flexible and Forward-Thinking Leader

The first story is that of Mariella Manca.[7] Her story is the story of an ordinary girl, an outsider, who became the wife of a local boss, and then led the clan once he was arrested.[8] She was rather good at it because she had been his partner in crime while he was free. She showed great criminal skills and vision in her leadership of her small clan. Known as a Zia, "Aunty," she was a strong-willed, determined young woman, who, at the age of twenty-five, successfully led a small emerging clan.[9] Today, she is a pentita, a state witness. When I interviewed her, she acknowledged fully her past saying, "*I was a Camorra woman.*"[10] Her account demonstrates her independence, her vision for her clan members, her charisma, and the respect granted her by the criminal underworld.

Born in 1984, she grew up in "*a simple context,*" in a small seaside town in the Bay of Naples. Hers was a "*normal*" extended family in which she was educated by her grandparents as her parents were too young when she was born. She was surrounded by her loving relatives, including her grandmother's brothers. She describes a "*happy childhood*," one with a strong female model, her grandmother who gave her "*a strong sense of maternal love and family (the values of the family are sacred).*"[11]

To attend secondary school, she returned to live with her parents closer to the city center. It was there that she met her future husband, Bruno.[12] She was eleven and he was fourteen. For her, he stood out because he was "*charismatic.*" Indeed, "*if there was a fight, he dominated the situation and he demanded respect. At school, things blossomed . . . and we started having a relationship.*"[13] She believes that she was attracted to him because "*he wasn't a normal guy,*" but also because she *was* "*attracted by his different lifestyle, that always attracted because any case the first boyfriend, the first . . . so, I didn't care who he was, who he wasn't.*"[14]

The relationship became serious even though her family did not approve. Mariella became pregnant at the age of fifteen and moved in with him and his family. She was made to feel very much at home by his parents as they only had sons, saying that "*they loved me like a daughter.*"[15] She is crystal clear that "*everything started from there.*"[16] What does she mean by "*everything*"? The answer is her Camorra activities and involvement. She explains, "*I was at home with them, I knew what they were doing. When I had to help my husband, I did.*"[17] In particular, when Bruno and his foot soldiers organized the local drug piazzas and market, she knew: "*It is a marketplace . . . I wanted to move up, so I followed that logic. . . . I followed that approach. . . . You do things . . . and you don't even realize what you're doing.*"[18]

She argues that her husband was his own man, although he got his drug supplies from other contacts: "*He was always on his own. Even though he had this market, he was never someone's boy. He had the market and he bought and sold by himself . . . so, it's also a family thing. He didn't feel like he was going to buy from people higher than him. It was a family thing.*"[19] Did she learn what to do from her husband as she was by his side? She did not quite see it that way: "*My husband and I were like that, equal. It's all a mental factor rather than appearance.*"[20]

After Bruno was arrested in 2010, Mariella was left on her own with her children and the clan. As she had an intuition that the police were on to them, she made the decision to stop all drug activities to deflate the situation: "*A little time passed and I ended everything, even the [drug] markets . . . so, at some point, I said let's get rid of the markets [drug piazzas].*"[21]

She independently did a risk assessment for her clan without any male influence. She felt that she was in charge, making decisions on her own for the survival of her clan. She was proactive to save her clan and did not wait for instructions from her husband in prison. She had no need for her husband's directives because she was equal to him, and he knew it. "*I did it. No. The only thing that he said to me was that he only trusted me, because I knew everything, where he got* [his drugs] *... who I had to pay, because I knew that those people had done something for him, so I was the one deciding.*"[22]

Did his family and foot soldiers only follow her orders because of the power she had from being his wife? This is a crucial question. They all knew that she was the one who could save the clan and make the best decisions. So, it might not have been only her authority and respect gained from her husband but also because she herself showed that she had great criminal intelligence, an ability to predict camorra dynamics, and efficient skills to run the clan's affairs.

Indeed, she organized all clan activities efficiently and its finances: "*I had to pay him, the lawyers, the families of the members who were in jail ... other guys who were out, logically, they could no longer work because, knowing that they were Bruno's boys, they couldn't go out normally one day and say now I'm going to work because they arrested my boss.*"[23]

Importantly, she states, "*For everything they needed, they came to me.*"[24] So, she managed a group of four active members but also had to deal with the growing pressure from Bruno's family and from her drug suppliers and protectors, the semilegitimate Davide family. They resented her because she was doing it on her own and was successful. She failed to fit in to their conceptions about hierarchy but carved out a criminal space for herself. She did not adopt masculine values and behavior, and this upset them as she challenged their own traditional attitudes. If anything, she was in fact very beautiful and feminine but used her intelligence, education, and know-how to strengthen her position, control the power relations that existed around her, and run the clan effectively.

Mariella showed agency in her feelings. Like many women who had husbands in prison for a long time, she got lonely. She met a man who made her feel special and loved. Perhaps, she fell in love with the idea of being in love. This love story turned sour. The clan soon found out, ambushed her and her lover, beating them badly, kicking her out of her home, and taking her children away from her. She became so desperate that she was arrested in 2012 at the age of twenty-six years. It did not take her long to decide to collaborate with the state because the clan had rejected her and had done everything possible to isolate her.[25] They did not accept her betrayal as a woman, although her husband seemed to understand and feared that her collaboration with the state would destroy the clan. Today, she is still very respectful of her husband, saying, "*I don't regret him, but I regret what we did.*"[26]

This story underlines that the Camorra family goes beyond narrow kinship ties and evolves through marriage creating new loyal relatives-cum-members. Mariella's story in particular shows how a young woman without blood ties to a clan but married to one of the emerging bosses can become a skillful proactive boss who shows a strong personality, independence of mind, great organizational skills, and full immersion into Camorra values. The clan itself was not automatically sexist but flexible and adaptable but she bothered them: she felt free from their control, failed to respect their strict rules, and lacked respect for them. Ultimately, she challenged the so-called male structures of the Camorra clan and showed that, maybe, they were not sufficiently robust themselves. Together with her husband, she managed the clan; she was a full partner in his leadership. But, once he was arrested, it was not his mother, father, or brothers who became the leader, but her, Mariella. She stepped up, took the initiative, led, and proved that a twenty-something female can be successful in this role, even if she was not born into a Camorra family.

Traditional and Tough Leader

Elena Rossi's life story reflects very similar features. It tells the story of long-time companion and criminal partner of a camorrista. If she had not been a great leader, the clan would not have survived as long as it has. Her presence may have been "invisible" until she was imprisoned in 2008, but it kept the clan together making it resilient and stable. Her power did not come from her relationship with her men (her husband, her sons, her brother-in-laws) but from her determined personality, her own safe pair of hands and her understanding of the criminal dynamics.

Elena, also known as *La signora del Male*, "the Evil lady" or "First Lady," was born in the mid-1950s in a small harbor town in the Bay of Naples. She met and married her husband in the 1970s with whom she had children. She proved to have a great criminal awareness and intelligence, making decisions when necessary for the good of the clan.

Between 1972 and 1973, the smuggling of cigarettes, or bionde, was a thriving activity in the town: indeed, it was considered to be the Italian capital of cigarette smuggling.[27] By the early 1980s, mass smuggling had died down substantially as routes moved south to Taranto, but criminal structures, reputations, and fortunes had been established. Her young husband was one such criminal who had made his name and money thanks to this activity. He, "*like many other Camorra leaders, started out smuggling cigarettes.*"[28] It is said that he grew up learning the trade from important and experienced smugglers. This had transformed him into a respected criminal player in the town and in the region; by the early 1980s he was already able to launder money into the legitimate economy.

Together, they had an extensive blood family (children, numerous nephews, and nieces as well as many grandchildren (including one, who was sent to prison as a minor). Elena also had two brothers and two sisters, who in time also became involved in her clan. It has been suggested that although "*she was the boss's wife, she could have been the boss.*"[29] Indeed, while its leader was in prison, serving a life sentence with periods in solitary confinement, the clan resisted and survived, even though it occasionally came under attack.

It was Elena who was at her husband's side during his successful criminal ascension, and I would argue that his success was also her success, and that the clan's longevity is in part thanks to her proactive criminal vision, as the boss has been locked in prison since 1991. She appears to be a "*strong woman* [with] *character, a strong personality, vulgar but powerful in her behavior and aggressive in her ways. . . . She dressed the part with her blond-dyed hair* [and] *challenging air.*"[30] Journalists have described her as "sharp," or *scaltra*, prudent and respected, with never a word out of place. A former clan member articulates one of the common contradictions that we encounter when we look at the role of Camorra women. According to him, on the one hand, Elena was "*kept . . . out of all discussions,* [because] *she* [was] *a woman,*" but at the same time, he argues that she was "*aware of the things her husband was involved in.*"[31]

Although she was only formally cited in a judicial proceeding in 1998, she was already involved in the clan's criminal strategies and had a criminal record well before then but had not officially served time in prison. In 1985, her presence was already noted: "*She was a front name and had shares in two companies.*"[32] In 1998, she was finally charged with 'mafia association' and violence for intimidating former clan members who were thinking about collaborating with the state, although she never served time for this.

Something happened between 1996 and 1997 during an important trial against the clan's leadership that would highlight her strategic and intelligent thinking.[33] Two loyal clan members started to have some serious thoughts about collaborating with the state. In order to protect the clan, Elena decided to influence their choices during the trial. She put pressure on their wives to go to the local newspaper and to publicly denounce and reject their husbands' decisions to become state witnesses. In this way, the wives publicly explained that they were asking for a *divorzio d'onore,* or "a divorce of honor" because they rejected their husbands and disagreed with their life decisions. This episode is one among many that highlights the resourceful, proactive, and original approach that Elena developed.

She lived in an elegant building built by a rich industrial family with a courtyard that became an ideal location for a clan to control the local community and district. Territory is fundamental for clans and the choice of this *palazzo* as the living quarters of many clan members, and its headquarters, its *roccaforte,* was instrumental. It was in the center of the town, close to the port, and was the home of all senior members. Over the years, the building played a crucial role in the clan's activities; it became almost an extra member. Elena lived on one of the lower floors, from where she controlled the comings and goings of clan members and the police. As it is believed she had police informers, it is even suggested that she "*receive*[d] *'tip offs'* [or *soffiate*] *from local law enforcement agencies*" when they were going to arrest clan members, to facilitate their getaway.[34] It was there, in this Camorra space that clan members made decisions; it was there that they met to discuss business and to plan murders. To make sure that it was extra safe, members built in their flats their own extensions and hideaways without asking for planning permission. In particular, they constructed special tunnels and flats for fugitives, connecting electricity illegally, so that they could hide and escape. In 2015, the criminal importance of the building was noted by the local judiciary who confiscated it officially because it was considered too dangerous and dilapidated. Consequently, 193 of its inhabitants were rehoused.

In 2008, Elena was finally arrested for "mafia association" and sentenced to ten years in prison. After seven years, although she was due to be released for good behavior, she was sentenced to another eleven years, to serve five. She clearly did not expect this: she collapsed when she heard that she had to remain in prison. These two investigations shone a light on her active role at the heart of the clan, even though many continued to insist that she was powerful only because of her relationship with her men (her husband and sons).

From the clan, she was paid a salary of 11,000 euros a month from the clan's kitty, an important sum underlining her crucial role at the heart of the clan and the importance of money for Camorra women.[35] As a former clan member remarked: "*For them, the main value in life is money.*"[36] She was involved at all levels of the clan's activities. She not only gave out orders; nothing happened without her approval, although officially it appeared as though it was her sons who took the decisions. At street level, she threatened shopkeepers and businessmen in the clan's extortion racket, she controlled and oversaw the drug activities, and collected money from the drug piazzas and distributed salaries to members. At home, she kept firearms, looked after fugitives and youngsters once crimes had been undertaken, and discussed new potential criminal business ventures: she "*makes her house available, attends meeting and drops off agreed sums of money, but most importantly, she participates actively because she is the wife and mother of camorristi.*"[37]

To guarantee the clan's survival, she was very hands on; she personally looked after the importation of drugs into the city. She received the delivery of the drugs and participated in the weighing of the doses and their packaging.[38] In prison, she discussed clan business and strategies, and it is believed that she received her husband's instructions. However, this is a male-centered approach. Laura Letto presents an alternative interpretation: "*So, the wife doesn't go home and implement what the husband says because even though he is the husband and gives orders, he has to stay in prison. Therefore, he needs to listen to the woman. It's true that they are the wi*[ves], *the daughter*[s] *but it is the wife and the daughter who keep the clan going.*"[39]

As a good matriarch, Elena imposed her will on clan activities and strategies: "*Everything about the life of the group, good and bad is communicated to her. She participates in everything with competence and awareness.*"[40] Thus, she sought to resolve arising criminal and personal issues, including situations close to her heart. It would have been dangerous to ignore her. This demonstrates that she controlled power relations as a strong woman. One classic example of this was when a local businessman complained that her nephew was not pulling his weight in his job: she "*gets involved with her usual theatrical style according to a game in which she replaces her son, in this case to defend the cause of her nephew . . . who works for Lello* [complicit businessman] *but who has missed many days of work. Her favorite nephew doesn't deserve to have his salary suspended, he is a good boy and well educated.*"[41]

The poor Lello could only agree, begging that in the future, her nephew actually turned up to work.[42] In other words, thanks to her specific request, her nephew had been paid for doing nothing, Lello wanted to get rid of him, but Elena had intervened to make sure that this did not happen.

State witnesses and antimafia prosecutors argue that she was not a leader: "*The leadership of her son . . . is crystal clear, he represents his father and brother across their territory, he is supported and helped by Elena.*"[43]

They argue that she was subordinate to her husband and sons, acting merely as a support system and only as their representative rather than as a player in her own right. In reality, she leads and has "*independent management powers,*"[44] which means that she had total autonomy to do what she wanted without ultimately needing the approval of men.

Indeed, she had individual power but as she systematically worked for the collective good of the clan and did everything she could to achieve this, her leadership features were diluted and it became easier to see her only as a soft and diplomatic "*mediator, liaising between prisoners and those free on the outside, guaranteeing them group unity and stopping possible disaggregation,*" rather than being an equal to the men.[45] Her criminal intuition and oversight which her son missed or neglected, were never appreciated. In this instance, her son "*underestimated*" a certain difficult emerging situation but she on the contrary insisted on acting fast to protect the clan. She was "*able to impose her will, forcing and obtaining for security reasons, the temporary suspension of drug dealing in piazzas.*"[46]

Elena also had her own agency and agenda. Her power was real, practical, and not just formal, that is, "*her opinion was indispensable, listened to with respectful submission.*"[47] She did have decisional power in the clan and was "*equal to, if not more important, than the male leaders.*"[48] Thus, she was a true matriarch, informed and up to date on all clan activities, including the dynamics of clan murders. She wore black and mourned the clan dead when necessary and appropriate to reinforce the image of a traditional southern Italian woman in the patriarchal public sphere while dominating the private sphere.

Quiet and Headstrong Leader

Valeria Nunzo also projected the traditional image of a southern Italian woman. She was a quiet Camorra widow or so it seemed. And yet, this was far from the truth. She was, in fact, determined, cool, and headstrong, a Camorra businesswoman who had shares in one of the most powerful drug importation cartels in Naples.[49] While the young hotheaded Turks lost control of the criminal situation around her, she remained calm and carried on in a difficult situation.

Valeria was born in the 1960s and had a large family: she had five siblings and five children. She became known as Zia because together with her sister they married two up-and-coming criminal brothers. Their younger brother was also involved with their husbands' activities, which made for the future basis of a strong Camorra family.

At its origin, this criminal family was a subgroup of a larger more established clan and they looked after the drug supply chain for their mother clan: they imported cocaine from South America via Spain into Italy. To do this, in 2000, the three men set up a companylike structure with two other outside investors to manage their drug business. In this way, they established a powerful drug clan from the suburbs of Naples. All five investors put money into the activity: 20 percent each, and each received 20 percent of the profits. This flow of money was what kept the larger clan alive and successful, but it angered the main leaders. This provoked a bloody war.

During this war, to keep safe and to avoid violent repercussions and being easy targets, many clan members, including the main bosses (and their families) went on the run and hid in Barcelona, Spain. It is not clear whether she moved to Barcelona full time during the war, but we know that both her and her children went regularly to Spain.

According to the Italian Finance Police, the Guardia di Finanza, during that war, Valeria seemed to have played an insignificant role and to have remained in the background, quasi-invisible and nonexistent. She was, after all, a Camorra widow enjoying the good life quietly and happily without drawing attention to herself as she lived off her husband's criminal activities. Indeed, she managed his shares of the international drug business but as a silent partner and not an "active" player. The only trace we have of her is in the antimafia prosecutor's attempt to figure out what clan members were actually doing in Spain apart from hiding and keeping safe. She was accused of being allegedly involved in the clan's money laundering activities in Europe, but ultimately found not guilty, and it was her sister, the wife of the boss, instead, who was found guilty of such activities in 2011.

From 2009 to 2010, the clan split as both historic leaders were arrested. As successors, they nominated two young Turks who were very confrontational and competitive, which led to many local tensions. Her sons led one branch and some sons-in-law led her brother's branch. Soon, the two branches started provoking each other and became very violent. This destructive behavior in the local district did not help the two branches flourish.

In 2011, she found herself managing two-fifths of the family drug business due to numerous arrests. And when in 2014, there were more arrests, she took up the reins of the two split branches of the clan after years of bitter infighting. She instantly became the head of the different subgroups and factions, unifying both branches into a single coherent and efficient clan. She decided to be a reconciliatory figure; she was very careful and had experience, knowledge, and vision. Where possible, she met rivals from the other branch to discuss activities and business. She was very diplomatic and regularly met representatives and leaders from other city clans to sort out arising problems and issues that could be bad for business. It could be argued that without her at the helm, the two clans would have disintegrated, but she cleared up the mess that the younger men had created.

What made Valeria a powerful figure in the clan was that she understood the complexities of the criminal underworld and took informed decisions, which made her authoritative and a force to be reckoned with. What made her all the more powerful was her overview of the drug market and shares in an international drug business; this gave her real economic influence. She now had full control over the three family shares of the cocaine company, her three-fifths. She was the only one who had direct contact and became the exclusive interlocutor of the two other investors who oversaw the importation of cocaine from Spain into Italy. By holding control of the drug market, she held the key to the clan's lifeline and became vital to all other activities and business. This was mostly luck and coincidence, but she made it work for her.

In the clan, she oversaw activities, resolved conflicts, made decisions independently, and used violence when necessary. Her managerial and leadership styles were different and refreshing. First, she mediated to keep the peace between clans and members, and then managed and led when she was the only one who could do so. She knew what to do and directed in a very clear way, as a mother, rather than in the style of young ambitious men. Perhaps being a widow allowed her more space and independence of action. She imposed her ideas but had a longer-term picture, which came with her maturity. She was discrete and focused, but also harsh, evil, and cruel. She did not hesitate to give orders to murder individuals who bothered the clan, but these were handled skillfully and out of sight from the general public.

In front of the clan's leadership power vacuum, she took control because she had to protect the clan's profits, territory, drug business and clan members. Valeria was more than ready for the challenge and was not just filling the role for the absent men or following their instructions. She was the ultimate leader and executive director of the clan, in the true sense of the word, administering activities with a variety of different responsibilities and tasks, ranging from drugs and extortion to politics. Because she was a widow, she did not have to report back to a husband, but in her prison visits discussed activities and business with her brother-in-law as an equal partner, not as his subordinate. In other words, she was capable in her own right.

Some may argue that she had inherited her husband or brother-in-law's capital, esteem, and reputation because she was his widow, and she automatically inherited the respect and authority he was due. She was described as "*one of the leaders because when she gives an order it is immediately implemented.*"[50] I believe that this is an oversimplification because, of her status, she enjoyed freedom including sexual freedom that married Camorra wives normally never have. Indeed, one pentito suggested that there existed the "*principle of the Camorra*" whereby none could go to the house of a woman if her husband was not there (or in prison), it was considered inappropriate, or at least this is what camorristi believed.[51]

Valeria was clever; she chose intelligent advisors who knew what they were talking about, so she made wise investment decisions. In early 2010s, she managed to understand the importance of unity and peace for business and therefore negotiated truce accords with different angry members of the clan to make way for peace, tranquility, good business, and money. She always talked one to one to clarify things, saying, "*We have clarified everything, I don't want to know any more about it.*"[52]

Judges identified a coherent strategy on her part whereby she reinforced and restructured the clan after a chaotic phase with internal wars and strife. It is alleged that she reorganized the clan by distributing clear roles to her trusted members. Her vision was for the long term and she slowly implemented her plans. The previous leaders, who were young men without the necessary experience, had been messy and haphazard in their approach, which was ultimately quite dangerous.[53] Instead, Valeria took her time, reflected, and sought to control both the criminal side of the operations as well as the economic activities. However, in a sexist world, this could never have been imagined. She was arrested in 2018.

In short, Valeria is quite emblematic of Camorra women because she was quasi-invisible and yet, she was a strong matriarch, who, because of her status as a Camorra widow, could essentially do as she wished.[54] She was so invisible that when out and about in her car and stopped by her lookouts, she became angry because they did not recognize her, saying *"but does that guy know that we rule here?"*[55] But her invisibility was in fact her strength.

Impetuous and Violent Leader

Nunzia D'Amico led the D'Amico clan in Ponticelli between 2009 and 2011. When Nunzia was murdered outside her front door in 2011 at the age of forty, the local paper, *Il Mattino*, ran a headline saying *"five bullets for Nunzia, murdered on her doorstep like a real* [male] *boss."*[56] She had been killed like a true male boss; she had been given all the respect of a man by being shot in broad daylight, in front of everyone.

Annunziata D'Amico was born in 1971. Her nicknames were Nunzia, la passillona ("black olives"), and Fraulella ("strawberry"). She was the eldest of six children. Her family lived in Ponticelli, a district in the southern suburb of the city, originating from a specific council estate, which was made up of several blocks of high-rise flats, enclosed and along a main road, Via Argine, that connects the industrial zone of Naples to Naples city center. Her estate was Parco Conocal. It forms part of the never-ending Ponticelli suburbs of Naples, with unceasing tower blocks of flats, small housing estates, new buildings, and unfinished projects.[57]

Nunzia made an important impact on her clan and on the Camorra when she reigned over the Conocal housing estate. During the early 2000s, the suburbs of Ponticelli and Barra were dominated by the Sarno clan and its allies, including Nunzia's brothers. Nunzia's story underlines how women can be powerful leaders even if not recognized as such. She was equal to her brothers but was criminally more astute. The Sarno clan was based in an estate called Rione de Gaspari, a few minutes away from the Conocal. This estate was made of smaller two- or three-story buildings with compact roads. The architecture is different from the Conocal housing estate and more condensed; the houses are closer together and the entrance to it is well-controlled.

This is where the Sarno clan played a central role in the local community; it controlled the drug market—jobs—and was able to distribute social housing after the earthquake in the 1980s—accommodation. The Sarno clan had emerged toward the end of the 1980s as part of the NF alliance and developed a coalition with the Misso-Mazzarella cartel.[58] This alliance gave the Sarno clan a certain amount of power and allowed it to expand outward toward the hinterland, where it sought allies and subordinates.

The D'Amico family was a subgroup of the Sarno clan in 2000. Antonio was their man in the Conocal housing estate. He set up a drug piazza for them under his building *vicino alla capella*, "near the church." He would sell the drugs that they provided and gave them a percentage of his profits. It was a man's world; drugs ruled the streets and the districts. Women were there but seen more as foot soldiers and sellers than anything else. The main boss was helped in his Camorra activities by his close relatives and extended family, including his parents, his siblings, and his in-laws; all of them worked with him in the drug piazza as the business was taking off.

When Nunzia's brothers were arrested in 2009, she became a fierce woman boss. Before their arrest, she was fully involved with them. Following their arrest, it was suggested that her husband formally took over the clan and that she was less involved, but this is an unfair reflection of events: *"In reality, when he* [her husband] *is free, he does everything that his wife Annunziata D'Amico tells him to do."*[59] Or again, *"If you took her and her partner, she was more important, Passillona. Passillona mattered in every aspect. He was a mere partner."*[60]

Nunzio grew criminally in parallel to her brother's own development: *"She thought like her brother did . . . they thought the same way. They had the same mindset."*[61] They were a partnership; she did not step in when the men were arrested but had always been there working by his side, even if invisible. For example, her brother cut up doses at her house as well as counting up the daily profits there. Once all the men were arrested, Nunzia had more freedom and acted as she wanted: *"Now, we are the Camorra. My husband is no longer here. Now, it is worse, there are the women. Here, we decide, not him."*[62]

She became the leader of the clan together with her sister-in-law, with whom it is said she did not get on very well. The two women ran all aspects of the organization together. Nunzia had a chauffeur-driven car at her disposal; her flat was the headquarters of the clan where everything was discussed and decided. She was in total control of all operations, even when violence had to be used to resolve an issue or dispute. She controlled everybody and everything.

Drugs were their main business but not the only one. By 2014, under her leadership, the clan managed forty drug piazzas. This business flourished around the Conocal housing estate; even her eldest son was allowed to have his own piazza, selling hashish and cocaine, while others had to pay her a tax on their profit as well as buying the drugs from her. It was not just one substance type; here, everything was available for those who came from outside to buy, that is, hashish, marijuana, cocaine, and heroin. Doses were regularly made up in her flat.

She controlled the extortion rackets in the neighborhood, and she was the one who decided who was allowed to rent or buy the council flats in the estate. She controlled the sales by taking a proportion of the transaction both from the buyer and seller, in this way becoming an illegal estate agent. She would hound out of the neighborhood those she did not like to allow people close to the clan or even clan members to move in. One of her sisters took over the local cleaning business whereby all citizens were forced to have their flats cleaned by them and had to pay seven euros a month. This company covered an extensive area. Even thieves had to give Nunzia a hundred euros a month to burgle flats; omertà and violence were important to the survival of the clan, and she did not hesitate to use aggressive and violent tactics if anyone bothered the clan or rebelled.

Nunzia's leadership style became evident when she went head-to-head with other clans; tensions grew with the local rival clan, especially when they came into the estate and threatened a clan member who was with her young daughter. While the men of the clan appeared less bothered by what had happened, she was furious and wanted blood. She immediately retaliated: "*We went out to kill . . . because the sister . . . sent him, because when the sister speaks, all the brothers listen.*"[63]

We can say that Nunzia D'Amico ordered the murder because she insisted that her brother do something; "*When they come, you need to go down, you need to go down . . . you need to do something. . . . Her husband did not speak in that moment because it is his wife who commands, he does what Nunzia D'Amico and her brother tell him to do. D'Amico listened to his sister and went downstairs.*"[64] Angela describes Nunzia's management style: "*And all the young girls involved . . . the boys who got involved. Not the least because when you get into these circles, they own you, they boss you around, they tell you what to do, they make you do what they want. . . . If you don't want to do it, they'll take your house or force your son to sell* [drugs]."[65]

What is fascinating about her leadership style is that she was very proactive and courageous. She did not shy away from using violence and used minors, if necessary. In particular, she had the respect from the women and from the men, although they did not really understand her. She had charisma, or at least, determination, and all the other members obeyed her: "*Passillona, you command me, I do what you tell me to do*" and "*he does not do anything without her say so* [her giving him instructions]."[66] Respect from others is also evident: "*Nunzia D'Amico reassured those present that she would resolve the problem.*"[67] "*Wait, I am coming now.*"[68]

The irony of Nunzia's story is that she was betrayed by women. She was careful about her own safety, but three women close to her clan had affairs with men from rival clans and ultimately provided them with vital information about her movements, which led to her murder. Facing her killers, she looked at them in the eyes and said "take off your balaclava . . . let me look at you in the face, let me see who you are.[69]" She was shot dead in front of her children.

Forceful and Determined Leader

Like Nunzia D'Amico, Eva Melliano has always been perceived as an authoritative figure. She was known as Lady Camorra, Zia, or Donna. She was the wife of a small-time camorrista, the lover a young charismatic camorrista, the mother of a camorrista killer and a camorrista herself. She had six children, four of whom have become involved in criminal activities.

Eva lived in the district of Ponticelli and became the boss of a small housing estate. Being fragmented, the clans in this part of the city come and go. After having been a member of the NCO, her husband passed into the ranks of the bigger Sarno Clan from the adjacent district, the De Gaspari Rione. One of her sons grew up in the clan as one of their killers but in 1998, he decided to split to set up his own autonomous clan.

Previously, during the early 1990s, she was believed to be a member of another local clan, and accredited with providing the clan with heroin and cocaine. She moved from group to group until her son organized his own group in the 1990s; she went from being a simple drug dealer to having more extensive activities. When her son received a life sentence for organizing an attack on his former boss that in fact murdered another relative, this provoked a bitter war between the established clan and the new emerging clan, at which point Eva became visible and powerful.

Eva's story once again highlights the informal sexual fluidity that exists in the Camorra and how sexual norms move beyond traditional values. Eva during the mid-1990s although still married, became romantically involved with a younger boss, from another district, who was on the run following the failure of his plan to ambush his rivals. He was much younger than her and also married to someone related to the Camorra, but it worked. They even had a child who would carry his Camorra heritage well. Interesting to note that a young member of the clan who dared to criticize her extramarital relationship as being "*a violation of the Camorra code*" was murdered by the clan.[70] She was arrested again in 2000.

She was released from prison in November 2009 after ten years in harsh prison conditions having been condemned as a mafia boss.[71] In less than eighteen months she was back inside because she had restarted her criminal activities and reinstalled her position of power in the local district, by raising money for her clan and extorting a local undertaker.[72]

Eva helped her son when he became a leader, and certainly she was more forceful and powerful when he was around, but she was the equal of any of the men who surrounded her. She started as a simple drug dealer and supplier, but then was able to become a leader of a small group focused on extortion rackets and drugs.[73] Her charisma, her strong character, and lack of fear reinforced her influence.[74]

Chaotic and Impulsive Leaders

Last but not least, an original case: a small and compact female clan. This group was made up of women who were neighbors in the district of the Rione De Gaspari of Ponticelli. They came to the fore and public notice in 2016. Often described as "women bosses," "Camorra mums," "Camorra bosses in skirts," they were not an official Camorra clan, but their behavior, actions, and activities can be seen as such and demonstrate true female Camorra power, in particular, their staunch defense of its code of honor and values. These women, with their younger male associates, were the bare criminal skeleton that remained standing once the dominant local clan was taken out by law enforcement agencies and decimated by the revelations from state witnesses, including the Sarno brothers, the top bosses in 2009. In 2021, this small clan is no more as its three or four principal female leaders are in prison for life. But its emergence and activities over a period of four to five years are significant as it underlines the continuous power of women.

According to the media, this group seems to have appeared out of nowhere overnight in 2010, but this is not really the case. This small group was in fact made up of a tight circle of women in their forties, who had always been involved in drug activities but quietly and invisibly in the background. They were always very active, keeping an eye on all the criminal activities in the district. They knew everyone's business.

These women were a mixed bunch from a poor suburb of Naples who initially just supported their sons, husbands, and the local clan. They then began to become organized and became leaders in their own right, because they could, and because, for a while, they were quite successful.

From the outside, it could be suggested that they inherited the clan and criminal space once a vacuum appeared following the decline of the traditional local clan. Nonetheless, the explanation has to be more nuanced because there were also a lot of emerging local male camorristi who could have filled that void or who could have eliminated these women. Instead, a kind of dream team of middle-aged women and younger and hungry male camorristi came together to reign in certain suburbs for three or four years.

The four main leaders had grown up together in difficult economic conditions, had a common past, and shared criminal activities. They were friends and relatives (two of them were cousins) but also related through their relationship with men. Two had a partner in common and so, their children were half-siblings. These women were recognized and well-respected figures in the local community, educated their children according to Camorra values, and had a substantial amount of social capital, accumulated from their households and their relationships with men which they transferred to their criminal activities. All of this they used wisely.

The female symbol of this clan was Nicoletta Grande. She had always been involved with the Camorra as her husband was a lifelong member of the local clan, and she was the mother of an emerging member. She brought up her two or three children on her own as her husband was often in prison. Her son soon learned the ways of the Camorra and became a killer for the Sarno clan. He was considered a "bad boy" and married the daughter of another boss to reinforce these criminal alliances. In 2019, he shocked the local clans, leaders, and his mother by deciding to collaborate with the state.[75]

Initially, these four women were simply a group of female middle-aged drug dealers in the suburb districts who became organized when necessary. Nicoletta, in particular, became a reliable, strong, and outspoken local drug dealer, who was not necessarily taken seriously by the local male clan. They did call on her when they needed to and to all effects, she responded. In this way, she gained respect and authority. She was taken seriously by acting without fear.

Although this group's roots were in the drug trade, they soon went beyond these activities because there was also the need to protect and defend all their criminal-business activities, their members, and the district from rivals. On one occasion, they turned up on the doorstep of a rival clan and refused their demands, thus showing courage and arrogance. They even went beyond just the talking. In 2016, they reacted when an ambitious camorrista from the city center of Naples sought new territory in their suburbs and started to bother them.

Together with their allies they agreed on what to do. They ordered, planned, and organized the camorrista's murder. Although they did not physically pull the trigger, they did everything else. The men provided the firearms and the killer. They organized every detail of the execution including the logistics, communication channels, recuperating the firearms, accompanying the killers, and hiding them after the act. They even acted as lookouts to inform the killers when the targets were arriving.[76] They organized every possible detail to be fully in control of the murder and its aftermath. Furthermore, this was not the only murder attack that they were involved in. A few years before, they were already involved in another murder. These women were devoted to the Camorra, its code of honor, and its cultural value system, perhaps more than men. Defenders of the Camorra status quo and all its tradition, even from prison they seek to have a voice in the local underworld. They have adapted to the times and now use social media regularly, with live broadcasts from inside prison and Tiktok video tributes posted on Facebook.

This clan may not have been very stable and on the retreat, but its appearance and actions show that there is no glass ceiling in Camorra clans. It could also be argued that these groups do not form part of the Camorra elite and the fact that they do like to get their hands dirty makes them an exception, but this is not the case. Women in Camorra elite families as has been discussed are also very active, have influence and a voice in Camorra activities and business. They are maybe less visible, but they are there.

Women Not Just "Bosses in Skirts"

The stories of women in this chapter have shown that gender is not a negative impediment to the involvement and social mobility of Camorra women: gender does not stop them from being valid powerful players and partners, and the organization does not discriminate against them. These stories underline how women can be at the level of the men and their equal partners. The life stories recounted here have illustrated how women have the capacity to manage "enterprise syndicates" (activities relating to business, money making activities) and "power syndicates" (activities relating to power and territory).[77] I believe that gender, together with social class and religion, can explain why women in the Camorra are powerful actors who have influence and who occupy a key position in the criminal underworld. Why we do not see them in this way is perhaps because of the sexist perceptions and cultural misogyny that are still present in Italy-Naples and in the world around the roles of women in OCGs. Contrary to the traditional and established images of the Camorra as a gendered criminal mafia with gendered stratification, I contest this portrayal and agree with Gribaudi that there are not distinct and different roles for men and women in the Camorra. Gender is unimportant.[78]

CHALLENGING TRADITIONAL MALE PERCEPTIONS OF CAMORRA WOMEN

One thing that occurred to me when I was analyzing my new material is the number of continuing perceptions, stereotypes, and myths that exist and how all the narratives around Italian mafias, organized crime, and women become distorted, manipulated, containing partial truths, sometimes even lies. This is why in this chapter I wish to discuss and challenge some of these established perceptions and narratives that came up time and time again in my interviews.

For too long Camorra women have been considered as footnotes to the transformation of the Camorra in the postwar period and not seen as actors with their own roles, space, and agency. They have been viewed solely as extensions of men, as objects or victims rather than players in their own right. They have been treated as subjects, instrumental players manipulated by their menfolk; they have been considered capable of criminal acts but only for short periods of time and only following the instructions of their men. They have been constantly presented, in black-and-white terms, as either hungry sexual objects or passive victims of abuse in a binary explanation of traditional gender and sexual roles and identities.

These male-constructed narratives are distorted, incorrect, and even false, since as we have seen, things are more complex, fuzzy, and nuanced than these narratives would have us believe. These women find themselves in a paradoxical situation constructed by civil society: they are represented as invisible in the Camorra space and passive in the clan, both enslaved and empowered at the same time.[1] Condemning women to the informal family, household, and private space, and concentrating only on formal rules and appearances in the public sphere to understand mafias and organized crime means that we fail to capture and grasp an important aspect of the criminal organization: the family setting. Women are in fact fundamental players in a complex historic, cultural, social, economic, and political context. This same society has difficulty recognizing their agency and accepting that their private power seeps into their performance in the Camorra.

Crime Markets/Groups versus Local Gender Orders

When looking for explanations about what determines gender inequality in crime groups, as we have seen, there are the three main schools of thought. First, crime markets such as drugs or human trafficking determine the number/roles of women in OCGs. Second, it is the organizational structure of the crime group. Last, the existing gender norms of a society explain the gender inequality and gender gap that supposedly exist. When I looked at my material, none of these theories explained what I was seeing, as all three approaches suggested that women had no agency of their own. These analyses always tied Camorra women's roles to their relationship to men, thus adopting a male-centered outlook. Women live and breathe patriarchal structures, and particularly so in Italy. However, this approach to patriarchy suggests that all forms of social, male-female interaction are constantly the same: a power relationship where men dominate and oppress women. This is not necessarily the case, nor systematic. Gender arrangements vary across time, culture, and countries, gender is not fixed, but fluid and "is inherently political" and constructed because "one is not born, but rather becomes a woman . . . one is not born masculine but has to become a man."[2]

As I have already argued, I believe that we must turn to the local gender orders that exist in Italy and Naples specifically, but also identify the Camorra's local gender regime to unpack the gender question and the notion of so-called gender inequality in the Camorra. It is by looking at these structures that perhaps we can understand the differences between gender dynamics in mafias and OCGs that are involved in similar criminal activities but where women may play different roles and have varying levels of power and influence.

It is in this messy cultural, social, and economic space of the Neapolitan public and private spheres that we need to look to better understand what is going on. In civil society, in the public sphere, the Camorra appears formally as "a male space only"—perhaps less than Cosa Nostra and the 'Ndrangheta, but the gender boundaries and roles in the private sphere are much more fluid, overlapping, and interwoven.[3] In particular, in the household, women are able to carve out their own space to have their own agency. They are able to counter and challenge patriarchal structures. Often, however, their agency does not mean a sisterhood of solidarity or feminist values that reject the masculine Camorra. Rather their behavior simply reinforces male criminal values and the clan. But these women do it on their own terms, they have their own ideas and their own agency. They are not the puppets of their men. They act like this because they believe in it.

Formally, the Camorra's local gender regime could be defined as patriarchal based on masculine values to the exclusion of women. It projects a masculine image, but this is more Camorra imaginary than fact. This is the image it projects to civil society, and it is the one civil society wants to see and accept. In reality, the Camorra's local gender regime is one based on the household where there are fluid arrangements of gender interaction and where a matriarchal model can become embedded. In this space, women have a voice, have an opinion, and can be respected because of the social capital they have gained there. This transfers into the Camorra allowing women to empower themselves to have agency to act and participate. Their agency, action, and involvement does not have to be a criminal act, but it does contribute to the criminal organization. This does not mean that the Camorra space is not a violent, brutish, and miserable place. It just means that the misogyny and gender inequality that is believed to govern the Camorra is in fact the rules and structures that govern Italian and Neapolitan civil society. Camorra masculinity is limited to the street; in the household it can be challenged and negotiated. The Camorra's local gender regime is gender fluid, flexible, with a lot of gender similarity.

In the Camorra, women can have roles as equal partners as has been suggested for other groups and markets.[4] In the Camorra's local gender regime, women are capable of navigating what looks like masculine structures but which in fact allow them to negotiate these criminal spaces to act. From the stories I collected, I can see that women can be successful in this environment not only because they are below the police/judicial radar but also because they are more discreet, efficient, effective, and risk averse. They fit into what is needed for the long-term survival of the family and clan because compared to men, they are less guided by self-interest and demonstrate more self-sacrifice for the collective good. Moreover, it is a recognized fact that "women work hard—twice as hard as men. All over the world, and for longer than records have been kept, that has been true."[5] Through my stories we can see the hard-working Camorra woman who operate and think for the collective, who provide support and assistance when needed for a criminal act or the criminal community. We also find strong, charismatic and powerful women who through the family find space to be successful in the Camorra as they have the social capital, capability, and intelligence to do so.[6]

So, the question arises as to why these women are not all victims and why they choose to become involved and accept the criminal Camorra life. This is a very relevant question because it is at the heart of understanding women's agency and how we explain their active and determined agency in the Camorra space. I suggest that there are a variety of reasons: either as a collective feeling of emotional attachment, of wanting money and a good life within the family setting (providing for others), or as part of an individual general survival strategy. In other words, women act and navigate the Camorra not as victims but as participants, they learn how to manage interpersonal formal and informal interactions in the household, but more importantly in the Camorra. Within more general societal patriarchal structures, these women are not held hostage to the Camorra group or individual members, but the capital and skills they collect in the family and household enable them to exist and survive in the crime group as recognized players. These dynamics are intricate and delicate to unpack but what is apparent is that women are not always victims without agency, and to consider them so removes our need to understand the complexity of their existence, their choices and how they can be helped.

The Public Sphere versus Private Sphere

When looking at the presence and roles of women in the Camorra, it soon became clear to me that there was a disjunction between public perception, institutional discourse, and reality. It is argued that Camorra women are irrelevant and unimportant. Where? How and to whom? Women are in fact present and active, but it depends on who is looking and where you are looking. When I zoomed in more meticulously on the Neapolitan postwar setting, the public sphere (NGOs, charities, the voluntary sector, and even the institutions) and the private sphere (family and friends) became a particularly important part of my analysis to explain the phenomenon. I soon realized that the repeated and accepted traditional narrative that in the Camorra women were agencyless and powerless and that they neither participated in criminal activities nor made criminal decisions, was the result of a constant male gaze, a male construct that was now presented as fact.

Siebert argues that the Sicilian and Calabrian mafias control the public and private spheres, which explains why they do not just "explicitly exclude women (whereas the public sphere is now accessible to both sexes) but also exert[s] a pervasive iron grip on the private sphere."[7] For the Neapolitan Camorra, things appear to be more subtle; the main difference is that the Camorra does not control nor dominate these two spheres and neither do men; women are present even though they are hidden by the men. The term *manosphere*, coined by Bates,[8] explains the Neapolitan public sphere but not the private sphere where the family and households are central. Understanding the specific dynamics of the Nea-politan private and public spheres (how they work, who is important, and what happens there) was essential for me to uncover and identify the true nature of the involvement and roles of women in the Camorra.

An influence that has to be considered in these spheres is religion. The Catho-lic religion is crucial in the Neapolitan private sphere. Without any question, the family is the most important institution of the private sphere and in Catho-lic teachings, fathers govern mothers and are esteemed. Therefore, Neapolitan and other southern Italian societies are often labeled "patriarchal" and based on familism. I dispute that this is the case in Naples and the South. Families and mothers are indispensable to the Neapolitan private sphere and this space is gen-dered. We could define this space as a *womenscape*, or even an *womenosphere*, where women have concrete influence and power.

Women in families are and remain paramount to the Camorra:

> Women as mothers play the central role here, forging, sustaining these relationships. Not surprisingly, women derive much of their self-esteem from their success in these tasks. This has important implications for women's agency, in that it is constrained by the practical and ideologi-cal conditions governing family life. But just as women uphold kinship and family and are limited by this responsibility, so too does the context of kinship offer different kinds of opportunities for women to exercise choice and control over their lives or push their potential to the limits of their circumstances.[9]

Essentially, to understand the Camorra, it is necessary to acknowledge the inter-penetration of the informal female-matriarchal private sphere "dominated by the figure of the mother"[10] with the formal male-patriarchal public sphere and how this plays out. I believe that women exist and dominate the private sphere, but that they become invisible in the patriarchal public sphere where men govern and dominate: "Discrimination against women occurs in the public sphere, whereas the private sphere is the place, par excellence, of women's power."[11]

The concept of a constructed "gendered society" permits us to frame the agency and power relations that explain why Neapolitan women are crucial play-ers in the Camorra, not only as loyal foot soldiers but also as headstrong leaders. They are the bedrock of this crime group.

Previous studies did not look closely enough at these gendered spheres, at the local culture and gender system to explain the role of women. We view the big-ger picture without looking at how the local public and private spheres may, in fact, shape and influence power relations. Despite the constructed male narrative, which tends to distort the situation and considers women as subordinate in both spheres, if we take a closer look at the Neapolitan gendered private sphere, we can see that women are equal partners.

The thrust of my argument remains that women have agency and power in the Neapolitan private sphere—where there is private governance—as this space is dominated by kinship, matriarchy, and religious structures. Perhaps it is an unacknowledged matriarchy, but it is matriarchy nevertheless, where women in the family as mothers are powerful actors as carers, advisers, helpers, and providers. Vincenzo Pirozzi articulates this point very succinctly when he explains that "I come from a matriarchal family because my father was always in prison, and I lived with my mother's family: seven sisters and two brothers. The head of the family was my grandmother, because my grandfather who led the family and brought the money home, died when I was only nine years old. From that day onwards, it was my grandmother who managed and organized the family but in reality, in many aspects, she has always been the true driving force."[12] The family becomes "an area of safety" governed by women.[13]

Indeed, since the 1861 Unification, Neapolitan civil society has constructed and portrayed a traditional patriarchal image of its society, structures, and institutions. But rhetoric and reality are very different. The Neapolitan public sphere is constantly represented as a patriarchal, patrilineal, and patricentric space where the father and male lines dominate the family structure, with wives and daughters being subordinates in the background. Man is the basic and main actor with women being insignificant. Laura Letto recalls her father's education and his patriarchal principles: "*He bought us up thinking that it is always the man who commands and who decides. And therefore, it is the father who rules. . . . A simple example, for all the money I had, if I wanted to go on holiday abroad, I was not free to decide whether to go on holiday. He always decided what I could and could not do.*"[14] He appeared and behaved as a traditional padre padrone, a father-boss.[15]

This was his worldview when in reality his women (his daughter, his ex-wife, his partner, and his lover) were fully involved in his clan and were not just auxiliaries.[16] Here, it is a man's world that dominates every level of society and discourse, without it being questioned. This maybe is merely an illusion. Men dominate to a certain extent the public sphere, and they think that they dominate the private sphere, but this is not systematically the case.

"Hegemonic masculinity" maybe an unhelpful concept here because it suggests that patriarchy and masculinity shape and influence all sectors of Neapolitan civil society, including the Camorra underworld, when I believe that these are negotiated spaces where power can be challenged, in particular, in the private sphere and in the household. In these spaces, different gender dynamics can be at play, which can explain why women may, in fact, have more power than is believed because they negotiate and contest the hegemonic masculine structures to empower themselves to act.

The Neapolitan private sphere is a female space, setting, and location, not a male-exclusive space and not a patriarchal and chauvinistic one. It is not a male-only society, whereas the Neapolitan public sphere remains dominated by men. In the family, the private space is the basic structure of the Camorra clans, from which criminal power is determined and which explains why women have an important role. Their family power overflows into the public sphere but it is rarely noted for what it is. This does not mean that domestic violence and abuse of women do not exist in the private sphere. But women manage to forge out a space where they can become respected, cherished, and esteemed. The private sphere is constantly neglected and ignored by many studies on organized crime because it is seen as irrelevant and, in any case, overrun by the public sphere.

On the contrary, I want to rethink and clarify which sphere we are talking about. The public sphere relies on the private sphere and so we need to analyze these interlinked relationships thoroughly to understand fully the power relations and domination that exist between people. So, first, these overlapping and interconnected relationships. Perhaps the boundaries are not as clear cut as is commonly believed and looking at them as interconnected gendered spaces might be more helpful to understand the power dynamics in Neapolitan criminal families.

When men go to prison, it is the women who visit and collect the instructions, which are then distributed to clan members on the outside. The private sphere of the family and women is completely hidden because, in the public sphere, it is the men who distribute instructions. Women are seen as the passive representatives of their menfolk, but this is far from the truth. Reality is more nuanced. For bosses who have been in prison for a long time, women are their lifeline to the outside world. Laura explained to me how she did not just fill her father's shoes:

> In the end, when my father was not there, even if I was the daughter of . . . I thought with my head. He was no longer there if he said, for example, the gun must be hidden in the floor. For me, the gun had to be hidden in another place, I hid it in another place because I was thinking with my own head. I am doing crime my way, I am managing the clan my way, I am managing the clan my way with my priorities, and no longer [his].[17]

Another good example is the murder of Maurizio Lutricuso, aged twenty-four. In 2016, he was murdered in the early hours, in Pozzuoli outside a night club, by young members of a city clan after an altercation about a cigarette. As the Polizia di Stato investigated the murder and one of the clan members went to the hospital because he had been shot in the foot, the women of the clan became active and responded to the needs of the male clan members who sought to organize and rationalize their approach to what had happened. One wife went straight to the police station in the middle of the night to gain information about the ongoing police investigation in order to give advice to the clan members, while other partners kept constantly in touch via SMS with the men who were on the run, to make sure that things were okay.[18]

When analyzing the Camorra, the importance of the private/public spheres dynamics must be taken into account. I hope I have shown that one must recognize the gender dynamics in these spheres and how they work: in other words, the local gender orders and regimes. The closer I looked, the more I could see that these spheres were particularly gendered: women in the private sphere, men in the public sphere; women have their own agency, which was autonomous from their men. It is these gendered spheres and interactions that give or not space to Neapolitan women in the Camorra. It is not the crime structure, market, or individuals that shape criminal roles, but the space and interactions women have in the private sphere that determine whether they manage to engage with or to dominate different power relations in the Camorra. This private sphere is so vibrant and forceful that it enables women not only to challenge the patriarchy in the household but empowers them to have their own agency in the criminal underworld. Their agency is in no way a sisterhood or a form of feminist liberation; if anything their agency upholds and reinforce the existing overarching patriarchal structures.

Masculine versus Feminine Roles and Values

An established and dominant narrative holds "that men and women are naturally different and have different intelligences, physical abilities, and emotional traits."[19] In the case of the Camorra, the image that is continuously perpetuated is one of weak and risk-averse Camorra women, with the odd exception, here and there. Although civil society and its traditional institutions (church, schools, media, to name but a few) dictate and reinforce the differences between the male and female values and roles, I found that on the ground these are interchangeable and that this division and the concept of male-domination are constructed.

The experiences of many Camorra women challenge the traditional binary gender roles established by civil society; their experiences challenge the notions of masculinities and femininities. This needs to be recognized not only in terms of leadership roles but also in their everyday duties and tasks. Biology may determine our physical sex, but civil society constructs our gender. Only behavior directly linked to procreation can be described as "masculine" and "feminine."

All the rest must be understood as culturally and socially constructed. Indeed, since the story of Adam and Eve, men and women have been put into socially constructed gender-specific categories in terms of their roles, behavior, and values. Traditionally, men and the notions of masculinity, maleness, manhood, manliness, or virility are seen in terms of being strong, dominant, brave, self-confident, competitive, assertive, aggressive, independent, and non-emotional whereas women, womanliness, or girlishness are considered weak, empathic, tender, kind, passive, gentle, sensitive, vulnerable, nurturing, and affectionate. In this way, people are socialized into gendered roles from an early age and branded with specific behavior and values. These socially constructed roles and values have been defined as "soft" in contrast to the "strong" roles and values identified as male. This has a constraining effect on our understanding because as Messerschmidt argues, "Criminology does not have the theoretical language capable of representing violence by women except to view it as totally abnormal; the view of violence by women is based on the view of male violence as 'macho, tough, aggressive.'"[20] However, I hope that my stories have illustrated how gender roles in the Camorra are more fluid than commonly believed and that there is much more similarity than differences.

In terms of masculine or feminine values, we can see how this works and how it has conditioned women's behavior rather than accepting that values are nongender specific and can be easily applied to different genders. For mafias, there has always been a narrative about "men being men" and "women being women"; traditional gender values have been applied inaccurately during the postwar period in order to reinforce the notions that mafia women were weak and vulnerable whereas mafiosi were strong, intelligent, and resilient.

Even Camorra women reinforce these stereotypes: Mariella Manca explained to me how she came to lead her clan: "*They never understood by themselves that I was a woman and that they were men. They made me behave like a man and they behaved like women.*"[21] In other words, in the clan values are fluid and do not reflect reality. Another example are the notions of honor and omertà, which have always been explained in relation to manhood and masculinity without trying to understand whether these notions cannot also belong to the female sphere, which they clearly can. Yet, another point of view, that of Angela Giallo, questions the very basis of these traditional stereotypes by stating that "*women are like men.*"[22] But as already argued, these clear-cut values may be unhelpful for the Camorra and an oversimplification.

Quite a lot has also been written about masculinity and masculine values in relation to female gang members, perhaps less about Italian mafia women. Most discussion has focused on the male-exclusive characteristics of the Italian mafias.[23] All the elements of masculinity block and renegade the feminine:

"Masculine ideology [and] mafia ideology exalts brotherhood between 'real men,' soldiers and combatants" thus highlighting how mafias have "contempt for the feminine" and "a radical ambivalence in relation to the feminine."[24] In other words, mafias are antiwomen and refute womanhood. Although mafia women "are always present," they are marginalized and excluded and become foreigners in the public sphere and are relegated to the private sphere, which is considered by many as an insignificant social space.[25]

It has also been argued that the complex relationship between gangs and women means that women must use masculine values and undertake "gender crossing" to be accepted.[26] Thus, women identify as male gang members if they want to be "one of the guys."[27] Others argue that young women construct a form of "bad girl femininity," which challenges traditional gender roles whereby they resort to violence and honor to gain status among male gang members.[28] Another approach suggests that women behave violently or "look bad" as part of a protective strategy to survive as they are at the bottom of the gang hierarchy.

We therefore have contrasting explanations. On the one hand, Italian mafias deny women their femininity and are antiwomen, while, on the other, the gang literature suggests that women seeking to gain status and recognition among their peers adopt masculine values to fit in and to be one of the guys. Neither of these analyses fits the new evidence I have collected.

In the case of the Camorra, Gribaudi argues that there is a "a man-woman social space in which moral codes, practices and roles fade into a nuanced continuum, from which people are free to glean elements with which to construct their own identity, even deciding to choose one that does not match their biological sex. This too is a feature of Neapolitan clans." She explains:

> Traditional codes of honor are certainly of no use to us in understanding the male-female relations within these criminal groups. The model followed by these women is not the "feminine" one of modesty and reserve (shame), but the manly one based on "respect," arrogance, and threat. . . . They [women] race around the neighborhood on powerful scooters, just like their male relatives. They are prepared to use violence personally, often taking up arms, and are ready to face prison no less than their husbands. And they give in to repentance much less often than their husband[s].[29]

Zaccaria elaborates on how Camorra women interpret male values: "It is clear that these [Camorra] women are able to translate feminine resources [physical beauty, charm, determination, organizing and managerial skills, blood kinship] into criminal resources, at times using violence without shame and playing on the double register/entente of tradition/modernity. But there is more."[30]

This suggests that men and women have different values which they use differently. She contrasts the values of the leader of the Moccia clan from Afragola in the province of Naples, Anna Mazza, to show how she uses them for the clan's benefit as well as her own. She "offers protection and solidarity, connecting with residents of the district, entering their homes. She presents herself as a godmother and witness to their weddings when they ask. This emotional bond provides at the same time for the Moccia clan a guarantee of loyalty and a recognition of power."[31]

The women of Ponticelli and Nunzia D'Amico are good examples of Gribaudi's male-female crime continuum: they use both masculine and feminine values and roles in their criminal identity.[32] Angela Giallo, our drug dealer from Ponticelli, elaborates on this when she suggests that these "[Camorra] *women wanted to be men*" because it was Neapolitan civil society that saw men as violent camorristi and to be recognized as a valid camorrista, you had to behave like a man: "*What I know is that women were supposed to cook Bolognese sauce.*[33] *They had to cook Sunday lunch. But now, women wanted to be men. They wanted to shoot, they wanted to kill, they wanted to do the same* [as the men]."[34] It is Neapolitan civil society that produces gender inequality, and this becomes gender differences in the Camorra. It is the public and private spheres that are considered male and, which as a result, project ideas and notions that are perpetually reinforced about weak and vulnerable females and strong and powerful men. However, Angela goes on to explain that her boss, Nunzia D'Amico, was "*a real Mafia woman. She's a man, she not a woman. She was a man. She just had to open her mouth and people would tremble in their shoes.*"[35] Moreover, "*she was always like that. She always managed her brother's affairs. She was always a girl who ran a Camorra business. Your life was in her hands. If she decided that you had to die, you would die, she wouldn't even ponder the idea.*"[36]

I believe very much that the Camorra is not a gendered organization because "the control, identity, meaning, actions, emotions and advantage" are not "patterned by distinguishing between male and female."[37] As I have already argued, a Camorra cultural value system exists in which values are appropriated and transformed into criminal values and resources by its members. These values are then transformed by both men and women and no such clear distinct gender values can be identified. Women use, understand, and appropriate these values, such as vendetta, honor, omertà, violence, and betrayal.

From my evidence, I would argue that Camorra masculine and feminine values and roles are fluid, interchangeable, and cannot be rigidly applied. Gribaudi correctly explains that the Camorra has always been more "gender fluid" compared to other Italian mafias.[38] The boss Mariella Manca argues that "*if a woman knows how to behave in certain ways, there is no difference between a man and a woman . . . because they have the same charisma; actually women have even a bit more. If a woman wants to, she can get everywhere.*"[39] The binary gender system is constructed by local society to reinforce the traditional status quo that "men should be men," strong and "women should be women," weak. As we have seen, Neapolitan cultural codes are very conventional and traditionalist. The Catholic culture, although declining in importance, still influences and shapes the outlook of many Neapolitans (for instance, homosexuality seen as a disease; the traditional roles of women; the importance of religious rituals such as christening, communion, and marriage).

Evidence for the Camorra shows that this is no longer applicable if it ever was. Violence and revenge are modern Camorra values that are interpreted by all, not only young men. These masculine versus feminine values have always been juxtaposed as separate, competing especially when it comes to the Camorra space, but this is not the case. There are many images of Camorra women being compliant and submissive to a so-called male criminal project when in fact they are the motor of the whole criminal operation.

Nunzia D'Amico is a classic example. It has been suggested that she sought to be a man with her masculine and violent behavior and her fondness for tattoos. Tattoos are perceived as symbols of virility and only belonging to the male domain. And yet, tattoos are not only for young men. Many women also have tattoos to underline and reinforce their total loyalty to the clan and its values.[40] As a tough leader Nunzia D'Amico wanted to be a better boss than her other male competitors. She had her own ideas and her own vision, she was self-confident, assertive, and aggressive about who controlled her neighborhood when she stated, "*We decide here, not him.*"[41] At the same time, she also lived her femininity to the full without the need to masculinize herself to gain status or to be respected by male clan members because her femininity was respected, loved, and admired. She had five children and was very feminine with black dyed hair, a tiny silhouette and sexy clothes like many other women from her district. She argued that "*I am a woman because externally I am a woman but inside, I feel like a man . . . I am no one's chick, and I have never been the woman of someone.*"[42]

She shows that masculine identity and female identity live side by side and intertwine, not conforming with traditional categories. Values are fluid and cohabit in different spaces and locations, not just among closed groups of men or women. Camorra women can be very sexy, sensual, and handsome while at the same time assertive, strong, and violent. They continuously look after their appearance with weekly visits to the hairdresser, manicures, and pedicures but when required can be forceful, bold, and violent.

Women can be just as evil, spiteful, power and money hungry, resentful, and unforgiving as men. Indeed, women want to show that they are just as good as men and show their hard side because that is what is important in Neapolitan society. There are many examples of women who appear cold and indifferent to emotions, lacking empathy, and even being complicit in the planning and elimination of their own partners: one woman was fully involved in the murder of her husband by her brothers, the leaders of the clan, while in another clan, one woman had her lover murdered by the local clan, but she carried on living in the district as though nothing happened and without it openly seeming to have an impact on her life.[43]

A revealing case is that women are just as fascinated by guns as men; they give out orders for murders as well as physically beating up and intimidating both female and male rivals. A good example of this is demonstrated by a small city clan. During 2014, this small clan from Forcella was led by three women and a brother-in-law.[44] They together ordered the murder of a young rival: one of the women ordered the crime, another was a lookout and the other hid the firearms. They even coined their road the "*street of death*" to underline what they did best, murder. It was a woman who ordered that Piero "*should be taken out*" and murdered.[45] This sentence uttered by a woman, summarizes all the evil, hate, and violence that women can have toward a rival clan. There were other Camorra women who took on manlike behavior and even became partners with other women. "'*A masculona*," "Big Man" is such an example. She became the partner of the widow of a local boss murdered in 2006.[46] Together, they led the clan and fought a war against a rival clan.[47] It shows that at all levels in the clans, women can "demonstrate" masculine values. The values of assertiveness, violence, innovation, and competition are not exclusively masculine as represented by newspaper articles and judicial and police investigations and can be equally applied to men and women.

It is striking to note how vigorous women can be against state witnesses, showing maybe more strength of character than their male counterparts. They have been the most assertively outspoken against them to protect clan members from "turning" and collaborating with the state. Even women not necessarily directly and fully involved in a clan have been ruthless. When the estranged wife of an important boss from the Casertano found out that her husband wanted to become a state witness, she did everything in her power to block him from siding with the state. She was outspoken, assertive, and clear: she would block his every move to collaborate with the state. Even his grown-up daughter stated that he should know that she would go and prostitute herself in the main piazza of Casal di Prinicipe if he abandoned the Camorra.[48] In 1998, Maria Licciardi, leader of the Secondigliano Alliance, who saw the potential danger of a former member and ally, Constantino Sarno, becoming a state witness, sought to buy him off.[49] She was arrested on her way to meet him, and it was discovered that she was going to offer him "*un millardo di lire*," a billion lire, to retract.[50] More recently, the Pazzignane clan have also adopted similar strategies to dissuade members from abandoning their clan.[51]

Beside expressing extreme loyalty to the clan, women feel entitled to receive respect back from clan members as wives. For instance, they automatically expect to receive their husband's salaries while they are in prison. In the Nuvoletta-Polverino clan, in 2015, some of the wives of the newly arrested members complained arrogantly about being abandoned by the clan and receiving no salary. On one occasion, Marina received only a hundred euros for her husband being in prison and sent them back in protest. On another occasion, Stefania implored her husband to make it clear to the clan that every Friday she should be able to go to the butcher and be given meat free of charge. In a city clan in 2019, the female relatives of some of the leaders made extravagant financial demands, expecting 500 euros a week, when the clan was in financial difficulty. They only slowly backed down and accepted a bit less money.[52] Eva is another useful example. She was the mistress of a subleader of the Moccia clan in Afragola. While her partner was in prison, it was his wife who helped him to manage his underlings. When he was released, he went and lived with his mistress and their child, leaving his wife.[53] His mistress, Eva, actively took over his wife's role and more. Many members noted her sense of entitlement and pompous behavior. She was arrogant and self-important in the way she managed instructions and the distribution of money.[54]

In the running of the clan's criminal activities, it is assumed that it is the bosses who are the driving force. My reading of the situation is different: it is actually the women who are innovative and creative compared to their male counterparts. The clans from Torre Annunziata and Ercolano have proved to be particularly innovational. Over the years, the Gionta clan adopted various original survival strategies that have proved very effective.[55] More recently, to facilitate the communication between the bosses in prison and the outside world, "a Gionta code" was developed in 2018.[56] It consisted of women organizing the prisoners to write instructions and orders for clan members on labels inside clothes that were then given to female relatives to be washed outside prison. In this way, messages passed from inside the prison to the outside world. There are also the more traditional techniques of women hiding and storing firearms and drugs in unusual places such as in the D'Amico clan, Mazzarella clan, or Elia clan.[57] These examples show that women have just as many creative ideas as their men.

The same can be said about the development of business strategies. When one looks closely at the different aspects of business activities one can see that women are just as competitive, if not more, as the men. Sisterhood is far from present, especially at the levels of the drug dealing piazzas. Nicoletta was ruthlessly competitive about her drug business, so much so that she led one of her rivals into a trap where she was murdered by the leaders of the Sarno clan because she started to collaborate with the state.[58] Why she did this can only be explained by her strong competitive nature and her survival instinct in the clan although she insists that she did not know what they had planned.[59]

Rather than arguing that women transform their female values into criminal values, I suggest the Camorra culture value system is one in which men and women interpret traditional values and transform them into criminal values that become forms of capital. I would argue that in the Camorra masculine and feminine values are not fixed nor binary. Civil society for too long has projected its image of traditional masculine and feminine onto the Camorra. Now, we need to question whether these gendered values are helpful in the context of Naples and organized crime in general.

Violence versus Negotiation

The notion of violence and the argument that Camorra violence is male only is a blanket argument used to the detriment of Camorra women and their agency. This argument suggests that these women are innocent and weak bystanders who are rarely involved in violent acts or involved in instigating them. This is an unfair portrayal but one that can be understood if we look at the facts. Italian statistics (2018–19) do show us that indeed murder is a male affair, with 96.6 percent of those sentenced between 2018 and 2019 being men compared to 3.4 percent who were women. The victims are also men: 204 men compared with 111 female.[60]

So, we need to unpack the term and meaning of violence in the Camorra context. Perhaps we need to consider mafia violence as gendered and nuanced, as this may help us to see women's violent features rather than condemning them to insignificance because they are not overtly nor visibly violent. For example, it is suggested that that men are more likely to react to social triggers, be aggressive, and use physical violence, leading to possible beatings and murder, compared to women. Whereas men might react more violently to certain situations, this does not make women less violent. Women's violence might more than just physical, it may also be psychological violence that they may use more freely and extensively compared to men.

In the criminal underworld, violence is a cherished value and a necessary resource that is most commonly associated with masculinity; it is a male value. Many scholars have identified it as the main explanation as to why women are excluded from OCGs, in other words, because of their so-called physical inability to do violence, women are thus subordinate to men. For a long time, there has been a general argument that women are less violent than men; this case has been made particularly for women in street gangs and OCGs, although it is now recognized that girls in street gangs can be violent.[61] In the criminal underworld, it is suggested that women use "soft skills," including negotiations rather than violence, to survive. Maybe they are more violence averse, want to take less risks, and think more, but we should also note that they do regularly order violent acts, beatings and even murders.

It is argued that "the ability to use violence to control and manage volatile situations is probably the most important defining element that relegates women to the margins of most illicit networks."[62] Women lack such qualities, they "have less exposure to opportunities for the display and use of violence and the mastery of weapons." An exception is in human smuggling networks, because these networks rely "on personal connections rather than violence."[63] Thus, it seems that women are more involved in human smuggling networks than in other criminal activities such as drug importation and dealing where violent confrontations are more frequent.

For the Camorra, it has been long and repeatedly argued that "violence cannot be delegated permanently. . . . As long as [Camorra] women need to delegate violence I doubt that matriarchy will replace patriarchy in mafia or camorra groups."[64] It is constantly suggested that women involved in Camorra violence are one-off, exceptional or "unique occurrence[s]" from which we cannot draw "precipitous conclusion[s]."[65]

Looking at my evidence and in the specific context of Naples and Campania, I have found this to be untrue and, in particular, that in the private sphere violence perpetuated by women does exist, physical and psychological. Women can also be violent in the street if we look close enough. We have difficulty talking about women as perpetrators of violence, but it is there whether they hand out beatings to relatives of state witnesses to intimidate them or seek out mistresses of clan members to publicly humiliate and rebuff them. Following the violent acts, the code of silence, omertà, kicks in and is respected so they get away with it. Women can be very determined, strong willed, and vindictive, they do not forget inappropriate behavior of clan members, and when necessary, they use violence for the clan's long-term survival or to resolve internal disputes. From this, they do not shy away.

Camorra women at all levels of clan activities command and use violence to impose their wills, whether for their criminal or personal projects. "It is not only in Naples city that the Camorra women are so ruthless."[66] Indeed, Camorra women in the city and province use violence when it is necessary to achieve their criminal objectives. Sometimes they use it in a symbolic way to give messages to their rivals but usually they use it to resolve clan-related issues. Often, for example, they are vital members of the support team providing crucial assistance to the killing squads, even if they don't directly pull the trigger. What is clear is that women are fully aware of their clan's violent and murderous projects, involved, and approve of them. This fact is consistently ignored or belittled in mainstream studies on the Camorra and organized crime, probably because they are only mothers, wives, daughters or sisters.

Women who get involved in the Camorra take it for granted that violence can be part of their way of life, either to survive or to demonstrate power. In many cases, girls grow up seeing and being victims of violence, thus becoming used to it. In this way, violence becomes "normalized." Fiora, the sister of a camorrista and sister-in-law of another important boss during the 1980s, like many other women, was regularly beaten by her husband because he had to show who was boss. Violence was also mentioned in the Giuliano clan: Luigi Giuliano, boss of the family, hit his niece while one of the daughters of another female leader was beaten up by a friend.[67]

Women leaders and managers often do not need to use violence themselves. There are many cases of women involved in the strategic planning of murders in which the actual act is carried out by killers. Nevertheless, they are capable of killing, when and if necessary. They can have a killer instinct like their male counterparts.

Margherita is a good case. She used violence. She was the wife of an alleged member of a local clan in Naples. While he was in prison, she had an extramarital affair with a younger lover from the Casalesi Confederation, who decided to leave her. In October 2018, she shot him dead in his car, not only because he no longer wanted to be with her but also because he had tried to steal some money from a company belonging to her camorrista husband. He had tried to be too clever, and Margherita did not hesitate to punish him for her own honor, love, and that of her brothers.[68]

For foot soldiers at the lower levels of the clan, violence is used as a free and frequent resource to impose the will of the clan and its rules. For example, Angela Giallo beat the clients who did not show her respect and wanted to pay less for a dose. She explains, "*I did it because I had to show it* [violence] . . . *if you are in the Camorra you have to be violent.*"[69] Other female clan members used baseball bats to get their way and to impose their laws on locals who challenged them.[70]

Women are aware that violence is not everything, and there are other skills they can and must use to navigate the Camorra space and criminal activities. As Laura remarked, you need more to be successful. She is very clear about the need to be thoughtful and intelligent in what you do. Whereas some women leaders such as Nunzia D'Amico (see chapter 7) were more prone to use violence, others used a more compromising and negotiated approach, which does not mean that they cannot order or use violence when they feel it is necessary or required.

Power versus Weakness

Power can be complex to define, but I hope this study has shown that power is multidimensional. Power in Italian mafias has always been identified as "male power" but in the case of the Camorra (and in the other Italian mafias too) power can also be "female power."

In this study, we have seen that women have different forms of power. They have power in the private sphere: power to influence and shape thinking, organize activities, and mold behavior. This also flows into the public sphere where men formally control relationships. "*Spending time with them, I believe that you acquire power*," says Laura Letto.[71] This is more than just the "temporary delegation of power" that Dino talks about.[72]

A crucial form of power is sex. It is rarely discussed but plays an important role, especially for women. In the case of men, they are often celebrated and respected for having mistresses: "Promiscuity for men is seen as actually preserving family unity since the implicit principle of the code is that 'boys will be boys.' Mafia men have mistresses, as men of power and influence often do."[73]

For a male camorrista to have a lover is a symbol of power. It is perceived as a positive fact and a sign of virility in the local community. Indeed, all bosses need to appear to be sexually powerful, even if this hurts their partner. When Giorgia Verde realized her husband had a lover, she was very upset. The sexual promiscuity of male camorristi is a common theme among journalists who constantly valorize this behavior: a top city boss had a particularly expensive mistress and the leader of the Caselese Confederation had two American lovers from the local NATO base. On the contrary, the sexual promiscuity of Camorra women is not considered in the same way: they are seen as *puttane* or *cagne*, prostitutes or whores. They are often ostracized by the local community for a while and have to beg for forgiveness in order to be accepted in again. Indeed, the image we have of Camorra women is that they are expected to remain faithful and loyal to their husbands locked up in prisons for years. Many women fit into this traditional model of obedience, loyalty, and servitude based on the image of marriage in the Catholic institution. Catholic teachings reinforce and work with Camorra values.

However, this is only a very small part of the wider picture. Women are never to stray or be tempted elsewhere, which for young women of sixteen to seventeen years of age is not necessarily easy. They are expected to become nuns waiting for their husbands to come out of prison or visit them forever onward because they are serving a life sentence. Those who remain totally faithful today are perhaps from a different generation, as Angela Giallo suggested: "*I think that only the older, traditional women respect. . . . a man, who is doing many years in jail. It is difficult for a woman . . . they would wait for him like gold. He's in jail for 20 years. He's in jail for 30 years."*[74]

Camorra men in the public sphere may seek to impose their so-called patriarchal model, but in fact Camorra women are sexually liberated and do what they want even if this results in dire consequences. Camorra women have asserted their sexual freedom, liberation, and power by for example, having extramarital affairs, even if the clan calls them to order, as was the case for Mariella Manca when her brothers-in-law beat her up for having a lover. When Nunzia D'Amico found out that her sister-in-law was cheating on her brother, she *"took it badly and beat her up."*[75] Same reaction to Angela Giallo's behavior when she had a new boyfriend while her husband was in prison doing time. She was threatened and told *"you are not a faithful wife."*[76]

Although rarely mentioned, I believe that Camorra women are in control of their sexual desires and gratification. This empowers them and means that they have power over their own bodies and destiny, which challenges traditional male power. Angela explains, *"Of course, they* [wives] *visit their husband in jail, but then their boyfriend is outside waiting for them. If the Hotel Faraone* [in Ponticelli] *could speak to you, so many women, wives. . . . In Ponticelli, if you could see how many wives of bosses went there, you'd say 'I really can't believe it.'"*[77]

So sexual obedience, one of the main values of patriarchy, has always been seriously challenged by Camorra women. Recently, it was revealed that Rita Longo had an affair with her daughter's husband, while Giorgia Verde also found comfort in a younger relative while her husband was in prison.[78]

Widowhood of course provides more freedom and fewer chains. Valeria Nunzo is a classic example; she had no constraining marital obligations and had a lover, moved in with him despite the fact that he was living with his wife.[79] When the widow of the brother of a boss from the Casalesi Confederation took on a new lover, the boss did not approve and tried to block her receiving her husband's salary from the clan.[80]

Traditional versus Modern Camorra Women

In the postwar period, there has been an ongoing debate about the traditional and modern Camorras. Traditional Camorra values centered on integrity, honesty, self-defense, generosity, honor, reputation, respect of rules, no violence, and hard work while modern Camorra values are greed, money, instant gratification, and violence. Both these sets of values have been labelled "masculine," but we can see that women respect and enact them on a daily basis.

Moreover, there is a delicate balance between the two systems and how women represent the contradiction of this hybrid Camorra, the Camorra that is both traditional and modern at the same time. Gribaudi argued that "these women reinterpret figures, roles and social codes whose root lies in a history and a tradition."[81] But, women, more than anyone in the Camorra, combine both traditional values and modern ways to create a vibrant and resilient criminal organization. Values include respect, honor, and revenge, but Laura Letto explains that "*the main basic value is to defend the weak*," describing a Robin Hood version of the Camorra to justify its violent behavior that women feel particularly in tune with.[82] Indeed, it is often argued that Camorra women are the most traditionalist of all, not wanting any form of change. Luciana Esposito has often explained how "the Camorra mothers of *Ponticelli* hold onto the notion of *omertà* and repeatedly tell her that if you want to help us, don't talk about the Camorra."[83] In other words, keep silent and shut up, perpetuating omertà.

Although the Camorra's cultural value system is evolving, Camorra women's values are still very much based on core traditional values, which remain strong and embedded in the local context. Rita Longo complained, "*I got angry with my partner because he had shown me no respect as the mother of his children and as a wife, I had lost everything.*"[84]

This is, in contrast with the younger generation of the so-called baby gangs who have

> a mentality that is completely different from the old school. For them, it's money, drugs . . . the only thing that matters for them is designer trousers, designer shirts . . . do you understand? And that's exactly what young people today are lacking, they don't have principles. For them killing a person for drugs is normal. 'Ah, you didn't pay me this thing?' To the wall! Or 'you annoy me. I don't like you'. They don't have any human values at all.[85]

One aspect of modernity that Camorra women seem to embrace is the use of new e-technologies. Social media are becoming more and more frequently used in Camorra clans, in particular to insult rivals and see what they are doing. The use of technology varies from simply using computers to playing video games as a way of relaxing and talking on social media: ("*They played video games at home using laptops and discussed various issues*") to a modern form of communication with clan members using social media.[86] Clans need to fill this virtual space with strong, aspirational, and symbolic messages. On social media, images of luxurious foreign holidays, evenings in night clubs, visits to VIP shops, and dinners in expensive restaurants are regularly posted to show young members the lifestyle they can aspire to. These carefully selected images are full of meaning, transforming clan members into idols and martyrs that can be admired by members inside and outside of prison. Camorra women also use social media like everyone else.

In common with the younger generation of men, women (including older women) use Facebook and Instagram to speak to each other and to those who are looking in but mainly to communicate inside a clan. Women do this to show off their lifestyles, their children, their wealth, and their grandchildren to each other while young men have used Facebook as a virtual piazza where clan members can insult and provoke each other. A specific form of communication appears; it is more a one-way exchange, a loudspeaker, rather than a channel of two-way friendly communication. This platform is often used to threaten and to intimidate rivals and women (for instance, former and potential girlfriends).[87]

In one case, a member of the Giuliano clan insulted and threatened the mother of his child as she left him. He encouraged his friends to do the same. In another, the sister-in-law of an important boss from the eastern suburbs of Naples, both under the state witness protection program, used Facebook in another and more imaginative way. In 2018, they streamed a live Facebook chat from their protected location at a bar taking a coffee and talking directly to their relatives who disagreed with their life choice as well as the local community.[88] Important coded messages full of symbolism and power were exchanged. She led the discussion.

YouTube has also been functionally used to give out coded messages. A good example is "the diva." She is an older lady who lives in the suburbs and appears to be close to clan members.[89] In the past, she has posted seven to eight videos on YouTube. They last a couple of minutes each and present her thoughts on different hot topics, such as what she thinks about the local state witnesses, and of what is going on in the criminal underworld. Her videos are powerful messages to clan members and the local community on what is what.

"Camorra 3.0" or "Criminal Google generation" are terms used to describe the latest modern and technologically advanced Camorra.[90] They have been explained as a way for male youngsters to get the most "likes" and to dominate in this virtual city; here they can spread their "toxic masculinity." Described as a male space, the online world is one where more and more young and aspiring male camorristi show off their qualities, skills, and their lifestyle. It is important for them to do this for their onlooking rivals, as they strut and preen in their branded clothes, their cars, and their Rolexes. Not only is this an online theater to put oneself in motion and be seen by others, but it also becomes a virtual battlefield where verbal abuse and provocations become common before breaking out onto the street or vice versa. TikTok rather than Facebook or Instagram has now become the common platform.

Women are also very active in this virtual world. They openly and publicly assert themselves in this new online world. They have clearly adapted to innovations in technology and use this medium to reinforce the power of the Camorra in this virtual territory where your appearance, your branded clothes, your choice of words, and the number of likes and from whom becomes vital not only for clan members but also for law enforcement agencies looking in. Domination of the digital world through TikTok is becoming a crucial existential tool for the Camorra and its women to affirm their power. Law enforcement agencies have started to develop internet and social media experts to analyze the cyber world of camorristi, to understand the power dynamics, the messages, and the possible repercussions out in the real world. Women are at the heart of this online world.

Agency versus Passivity

When I started to take a closer look at women in criminal organizations, one thing that struck me was the constant male gaze (whether by women or men) being used to analyze the role and presence of women. They were either portrayed as "victims" or "subjects." As far as I could see, there was one clear concept that was missing from the debate around women's involvement in criminal activities, that is, the notion of "agency." Nowhere could I find women having their own agency, or having it acknowledged as such. In other words, their own female capacity to act without external help, suggestions, or patronage. Women in the literature and judicial-police reports were never in control of their own criminal activities. They totally lacked their own agency and were in complete subordination to men.

Recently, Ingrasci who studied women in the Sicilian Cosa Nostra and the Calabrian 'Ndrangheta did elaborate on the notion of agency.[91] She broke it down into three different forms of agency: conformist, compliant, and transformative. She argues that, as well as vulnerabilities, women have "soft powers" that they have started to use in these different forms of agency. Ultimately, she argues that there were general indicators—"the persistence of patriarchal relations and women's economic dependence, temporary allocation of power to women during periods of emergency, use of female labor in low profile jobs, and exclusion of women from career opportunities—which suggested that the increasing public presence of women in the mafias, beyond mere supportive and private roles, was the result of a process of female pseudo-emancipation."[92] I do not believe that the term *agency* can or should be broken down because women either act of their own accord on their own initiative or they are forced or intimated to do so by others and therefore, this becomes pressurized, forced behavior.

The term *agency* has no real antonym, perhaps the word *nonparticipant* could be useful, but this does not really capture the total indifference as opposed to active positive agency. Perhaps the dichotomy active (agency) versus passive (nonparticipant) renders this difference better. So, agency must be seen as being hands-on, active immersed participation, influencing others, speaking out, undertaking intentional and explicit acts that women have decided by their own volition. For me, thus, agency can only be an absolute term and doesn't have various levels of agency: agency means initiating and deciding to act of one's own accord without the influence of (male) others. You cannot have negative agency whereas you can be a nonparticipant with tacit complicity, and your presence can be a form of approval and support even though you do not actively participate. This indeed is a very delicate and nuanced debate.

From the evidence, there are different types of Camorra women, not only women actively involved in Camorra activities but also women who are there, passively, and acquiescently, living a neutral presence in a complex criminal space. These women appear to live a parallel existence to that of the clan and its members, but in the same criminal space. However, these Camorra women, who live in the same Camorra space, underpin the group's presence and activities and are a shadow on proceedings and developments. Their presence is never neutral; even indifference is a form of complicity and acceptance in that Camorra space. There are different forms of agency, neutrality, passivity, and cohabitation.

When thinking about the role of women, agency is vital to consider and to recognize here. For too long, Camorra women have been denied their own agency and intelligence. Women have agency in their victimhood but not in their criminality. Women make decisions in the Camorra and have been doing so since its beginning. For too long, Camorra women have been downgraded to second-rate citizens by male scholars and investigators. For too long, we have all believed the narrative that the Camorra and institutions have fed us, but also that Neapolitan and Italian society has projected for us.

The more one thinks about the role of women in the Camorra, the more one realizes that participation-involvement must be seen as a spectrum: women are not necessarily in full control of activities and members, but neither are they insignificant or absent. They are there, and they know what is going on. *Agency* is a term rarely found in the literature on the role of women in OCGs. In particular, the notion of "criminal agency" is missing, by which I mean "the capacity, the condition or state of acting or of exerting power" independently to undertake their own criminal acts and behavior.[93] Criminal agency conveys the idea of individual life choices and self-subjecthood to undertake crime, not conformist or compliant agency.[94] If we do find the term *agency*, it is then followed by the word *emancipation* as though women's agency only came about because of emancipation in civil society at large and in relation to men.

As a result, the traditional image of Camorra women is that they float in a neighborhood, in a country, in a market, and in a crime organization, and that everything is decided for them. That they have no voice, that they have no understanding or agency, that they are controlled by men. This description may be put forward because the primary material analyzed is male-articulated, and consequently, the true nature of the gender regime of the Camorra is missed. It could even be argued that this is a simple analysis produced both by law enforcement agencies and researchers. From the different stories recounted here, we see that it is the women who have the strategic intelligence to be proactive in their decision-making rather than waiting for things to happen. This is the case not only at leadership level but also for the small-time foot soldiers who appear to be insignificant but whose decisions become pivotal for the control of the territory and the clan's economic survival.

At the end of the spectrum, we find the concept of passivity. This needs to be defined and refined. Passivity is defined by the *Merriam-Webster* as "the quality or state of being passive" and passive means "not active or operating: inert," or, in other words, inaction.[95]

Through my stories, I have seen different forms of passivity but there are two main distinct forms that predominate. Both forms mean involvement:

1. A so-called neutral and indifferent passivity, not engaging and doing nothing; they exist in the Camorra space but do nothing one way or the other. Not leaving can be seen as acceptance and a form of endorsement; they bring up the children.
2. A tacit and complicit passivity, a hint of help or some kind of help/support; they exist in the Camorra space but make sure their supposed passivity does not hinder or block the criminal behavior of the clan. If anything, it might help.

These insiders-outsiders are "*the camorrista's wives who do not share and who at the same time do not contrast their activity, those who strongly hold their own children outside of the activities while staying next to their partners are always in the criminal organization, but it is as though they live outside it.*"[96]

Their presence shows acceptance, knowledge, and complicity. The image of passive Camorra women is the norm in society, with men protecting them from crime and society at large. Men believe that it is their traditional role to protect women and to keep them out of certain activities, and therefore, they are seen as passive actors. This form of passivity, even, if it is a kind of indifference, still means supporting and not hindering criminal activities.

The boss, Giuseppe Sarno, maintained that he "*never said anything near my wife . . . I have never spoken about these things to my wife.*"[97] This means that he kept up the traditional image of a man protecting his wife from criminal activities, but she shared his life. So, how would she not have known? This remains ambiguous and ambivalent. Francesca Francetti argues that "*there are many types of women . . . if we're talking about women who are still with their husbands after many years, in my opinion it's because they like this life. I'm sorry to say because we are women. They like this life.*"[98] She must also have some understanding of the dynamics that surrounded her.

Rita Longo is a good example as she embodies both agency and tacit passivity. She always talked about her partner as a patriarchal figure and in her interview with me, she had difficulty articulating the true nature of her role in the clan. She was adamant that "*no, I didn't participate in anything, meetings with the group, entrepreneurs, or politicians . . . my role was to be the mother of the kids . . . no, I don't feel involved in this thing . . . I'm passive, yes.*"[99]

Indeed, for a long time, she accepted her fate with passivity and her degrading situation for the love of her children. Even when she found out that he had a mistress, she stayed, saying, "*I even thought about leaving home, but I didn't because the children were small.*"[100] Even after being beaten and humiliated by her son-in-law, on more than one occasion, she accepted the violence and stayed: "*He told me off and violently slapped me accusing me of having a relationship with the doctor GC. He said, and I quote . . . 'Now I will show you where I send GC'* [a threat of violence]."[101]

Although, she did react on another occasion, her general behavior was passive. When she became involved in the money laundering operations of the clan, transferring money to different members and clearly participating, she claimed she did not know where the money came: "*I don't know where this other money, given to me by my brother-in-law, came from.*"[102] But when she visited her partner in high-security prisons, she became his go-between and representative in the outside world. She must have known exactly what she was doing: "*We were able to communicate via hand gestures and traditional signals and I became very good at understanding what he wanted.*"[103]

Obviously, there were aspects that she was not involved in but in reality, she was part of the management group looking after her family network and its criminal activities, whether her partner was in or outside of prison. Although she portrays herself as "*the passive wife,*" her actions illustrate a different story: "*In this part of the* [prison] *discussion I informed my partner that his daughter . . . was demanding half of my 'salary' and that I didn't want to give her the money because I needed to look after the other two children.*"[104]

When the situation became critical for her, and she decided to leave and collaborate with the state; her explanations highlight that she was aware of her surrounding criminal context and her actions within it: "*I want to make this clear that before leaving Casal* [her hometown], *I visited his brothers and asked them for ten thousand euros, but they refused because they said they had problems with the bank. I must add that on other occasions, I had already asked for a money loan when I needed to pay my husband's lawyers and the usual common kitty had not yet been collected.*"[105] So, it is difficult to assert that women are passive.

Wives enter knowingly into a partnership, they understand their husband's criminal projects, and become essential parts of the Camorra criminal project. I should underline that wives are more often "'*more intelligent*' *and therefore active because they* '*know*[s]."[106] It is even suggested that men look for this kind of woman. The thinking is: "*My father was in jail, no one could support him. I had to start pursuing a criminal life. And to do that, I needed a housewife who could be my partner . . . because a camorrista must have a wife.*"[107] When one member of the Amato-Pagano clan was invited to go to Spain, he quickly answered, "*But I love my wife and children*" and so was told to take them with him abroad.[108] This underlines the fact that his wife was part of his criminal future.

In the same way, Teresa's husband got involved in the cigarettes smuggling contraband trade in the 1980s, but he soon became a full-time Camorra member and capo zona for the Mariano clan of the Spanish Quarter.[109] He was much respected by the local community. She explains that "*they loved him*" because he provided calm in the district.[110] Nevertheless, she is clear that as his wife, she was fully complicit in his Camorra activities and existence: "*We got ourselves into a mess, me, and him. Not a small one. There was no turning back now. . . . Anyway, we were both irresponsible, me and him. From the beginning, I realized that my husband was with these people . . . I started to understand many things. I understood. But by now we were too involved, because when you get into this thing, you can't get out afterwards. . . . You don't get out easily. You don't leave.*"[111]

A *pentito* explains the role of the wife in the wife-husband partnership in even more basic terms: "*We went to talk with his wife. . . . You must not be shocked by this because very often it is the women and wives of the bosses who manage together with their husbands or other clan members, and then they assume a leadership role when the husband or partner are unable to for whatever reason.*"[112]

In this particular case, the wife happened to be the daughter of an important Camorra member, but even women who are not born into a crime family understand.

Confirming this, the wife of one of the brothers of a top boss, reflects about her life choices: "*I married* [him] *knowing full well what was going on . . . I do not blame anyone, I am fully responsible, maybe I made a mistake somewhere.*"[113]

So does Francesca Francetti: "*So, I knew everything. I was living with them more and more, as I was his wife . . . I would see everything. I am not a fool. I knew what they were planning at that moment, what they were doing. It's the role of a wife to witness these things. And as I told you, we would go to bed and maybe, he would tell me about his day. So, I knew everything.*"[114]

Contradicting again gender expectations about women being passive, I found that it was not only the wives but also the daughters who buy into their parents' criminal project. Laura Letto explains again that she knew, and she did what she thought was best:

> *In the end, when my father was not there, even if I was the daughter, I thought with my head. He was no longer there if he said, for example, the gun must be hidden on the floor. For me the gun had to be hidden in another place, I hide it in another place because I am thinking with my head. I am doing crime my way, I am managing the clan my way, I am managing the clan my way with my priorities, and no longer* [his].[115]

In Camorra clans, according to previous research, a marked gender stratification and a clear gender gap exists between men and women, but I found that this was not the case, that it was a projection and construction by the outside world on how the Camorra's gender dynamics should be. As I have shown, a closer look reveals that women do not have specific gendered activities, apart perhaps from pulling the trigger, that they are essential to Camorra's success, neither marginalized nor stratified out of discussions.

A spectrum of female mafia involvement within Camorra space is necessary and helpful to recognize that they do have agency, criminal agency. We can imagine active women at one end and nonparticipant-passive women at the other. To be more precise, we have women who have active participation, influencing others, speaking out in favor of activities. These women clearly have independent agency and free will to be involved in criminal activities. At the other end of the spectrum, nonparticipants, women with no involvement or interest in activities, completely opting out of activities and behavior, refuse to participate in any way.

I think that one must add that between active participation and nonparticipant behavior, there is another kind of involvement: ambiguous indifferent behavior. These women are passive observers and bystanders who may benefit from their husband's activities, their indifference thus becomes a form of complicity, passive complicity. So, we have three categories of female involvement: (1) agency (active participation), (2) passive complicity (interested neutrality), and (3) no involvement and indifference (nonparticipation). Giving women agency in the way we have means moving away from the traditional male gaze to reconceptualize the Camorra space as a space shared with women as equals.

The Need to "Engender" the Study of Mafias and Organized Crime

In this study, I have shown and analyzed the agency of women, the positive and proactive criminal agency of women in the Camorra. Able, intuitive, independent, and in full control of their criminal lives and decisions, these women are capable of acting and deciding at all levels, when they need to. They negotiate and bargain with the traditional patriarchy in civil society and in the Neapolitan household, which they make their own. From this, they gain capital that empowers them to become criminal interlocutors, allies, and partners. The capital gained in the household transfers or seeps into the Camorra structure and space. But, because of the traditional image imposed on women by civil society and law enforcement agencies, they are an invisible labor force. Francesca Francetti remains a relevant example. She became involved in criminality fully aware of what she was doing but she also decided to opt out: she constantly encouraged and pleaded with her partner, a camorra boss, to change his life until he finally did: "*I am also a witness of my own story*."[116] Her *own* story with her *own* decisions and choices whether good or bad. Women should be studied as an essential and integral feature of the Neapolitan Camorra and Italian mafias if we are serious about tackling these criminal dynamics. We can only do this if we adopt a holistic approach that includes all aspects, structures, and spaces of the crime group and a clear understanding of gender as we have constructed it.

CONCLUSION

Recontextualizing the Debate about Women in the Camorra

The official (male) history of the Neapolitan Camorra is one that holds that "the underpinning belief is that women are and always have been on the margin of these stories."[1] Immediately, we automatically have an image of Camorra women as powerless and submissive beings trapped within patriarchal structures and hierarchies of masculinity. I hope that this study has contributed to demonstrating that this is not the case. The life stories of all the women I have come across show that this generalization is unhelpful when thinking about Camorra women. Women are systematically ignored in general history books on organized crime and in those on the Neapolitan Camorra, and yet, the women in this study have shown how they are "active agents of history," of their history, good or bad.[2] Perhaps they have been ignored because scholars focused too much on male centric categories (organizational structures, market opportunities, and social change) and did not see the influence that culture had in shaping and directing behavior, organizations, structures, institutions, and opportunities. Perhaps, they did not consider how "gender" is constructed and produces gender orders and gender regimes; in our case the Neapolitan gender order and the local Camorra gender regime, which may not be as they appear.

Our bias, our myths—"myths are a mirror of us after all"—stereotypes and misunderstandings of Camorra women reflect how civil society views women in general, being only a mirror of the public sphere, which maintains a patriarchal framework.[3] In the private sphere, the situation is less straightforward, patriarchy is more fluid, and women in the family, and thus in the household, are more important than is acknowledged because they occupy this physical, economic, and emotional space bargaining with patriarchy, making it their own, contesting male-influenced boundaries, rules, and authority. Women can carve out a space for themselves where they are not systematically oppressed but where they can become empowered and use their agency. Women seen in this way must be considered the key to the power of the Neapolitan Camorra and are its very backbone and motor.

By redressing the balance and shining a light on these women who, for too long, have been relegated to the background and considered as second-rate figures, I hope that I have modified the perception people normally have of them. In the Neapolitan context, mafia women are just as violent, active, money hungry, and exploitative as men, if not more. There exists no sisterhood here, in the sense that women do not necessarily look out for each other but look out for themselves, their families, and their clans.

Neapolitan civil society has been incapable or unwilling to face this reality, as though by doing so would have weakened and diminished its masculinity. Camorra women, driven by their modern cultural value system, are like this because of the space they occupy in the Neapolitan private sphere. Here, women deal with poverty, inequality, limited opportunities, poor access to education but also greed and wealth, and they make the choice that criminality can be a way of surviving or helping them live the life they want.

Power and money are the two fundamental values, for both men and women, women being, after all, their partners in crime. Violence is used to achieve these ends. Violence is not male exclusive; women use it freely and without hesitation. Therefore, Camorra women are equal to, if not more central than, men in the private sphere. However, it is the public sphere that remains formally patriarchal, and this is what civil society sees, projects, and accepts. Women are the embodiment of both good and evil; that is why the future of the Camorra is in their hands as Mariella argues, women *"are smarter. . . ."*[4] To update a 1970s feminist slogan: "*Tremate, tremate, le straghe sono tornate*" ("Tremble, shiver, the witches have returned") to be relevant for the Camorra: "*Tremate, tremate, le straghe non sono mai andate via!*" which translates as "be careful, be careful, the witches never went away!"[5]

If my reflections were to stop here it would still leave my picture incomplete. I have used a gendered lens to look at women in the Camorra, and I concentrated on identifying those who were active and whose agency emanated from their power in the household to challenge the mainstream notion that the Camorra is a male-dominated world. This allowed me to show the variety and extent of women's criminal agency and power that does not easily fit with established categories and labels. Within the Neapolitan household, women contest and bargain with patriarchy to establish informally their matriarchal structures and this empowers them. Their social capital becomes criminal capital. In effect, some, more than we think nor want to accept, are equal partners and not scapegoats or eccentrics.

We must not forget that historical, cultural, economic, and geographical gender variations matter because a diversity of gender patterns can be found across time, history, and cultures. Therefore, the Camorra's local gender regime is just as important to understand if we want to unpack women's agency within the Camorra. I did this by telling women's life stories where possible to underline that they are not all victims, anything but. . . . They have choices, and they make decisions, they use their agency, and they reinforce their capital whether for their own interests or those of the collective good of the clan. These women and their agency are fundamental to the Camorra's continuing success.

But these women are not the only ones to inhabit the Camorra space. There are women who explore the different options within their daily context, who also have agency and make difficult choices and who choose differently; theirs is not criminal agency. They choose between darkness and fear, or between light and hope. Many choose the Camorra as we have seen, but many also choose to opt for light, hope, and walk away, even if this makes their lives even more complicated and arduous for them. They can opt out and they do opt out. It would be unfair not to give a voice to these many women who live and cohabit in the Camorra space without being active or complicit in camorra activities, who reject criminal agency but who are just there, living perhaps with many contradictions. They live in the dark Camorra space while rejecting its subjugation.

During my research I came across many of them. So, here is my gallery of women who chose not to interact with the Camorra. Women from the Soccavo–Rione Traiano district (see figure I.1) explain what living with the Camorra means on a daily basis; for them, it is "cohabitation" and living in a criminal space. One woman explained:

> *My husband and my eldest son, who is twelve years old, we are afraid. We lock ourselves inside at home. We clamp up. We are afraid to talk to people, because we believe there is nothing else we can do. But it's not a good situation. Because when these things happen, we're not fine. We are quiet people, we have no problems, we never argue with anyone, but unfortunately, we are in it. We live there, and . . . let's say that we get on with it. We don't like it, though . . . and that's it . . . it is about coexisting with this bad situation. You are always exposed."*[6]

She continues, "*Even if I go out to do some shopping or buy something, I have to look behind me. I have to see if the situation is quiet. I have to see if I can take my son with me. I have to look out for so many things."*[7]

Another woman adds, "*What makes me most disheartened is not so much the single event of violence, but the fact that it is everywhere. It is in everything you do. In every shop . . . the normality of it. In the sense that everything is connected. Sure, the owner of the petrol pump might not be a Camorrista per se, but he keeps the weapons . . . do you know what I think is absurd? . . . that this fear becomes normal . . . you don't even notice it anymore . . . that's very common.*"[8] A third one explains, "*So, what I want to say is, you can mind your own business, but you always have to hope it doesn't happen to you.*"[9]

Living and cohabiting with the Camorra can become normalized. These women express that they are constantly living in fear, looking over their shoulder, and in dread of being in the wrong place at the wrong time. However, they ignore these concerns and look straight ahead.

For a couple of years, Teresa lived the "*Camorra high life*" as she was a traditional mafia wife. She accompanied her husband throughout his life and criminal career. She was not ignorant, indifferent, or passive. They lived together through highs and lows; she was with him while he was a trusted lieutenant to the Mariano brothers during the NCO versus NF war, and she is still with him today. She remained his rock while he was a lifer.[10] Initially, the clan looked after her and her five children. "*I didn't understand much of all this. Anyway, they* [clan] *came in and hired a lawyer and gave me 100,000–150,000 Italian lira a week.*"[11]

Then, her husband decided that she would be better off without him, saying "*Now this is a decision you have to make; leave me because I wasn't a good husband.*"[12] They decided to walk away from the Camorra together and she explains: "*My love never vanished. Anyway, I didn't accept this. I kept standing by his side and then, together we took this* [decision to leave the clan and I refused their financial support].*"[13]

Once, they had made this decision together, he was clear. Teresa recounted his words:

> "*Teresa, you have to do something. You don't have to let anyone come to the house and you have to stop taking money. . . . But you have to do me a favor, get away from those people. Don't take anything anymore because now, slowly, our children will grow up and I don't want them to go down the same path.*" So, I did. But it was hard. It wasn't easy for me . . . I had to scrape together some money to keep my husband in jail and to raise my children . . . and for house expenses . . . my life was bad. You don't know what my life was like. You can't even imagine. Life is too complicated, even today.[14]

Currently, Teresa lives a life of economic hardship but has been successful in keeping her five children away from the Camorra.[15]

Lucia is a well-respected woman who has lived in the Camorra space for the last eighty years. She has been a witness to much of its postwar transformation without necessarily realizing it. Each phase of her life has been marked by men, her father, her husband, her brother, and her brother-in-law. She explains that *"in my life, I have tried on everything. I would like to write a book* [about it and] *I would call it 'a very tight dress.' It is a very tight dress that I have found myself wearing* [all these years]. *It was put on me by both my family and my husband."*[16]

Her father was a respected guappolike figure. Her husband was involved with his brother, a renowned Neapolitan and international drug baron, and her younger brother was close to the Alfieri Confederation.[17] Both her husband and brother were murdered by the Camorra in the 1990s. She would have had good reason to swear revenge or to flee Naples and yet, she decided to do neither. She explains:

> *I gathered my children* [and said], *"Kids, this is the situation. Do you want us to leave?" None of them said yes. They said no. So, I said, "I'll stay too. I won't leave you. So, let's be ready for anything." And I told the judge, "Dottore, I'm on the first floor in Piazza GDA 16. If they want to retaliate again, they know where to find me." And I told my children, be ready, because . . . I know that they had murdered my husband out of vendetta because they knew how much he cared for his brother. The judge said, "But you know better than me; some fanatic might come out of the blue and then . . ." "Dottore, all the lives they've taken from me . . . they took my brother, they took my husband. I don't think there's anything else for them to do."*[18]

Although in potential danger, she stayed in Naples, carried on with her life and educated her children outside the Camorra. It could be debated that she could do that because she was financially secure and had no need to act out her revenge. But it could also be argued that when she was finally on her own, she chose life and hope, as she could afford to do so.

While reading through the investigations on the Sarno clan, I found the forgotten story of Anna Sodano, a drug dealer from Rione De Gaspari. Having chosen life outside of the Camorra, she disappeared at the age of twenty-seven. Called "Nannina," she was married to Gaetano, a member of the Sarno clan, with whom she had three children.[19] Gaetano introduced her to drug dealing and then, she started transporting firearms for the clan; she actually *"got good at it"* (*"era un vero intenditore"*).[20] All this changed when her husband was arrested in 1997. Anna got scared, became restless, or quite simply fell for someone who was not a clan member and who made her feel giddy and happy.[21] All these thoughts and emotions pushed her to make a decision: she wanted to collaborate with the state because as she herself put it succinctly: "*I am alone. I can't do this anymore.*"[22]

She turned her back on her husband and the clan. But she was tortured by this decision, saying, "*I am scared that they will kill me.*" When she was about to be taken away by the police authorities, she got a phone call from one of her friends who lured her back to Rione De Gaspari with the promise that the clan would leave her alone and do her no harm. Unfortunately, she did not realize that she posed a threat to the clan, that not only because of what she had already told judges but because she also represented freedom and independence of mind and hope. The clan got rid of her in a "*morta bianca*" or a "*lupara bianca*," "a white death," an act of disrespect, she disappeared without trace. Her body was never found; it was suggested that they finished her off in a cement mixer.[23]

Gina was eighteen years old and lived in the center of Naples. She appears in a recent judicial investigation on city clans. She was the former girlfriend of a so-called baby boss from Naples city center. Her voice, her presence, and her relationship emerge only through a police investigation.[24] Practically nothing is known about her apart from her conversations, her thoughts and her advice to a baby boss, her former boyfriend. She lived in the Camorra space, but she did not pursue its logic nor follow her man obediently. Gina spoke out, she had an opinion, she had views, and she represented an alternative to the Camorra's way. She articulated a female view in the Camorra space without being visible in the public sphere. Her words are strong while showing that she is not ignorant, for instance, asking, "*But do you think I have just fallen out of the clouds?. . . Do you think I am stupid?*"[25]

She gives her former boyfriend advice and warns him against his Camorra future "*I want to say one thing. Do you realize what you are doing with your life? . . . I was by your side for a long time . . . but it is not worth it, believe me. . . . I gave you advice, but you did not want to listen to me. . . . A lot of people do not want to see me with you because they know that you are bad.*"[26]

Then, she accepts that he wants that kind of criminal life and that she cannot save him because of who she is, realizing "*so, the problem was me. . . .*"[27]

"*How dare you take the piss out of me and call me up?*"[28]

She remains lucid, claiming, "*You are a dead man walking,*" but believed that each individual can have agency.[29]

"*Here everyone decides the kind of life they want to lead. . . .*

I repeat, this is your life. . . .

Yours is a choice about the type of life you want to lead."[30]

She lived in the Camorra space and knew the Camorra way of life, but she also knew that it was not for her, crying *"You disgust me, you make me sick, you are rubbish!"*[31] She was frank and articulate at rejecting her boyfriend's choices and his life. She did not follow nor seek to trap her man but to save him and to show him an alternative path. She chose love, light, and hope and walked away from him, his life, and his Camorra future.

I was able to meet Mira, a very special person. She is free and not involved with the Camorra. Yet, she is the great-niece of a mafia boss and the niece and cousin of the new generation of a Camorra clan. Her mother is from a Camorra family, and her father collaborates with them. She works in local community projects to get out of her close proximity to Camorra activities, although she exists in both the Camorra space, which is her family and her private space and in the public arena in which she openly fights the Camorra. Mira has to all effects turned her back on the Camorra but cannot cut herself off totally from her roots. She lives the daily routine of the Camorra clan and knows about it while positioning herself above and away from it. She rejects it in her behavior and actions but is still profoundly influenced and shaped by this local context and physical space, which are hers and that of the Camorra. She cannot leave even if she has turned her back on it.

These alternative voices are just as important as those of true Camorra women, but they are also often ignored because of the complexity and contradictions they reveal. More simplistic and fashionable narratives predominate but we must not forget (and must emphasize) how for Neapolitans, the Camorra is not a glamorized TV series or a Hollywood film but a daily way of life. For hundreds of women in Campania, it is a route out of poverty and a survival strategy when, to them, there seems to be no viable alternative.

The Camorra, in its most basic form, is a group of people made up of human relations and emotions. They are individuals with the same emotions, fears, thoughts, and reactions as the rest of us. They are neither more different nor more special than us, but follow violent criminal rules of behavior in order to survive, to make money, or to attain power. If they want to provide for their family and have money to survive, women often do not feel that they have a choice.

During the 1950s, they were a kind of Mother Courage in their own lives, stating "pride isn't for the likes of us. You eat dirt or you go down," emphasizing their involvement in survival and criminal strategies, including decisions, help, and advice to emerging camorristi.[32] Today, Neapolitan women remain these Mother Courage figures, who are the active, solid, and hidden foundation of Camorra families. From the criminal elite city clans to the hard-grafting suburb clans to the province, women are the necessary and unacknowledged partners in crime. There is no glass ceiling, just invisible labor, and a sexist civil society.

Notes

PREFACE AND ACKNOWLEDGMENTS

1. Mary Beard, *Women and Power, A Manifesto Updated* (London: Profile Books, 2018), 4.

2. See P. A. Allum, *Politics and Society in Post-War Naples* (Cambridge: Cambridge University Press, 1973).

3. See Felia Allum, *Camorristi, Politicians, and Businessmen: The Transformation of Organized Crime in Post-War Naples* (London: Routledge, 2006).

4. See Felia Allum, *The Invisible Camorra: Neapolitan Crime Families across Europe* (Ithaca: Cornell University Press, 2016).

5. IJPL1. Regarding this quote and others like it throughout the book, I have put in *italics* the quotes from my primary sources—interviews and judicial material—to highlight these voices.

6. The Massacre of the Fontanelle was a shoot-out that took place on April 22, 2016. See Luciana Esposito, "Rione Sanità, 'La 'Strage delle Fontanelle,'" Napolitan.it, April 22, 2017, https://www.napolitan.it/2017/04/22/63085/strage-delle-fontanelle/.

7. See Daniela De Crescenzo, "La ferocia di Mamma Camorra: 'Devono sentire lo stesso dolore,'" *Il Mattino,* May 10, 2016, https://www.ilmattino.it/napoli/cronaca/la_ferocia_di_mamma_camorra_devono_sentire_lo_stesso_dolore-1722270.html.

8. See De Crescenzo, "La ferocia di Mamma Camorra"; See "Napoli. La vedova del boss: 'Così ho visto uccidere mio marito,'" Metropolisweb, September 14, 2016, https://www.metropolisweb.it/metropolisweb/2016/09/14/napoli-la-vedova-del-boss-cosi-ho-visto-uccidere-mio-marito/.

9. See De Crescenzo, "La ferocia di Mamma Camorra"; See Angela Marino, "Faida di Camorra, La vendetta del boss: 'Gli uccidiamo pure le creature di quattro anni,'" Fanpage. it, May 16, 2016, https://napoli.fanpage.it/faida-di-camorra-la-vendetta-del-boss-gli-uccidiamo-pure-le-creature-di-quattro-anni/. She says, "They will come for me." In this sentence, there is clearly the idea that because she is a woman, they would come for her. See notebook 11.19.

10. When Ferrell writes about the absent, he refers to "undocumented migrants, ex-cons, registered sex offenders, nocturnal graffiti writers, homeless urbanites, freight-hopping gutter punks" (Jeff Ferrell, "Ghost Method," in *Ghost Criminology: The Afterlife of Crime and Punishment,* edited by Michael Fiddler, Theo Kindynis, and Travis Linnemann [New York: New York University Press, 2022], 67). The more I thought about it, the more I realized that Camorra women (and Italian mafia women in general) were treated in this same way; they are ghosts for mainstream society. Thus, without realizing it, I adopted Ferrell's "ghost" thinking and methodology about women who have been ignored and excluded from records and accounts. It became clear to me the importance of the absent, those people who have, for whatever reasons, had "an imposed invisibility" (Ferrell, "Ghost Method," 69). To better understand these women, I would need "an ability to look past the overwhelming immediacy of presence to see those not allowed to be present, a willingness to unearth the residues of embedded exclusion" (Ferrell, "Ghost Method," 72).

11. In this study, I used Connell's definitions of gender: "Gender is above all, a matter of the social relations within which individuals and groups act. . . . Gender must be

understood as a social structure. It is not an expression of biology, nor a fixed dichotomy in human life or character. It is a pattern in our social arrangements, and in the everyday activities or practices which those arrangements govern." Raewyn Connell, *Gender, Short Introduction,* 2nd ed. (Cambridge: Polity Press, 2009), 10.

12. See Beard, *Women and Power;* Caroline Criado Perez, *Invisible Women: Exposing Data Bias in a World Designed for Men* (London: Vintage, 2019).

13. Joanna Belknap, *The Invisible Woman: Gender, Crime, and Justice* (Belmont, CA: Wadsworth, 2001), xv, xvi.

14. Michael A Ledeen, *Virgil's Golden Egg and Other Neapolitan Miracles: An Investigation into the Sources of Creativity* (London: Routledge, 2017).

15. Nagaire Naffine, *Female Crime: The Construction of Crime* (London: Allen & Unwin, 1987), 62–63.

16. Connell, *Gender, Short Introduction,* 62.

17. Clarice Feinman, *Women in the Criminal Justice System* (Santa Barbara, CA: ABC-CLIO, 1986).

18. Felia Allum, *Camorristi, Politicians;* and Felia Allum, *The Invisible Camorra.*

19. To be clear, I am using the term *agency* in this study to mean both the capacity to act independently but also to undertake criminal acts/participating in criminality of one's own free will. See also Martha C. Nussbaum, *Creating Capabilities: The Human Development Approach* (Cambridge, MA: The Belknap Press of Harvard University Press, 2011).

20. P16; see also Robin Pickering-Iazzi's *The Mafia in Italian Lives and Literature, Life Sentences and Their Geographies* (Toronto: University of Toronto Press, 2015), for other stories of women who have been "removed" by Italian mafias.

INTRODUCTION

1. A police officer from the Squadra Mobile, the flying squad of Naples, recalls how they were going around Naples checking on criminals who had to respect specific rules. When they arrived, the wife of the boss was in the street and started hurling abuse at the police officers. The boss appeared at the window and ordered his wife to "Stai zitta!" ("Shut up and be quiet") (IJP9). The officers interpreted his as a put-down, but it might have been something else: it might have been a request to keep back and not get involved or show oneself (IJPL9 & IJPL10). This telling episode provided me with a glimpse of the power dynamic between husband and wife in the Camorra. To the outside world, the man wanted his wife to appear silent but between them she clearly had a voice.

2. Annalisa Casini, "Glass Ceiling and Glass Elevator," in *The Wiley Blackwell Encyclopaedia of Gender and Sexuality Studies,* 5 vols., edited by Nancy Naples, Renee Hoogland, C. Wickramasinghe, Wong Maithree, and Wai Ching Angela (Oxford: Blackwell, 2015), 1–2, http://hdl.handle.net/2078.1/168048.

3. See Roberto Saviano, *Gomorrah: Italy's Other Mafia* (London: Macmillan, 2007); Roberto Saviano, *La Paranza dei bambini* (Roma: Feltrinelli, 2016). See *ES17,* a 2018 documentary based on an idea by Roberto Saviano. See *Gomorrah* (2008), directed by Matteo Garrone, Rai Cinema, Rome.

4. IPO3.

5. IJPL14.

6. IJPL13.

7. IPO3.

8. See Isaia Sales, *Le strade della violenza: Malviventi e bande di camorra a Napoli* (Napoli: L'Ancora del Mediterraneo, 2006); Gabriella Gribaudi, "Donne di camorra e identità di genere," in *Donne di Mafia,* Meridiana Rivista di Storia e Scienze Sociali, 67, edited by Gabriella Gribaudi and Marcello Marmo (Roma: Viella, 2010), 145–154;

Gabriella Gribaudi, "The Use of Violence and Gender Dynamics within Camorra Clans," in *Mafia Violence*, edited by Monica Massari and Vittorio Martone (Abingdon: Routledge, 2019), 236–249.

9. See Anna Maria Zaccaria, "Donne di camorra," in *Traffici criminali: camorra, mafie e reti internazionali dell'illegalita*, edited by Gabriella Gribaudi (Turin: Bollati Boringhieri, 2009), 280–309; Anna Maria Zaccaria, "L'emergenza rosa: dati e suggestioni sulle donne di Camorra," in *Donne di Mafia*, Meridiana Rivista di Storia e Scienze Sociali, 67 edited by Gabriella Gribaudi and Marcella Marmo (Roma: Viella, 2010), 155–173; Anna Maria Zaccaria, "Donne fuori luogo, Camorra e profili femminili." *Fuori Luogo: Journal of Sociology of Territory, Tourism, Technology* 1, no. 1 (2017): 81–99.

10. See Mo Hume and Polly Wilding, "Beyond Agency and Passivity: Situating a Gendered Articulation of Urban Violence in Brazil and El Salvador," *Urban Studies* 57, no. 2 (2020): 249–266; Lirio Gutiérrez Rivera and Luisa Delgado Mejía, "Agency in Contexts of Violence and Crime: Coping Strategies of Women Community Leaders vis-à-vis Criminal Groups in Medellín, Colombia," *Journal of Illicit Economies and Development* 4, no. 3 (2022): 282.

11. Filippo Beatrice, "Uno stile tipicamente aziendale (Il modello impresa e la criminalità camorristica)," in *Questione giustizia*, bimestrale promosso dalla Magistratura Democratica (Milano: Franco Angeli), Fascicolo 3 (2005) cited in Sales, *Le Strade della violenza*, 240.

12. See Felia Allum, "Doing It for Themselves or Standing In for Their Men? Women in the Neapolitan Camorra (1950–2003)," in *Women and the Mafi*, edited by Giovanni Fiandaca (Amsterdam: Springer, 2007), 9–17.

13. Felia Alum and Irene Marchi, "Analyzing the Role of Women in Italian Mafias: The Case of the Neapolitan Camorra," *Qualitative Sociology* 41, no. 3 (2018): 361–380.

14. See Leandro Del Gaudio, "Camorra, le mogli dei boss sono i loro Avatar: così reggono i clan," *Il Mattino*, March 4, 2022, https://www.ilmattino.it/napoli/cronaca/camorra_mogli_boss_avatar_napoli-6540571.html.

15. T59, 345.

16. Cynthia Fuchs Epstei, "Great Divides: The Cultural, Cognitive, and Social Bases of the Global Subordination of Women," *American Sociological Review* 72 (2007): 1–22, quoted in Connell, *Gender*, 62.

17. Thomas Belmonte, *The Broken Fountain* (New York: Columbia University Press, 2005), 92.

18. IPO6.

19. See Vanessa Thorpe, "How William Blake's Wife Bought Colour to His Works of Genius,"' *The Guardian*, September 7, 2019. https://www.theguardian.com/culture/2019/sep/07/william-blake-wife-catherine-brought-colour-works-of-genius-tate-britain.

20. Thorpc, "How William Blake Wife Bought Colour."

21. Rory Carroll, "*Italy's Most Wanted Mamma*," *The Guardian*, June 20, 2000, https://www.theguardian.com/g2/story/0,,338148,00.html. Philip Jacobson, "*Godmother Sends Deadly Message to Her Mafia Rivals*," *The Telegraph*, June 25, 2000, https://www.telegraph.co.uk/news/worldnews/asia/1344933/Godmother-sends-deadly-message-to-her-Mafia-rivals.html.

22. T12.

23. Carroll, "Italy's Most Wanted."

24. See IC8—prison letter from G. Panzuto to author, July 13, 2020.

25. See IC8.

26. Carroll, "Italy's Most Wanted."

27. Teresa Principato and Alessandra Dino, *Mafia donna: le vestali del sacro e dell'onore*, vol. 20 (Palermo: Flaccovio Editore, 1997); Ombretta Ingrascì, "Women in the

'Ndrangheta: the Serraino-Di Giovine Case," in *Women and the Mafia*, edited by Giovani Fiandaca, (New York: Springer, 2007), 47–52; Ombretta Ingrascì, "Donne, 'ndrangheta, 'ndrine. Gli spazi femminili nelle fonti giudiziarie," in *Donne di Mafia,* Meridiana Rivista di Storia e Scienze Sociali, 67 edited by Gabriella Gribaudi and Marcella Marmo (Roma: Viella, 2010), 35–54; Ombretta Ingrascì, *Gender and Organized Crime in Italy: Women's Agency in Italian Mafias* (London: Bloomsbury Academic, 2021).

28. P2, 78–79.

29. Felice Carabellese, Alan R. Felthous, Domenico Montalbò, Donatella La Tegola, Fulvio Carabellese, and Roberto Catanesi, "The Psychopathic Dimension in Women of Mafia." *International Journal of Law and Psychiatry* 74 (2021), 5.

30. IC3, 30.

31. Renata Siebert, *Secrets of Life and Death: Women and the Mafia* (London: Verso, 1996); Ingrasci, *Gender and Organized Crime*; Alessandra Dino, "Women and Transnational Organised Crime: The Ambiguous Case of the Italian Mafias," in *The Routledge Handbook of Transnational Organized Crime*, edited by Felia Allum and Stan Gilmour, 2nd ed. (Abingdon: Routledge, 2022).

32. I have always asked myself whether and how I should tell these stories. If I remove the names, they might lose their relevance, but as it is the social behavior, interaction and relationships, and their meanings that I am interested in, the specific names are of no real relevance. It is what they represent and how I can understand and analyze them that is important. Moreover, my analysis is sociological, which can include alleged illegal and semilegal behavior, and it is delicate to make these kinds of statements. This is why in this study I have decided to change the names.

33. T54, 560.

34. IC5, 25.

35. IC4, 57.

36. IC6.6, 5.

37. IC5, 10.

38. Valeria Pizzini-Gambetta, "Women and the Mafia: A Methodology Minefield," *Global Crime* 9, no. 4 (2008): 351.

39. Anne Campbell, *The Girls in the Gangs*, 2nd ed. (London: Blackwell, 1984), x and 281.

40. Joan Wallach Scott, *Gender and the Politics of History*, Rev. ed. (New York: Colombia University Press, 1999); Maria Mies, *Patriarchy and Accumulation on a World Scale: Women in the International Division of Labour* (London: Bloomsbury, 2022).

41. Scott, *Gender and the Politics*, 18–19.

42. Scott, *Gender and the Politics*, 18–19.

43. Campbell, *The Girls in the Gang*, 281.

44. See Isaia Sales, *La Camorra e le Camorre* (Roma: Editori Riuniti, 1988).

45. Istat, "Il Censimento permanente della popolazione in Campania." 2019, https://www.istat.it/it/archivio/253433.

46. See P. A. Allum, *Politics and Society in Post-War Naples* (Cambridge: Cambridge University Press, 1973).

47. Allum (*Politics and Society*) identified parallel economic systems in Naples during the 1950–60s: *"gemeinschaft"* and *"gesellschaft"*: community versus self-interest.

48. Camera di Commercio di Napoli, 2018. *Profilo economico della provincia di Napoli,* https://www.na.camcom.gov.it/index.php/crescita-dell-impresa/informazioni-statistiche-ed-economiche/profilo-economico-della-provincia-di-napoli.

49. Victoria Goddard, *Gender, Family, and Work in Naples* (London: Berg, 1996), 205.

50. See Xan Brooks, "Sofia Loren: The Body Changes, the Mind Does Not," *The Guardian*, November 6, 2020, https://www.theguardian.com/film/2020/nov/06/sophia-loren-the-body-changes-the-mind-does-not.

51. Goddard, *Gender, Family and Work*, 205–229.

52. Mohammed Rahman, Robert McLean, Ross Deuchar, and James Densley, "Who Are the Enforcers? The Motives and Methods of Muscle for Hire in West Scotland and the West Midlands," *Trends in Organized Crime* 25, no. 2 (2020), 2.

53. See Federico Varese, ed., *Organized Crime* (London: Routledge, 2010).

54. Fabio Armao, "Why Is Organized Crime So Successful," in *Organised Crime and the Challenge to Democracy*, edited by Felia Allum and Renata Siebert (Abingdon, UK: Routledge, 2003), 27–38.

55. Alison Jamieson, *The Antimafia: Italy's Fight against Organized Crime* (New York: Macmillan Press, 2000), xxi.

56. Jamieson, *The Antimafia*, xxi.

57. IPO1. Sales, *Le strade della violenza*, 1.

58. See Diego Gambetta, *The Sicilian Mafia: The Business of Private Protection* (Princeton: Princeton University Press, 1993); Federico Varese, *The Russian Mafia: Private Protection in a New Market Economy* (Oxford: Oxford University Press, 2001); Maurizio Catino, *Mafia Organizations* (Cambridge: Cambridge University Press, 2019).

59. Luciano Brancaccio, *I clan di camorra: Genesi e storia* (Rome: Donzelli, 2017).

60. Luciano Brancaccio, "Violent Contexts and Camorra Clans," in *Mafia Violence, Political, Symbolic, and Economic forms of violence in Camorra clans,* edited by Monica Massari and Vittorio Martone (Abingdon, UK: Routledge, 2019), 135.

61. Brancaccio "Violent Contexts," 144.

62. See Brancaccio, "Violent Contexts"; Luciano Brancaccio and Vittorio Martone, "The Camorras in Naples and Campania: Business, Groups, and Families," in *Italy Mafias Today*, edited by F. Allum, I. Clough Marinaro, and Rocco Sciarrone, (Cheltenham: Edward Elgar, 2019), 30–46.

63. DIA, Relazione del Ministro dell'Interno al Parlamento, Attività svolta e risultati conseguiti dalla Direzione Investigativa Antimafia, II Semestre, 2019, 4.

64. Brancaccio, *I clan di camorra*; Brancaccio, "Violent Contexts"; Brancaccio and Martone, "The Camorras in Naples."

65. Beatrice, "Uno stile tipicamente aziendale; Allum, *The Invisible Camorra*.

66. Brancaccio, "Violent Contexts," 137.

67. IC6.1, 10.

68. See T2 & CDA2.1, and T3 & T4.

69. Giovanni Melillo, "Organizzazioni criminali, modelli di impresa e mercati," in *Organizzazioni criminali: Strategie e modelli di business nell'economia legale*, edited by Stefano Consiglio et al. (Rome: Donzelli editore, 2019), 3–21.

70. Pizzini-Gambetta, "Women and the Mafia," 352.

71. Pizzini-Gambetta, "Women and the Mafia," 351–352.

72. Enzo Ciconte, *Riti criminali: i codici di affiliazione alla'ndrangheta* (Soveria Mannelli: Rubbettino Editore, 2015).

73. See T6.

74. IC1, 5.

75. Maarja Saar and Hannes Palang, "The Dimensions of Place Meanings," *Living Reviews in Landscape Research*, 3, no. 3 (2009): 6–7.

76. Jorgensen and Stedman, quoted in Saar and Palang, "The Dimensions of Place," 7.

77. See Allum, *The Invisible Camorra*.

78. Saar and Palang, *The Dimensions of Place*, 6.

79. Brancaccio, "Violent Contexts," 148.

80. Yusuf Bakkali, "Life on Road: Symbolic Struggle and the Munpain," PhD diss., Sussex University, 2017, 53. See also Nikki Jones, *Between Good and Ghetto: African America Girls and Inter-City Violence* (London: Rutgers University Press, 2010), 9.

81. IJPL5.

82. See Anne Parsons, *Belief, Magic and Anomie: Essays in Psychosocial Anthropology* (New York: Free Press, 1969).

83. Bakkali, *Life on the Road*, 25.

84. Luciana Esposito, "Il significato che la camorra attribuisce ai fuochi d'artificio," June 27, 2016, Napolitan.it, https://www.napolitan.it/2016/06/27/46891/fuochi-dartificio/.

85. T10 & P15.

86. See Felia Allum and Luca Palermo, "Street Art: Young Italians Shake Camorra's Hold on Public Space," *The Conversation*, November 15, 2017.

1. LISTENING TO WOMEN'S VOICES

1. For a week in mid-September 2020 (Monday to Friday, September 14–18), I lived in a flat that gave directly onto Piazza Carolina in the city center of Naples to observe the general behavior and activities in this public space. I noted the daily activities of groups, their gender, and times for five days continuously during the week (not the weekend) to see whether a pattern of gendered activities emerged. This was before children went back to school in late September. The point of the observation: to note the regularity of daily activities, the gender of the groups, and their use of the public space during the working week.

2. See notebook 9.21.

3. Rosalind Coward, *Patriarchal Precedents, Sexuality and Social Relations* (London: Routledge, 1983), 240.

4. Coward, *Patriarchal Precedents,* 183, 285.

5. Mies, *Patriarchy and Accumulation*. Maria Ridda in her book *Criminality and Power in the Postcolonial City Mapping the Mean Streets of Mumbai and Naples* (Abingdon: Routledge, 2023) discusses "masculine patriarchy." This is a helpful concept to understand civil society in Naples.

6. See for example, Paul Cockshott, *How the World Works: The Story of Human Labor from Prehistory to the Modern Day* (New York: Monthly Review Press, 2019).

7. Michael S. Kimmel, *The Gendered Society* (New York: Oxford University Press, 2000).

8. Paul Mazerolle, "The Poverty of a Gender Neutral Criminology: Introduction to the Special Issue on Current Approaches to Understanding Female Offending," *Australian and New Zealand Journal of Criminology* 41, no. 1 (2008), 2.

9. Dina Siegel, "Women in Transnational Organized Crime," *Trends in Organized Crime* 17, no, 1–2 (2014), 56.

10. Siegel, "Women in Transnational Organized Crime," 56.

11. Federico Varese, *Mafia Life; Love, Death, and Money at Heart of Organised Crime.* (London: Profile Books, 2017), 122.

12. Varese, *Mafia Life*, 121.

13. Varese, *Mafia Life*, 122.

14. See Brooke Ackerly and Jacqui True, *Doing Feminist Research in Political and Social Science* (London: Palgrave Macmillan, 2010).

15. Anthony Giddens, *The Constitution of Society: Outline of the Theory of Structuration*. Cambridge: Polity Press, 1986; see Felia Allum, *Camorristi, Politicians*. See also Nussbaum, *Creating Capabilities*.

16. Nita Luci, "Endangering Masculinity in Kosova: Can Albanian Women Say No?" *Anthropology of East Europe Review* 20, no. 2 (2002), 73.

17. Raewyn Connell. *Gender*, 11.

18. See Jana Arsovska and Felia Allum, eds., "Women and Transnational Organized Crime," Special Issue, *Trends in Organized Crime* 17, no. 1 (2014): 1–15; Margaret E. Beare, *Women and Organized Crime*; Dina Siegel, "Women in Transnational Organized Crime"; Chris M. Smith, *Syndicate Women: Gender and Networks in Chicago Organized Crime* (Berkeley: University of California Press, 2019); Rossella Selmini, "Women in Organized Crime," *Crime and Justice* 49, no. 1 (2020): 339–383; and Anqi Shen, "Women Who Participate in Illegal Pyramid Selling: Voices from Female Rural Migrant Offenders in China," *Asian Journal of Criminology* 15 (2020): 91–107.

19. Geert Hofstede and Willem A. Arrindell, *Masculinity and Femininity: The Taboo Dimension of National Cultures* (London: Sage, 1998), 6.

20. Parsons, *Belief,* 95, 94.

21. Antonio Nicaso and Marcel Danesi, *Organized Crime: A Cultural Introduction* (Abingdon, UK: Routledge, 2021).

22. Deniz Kandiyoti, "Bargaining with Patriarchy," *Gender and Society*, vol 2, n. 3 (1988): 285.

23. See Selmini, *Women in Organized Crime.*

24. Meda Chesney-Lind and Lisa Pasko, *The Female Offender: Girls, Women and Crime* (Thousand Oaks: Sage, 2004), 4.

25. In this study, I adopt a general intersectional framework that focuses specifically on gender while acknowledging the importance of other structural categories (e.g. class, culture, nationality, sexuality, political structures). I accept the importance of the other social markers but want to focus specially on gender.

26. Doing research on organized crime and Italia mafias is a very reflective process that takes time. The Leverhulme Major Research Fellowship has enabled me to continue collecting material about Camorra women as part of my general project on women in TOC. I thought I would deal with this topic after I had completed my general comparative project, if I could. It was not really a concrete project. However, on a visit to Naples in October 2018, Professor Isaia Sales, suggested that I write about women in the Neapolitan Camorra because I had so much material and, as a foreign woman, I might see things that Neapolitans and Italians might not appreciate or comprehend. So, it became a serious project I wanted to do. Then, COVID hit in March 2020, and it made sense for me to begin writing, as all of my other activities, in particular the collection of data, stopped for a while. This aspect of the Camorra has preoccupied me for a long time, and it has been good to focus and think it through properly. Doing research on organized crime and Italian mafias continues to be for me a reflection about life in the twenty-first century.

27. Patricia Rawlinson, "Mafia, Methodology, and Alien Culture," *Doing Research on Crime and Justice*, edited by Roy E. King and Emma Wincup (Oxford: Oxford University Press, 2000), 353.

28. James Windle and Andrew Silke, "Is Drawing from the State 'State of the Art'? A Review of Organised Crime Research Data Collection and Snalysis, 2004–2018," *Trends in Organized Crime* 22, no. 4 (2019), 396.

29. See William F. Whyte, *Street Corner Society: The Social Structure of an Italian Slum* (Chicago: University of Chicago Press, 2012); Dick Hobbs, *Lush Life: Constructing Organised Crime in the UK* (Oxford: Oxford University Press, 2013); Sudhir Venkatesh, *Gang Leader for a Day: A Rogue Sociologist Takes to the Streets* (London: Penguin, 2008); Sudhir Venkatesh, *Floating City: A Rogue Sociologist Lost and Found in New York's Underground Economy* (London: Penguin, 2013); Brendan Marsh, *The Logic of Violence: An Ethnography of Dublin's Illegal Drug Trade* (Abingdon: Routledge, 2019).

30. See for example, Antonio Bosisio, Giovanni Nicolazzo, and Michele Ricciardi, "I cambi di proprietà delle aziende italiane durante l'emergenza Covid-19: trend e fattori di

rischio," *Transcrime*, 2021, https://www.transcrime.it/wp-content/uploads/2021/05/
Ownership-changes-report-1.pdf. See Carlo Morselli, ed., *Crime and Networks* (Abing-
don, UK: Routledge, 2013); Carlo Morselli, ed., *Inside Criminal Networks*, vol. 8 (New York:
Springer, 2009); David Bright, Johan Koskinen, and Aili Malm. 'Illicit Network Dynamics:
The Formation and Evolution of a Drug Trafficking Network," *Journal of Quantitative
Criminology* 35, no. 2 (2019): 237–258.

31. See Laurel Richardson, *Fields of Play: Constructing an Academic Life* (New Brunswick, NJ: Rutgers University Press, 1997); Kriste Ghodsee, *From Notes to Narrative: Writing Ethnographies That Everyone Can Read* (Chicago: Chicago University of Press, 2016);
Paul A. Thompson, "Pioneering the Life Story Method," *International Journal of Social
Research Methodology* 7, no. 1 (2004): 81–84.

32. Patricia Rawlinson, "Mafia, Methodology," 354.

33. See Flavia Dzodan, June 7, 2020, https://twitter.com/redlightvoices.

34. Ackerly and True, *Doing Feminist Research,* 10.

35. Erlinda C. Palaganas, Marian C. Sanchez, Visitacion P. Molintas, and Ruel D. Caricativo, "Reflexivity in Qualitative Research: A Journey of Learning," *Qualitative Report* 22,
no. 2 (2017), 430.

36. Some suggest that it is possible to research neatly and in a neutral way but the
more I have done research on organized crime, the more I have realised that we frame our
points of view and our analysis on the basis of our experiences and sensitively. Research
can never be neutral.

37. John F. Gallhier and James A. Cain, "Citation Support for the Mafia Myth in Criminology Textbooks." *American Sociologist* 9, no. 2 (May 1974): 73, quoted in Windle and
Silke, "Is Drawing from the State," 408. Dick Hobbes and Georgios Antonopolous, 2014,
98, quoted in Windle and Silke, "Is Drawing from the State," 408.

38. Belknap, *The Invisible Woman*, 20.

39. Richard Tewksbury, "Qualitative Versus Quantitative Methods: Understanding
Why Qualitative Methods Are Superior for Criminology and Criminal Justice," *Journal of
Theoretical and Philosophical Criminology* 1, no. 1 (2009): 38.

40. See Allum, *The Invisible Camorra*.

41. Bruce Berg, *Qualitative Research Methods for the Social Sciences*, 6th ed. (Boston:
Pearson Education, 2007), 3.

42. Tewksbury, "Qualitative Versus Quantitative Methods," 39.

43. Kathleen Daly and Meda Chesney-Lind, "Feminism and Criminology," *Justice
Quarterly* 5, no. 4 (1988): 519.

44. DIA Semestrial reports of 2020, see https://direzioneinvestigativaantimafia.
interno.gov.it/relazioni-semestrali/. I also collected extensive judicial material from
DNAA, the Polizia di Stato, the Guardia di Finanza and the Carabinieri.

45. Lawrence A. Palinkas, Sarah M. Horwitz, Carla A. Green, Jennifer P. Wisdom, Nai-
hua Duan, and Kimberly Hoagwood, "Purposeful Sampling for Qualitative Data Collection and Analysis in Mixed Method Implementation Research," *Administration and Policy
in Mental Health and Mental Health Services Research* 42 (2015): 533.

46. Helen Kara, *Creative Research Methods in the Social Sciences: A Practical Guide*
(Bristol: Policy Press, 2015), 102.

47. Pizzini Gambetta, "Women and the Mafia," 352.

48. "Sociobiography" is defined as "a second type of qualitative research procedure,
which, again, may take the form of a case study, is the examination of life histories, or partial or total biographies of individuals. We mean here biography not in the conventional
sense of the term, such as biography of Franklin Roosevelt, but rather the 'sociobiography'
of a particular social type or social role." Anthony M. Orum, Joe R. Feagin, and Gideon
Sjoberg, "Introduction: The Nature of the Case Study," in *A Case for the Case Study*, edited
by Orum, Feagin, and Sjoberg (Chapel Hill: University of North Carolina Press, 1991), 4.

49. Campbell, *The Girls in the Gangs,* xi.

50. James L. Peacock and Dorothy C. Holland, "The Narrated Self: Life Stories in Process," *Ethos* 21, no. 4 (1993), 371.

51. See https://www.merriam-webster.com/dictionary/agency.

52. Power here means "the ability to achieve a desired outcome, sometimes referred to in terms of the 'power to' do something and I also add the political aspect which sees power as a relationship, in terms of 'the ability to influence the behaviour of others in a manner not of their [necessary] choosing'" (Andrew Heywood, *Key Concepts in Politics,* [Basingstoke: Palgrave 2000], 35). By "power relations," I use the definition, "Power relations are relationships in which one person has social formative power over another and is able to get the other person to do what they wish." http://kgsvr.net/dooy/power.html. The power relation is not an equal partnership. There is one person who dominates/shapes the relationship.

53. Like Siebert, I preferred to give space to those who contributed firsthand testimony: interviews, stories, and comments (*Secrets of Life and Death*, 7).

54. Natalie Haynes, *Pandora's Jar: Women in the Greek Myths* (London: Picador, 2020), 288.

55. John Van Maanen, *Tales of the Field: On Writing Ethnography*, 2nd ed. (Chicago: Chicago University Press, 2011).

56. Paolo Campana and Federico Varese, "Studying Organized Crime Networks: Data Sources, Boundaries and the Limits of Structural Measures," *Social Networks*, 2020, 25, file:///Users/mlsfsa/Downloads/Campana-and-Varese_2020_Studying_organized_crime_networks__-3.pdf.

57. Jennifer Fleetwood and Gary R. Potter, "Ethnographic Research on Crime and Control: Editors' Introduction," *Methodological Innovations* 10, no. 1 (2017): 1–4.

58. Campbell, *The Girls in the Gangs*, vii–viii.

59. IC6.5, 1.

60. This makes me think of Rawlinson when she writes, "It is worth remembering that in the study of organized crime official documentation has been partisan and ill-informed" ("Mafia, Methodology," 357).

61. Iddo Tavory, "Interviews and Inference: Making Sense of Interview Data in Qualitative Research." *Qualitative Sociology* 43, no. 4 (2020), 462.

62. Joe L. Kincheloe, "On to the Next Level: Continuing the Conceptualization of the Bricolage." In *Key Works in Critical Pedagogy* (Leiden: Brill, 2011), 327.

63. Kincheloe, "On to the Next Level," 327.

64. Kara, *Creative Research Methods*, 27.

65. Judicial/police investigations/transcripts/reports/sentence/wire taps, etc. Many of these documents I have already used for my two previous books on the Camorra: F. Allum, *Camorristi, Politicians*; and F. Allum, *The Invisible Camorra*. See *L'Emeroteca Biblioteca Tucci* [Napoli] webpage, https://www.emerotecatucci.it/it/home/. *L'Emeroteca* is located in the main post in the city center. See Studio Legale Pecoraro website, http://www.studiolegalepecoraro.it/lo-studio/. Gennaro Pecoraro was a key criminal lawyer during the 1950s. I interviewed him during the 1990s, and he already had a lot of information about the women I was interested in then. I approached his son to ask whether there was any more material, and he let me see some of the court documents for the Maresca-Orlando trial.

66. Tavory, "Interviews and Inference," 450.

67. Barbara Sherman Heyl, "Ethnographic Interviewing," in *Handbook of Ethnography*, edited by Paul Atkinson, Sara Delamont, Amanda Coffey, John Lofland, and Lyn Lofland (London: Sage, 2001), 380.

68. The antimafia prosecutors of the Naples Antimafia Directorate (DDA) have been particularly open and kind to engage in discussions with me over the last twenty years:

to mention only a few: Giovanni Melillo, Giuseppe Borrelli, Filippo Beatrice, Antonella Fratello, Maria Di Mauro, Ida Frongillo, Vincenza Marra, Maurizio De Marco, Ida Teresi, Luigi Landolfi, Michele del Prete, Marco Del Gaudio, Sergio Amato, Pierpaolo Fillippelli, Vincenzo D'Onofrio, Enrica Parascandolo.

69. See *L'Orsa Maggiore, Cooperativa Sociale*, http://www.orsamaggiore.net/. This NGO has various projects across Naples. I visited the ones in Rione Traiano and Posillipo. The "mother-toddler" group was based in Traiano. Il Rione Traiano is a subdistrict of the larger Soccavo district, which is to the southwest of Naples, beyond the district of Fuorigrotta with the San Paolo Stadium and university buildings. It is considered a relatively poor district, with high-rise council housing mostly built during the 1960s. It has few proper services apart from the Circumflegrea Train, which connects it to Naples city center. In 2016, it became a drug hub as other districts were heavily targeted by law enforcement.

70. ICS3, ICS4, ICS5 & ICS7.

71. The middle school, Scuola media, Istituto Comprensivo Borsellino, Via Enrico Cosenz, 13, 80142 Napoli NA, Italy. This school is located near the Central Station.

72. These interviews have been fundamental moments for me as they allowed me to collect an insider's perspective to my research questions but also to listen and reflect with women who had been in the thick of Camorra activities only a few years earlier. Interviews with six Camorra state witnesses, pentite, has allowed me to collect new material but also gain the all-important insider's perspective. Some of their ideas intrigued me and sent me on another research trail.

73. These Camorra women represented very different Camorra spaces: from Casal di Principe; from Ercolano, Santa Maria Capua Vetere; from Mondragone; from Ponticelli.

74. The request of accessing former camorristi who live under protection can be quite a long process and take a couple of months. On occasions, the state refuses access and on another occasion, the women refuse to meet and talk.

75. Camera dei Deputati, XVI Legislatura, Relazione sui programmi di protezione, sulla loro efficacia, e sulle modalita generali di applicazione per coloro che collaborano con la Giustizia, (Secondo Semester 2018), Doc XCI, 1, trasmessa il 13 agosto 2019), 58.

76. Dina Siegel, "Conversations with Russian Mafiosi," *Trends in Organized Crime* 11, no. 1 (2008), 21.

77. Windle and Silke, "Is Drawing from the State," 405.

78. Signora Teresa (68) and Signora Lucia (81). Twenty years between them, but still resilient. They have cohabited with the Camorra and explained to me how and why. See Felia Allum, "Married to the Mob: What the Lives of Two Camorra Women Tell Us about How to Challenge the Power of the Mafia," *The Conversation*, December 18, 2022, https://theconversation.com/married-to-the-mob-what-the-lives-of-two-camorra-women-tell-us-about-how-to-challenge-the-power-of-the-mafia-193924.

79. See IC8 and IPO2.

80. IPO5.

81. Siegel, "Conversations with Russian," 29.

82. Von Lampe, Klaus, "Introduction to the Special Issue on Interviewing 'Organized Criminal,'" *Trends in Organized Crime* 11, no. 1 (2008), 3.

83. Tavory, "Interviews and Inference," 457.

84. Tavory, "Interviews and Inference," 458.

85. Tavory, "Interviews and Inference," 458.

86. Rawlinson, "Look Who's Talking, Interviewing Russian Criminals," *Trends in Organized Crime* 11, no. 1 (2008), 19.

87. Windle and Silke, "Is Drawing from the State," 403.

88. ICS7. ICS4 & ICS5. ICS1, ICS2 & ICS6.

89. ICS3, ICS4 & ICS5.

90. E. Lenz Kothe, "Inquiry While Being in Relation: Flâneurial Walking as a Creative Research Method," in *The Flâneur and Education Research: A Metaphor for Knowing, Being Ethical and New Data Production*, edited by Alexandra Lasczik Cutcher and Rita Irwin (London: Palgrave Pivot, Cham, 2018), 55.

2. WOMEN AND THE EMERGING POSTWAR CAMORRA

1. Even one of his sisters, a nun, will keep an eye on him: "Sister Emilia, who at the right moment will give him full support." Marisa Figurato and Francesco Marolda, *Storia di Contrabbando, Napoli 1945–1981* (Napoli: Tullio Pironti Editore, 1981), 80. For Lucky Luciano, see Francesco Li Volti, "Quando Lucky Luciano viveva a Napoli, nella sua casa in Via Tasso 484," May 19, 2020, https://storienapoli.it/2020/05/19/lucky-luciano-la-sua-casa-in-via-tasso/.

2. Marc Monnier (1863), cited in Marc Monnier, *La Camorra* (Perugia: Edizioni di Storia e Studi Sociali, 2014), 78.

3. Tom Behan, *The Camorra* (London: Routledge, 1996), 210n6. It is worth noting how in the second edition (2002) of Behan's book, now entitled *See Naples and Die: The Camorra and Organised Crime,* this footnote (now 302n4) was changed slightly. It now reads: "The use of the masculine pronoun here and elsewhere is deliberate. However, in recent years female activity with Camorra gangs, involving women such as Rosetta Cutolo and Maria Licciardi has occurred at a far higher level than that of Sicilian Mafia women within the mafia. See C. Longrigg (1997) and R. Siebert (1996)" (Behan, *See Naples and Die*, 302).

4. Saviano, *Gomorrah,* 141.

5. See Silvana Mazzocchi, "Ninetta e le altre," *La Repubblica, Palermo,* March 4, 1994, https://ricerca.repubblica.it/repubblica/archivio/repubblica/1994/03/04/ninetta-le-altre.html?ref=search.

6. Gribaudi in Clare Longrigg, *Mafia Women* (London: Vintage, 1997), 51.

7. Gabriella Gribaudi, *Donne, Uomini, Famiglie: Napoli nel Novecento*, vol. 1 (Napoli: L'Ancora del Mediterraneo, 1999), 45.

8. Gribaudi, *Donne, Uomini, Famiglie*, 46.

9. Cited in Siani, *Giancarlo Siani: Il Corraggio della Cronaca*, edited by Amato Lamberti (Salerno: Metafora Edizioni, 1991), 44.

10. See also Figurato and Marolda, *Storia di Contrabbando.*

11. The law was out of sync with social and criminal behavior. Pre-1982, criminal codes assessing penalties for mafia-type crime did not exist, and therefore Camorra bosses were prosecuted for individual crimes such as murder or drug trafficking but not mafia association or mafia membership (and therefore, belonging, participating to a criminal organization). Mafia membership became a formal crime in September 1982 and before then, legally mafias and Mafiosi did not exist. This makes our analysis of the role of women during the 1950s in this chapter even harder and more complicated.

12. Interview with lawyer Renato Pecoraro (IJP8) between 1997 and 1998. He was the lawyer of Pupetta Maresca during the 1950s, and therefore, I was able to go back and use this interview and capture his voice as a direct participant.

13. Allum, *Camorristi, Politicians*; Allum, *The Invisible Camorra.*

14. See Dario Del Porto and Conchita Sannino, "Camorra, scacco agli affari della famiglia Moccia. Blitz con 45 ordinanze," La *Repubblica, Napoli*, January 23, 2018, https://napoli.repubblica.it/cronaca/2018/01/23/news/camorra_gli_affari_della_famiglia_moccia_blitz_con_45_ordinanze-187082148/. P13, 19.

15. See news reports from March 19, 2017, http://cronaca.il24.it/muore-anna-mazza-la-vedova-moccia-quella-paura-la-possibile-confisca-della-casa/.

16. P13, 14.

17. P13, 19, and P13, 20.

18. P13, 20.

19. P13, 91–93.

20. Longrigg, *Mafia Women*; Milka Khan and Anne Véron, *Women of Honor: Madonnas, Godmothers, and Informers in the Italian Mafia* (Oxford: Oxford University Press, 2017); Barbei Latza Nadeau, *The Godmother: Murder, Vengeance, and the Bloody Struggle of Mafia Women* (London: Penguin, 2022).

21. See Allum, *Camorristi, Politicians*.

22. See Hans Magnus Enzensberger, "Pupetta Maresca: L' angelo del crimine che sparò per amore," *La Repubblica*, August 15, 1998, https://ricerca.repubblica.it/repubblica/archivio/repubblica/1998/08/15/pupetta-maresca-angelo-del-crimine-che.html. In January 1956, her father Alberto was arrested (*Il Mattino*, January 15, 1956) as was her uncle, Vincenzo, later in March 1956 after seven months of being on the run. He was wanted for attempted murder after a feud (*Il Mattino*, March 23, 1956).

23. Known as *I Lampetielle*, the Maresca family "originated from a terrible branch of crime" that followed "antique criminal customs" such as getting the youngest person to shoot (in this way avoiding prosecution) (Longrigg, *Mafia Women*, 19).

24. See *Reality Car 3ª Puntata—Pupetta Maresca*, February 24, 2018, https://www.youtube.com/watch?v=B6f8DJvzYMM.

25. See also Garone's film *Gomorrah* (2008) and the TV series *Gomorrah* (2014–21).

26. MI2 and MI3; MI2, 53.

27. IJPL8.

28. Enzensberger, "Pupetta Maresca."

29. PG1, 29.

30. IJPL8.

31. CDA1.1, 37. See Allum, *Camorristi, Politicians*.

32. T1,1.

33. See T1.1; CS2, CS3, CS4.

34. PG1, 2

35. PG1, 90.

36. T1.2.

37. CA1, 38, 66.

38. CA1, 71.

39. CA1, 38.

40. PG1, 18.

41. PG1, 18.

42. CA2.

43. PG1, 40.

44. CD1, 16

45. See *Reality Car 3rd Puntata—Pupetta Maresca*.

46. IJPL6, CS3 & CS4. CS1, 12.

47. CDA1.2.

48. PG1, 38.

49. IJPL8.

50. Enzensberger, "Pupetta Maresca"; Allum, *Camorristi, Politicians*.

51. PG1, 15.

52. See C3. At the beginning of the 1980s, Ammaturo was a member of the NF against Raffaele Cutolo's NCO. Ammaturo was very protective of Pupetta: "*Ammaturo had wounded the 70 year old camorrista Felice Malventi (father of Antonio Malventi and father in law of Antonio Ammaturo, brother of Umberto Ammaturo) because he had not*

showed Assunta Maresca (Pupetta) enough authority because she was a woman" (QR, 393). During her time with Ammaturo, Pupetta was involved in different criminal events not as a passive actor but as an active agent. Pupetta entered this relationship on her terms with a criminal past and reputation that all respected. She was considered very pretty and charismatic.

53. IC11, 10–11.

54. See "Tagliai la testa a Semarari aveva tradito il nostro accordo, Intervista al Boss, Elio Scribani," *La Repubblica*, May 25, 2010, https://napoli.repubblica.it/cronaca/2010/05/25/news/boss_ammaturo-4312237/.

55. C1, 32.

56. C1, 33.

57. Q1, 5.

58. Sergio De Gregorio, *I Nemici di Cutolo* (Napoli: Tullio Pironti, 1983), 34.

59. Listen to Pupetta Maresca during a trial where she holds her own, *Umberto Ammaturo, Maresca + 2 Imputati in base al 416 bis accusati da pentiti*, 30.9.1986, https://www.radioradicale.it/scheda/17904/umberto-ammaturo-maresca-2-imputati-in-base-al-416bis-accusati-da-pentiti.

60. Her father, Alberto, was a smuggler working on his own but not with a clan and her younger brother was associated with various clans, including the Alfieri Confederation during the 1980 and 1990s.

61. One of her brothers, Angelo, was the Communist mayor of Marano between 1953 and 1956 (see Allum, *The Invisible Camorra*, 92–94).

62. CS2, CS3 & CS4; see Allum, *Camorristi, Politicians*.

63. IJPL3 & IJPL4.

64. IJPL4.

65. T2, 216.

66. T2, 216.

67. T2, 216.

68. De Gregorio, *I nemici di Cutolo*, 89.

69. Forcella, a badly bombed district at the heart of the city was described as a 'open land for smugglers' where families sought to survive (see figure I.1).

70. Nunzio Giuliano, *Dario di una Coscienza a cura di Maria Rosaria Riviecco and Roberto Marrone* (Napoli: Tullio Pironti, 2006), 46–47.

71. Six boys and five girls: Luigi, Carmine, Salvatore, Raffaele, Guglielmo, Erminia, Anna, Patrizia, Silvana, Antonietta, and Nunzio Giuliano.

72. Giuliano, *Dario di una Coscienza*, 47.

73. Figurato and Marola, *Storia di Contrabbando*, 237.

74. *Cronache di Napoli,* September 29, 2009, 14.

75. Figurato and Marola, *Storia di Contrabbando*, 5.

76. She died from an apparent heart attack the day the police came looking for her sons: "She heard the gunshots and crashed.... She feared for her sons say friends and relatives" (*Il Mattino,* September 29, 2009) 35; De Gregorio, *I Nemici di Cutolo*.

77. *Il Mattino,* September 29, 2009, 35

78. Q1.1.

79. F. Allum, *Politicians, Camorristi*, 103.

80. Figurato and Marola, *Storia di Contrabbando*, 139.

81. Longrigg, *Mafia Women*, 41.

82. See *France Soir*, April 18, 1984.

83. Giorgio Mottola, *Camorra Nostra* (Roma: Sperling & Kupfer, 2017).

84. MI1.

85. *Il Mattino*, April 18, 1984.

86. QR1, 491.
87. Q2, 9.
88. T1, 9
89. QR1, 327. TGIM1, 116.
90. QR1, 328.
91. QR1, 446.
92. CAN1, 13.
93. CAN1, 13.
94. QR1, 446–447.
95. QR1, 446–447.
96. QR1, 446–447.
97. QR1, 336–337; 17.
98. CAN1, 9.
99. QR1, 447.
100. CAN1, 13.
101. QR1, 326.
102. QR1, 441.
103. QR1, 444.
104. QR1, 444.
105. CAN2, 22.
106. No major law enforcement agency or Naples tribunal have their own archive in Naples open to the general public. There is an archive of Neapolitan judicial documents that have been sent to Perugia to be archived but this makes access complicated. In order to put these stories together, I have used multiple sources (police reports, judicial sentences, newspaper articles, interviews) to make the chronology coherent, but I have also had a bit of luck and intuition.

3. WOMEN IN THE CAMORRA SPACE

1. See "Rinascita, il ruolo di Emanuele Mancuso: 'Con il cellulare trovavo le telecamere,'" Zoom24.it, 4 April 2021, https://www.zoom24.it/2021/04/04/rinascita-il-ruolo-di-emanuele-mancuso-con-il-cellulare-disattivavo-le-telecamere/.
2. 1C1, 22, 23, 1.
3. See Antonello Ardituro, *Lo Stato non ha vinto: la camorra oltre i casalesi* (Rome: Gius. Laterza & Figli, 2015).
4. Michael Moran, *Politics and Governance in the UK* (Basingstoke, UK: Palgrave Macmillan, 2005), 3.
5. T24.
6. Diego Gambetta, *The Sicilian Mafia: The Business of Private Protection* (Princeton: Princeton University Press, 1993), 77.
7. See P8.
8. T31.
9. See Allum, *Camorristi, Politicians*.
10. P9, 864; P11.
11. See Q9; and Roger-Louis Bianchini, *Mafia Argent et Politique: Enquête sur des liaisons dangereuses dans le Midi* (Paris: Editions des Seuils, 1995); Allum, *The Invisible Camorra*.
12. See Badolati, *Le 'Ndrangheta dell'Est: Profili Internazionali della Mafia Calabrese* (Coesenza: Luigi Pellegrini Editore, 2017), who clearly shows that 'Ndrangheta bosses also get involved with non-Calabrian, foreign women.

13. See Marco Jacquemet, "Namechasers," *American Ethnologist* 19, no. 4 (1992): 733–748; Marco Jacquemet, *Credibility in Court: Communicative Practices in the Camorra Trials*, vol. 14 (Cambridge: Cambridge University Press, 1996); Diego Gambetta, *Codes of the Underworld* (Princeton: Princeton University Press, 2011).

14. IC8.

15. P12.

16. T32, 180–181.

17. T50, 79. T23, 746.

18. P10, 219.

19. Antonio Nicaso and Marcel Danesi, *Made Men: Mafia Culture and the Power of Symbols, Rituals, and Myth* (Maryland: Rowman & Littlefield, 2013), 43.

20. Judith Aldridge, Juanjo Medina, and Robert Ralphs, *Youth Gangs in an English City: Social Exclusion, Drugs and Violence: Full Research Report ESRC End of Award Report* (RES-000–23–0615. Swindon: ESRC, 2007), 20; John Pitts, *Reluctant Gangsters: Youth Gangs in Waltham Forest* (Bedfordshire, UK: University of Bedfordshire Press, 2007), 40, https://www.wfcw.org/docs/reluctant-gangsters.pdf; Keith Kintrea, Jon Bannister, Jon Pickering, Maggie Reid, and Naofumi Suzuki, "Young People and Territoriality in British Cities," Joseph Rowntree Foundation 6 (York, UK: 2008), 26, https://herd.typepad.com/files/2278-young-people-territoriality.pdf; Densley, quoted Simon Harding, *The Street Casino* (Bristol, UK: Bristol Policy Press, 2014), 221.

21. Mary Dodge, "Women and White-Collar Crime," in *Oxford Research Encyclopaedia of Criminology and Criminal Justice* (Oxford: Oxford University Press, 2019), 1.

22. Vincenzo Ruggiero, *Organized and Corporate Crime in Europe: Offers That Can't be Refused* (Aldershot, UK: Dartmouth Publishing, 1996).

23. Zaccaria, "Donne fuori luogo," 81.

24. Siebert, *Secrets of Life*, 7–8.

25. Siebert, *Secrets of Life*, 7.

26. Dino, "Women and Transitional Organised Crime," 356.

27. Siebert, *Secrets of Life*, 14, 25.

28. Dino, "Women and Transitional Organised Crime," 355.

29. Kandiyoti, "Bargaining with Patriarchy."

30. Giovanni Falcone with Marcelle Padovani, *Men of Honour: Truth About the Mafia* (London: Time Warner Paperbacks, 1993); Rocco Sciarrone, ed., *Alleanza nell'Ombra, Mafie ed economie locali in Sicilia e nel Mezzogiorno* (Roma: Donzelli editore, 2011); Rocco Sciarrone, "Mafie, relazioni e affair nell'area grigia," in *Alleanza nell'Ombra, Mafie ed economie locali in Sicilia e nel Mezzogiorno*, edited by Rocco Sciarrone (Roma: Donzelli editore, 2011), 3–43.

31. Italo Pardo, *Managing Existence in Naples: Morality, Action and Structure*, vol. 104 (Cambridge: Cambridge University Press, 1996), 20.

32. Nicaso and Danesi, *Made Men: Mafia Culture*, 22.

33. Vincenzo Ruggiero, "Introduction-Fuzzy Criminal Actors," *Crime, Law, and Social Change* 37, no. 3 (2002): 177–190.

34. Ruggiero, "Introduction-Fuzzy," 186.

35. My emphasis. See NCA's report "High End Money Laundering, Strategy and Action Plan," December 2014, https://www.nationalcrimeagency.gov.uk/who-we-are/publications/16-high-end-money-laundering-strategy/file.

36. See NCA's "National Strategic Assessment of Serious and Organised Crime 2018," https://www.nationalcrimeagency.gov.uk/who-we-are/publications/173-national-strategic-assessment-of-serious-and-organised-crime-2018/file.

37. Michael Levi, Hans Nelen, and Francien Lankhorst, "Lawyers as Crime Facilitators in Europe: An Introduction and Overview," *Crime Law and Social Change* 42 (2005):

117; Felia Allum, Rossella Merlino, and Alessandro Colletti, "Facilitating the Italian Mafia: The Grey Zone of Complicity and Collusion," *South European Society and Politics* 24, no. 1 (2019): 83.

38. Pizzini-Gambetta, "Women and the Mafia," 351.
39. Sciarrone, "Mafie, relazioni e affari."
40. Sciarrone, "Mafie, relazioni e affari."
41. see Allum, *The Invisible Camorra.*
42. Allum, *The Invisible Camorra*, 91.
43. Sciarrone, "Mafie, relazioni e affari."
44. Sciarrone, "Mafie, relazioni e affari."
45. T44.
46. T44.
47. Tr2-1, 5.
48. see Tr2-1, 2.
49. See Leandro Del Gaudio, "Camorra e appalti in ospedale: 'Soldi, auto e vacanze? Sono per lady Monaldi,'" *Il Mattino*, October 23, 2021, https://www.ilmattino.it/napoli/cronaca/camorra_a_napoli_ultime_notizie_oggi_arresti_spalti_in_ospedale-6275223.html.
50. T66, 337.
51. T66, 317.
52. See T34.
53. T34, 689.
54. T34, 689.
55. T34, 690.
56. C6.
57. Q7.
58. T66, 343.
59. T66, 77.
60. T12, 156.
61. T42.
62. P3, 13–14.
63. P3, 100.
64. T38, 49.
65. See "Arrestato affiliato dei Casalesi: ritenuto vicino a Setola," Ottopagine.it-Caserta, April 5, 2016, https://www.ottopagine.it/ce/cronaca/71745/arrestato-affiliato-dei-casalesi-ritenuto-vicino-a-setola.shtml. He was arrested as he needed to serve eleven years for Mafia association and extortion.
66. T21, 259.
67. T23.
68. P9, P11.
69. P9, 4; P11.
70. P9, 12.
71. P11.
72. T11; T12.
73. Q7.
74. See P10, P12 & T55.
75. P12, 188.
76. P12, 187.
77. P12, 188.
78. T12.
79. P12,160.

4. WOMEN AND THE CAMORRA'S CULTURAL VALUE SYSTEM

1. Felia Allum, "Becoming a Camorrista: Criminal Culture and Life Choices in Naples," *Journal of Modern Italian Studies* 6, no. 3 (2001): 324–347; Allum. *Camorristi, Politicians.*

2. See Allum, "Becoming a Camorrista." Some also call this "a criminal identity," but I think it is more subtle than this. It is not just criminal values; it is a mixture of values that create a sense of belonging. Antonio Nicaso and Marcel Danesi (*Organized Crime: A Cultural Introduction* [Abingdon: Routledge, 2021]) refer to the "symbolic capital" of the Calabrian mafia and argues that it is the women who transmit cultural values to their children.

3. Peter Reuter and Letizia Paoli, "How Similar Are Modern Criminal Syndicates to Traditional Mafias?" *Crime and Justice* 49, no. 1 (2020), 226.

4. See citation of Clarke et al. in Bakkali, *Life on Road: Symbolic Struggle.*

5. IC11, 3.

6. See "Lungomare violento, presi gli autori del pestaggio a poliziotto e moglie," *Il Mattino,* November 14, 2017, https://www.ilmattino.it/napoli/cronaca/lungomare_violento_presi_gli_autori_del_pestaggio_a_poliziotto_e_moglie-3366008.html.

7. Brancaccio, "Violent Contents," 135.

8. IC4, 33.

9. IC4, 6.

10. See Allum, "Becoming a Camorrista."

11. Term used by Giuseppe Galasso in P. A. Allum, ed., *Giuseppe Galasso, Intervista sulla storia di Napoli* (Bari: Laterza, 1978), 285.

12. Antonio Cottino, "Sicilian Cultures of Violence: The Interconnections between Organized Crime and Local Society," *Crime, Law and Social Change* 32, no. 2 (1999), 112.

13. IC5, 28.

14. IC6.1, 21.

15. IC1, 11

16. Dino, "Women and Transitional Organised Crime."

17. IC1,11.

18. Allum. *Camorrsiti, Politicians*, 62.

19. See SMCV2.

20. IC5.1, 4.

21. Belmonte, *Broken Fountain*, 53.

22. Goddard, *Gender, Family and Work,* 179.

23. Belmonte, *Broken Fountain*; Goddard, *Gender, Family and Work,* 229.

24. Quoted in Belmonte, *Broken Fountain,* 91.

25. Parsons, *Belief,* 97.

26. Parsons, *Belief,* 97.

27. My emphasis. Belmonte, *Broken Fountain,* 93.

28. Belmonte, *Broken Fountain,* 94.

29. Belmonte, *Broken Fountain,* 92.

30. Goddard, *Gender, Family and Work*, 194.

31. Pardo, *Managing Existence*, 99.

32. Goddard, *Gender, Family and Work,* 227.

33. Nicaso and Danesi, *Organized Crime.*

34. Nicaso and Danesi argue that "the Camorra either shuns or discourages the same sense of kinship bonds. Family ties are important, but they are not essential" (2021, 24). I disagree with this analysis.

35. Brancaccio, *I clan di camorra;* Brancaccio, "Violent Contexts."

36. See CA2.1; Allum, *Camorristi, Politicians*; T2.

37. Brancaccio, "Violent Contexts"; Brancaccio and Martone, "The Camorras in Naples"; Allum, *The Invisible Camorra*; IC1, 1.

38. IC1, 10.

39. Brancaccio, "Violent Contexts," 136.

40. Meintje Van Dijk et al., "Intergenerational Continuity of Crime among Children of Organizational Crime Offenders in the Netherlands," *Crime, Law and Social Change* 77, no. 2 (2021): 211.

41. Van Dijk et al., "Intergenerational Continuity," 2021.

42. IC3, 3.

43. IC3, 3.

44. P7, 309.

45. Q3, 120.

46. C4, 353.

47. C4, 443.

48. See Emanuela Condè, "Colpo alla camorra: arrestata la mamma di un affiliato al clan De Micco," January 30, 2018, https://www.ilmeridianonews.it/2018/01/colpo-alla-camorra-arrestata-la-mamma-di-un-affiliato-al-clan-de-micco/; See Giancarlo Tommasone, "Mala dell'area orientale, scarcerata Carmela Ricci: torna a Ponticelli," October 31, 2020, https://www.stylo24.it/mala-dellarea-orientale-scarcerata-carmela-ricci-torna-a-ponticelli/.

49. T27, 1308–1309.

50. T27.

51. IC1, 1.

52. IC1, 1.

53. T26, 45.

54. T54.

55. T54; T32, 36.

56. CDA2.3.

57. T4, 132.

58. T54, 27.

59. IC4, 53.

60. IC6: IC8, 20.

61. IC7, 5.

62. IC3, 3.

63. T66; T50.

64. P16, 562.

65. T54, 303, 320, 348, 369.

66. T54, 369.

67. IC1–2, 25.

68. T20, 28.

69. T20, 30.

70. T20, 31–32.

71. There are some children who have managed to turn their back on their father's world, but this often occurs with the help of a mother who can break with Camorra values. Maldresto, a Neapolitan singer and poet, son and nephew of Tommaso and Maurizio Presiteri, an important Camorra boss from Scampia, now a state witness. Maldresto managed to move away and have a distinguished singing career (see http://www.ilgiornale.it/news/sono-sfuggito-camorra-mamma-mi-ha-portato-sanremo-1588633.html).

72. Sales, *La Camorra*.

73. Saviano, *La Paranza*.

74. See De Gregorio, *I nemici di Cutolo*; Behan, *The Camorra*.

75. T54, 277.
76. T50.
77. IC4.
78. T62.
79. T62, 53.
80. T62, 52.
81. T62, 57.
82. ICS3.
83. IC1, 5–6.
84. IC1, 6.
85. ICS1.
86. ICS6.
87. IC4, 35.
88. IC2, 23.
89. T50, 572.
90. See T38.
91. T38, 32.
92. IC4.
93. T20.
94. T20, 17.
95. Gribaudi and Marmo, eds., *Donne di Mafia;* Gribaudi, "Donne di camorra."
96. Gribaudi, "The Use of Violence," 9.
97. "She was murdered as a man: because the Camorra has one way to kill women and one way of killing men. They murdered Giovanna as a man," https://www.dagospia.com/rubrica-29/cronache/storia-gio-gio-giovanna-arrivoli-aspirante-boss-transessuale-124588.htm, May 12, 2016, DagoSpia.com.
98. IC5.1, 2.
99. See "Arrestato boss della Camorra preso seguendo l'amant,"' *La Repubblica*, March 13, 2004, https://www.repubblica.it/2004/c/sezioni/cronaca/schiarresto/schiarresto/schiarresto.html.
100. See "Camorra, arrestato il boss. Cimmino: incastrato da amante gelosa," *Il Gazzettino Vesuviano*, July 10, 2015, https://www.ilgazzettinovesuviano.com/2015/07/20/camorra-arrestato-il-boss-cimmino-incastrato-da-amante-gelosa/.
101. See "Gli appalti pubblici della camorra: la moglie e l'amante dal boss unite dall'amore e dal 'pizzo,'" *Il Mattino*, June 4, 2019, https://www.ilmattino.it/napoli/cronaca/torre_greco_appalti_pubblici_camorra_moglie_amante_boss-4536213.html.
102. As defined by Merriam-Webster, https://www.merriam-webster.com/dictionary/power.
103. IC3, 25.
104. IC2, 33.
105. IC2, 18.
106. IC5, 20.
107. T54, 249.
108. T54, 249.
109. T54–1, 27–28.
110. IC4, 32.
111. IC2, 12.
112. IC4, 32.
113. IC5, 20.
114. IC2, 25.

115. IC2, 26, 33.

116. Rita argued that she was given 10,000 euros on the thirteenth of every month ("her husband's monthly wage") and with that money she had to look after her family (IC1, 8).

117. IC1, 9.

118. IC11.

119. IC1, 33.

120. IC5, 20.

121. T52, 292; IC5, 21.

122. IJPL7.

123. IC2, 16.

124. IC2, 17.

125. IC4, 2, 3.

126. P12, 119.

127. T29, 20.

128. T60, 18.

129. T60, 18.

130. P12, 127.

131. T60, 70; T60, 73.

132. IC1.

133. T17, 459.

134. T11; Q7, 254; P10, 411.

135. P10, 411.

136. T32, 425–426.

137. T58, 12–13.

138. T58, 40.

139. IC1.

140. IC4, 32.

141. IC6.6, 21; IC3, 27–28.

142. SMCV3, 313.

143. Pizzini-Gambetta, "Women in Gomorrah," 270.

144. IC6.6, 1.

145. IC6.6, 12.

146. T32, 65.

147. T54, 29–30.

148. T4, 399.

149. T29, 152–154, 150; P5, 14, 18; Q5.

150. T61, 60.

151. T54, 1044.

152. T66, 49.

153. Luciana Esposito, "Ponticelli: ecco come la "Lady camorra del Lotto O" commentò la morte dell'innocente Colonna e del boss dei Barbudos," September 23, 2019, Napolitan.it, @ https://www.napolitan.it/2019/09/23/91600/lady-camorra-lotto-o/; T60.

154. T29, 179.

155. see Tr3.

156. T11, 105.

157. T11, 177–178.

158. T41, 404–405.

159. T29, 139.

160. IC6.6, 18.

161. T54, 3.

162. See T6.
163. IC4, 42.
164. T5, 53.
165. T38, 4.
166. T11, 179.
167. T59, 22.
168. T59, 30.
169. IC6.1 and IC6.6; P10, 139.
170. P10, 919.
171. Q8, 73.
172. T9, 23.
173. T9, 27–28.
174. P3, 131, 136; P3, 136.
175. P3.
176. See "Camorra, ucciso un 20enne. Era un testimone scomodo," *Il Format*, May 2, 2019, https://ilformat.info/camorra-ucciso-un-20enne-era-un-testimone-scomodo/.

5. HARD-WORKING FOOT SOLDIERS

1. A note about methodology: foot soldiers are particularly difficult to analyze because of the lack of material on them as they are not leaders and therefore also considered perhaps less important for the prosecution.
2. See *Gomorrah*, the TV series (2014–21); Roberto Saviano (creator), Stefano Sollima, Claudio Cupellini, Francesca Comencini, Claudio Giovannesi, Marco D'Amore, Ciro Visco, and Enrico Rosati. See the trailer for season 5: https://www.youtube.com/watch?v=2eJc7DTCsrc. See also *ES17, Dio non manderà nessuno a salvarci* (2018). A documentary from an idea of Roberto Saviano, written by Diana Ligorio and Conchita Sannino; Emiliano Bechi Gabrielli (editor), https://www.youtube.com/watch?v=2nKvuIchQbE 9.8.2020.
3. See *Robinù, i veri ragazzi di Gomorra* (2016), documentary by Michele Santoro, https://www.youtube.com/watch?v=QU5uBTAHPwM.
4. Gribaudi, *Donne, Uomini, Famiglie*.
5. IC6.6, 10; IC6.6,19.
6. IC6.4, 7.
7. IC6.6, 1, 14.
8. See Allum, "Becoming a Camorrista"; Allum, *Camorristi, Politicians*.
9. IC2, 36.
10. T7.
11. See Q3; Q4; T70; Q6.
12. T7.
13. T9.
14. T9; T7. See video—*Camorra Ponticelli: più di 5 secoli di carcere per il clan D'Amico del Rione Conocal*, Luciana Esposito, July 27, 2019, https://www.napolitan.it/2019/07/27/90109/condanne-clan-damico/; see *Camorra Ponticelli: più di 5 secoli di carcere per il clan D'Amico del Rione Conocal*, *Cronache delle Campania*, December 1, 2018, https://www.cronachedellacampania.it/2018/12/pure-noi-femmine-ci-mettiamo-le-pistole-addosso-e-andiamo-a-sparare-il-processo-al-clan-damico-di-ponticelli-guidato-dalle-donne/.
15. P10, 509.
16. T54 and T56.
17. T54, 656.

18. C4, 53.
19. See C4, 59–60.
20. C4, 273.
21. Alessandro Colletti, *Il Welfare e il suo Doppio, Percorsi Etnografici nelle Camorre del Casertano* (Milan: Ledizioni, 2016).
22. C4, 303.
23. IC6.3, 8.
24. This group and its members can be defined more as a "drug association" than a "Camorra association."
25. See T56.
26. IC5, 20.
27. T50, 170.
28. IJ1.
29. IC6.2, 1.
30. IC6, 1.
31. IC6.2, 2.
32. IC6.3, 10.
33. IC6.3, 2.
34. IC6.3, 23.
35. IC6.4, 2.
36. IC6.5, 1.
37. IC6.5, 3.
38. IC6.4, 8.
39. IC6.4, 4.
40. IC6.3, 23.
41. IC6.3, 1.
42. Jason Pine, *The Art of Making Do in Naples* (Minneapolis: University of Minnesota Press, 2012).
43. IC6.4, 4.

6. EFFICIENT MANAGERS

1. Allum and Marchi, "Analyzing the Role of Women."
2. IPO4.
3. T65, 65.
4. T65, 65.
5. T65, 291.
6. T34, 632.
7. T34.
8. See T55.
9. Longrigg, *Mafia Women*, 55.
10. T46, 40.
11. T16, 54.
12. T5, 37.
13. T5, 38.
14. T5, 37.
15. T5, 52–53.
16. T5, 55.
17. See CDA2.2.
18. T29, 41.
19. T29, 60.

20. T29, 73.
21. T29, 95, 73.
22. P16, 62.
23. T41, 405.
24. T41.
25. IC2, 8.
26. IC2, 3.
27. IC2, 21.
28. IC2, 21.
29. T38, 11.
30. IC2, 15.
31. IC2, 25.
32. T38, 1.
33. T38, 14; 11.
34. T38, 15.
35. T38, 15.
36. IC2, 36.

7. STRATEGIC AND INTELLIGENT LEADERS

1. See T33 and T51.
2. IC2, 25.
3. IC4, 9; IC4, 11.
4. IC4, 41.
5. *Il Prezzo*, Rai 3, September 19, 2018.
6. The different documents I have used to reconstruct crucial moments in their lives come from investigative files and sentences, police documents, press reports, policy documents, and interviews with privileged observers. A variety of documents have been used at all times, and I have not limited myself to one single document but have sought to draw on different perspectives on these women's lives.
7. In December 2017, I traveled to Turin to meet Mariella. We met in a big office at the top of a large staircase in a police office in the town. Before I met her, her minder mentioned that she had had cold feet that morning but had finally decided to come. When I finally met her, I realised why she would think twice: she was heavily pregnant and quite rightly would rather have been somewhere else than "interrogated" by me. But she kindly indulged me. She opened up and shared her story with me and we had an insightful discussion.
8. T37, T43, and T45.
9. See https://tvzap.kataweb.it/programma/stagione/1/207410/; *Les Reines de la mafia*, documentary, https://television.telerama.fr/tele/documentaire/les-reines-de-la-mafia,25718711,episodes.php.
10. IC4, 27.
11. IC4, 2; IC4, 2.
12. IC4, 3.
13. IC4, 5.
14. IC4, 5; IC4, 3.
15. IC4, 2, 57.
16. IC4, 5.
17. IC4, 4
18. IC4, 4.
19. IC4, 4.

20. IC4, 5.
21. IC4, 8.
22. IC4, 8.
23. IC4, 5.
24. IC4, 15.
25. see Felia Allum and Anna Mitchell, *Graphic Narratives of Organised Crime, Gender and Power in Europe: Discarded Footnotes* (London: Routledge, 2022)—her story here is in chapter 4.
26. IC4, 2.
27. Figurato and Marolda, *Storia di Contrabbando.*
28. Siani, *Giancarlo Siani*, 48.
29. IJPL2.
30. IJPL2.
31. IC13.
32. Siani, *Giancarlo Siani,* 61.
33. I attended this trial during the late 1990s–2000s, which was held inside Naples prison, Poggioreale, Aula Bunker, aula Ticino 3, which is the smallest of the three court rooms. The clan's leadership was all on trial.
34. T42, 457.
35. T42, 455.
36. IC9.
37. T42, 44; T42, 173.
38. T42, 451.
39. IC2, 24.
40. T42, 172.
41. T42, 172.
42. T42, 172.
43. T42, 108.
44. T42, 447.
45. T42, 447
46. T42, 465.
47. T42, 465.
48. T42, 465.
49. IJP12.
50. T67, 48.
51. T16, 26.
52. T67, 48.
53. See P17, T49, and Q8.
54. IJPL12.
55. T67, 53.
56. See Leandro Del Gaudio, "Cinque colpi per Nunzia uccisa sulla porta di casa come un vero bos,"' *Il Mattino*, October 11, 2015, https://www.ilmattino.it/napoli/cronaca/cinque_colpi_nunzia_uccisa_sulla_porta_di_casa_un_vero_boss-1289746.html.
57. A new hospital, L'Ospedale Del Mare has just been built between Ponticelli, Rione Lotto 0 and Barra as a new investment in the area as a boast to the economy. But, up until now, this area has been difficult of access by public transport; by car, all is easy.
58. Q3, Q4, and Q6.
59. T56, 1172.
60. IC6.6, 3.
61. IC6.6, 3.
62. T56, 254, 256.

63. T56, 53.
64. T56, 1168.
65. IC6.6, 1.
66. T54, 370, 498.
67. T54, 282.
68. T54, 283.
69. T65. See "Un anno fa veniva uccisa Nunzia D'Amico: ecco come quell'agguato ha cambiato il clan," *Redazione Napolitan*, October 10, 2016, https://www.napolitan.it/2016/10/10/53741/annunziata-damico-2/. *'lievet' stu cos' 'a faccia . . . fatti guardare in faccia, fammi vedere chi sei!'*
70. See "Ponticelli, 10 anni di orrendi delitti cadaveri smembrati e sciolti nell'acido," *La Repubblica*, December 21, 2010, https://ricerca.repubblica.it/repubblica/archivio/repubblica/2010/12/21/ponticelli-10-anni-di-orrendi-delitti-cadaveri.html.
71. IJPL11.
72. T22.
73. T22, T36, and T35.
74. IJPL11.
75. See Luciana Esposito, *Nell'Inferno della Camorra di Ponticelli, Napolitan* (Napoli: Cronisti Scalzi, 2022), for a detailed description and analysis of this Camorra.
76. T60, 13.
77. See Gribaudi, "Donne di camorra."
78. Gribaudi, "Donne di camorra."

8. CHALLENGING TRADITIONAL MALE PERCEPTIONS OF CAMORRA WOMEN

1. Jane Schneider and Peter Schneider, "Mafia, Antimafia, and the Plural Cultures of Sicily," *Current Anthropology* 46, no. 4 (2005): 50.
2. Connell, *Gender*, 7.
3. IJPL13.
4. see Dina Siegel and Sylvia de Blank, "Women who Traffic Women: The Role of Women in Human Trafficking Networks—Dutch Cases," *Global Crime* 11 (2010): 436–447; Jana Arsovska and Popy Begum, "From West Africa to the Balkans: Exploring Women's Roles in Transnational Organized Crime," *Trends in Organized Crime* 17 (2014): 89–109.
5. Naomi Wolf, *The Beauty Myth* (London: Vintage Books, 1991), 22.
6. IJPL6.
7. Siebert, *Secrets of Life*, 15.
8. See Laura Bates, *Men Who Hate Women: From Incels to Pickup Artists, the Truth about Extreme Misogyny and How It Affects Us All* (London: Sourcebook, 2020).
9. Goddard, *Gender, Family and Work,* 179–180.
10. Goddard, *Gender, Family and Work,* 227.
11. Sabina Garofalo and Giovanna Vingelli, "Masculinity in Crisis? Men's Accounts of Masculinity, Power and Gendered Relations in Contemporary Cosenza," *Reimagining Masculinities: Beyond Masculinist Epistemology*, edited by Frank G. Karioris and Cassandra Loeser (Oxford: Inter-Disciplinary Press, 2014), 148.
12. Dario Cirrincione, *Figli dei Boss* (Milano: San Paolo, 2019), 69.
13. Goddard, *Gender, Family and Work,* 227.
14. IC2, 32.
15. IC2, 2.
16. T38.
17. IC2, 24.

18. T65.

19. Connell, *Gender*, 62.

20. Quoted in Sharon Grace, Maggie O'Neill, Tammi Walker, Hannah King, Lucy Baldwin, Alison Jobe, Orla Lynch, Fiona Measham, Kate O'Brien, and Vicky Seaman. *Criminal Women: Gender Matters* (Bristol: Bristol University Press, 2022), 39.

21. IC3, 19.

22. IC6.6, 6.

23. See Siebert, *Secrets of Life*.

24. Siebert, *Secrets of Life,* 25, 27.

25. Dino, "Women and Transitional Organised Crime."

26. Ross Deuchar, Simon Harding, Robert McLean, and James A Densley, "Deficit or Credit? A Comparative, Qualitative Study of Gender Agency and Female Gang Membership in Los Angeles and Glasgow," *Crime and Delinquency* 66, no. 8 (2020): 1087–1114.

27. Jody Miller, *One of the Guys: Girls, Gags, and Gender* (Oxford: Oxford University Press, 2001).

28. James W. Messerschmidt, "On Gang Girls, Gender and a Structured Action Theory: A Reply to Miller," *Theoretical Criminology* 6, no. 4 (2002): 461–475.

29. Gribaudi, "The Use of Violence," 247.

30. Zaccaria, "Donne fuori luogo," 87.

31. Zaccaria, "Donne fuori luogo," 91.

32. Gribaudi, "The Use of Violence."

33. IC6.6, 1.

34. IC6.6, 1.

35. IC6.5, 1.

36. IC6.5, 1–2.

37. Belknap, *The Invisible Woman*, 12.

38. Gribaudi, "Donne di camorra"; Gribaudi and Marmo, *Donne di Mafia.*

39. IC3, 34.

40. See Luciana Esposito, "Tatuaggi e camorra," *Redazione Napolitan*, June 4, 2016, https://www.youtube.com/watch?v=L2t590UZ8l0.

41. T54, 3.

42. T54, 3.

43. T29, 179.

44. See Luciana Esposito, "Le Scianel della camorra prestate a Gomorra: le donne del clan Buonerba," *Napolitan.it*, July 1, 2017, https://www.napolitan.it/2017/07/01/66131/clan-buonerba/.

45. See Luciana Esposito, "Le Scianel della camorra prestate a Gomorra."

46. See Conchita Sannino, "Presa la donna boss di Qualiano," *La Repubblica*, June 27, 2012, https://ricerca.repubblica.it/repubblica/archivio/repubblica/2012/06/27/presa-la-donna-boss-di-qualiano.html. See Simone Di Meo, "Qualiano: Le Tappe della 'Guerra di Camorra' scoppiata dopo la morte del boss 'O Mussuto," *Redazione Internapoli*, June 6, 2008, https://internapoli.it/12290-qualiano-le-tappe-della-guerra-di-camorra-scoppiata-dopo-la-morte-del-boss-o-mussuto/; see also "Camorra, in manette 66 affliati alla cosca Pianese-D'Alterio. In manette anche la donna a capo del clan," *Il Sole 24 Ore*, June 26, 2012, https://st.ilsole24ore.com/art/notizie/2012-06-26/camorra-manette-affiliati-cosca-162141.shtml?uuid=AbOPbZyF&refresh_ce=1.

47. See "Camorra a Qualiano. Faida d'Alterio-Pianese, clamorosa sentenza su 4 omicidi che hanno insanguiato la citta," *Redazione Internapoli*, September 15, 2016, https://internapoli.it/47404-camorra-a-qualiano-faida-dalterio-pianese-clamorosa-sentenza-su-4-omicidi-che-hanno-insanguinato-la-citta/.

48. See T30.

49. T11.

50. See "Un miliardo di lire per corrompere il boss pentito," *Redazione, Stylo24*, June 10, 2018, https://www.stylo24.it/un-miliardo-lire-corrompere-boss-pentito/.

51. See T60; T61; and T68.

52. T65.

53. T70.

54. T70.

55. T51.

56. See "Messaggi cifrati nei vestiti dei detenuti: Polizia penitenziaria scopre il codice Gionta, sentenza definitive," *Penitenziaria.it*, July 16, 2018, https://www.penitenziaria.it/carceri/messaggi-cifrati-nei-vestiti-dei-detenuti-polizia-penitenziaria-scopre-il-codice-gionta-sentenza-d-993.asp.

57. T57; P4; and P16.

58. T14.

59. T14.

60. Istat, Comunicato Stampa, *Autori e Vittime di Omicidio* 2021, https://www.istat.it/it/archivio/253296.

61. See Nikki Jones, "Working 'the Code': On Girls, Gender, and Inner-City Violence," *Australia and New Zealand Journal of Criminology* 4, no. 1 (2008): 63–83; Nikki Jones. *Between Good and Ghetto: African America Girls and Inter-city Violence* (New Brunswick, NJ: Rutgers University Press, 2010); Mark S. Fleisher, *Dead End Kids: Gang Girls and the Boys They Know* (Madison: The University of Wisconsin Press, 2000).

62. Sheldon X. Zhang, Ko-Lin Chin, and Jody Miller, "Women's Participation in Chinese Transnational Human Smuggling: A Gendered Market Perspective," *Criminology* 45, no. 3 (2007): 734.

63. Zhang, Chin, and Miller, "Women's Participation," 701.

64. Pizzini-Gambetta, "Women in Gomorrah," 270.

65. Pizzini-Gambetta, "Women in Gomorrah," 270.

66. Sales, *Le strade della violenza*, 230.

67. Tr3 and Tr4.

68. See Fulvio Bufi, "Passione e camorra: uccise l'amante che la lasciò, catturata moglie del boss," *Il Corriere della Sera*, Cronache, Caserta, February 27, 2020, https://www.corriere.it/cronache/20_febbraio_27/passione-camorra-uccise-l-amante-che-lascio-catturata-moglie-boss-dfb72216-599f-11ea-af71-899699a3d6d8.shtml; "Arrestata Rita Mango per aver ucciso l'amante che voleva lasciarla," *Redazione, Radio Prima Rete*, February 27, 2020, http://www.radioprimarete.it/2020/02/arrestata-rita-mango-per-aver-ucciso-lamante-che-voleva-lasciarla/; Valerio Papadia, "Camorra, uccise l'amante che rubava dalle case del clan: arrestata moglie del ras dei Lo Russo," *Fanpage.it*, February 26, 2020, https://napoli.fanpage.it/camorra-uccise-lamante-che-rubava-dalle-casse-del-clan-arrestata-moglie-del-ras-dei-lo-russo/.

69. IC6.6, 22; IC6.6, 21.

70. T54, 220.

71. IC2, 18.

72. Dino, "Women and Transitional Organised Crime."

73. Nicaso and Danesi, *Made Men*, 41.

74. IC6.6, 13.

75. IC6.6, 13.

76. IC6.6, 13.

77. IC6.6, 13.

78. See the Rai TV program, *Belve*, presented by Francesca Fragnani, shown on June 4, 2021, https://www.raiplay.it/video/2021/05/Belve-Puntata-del-04062021-35cf54ed-9f9a-4b25-b754-fc07e2dfaa25.html.
79. IJPL12.
80. T17, 460
81. Gribaudi, "The Use of Violence," 247.
82. IC2, 4.
83. See Luciana Esposito, "Le mamme della camorra" del Rione De Gaspari di Ponticelli," *Napolitan*, October 6, 2017, https://www.napolitan.it/2017/10/06/69296/le-mamme-della-camorra-del-rione-de-gasperi-ponticelli/.
84. Tr2–3, 11.
85. IC3, 4.
86. T54, 2.
87. In one case, a clan member who was involved with a minor also communicated to her via Facebook: https://www.ilfattoquotidiano.it/in-edicola/articoli/2016/12/11/io-violentata-a-15-anni-dal-boss-quello-ci-spara-e-siamo-da-soli/3250859/.
88. See video—Luciana Esposito, "La diretta facebook di Peppe Sarno e Patrizia Ippolito finisce nel mirino del pool anticamorra, aperta un'indagine," *Napolitan*, October 11, 2018, https://www.napolitan.it/2018/10/11/82295/pool-anticamorra-diretta-facebook-sarno/?fbclid=IwAR2DusvQXqQTFrtpX9nbu00l2zvsYTsCcrb2DjkvN-2lEAeAUySuZA-fXOc.
89. See Luciana Esposito, "Camorra Ponticelli: I clan alleati affidarano la replica al video dei Sarno a 'Pina la diva' da casa Minchini," *Napolitan.it*, January 20, 2021, https://www.napolitan.it/2021/01/20/105819/camorra-ponticelli-clan-alleati-affidarono-la-replica-al-video-dei-sarno-pina-la-diva-casa-minichini/.
90. See Simone Di Meo, "Camorra 3.0, quando i boss sfidano la legge sui social network, Ormai è tutto il sistema malavitoso a comunicare tramite internet," *Il Quotidiano del Sud,* May 13, 2019, https://www.quotidianodelsud.it/laltravoce-dellitalia/le-due-italie/2019/05/13/camorra-30-quando-i-boss-sfidano-la-legge-sui-social-network-ormai-e-tutto-il-sistema-malavitoso-a-comunicare-tramite-internet/; Marcello Ravveduto, "L'imaginaire de la Google generation criminelle: les profils Facebook des jeunes de la Camorra," *Cahiers de Narratologie. Analyse et théorie narratives* 36 (2019), https://journals.openedition.org/narratologie/9942.
91. Ingrasci, *Gender and Organized Crime.*
92. Ingrasci, *Gender and Organized Crime,* 7.
93. Definition taken from https://www.merriam-webster.com/dictionary/agency.
94. Ingrasci, *Gender and Organized Crime.*
95. Definition taken from https://www.merriam-webster.com/dictionary/passive#h1.
96. T59, 98.
97. T20, 15.
98. IC5, 20.
99. IC1–2, 16.
100. Tr2–4, 3.
101. Tr2–3, 6–7.
102. Tr2–2, 2.
103. Tr2–4, 4.
104. Tr2–2, 2.
105. Tr2–3, 15.
106. T50, 1292.
107. IC5, 10.
108. T18, 92.

109. See also Allum, "Married to the Mob."
110. IC11, 6.
111. IC11, 6.
112. P10, 874.
113. T59, 23.
114. IC5, 14.
115. IC2, 24.
116. IC5, 3; T47.

CONCLUSION

1. Haynes, *Pandora's Jar*, 286.
2. Scott, *Gender and the Politics,* 18.
3. Haynes, *Pandora's Jar*, 286.
4. IC3, 57.
5. *"Tremate, tremate, le streghe sono tornate,"* was a famous and important 1970s slogan of the Italian feminist movement.
6. ICS1, 1.
7. ICS1, 5.
8. ICS1, 1.
9. ICS1, 5.
10. See Allum, "Married to the Mob."
11. IC10, 11.
12. IC10, 11.
13. IC10, 11.
14. IC10, 6.
15. Allum, "Married to the Mob."
16. IC11, 6.
17. See T2 and CDA2.1.
18. IC11, 10.
19. He would be murdered in 2000 by the Sarno clan as he was perceived as unreliable and could not be trusted.
20. T69, 338.
21. The question of whether she had a new love interest is unclear. She maintains she did not, but the clan and judicial authorities suggest that she did.
22. Tr1, 12.
23. P14, 55.
24. T50.
25. T50, 460, 461.
26. T50, 596, 522, 521, 460.
27. T50, 522.
28. T50, 525.
29. T50, 595, 600.
30. T50, 520, 523, 562.
31. T50, 563.
32. Belmonte, *Broken Fountain,* 117.

Glossary

Camorra War	war between Camorra clans
camorrista/i/e	member of a Camorra family/clan
Carabinieri	Italian police
cassa comune	common fund of the clan
Collaboratore di giustizia	state witness, turncoat, informer, queen's witness (see *pentito/pentita*)
Cosa Nostra	Sicilian Mafia that originated and has its roots in Sicily
guappo	old-time criminal with traditional values
Guardia di Finanza	Italian finance police
latitante	fugitive from the law
Legge Rognoni-La Torre	Italian law (648/1982) that established "mafia association" as a crime
Mafia association	group of people who belong to a mafia clan/the crime of belonging to a mafia clan (art. 416-bis)
Mezzogiorno	southern Italy
Misso-Mazzarella cartel	Camorra alliance made of the Misso and Mazzarella clans (2000s)
morte bianca/lupara bianca	when a body disappears without a trace and is never found
'Ndrangheta	Calabrian mafia that originated and has its roots in Calabria
omertà	law of silence
Paranza dei bambini	gang of children
pentito/pentita	*camorrista* who becomes a state witness
Polizia di Stato	Italian National Police
Questura	police headquarters/precinct/police force
Rione	district of a town
Secondigliano Alliance	Camorra alliance made up of three Camorra families: Licciardi clan, Mallardo clan, and Contini clan (2000s)

Bibliography

Fieldnotes

Notebook 11.19   Notes on trial contro Molli + 5: November 1, 2019, Naples Court, observation notes.

Notebook 9.20   Photos and Observation of Piazza Carolina, Naples, September 14–18, 2020.

Interviews

Camorra world (IC)

IC1	Rita Longo, Rome, October 30, 2012
IC2	Laura Letto, Naples, December 27, 2012
IC3	Giorgia Verde, Bologna, December 19, 2015
IC4	Mariella Manca, Torino, December 18, 2017
IC5 and IC5.1	Francesca Francetti, Torino, October 25 2018
IC6.1–IC6.6	Angela Giallo, Rome, October 30, 2019
IC7	Giovanni Messina, De Sena clan, Naples, April 25, 2012
IC8	Gennaro Panzuto, Piccirrillo clan, prison letters, 2019–20
IC8.1	Gennaro Panzuto, ongoing conversation, Naples, 2019–24
IC9	Salvatore Migliorino, Gionta clan, Naples, September 22, 1997
IC10	Teresa, Naples, July 29, 2022
IC11	Lucia, Naples, June 19, 2020

Civil Society Associations (ICS)

ICS1	Focused group discussions 'Mamme e Bambini', *L'Orsa Maggiore coop. soc, Rione Traiano*, April 17, 2019
ICS2	Focused group discussion, "Mamme e Bambini', L'Orsa Maggiore coop. soc, Rione Traiano, December 17, 2019
ICS3	Social worker, L'Orsa Maggiore coop. soc, April 17, 2019
ICS4	Suore Rita, La Torretta, Naples October 2, 2018, September 16, 20
ICS5	Suore Michelina, Mattedei, Naples, 2019–22
ICS6	Focused group, school children 13–14 years old, 31st Istituto Comprensivo Paolo Borsellino, Naples, April 16, 2019
ICS7	School teacher, 31st Istituto Comprensivo Paolo Borsellino, Naples, April 16, 2019

Italian Judiciary, Police and Lawyers (IJPL)

IJPL1	Antonella Fratello, Naples, November 14, 2018
IJPL2	Rosamaria D'Antonio, Rome, email, April 26, 2020

IJPL3	Maria Di Mauro, Naples, November 15, 2018
IJPL4	Giuseppe Borrelli, Naples, April 15, 2019
IJPL5	Filippo Beatrice, Naples, discussions (2011–18)
IJPL6	Ida Frongillo, Naples, June 6, 2020
IJPL7	Stefania Castaldi, Naples, February 24, 2011
IJPL8	Avv. Renato Pecoraro Naples, January 14, 1997
IJPL9	Squadra Mobile 1—Naples, November 22, 2018
IJPL10	Squadra Mobile 2—Naples, November 22, 2019
IJPL11	Giovanni Corona, Naples, e-mail, June 19, 2020
IJPL12	Maurizio De Marco & Vincenza Marra, Naples, December 18, 2018
IJPL13	Alessandra Camassa, Zoom, April 29, 2021
IJPL14	Giovanni Melillo, Naples, December 18, 2019

Privileged Observers (IPO)

IPO1	Isaia Sales, author and professor of criminology, Naples, October 15, 2018
IPO2	Massimo Ammaturo, son of Camorra family and now successful businessman, Naples, ongoing discussions, 2020–23
IPO3	Antonio Nicaso, author and mafia expert, discussion, November 19, 2020
IPO4	Sabrina Garofalo, researcher, February 2, 2021
IPO5	EM, former member of the Calabrian Mancuso clan, today state witness, March 30, 2020
IPO6	Elaine Carey, professor of history and dean of the College of Arts and Sciences at Oakland University in Rochester, Michigan, discussion, February 19, 2022

Judicial and Police References

Judicial and police sources used in this study: police investigations, sentences, appeal documents, arrest warrants, confiscation warrants, intercepts, and indictments.

Corte d'Appello, Appeal Court, Naples (CAN)

| CAN1 | Corte d' Appello di Napoli, Zaza, November 12, 1992. File on Michele Zaza. |
| CAN2 | Corte di Appello di Napoli, Decreto nei confronti di Zaza Michele, VIII Sezione penale, December 19, 1992 [decree of the Court of Appeal]. |

Corte di Appello, Appeal Court, Rome (CA)

| CA1 | Corte di Assise d' Appello di Roma, Sentenza contro Orlando Carlo Gaetano + 2, SC n. 33/63 Reg.Gen., n. 53/64 Reg.Sent. December 12, 1964, Roma [sentence]. |
| CA2 | Motivi di appello per Ciro Maresca contro la Sentenza del May 16, 1959 e del March 12, 1960 (avv, Fusco, avv. Gianuzzi Savella + avv. Botti) [grounds for the appeal]. |

Corte d'Assise, Assize Court, Naples (CDA)

CDA1.1   Corte di Assise di Napoli, Sezione II, Sentenza a carico di Orlando
Carlo Gaetano + 3, Sentenza n. 29/59, May 16, 1959 [sentence].

CDA1.2   Corte di Assise di Napoli, Sezione II, motivi di appello per Maresca
Assunta contro Sentenza del May 16, 1959, 1–15 (avv. Pecoraro +
avv. De Gennaro) [grounds for the appeal].

CDA2.1   Corte di Assise di Napoli, I Sezione, Sentenza nei confronti di Alfieri
Carmine + altri, procedimento n. 11/95 RG, November 14, 2000
[sentence].

CDA2.2   Corte di Assise di Napoli, III Sezione, Sentenza nei confronti di
Bocchetti Gaetano + 32, n. 39244/00, n. 43/01 RG, n. 31/03 R.sent.,
May 19, 2003 [sentence].

CDA2.3   Corte di Assise di Napoli, Sezione I (ex-IV), Sentenza nella causa
contro Salvatore Di Micco + 3., 28/15, 3/18 R. sent., n. 6303/15
RGNR, February 28, 2018 [sentence].

Corte di Cassazione, Supreme Court, Rome (CS)

CS1   Corte di Cassazione, per ottenere la rimessione del procedimento
penale a suo carico, Gaetano Orlando, April 27, 1959 [decision].

CS2   Corte di Cassazione, ricorre Gaetano Orlando, 1–15, Napoli,
April 29, 1959 [sentence].

CS3   Corte di Cassazione, I Sezione Penale, Sentenza nei confronti di
Orlando Carlo Gaetano + 1, udienza del May 15, 1963, Roma
[sentence].

CS4   Corte di Cassazione, I Sezione Penale, memoria in difesa di Orlando
Carlo Gaetano, udienza del December 1, 1965, Roma, 1–24 [defense
statement].

Procura Generale, Prosecution's Office at the Court of Appeal, Naples (PG)

PG1   Procura Generale della Repubblica, Napoli, Motivi del ricorso
per Cassazione contro la Sentenza pronunciata il 15 dicembre
1960 dalla Sezione I della Corte di Assise di Appello di Napoli nel
procedimento penale contro Orlando Carlo Gaetano, Maresca
Assunta e Maresca Ciro, 1–150 [grounds for the appeal to the
Supreme Court].

Procura della Repubblica, Prosecutor's Office, Naples (P)

P1   Procura della Repubblica presso il Tribunale di Napoli—Direzione
Distrettuale Antimafia (DDA), procedimento n. 12234/R/94
RGNR, n. 533/94 DDA, richiesta di applicazione di misure cautelari
personali a carico di Allegro Fabio + 43, October 22, 1996 [Request
for arrest warrant].

P2   Procura della Repubblica presso il Tribunale di Napoli—DDA,
richiesta di applicazione di misure cautelari contro Gaetano
Bocchetti + 40, procedimento n. 2504/R/97 DDA, 1997 [request for
arrest warrant].

P3   Procura della Repubblica presso il Tribunale di Napoli—DDA,
      richiesta per l'applicazione di misure cautelari nei confronti di
      Apicella Pasquale e altri, procedimento n. 10085/99 RGNR (stralcio
      del procedimento n. 3615/R/93 [arrest warrant].
P4   Procura della Repubblica presso il Tribunale di Napoli—DDA,
      Decreto di fermo di indiziato di delitto nei confronti di Albino
      Gennaro + 12, n. 60455/02/R RGNR, January 14, 2005 [Request for
      arrest warrant].
P5   Procura della Repubblica di Napoli—DDA, Decreto di fermo di
      indiziato di delitto, nei confronti di Salvatore Terracciano + 14,
      April 12, 2006 [arrest order].
P6   Procura della Repubblica presso il Tribunale di Napoli—DDA,
      Decreto di fermo di indiziato di delitto nei confronti di Mazzarella
      Gennaro + 20, RG 66184/04 Mod 21, November 25, 2006 [arrest
      order].
P7   Procura della Repubblica presso il Tribunale di Napoli—DDA,
      Decreto di fermo di indiziato di delitto nei confronti di Di
      Biase Luigi +18, 46606/05Mod 21, March 26, 2007 [arrest
      warrant].
P8   Procura di Repubblica presso il Tribunale di Napoli—DDA, Decreto di
      fermo di indiziato di delitto, Decreto di sequestro preventivo urgente
      ex art. 321 c.p.p. e 12 sexies legge 356/92, Decreto di perquisizione
      personale e locale nei confronti di Candurro Vincenzo + 30,
      procedimento n. 60455/02 Mod. 21, January 24, 2008 [arrest, search
      and seize order].
P9   Procura della Repubblica presso il Tribunale di Napoli—DDA,
      Decreto di fermo di indiziato di delitto nei confronti di Caputo
      Carmine + 10, procedimento n. 21944/2009 RGNR, January 27,
      2011 [arrest order].
P10   Procura della Repubblica presso il Tribunale di Napoli—DDA,
      richiesta di applicazione di misure cautelari personali nei confronti
      di AIETA Antonio + 102, procedimento n. 17982/05 RGNR,
      December 19, 2011 [request for an arrest warrant].
P11   Procura della Repubblica presso il Tribunale di Napoli—DDA,
      richiesta di applicazione di misure cautelari personali nei confronti
      di Albino Anna + 55, procedimento n. 38721/12 RGNR, October 12,
      2012 [request for an arrest warrant].
P12   Procura della Repubblica presso il Tribunale di Napoli—DDA,
      richiesta di applicazione di misure cautelari personali nei confronti
      di Contini Edoardo + 83, procedimento n. 17982/05/R RGNR,
      December 22, 2012 [request for an arrest warrant].
P13   Procura della Repubblica presso il Tribunale di Napoli—DDA,
      richiesta di applicazione di misure di prevenzione, sequestro e
      confisca dei beni nei confronti di Esposito Salvatore, n. 79/2013
      RGMP, March 19, 2013 [request for a non-conviction-based asset
      forfeiture warrant].
P14   Procura della Repubblica presso il Tribunale di Napoli—DDA,
      memoria del pubblico ministero, procedimento nei confronti di
      Adamo Ferdinando + 14, procedimento n. 16635/12 RGNR, May 4,
      2014 [statement of the public prosecutor].

P15   Procura della Repubblica presso il Tribunale di Napoli—DDA, richiesta per l'applicazione di misure cautelare personale nei confronti di Nuvoletta Giovanni + 5, n. 15505/13/21 RGNR, February 18, 2015 [request for an arrest warrant].

P16   Procura della Repubblica presso il Tribunale di Napoli, DDA—procedimento nei confronti Antonio + 48, January 2017 [request for an arrest warrant].

P17   Procura della Repubblica presso il Tribunale di Napoli, DDA, fermo di indiziato di delitto, nei confronti di Mario Abbatiello + 25, n. 44438/08 RNRT, January 18, 2010 [arrest warrant].

Tribunale di Napoli, Naples Tribunal (T)

T1.1   Tribunale di Napoli, Sentenza contro Orlando Gaetano + 6, n. 20076/252 Reg.Gen, n. 939/55 Reg Gen, July 17, 1957 [sentence].

T1.2   Tribunale di Napoli, procedimento penale a carico di Maresca Assunta + 1, relazione di consulenza tecnica medico-legale, prof. dott. Francesco Tarsitano, 1–23, 1957 [medical forensic report].

T1   Tribunale di Napoli, Ufficio Misure di Prevenzione, nei confronti di Zaza Michele + 6, n. 0220176 MP, January 10, 1985 [preventative measures].

T2   Tribunale di Napoli, Ufficio del Giudice per le Indagini Preliminari, Ordinanza di custodia cautelare in carcere nei confronti di Agizza Antonio + 100, n. 9086/R/92 RGPM, September 19, 1994 [arrest warrant].

T3   Tribunale di Napoli, Ufficio del Giudice per le Indagini Preliminari (GIP), Sezione II, Ordinanza custodia cautelare in carcere nei confronti di Abbate Antonio + 142, n. 3615/R/93 R.PM, n. 4458/95 A R.GIP, July 27, 1995 [arrest warrant].

T4   Tribunale di Napoli, Ufficio GIP, Sezione II, Ordinanza custodia cautelare in carcere nei confronti di Baldascino Antonio + altri, n. 3615/R/93 R.PM, n. 2667/96 A Reg. GIP., May 27, 1996 [arrest warrant].

T5   Tribunale di Napoli, Ufficio GIP, Ordinanza applicativa della misura cautelare della custodia in carcere nei confronti di Mazzarella Michele + 4, Proc.pen. 8750/R/99, n. 30331/00 Gip, n. OCC /2001, 2001 [arrest warrant].

T6   Tribunale di Napoli, Ufficio GIP, Sezione I, Ordinanza di   misura cautelare nei confronti di Graziano Adriano + 14, n. 8440/98, n. 3275/99 R.GIP, n. 282/02 R.OCC, June 20, 2002 [arrest warrant].

T7   Tribunale di Napoli, Sezione GIP, Ufficio VI, Ordinanza di custodia cautelare in carcere contro Caldarelli Raffaele + 6, n. 2504/97 R.PM, n. 93643/02 R.GIP, n. 297/02 R.OCC, July 1, 2002 [arrest warrant].

T8   Tribunale di Napoli, Ufficio GIP, Sezione III, Ordinanza di custodia cautelare in carcere nei confronti di Alfiero Massimo + 42, n. 7141/96 RGNR n. 740299 R.GIP. January 2, 2003 [arrest warrant].

T9   Tribunale di Napoli, Ufficio GIP, Sezione XXXIII, Ordinanza di applicazione e di parziale rigetto di misure coercitive personali e reali, nei confronti di Luciano Divano + 23, proc. n. 9604/01

RGNR, n. 4743/02 R.GIP, n. 46/03 R.OCC, January 24, 2003 [arrest warrant].

T10   Tribunale di Napoli, Ufficio GIP, Sezione II, Ordinanza di custodia cautelare in carcere di Addeo Giuseppe Salvatore, n. 5709/97 RGNR, n. 6851/99 R.GIP, n. 498/03 R.mis.caut, March 14, 2003 [arrest warrant].

T11   Tribunale di Napoli, VII Sezione Penale, Sentenza, May 16, 2003, Licciardi [sentence].

T12   Tribunale di Napoli, Ufficio GIP, Sezione XXXIII, Ordinanza di applicazione e di parziale rigetto di misure coercitive personali nei confronti di LICCIARDI Vincenzo + 96, Proc. n. 57523/00 RGNR, n. 100839/01 R.GIP, July 5, 2004 [arrest warrant].

T13   Tribunale di Napoli, Ufficio GIP, Sezione XXVII, Sentenza nei confronti di Mazzarella Michele, proc. n. 18476/06 RGNR, n. 2231/06 RGIP, reg.sent. n. 1455/06, July 31, 2006 [sentence].

T14   Tribunale di Napoli, Sezione GIP, Ufficio XII, Ordinanza di applicazione di misure cautelari personali e reali e di parziale rigetto nei confronti di Andreozzi Salvatore + 18, n. 49946/03 RGNR, March 22, 2007 [arrest warrant].

T15   Tribunale di Napoli, Sezione GIP, Ufficio XII, Ordinanza di applicazione di misure cautelari personali e reali e di parziale rigetto nei confronti di Conte Ugo + 19, n. 49946/03 RGNR, December 29, 2007 [arrest warrant].

T16   Tribunale di Napoli, Sezione GIP, Ufficio XXVI, Ordinanza applicativa di misure cautelari personali nei confronti di Allagrande Maria + 21, n. 43915/02 RGNR, April 22, 2008 [arrest warrant].

T17   Tribunale di Napoli, Sezione GIP, Ufficio II, nei confronti di IOVINE Antonio + 97, n. 28515/03 RGNR, n. 29166/04 R.GIP, April 28, 2008 [sentence].

T18   Tribunale di Napoli, Sezione GIP, Ordinanza di custodia cautelare, nei confronti di Abete Mariano + 113, n. 19964/2005 RGNR, n. 17669/06 R.GIP, March 30, 2009 [arrest warrant].

T19   Tribunale di Napoli, Sezione GIP, Decreto di sequestro preliminare a carico di Mariano Abete + 20, n. 19964/05 RGPM, n. 17669/06 R.GIP, March 30, 2009 [Preliminary asset seizure warrant].

T20   Tribunale di Napoli, Sezione GIP, Ufficio I, nei confronti di Sarno Antonio + 4, n. 31751/04 RGNR, n. 24052/05 R.GIP, July 24, 2009. [arrest warrant].

T21   Tribunale di Napoli, Ufficio GIP, Sentenza nei confronti di Alluce Antonio, December 17, 2009 [sentence].

T22   Tribunale di Napoli, Sezione GIP, Ufficio II, nei confronti di Teresa De Luca + 2., n. 31751/04 RGNR, n. 24052/05 R.GIP., n. 879/09 R.OCC. December 30, 2009 [arrest warrant].

T23   Tribunale di Napoli, Sezione GIP, Ordinanza applicativa di misure cautelare e di sequestro preventivo nei confronti di Beneduce. Gaetano ed altri, n. 118229/00 RGNR, n. 80547/01 R.GIP, 26.11.2009, May 22, 2010; September 6, 2010 [arrest and preliminary asset seizure warrant].

T24   Tribunale di Napoli, Ufficio Giudice per le Idagine Prelimiari, 39 Sezione, Ordinanza di Applicazione di Misure coercitiva nei confronti di Enzo Barattolo + 30, n. 28398/19 (e riunito 3300/21)

	RGR, n. 5003/21 RGGIP, n. 405/22 R mis. Caut, November 25, 2022 [arrest warrant].
T25	Tribunale di Napoli, VI Sezione, Sentenza, n. 61015/08, n. 18566/09 RG. Trib, April 30, 2010 [sentence].
T26	Tribunale di Napoli, Sezione GIP/GUP, Ufficio XLII, richiesta di applicazione di misura cautelare nei confronti di Matola Giorgio e 5, proc. n. 34529/09 RGNR, May 19, 2010 [arrest warrant].
T27	Tribunale di Napoli, Sezione GIP/GUP—Ufficio 32, Sentenza contro Amato Raffaele + 51, Nr. 50426/09 R.G. P.M, May 20, 2010 [sentence].
T28	Tribunale di Napoli, Sezione GIP, Ufficio XVII, Ordinanza di custodia cautelare in carcere nei confronti di D'ANIELLO Carmine + 14, n. 10528/98 RGNR, n. 5977/07 R.GIP, May 20, 2010 [arrest warrant].
T29	Tribunale di Napoli, Ufficio GIP, Sezione IV, Ordinanza applicativa della custodia cautelare in carcere nei confronti di AMBROSANIO Gennaro + 19, n. 32253/2010 NGNR, n. 42263/2010 R.GIP., n. _____/2010 o.c.c, September 24, 2010 [arrest warrant].
T30	Tribunale di Napoli, Sezione GIP/GUP, Ufficio XLII, applicazione di misura cautelare nei confronti di Alessandro Cirillo + 8, proc. 54897/08 RGNR, n. 657/10 R.OCC., October 12, 2010 [arrest warrant].
T31	Tribunale di Napoli, Sezione GIP/GUP, Ufficio XXXII, Sentenza contro Mariano Abete + 6, n. 10585/10 + 20702/10 RGNR, n. 10607/10 R.GIP, October 22, 2010 [sentence].
T32	Tribunale di Napoli, Sezione GIP, Ufficio XXXVI, Ordinanza applicativa di misura cautelare nei confronti di Vincenzo Ferraro + 22, n. 53942/07 RGNR, n. 9005/10 R.GIP, n. 339/11 R.OCC [arrest warrant].
T33	Tribunale di Napoli, Sezione GIP, Ufficio II, procedimento penale nei confronti di De Cicco Annamaria + 24, February 4, 2011 [arrest warrant].
T34	Tribunale di Napoli, Ufficio GIP, procedimento penale n. 21944/2009 a carico di Albino Anna + 83, February 9, 2011 [arrest warrant].
T35	Tribunale di Napoli, Sezione GIP, Ufficio II, procedimento penale nei confronti di Terracciano Raffaele + 2, n. 31751/04 RGNR, n. 24052/05 R.GIP, n. 163/11 R.OCC, March 10, 2011 [arrest warrant].
T36	Tribunale di Napoli, Sezione GIP, Ufficio II, procedimento penale nei confronti di De Luca Teresa + 5, n. 31751/04 RGNR, n. 24052/05 R.GIP, n. 27/10 R.OCC, March 10, 2011 [arrest warrant].
T37	Tribunale di Napoli, Sezione GIP, Ufficio XXV, Sentenza a seguito di rito abbreviato nei confronti di Danese Natale., n. 39259/10 RGNR, n. 21937/09 R.GIP, n. 846/2011 Reg.Gen.Sent., May 2, 2011 [sentence].
T38	Tribunale di Napoli, Sentenza nei confronti di Maio Emilia + 1, n. 26137/10 RGPM, n. 26740/10 R.GIP, May 31, 2011 [sentence].
T39	Tribunale di Napoli, Ufficio GIP, Ufficio XVI, Ordinanza applicativa della misura cautelare della custodia in carcere nei confronti di Vincenzo Accetta +113, n. 31215/2007 RGNR, n. 53619/2007 R.GIP, June 22, 2011 [arrest warrant].

T40   Tribunale di Napoli, X Sezione Distrettuale, riesame provvedimenti restrittivi, libertà personale e sequestri, Ordinanza nell'interesse di Letizia Alfonso, n. 2528 RGNR PM n. 93/86/11 personali, part 1 and part 2, December 27, 2011 [Review warrant of an arrest warrant].

T41   Tribunale di Napoli, Ufficio GIP, Sezione IV, procedimento penale nei confronti di Michele Barone + 29, n. 29752/2007 RGNR, n. 25265/2008 R.GIP, n. 22/2012 R.OCC, January 11, 2012 [arrest warrant].

T42   Tribunale di Napoli, Sezione GIP, Ufficio II, procedimento nei confronti di Gionta Pasquale + 10, n. 20384/07 RGNR, n. 20186/07 R.GIP, March 26, 2012 [arrest warrant].

T43   Tribunale Di Napoli, Ufficio GIP, Sezione IV, Ordinanza applicativa della misura cautelare della custodia in carcere e di rigetto di misura cautelare nei confronti di Ciro Dantese + 8, n. 29752/2007 RGNR, n. 25265/2008 R.GIP, n. 737/2012 R.OCC, November 26, 2012 [arrest warrant].

T44   Tribunale Di Napoli, Ufficio GIP, Sezione XXIII, procedimento nei confronti di Acampora Raffaele + 38, n. 7195/2012 RGNR, n. 4994/13 R.GIP, July 17, 2013; November 30, 2013; December 5, 2013 [arrest warrant].

T45   Tribunale di Napoli, Ufficio GIP, Sezione XXXII, Ordinanza di applicazione di misure cautelari nei confronti di Danese Natale + 3, December 12, 2014 (Danese/Madonna) [arrest warrant].

T46   Tribunale di Napoli, Ufficio GIP, Sezione IX, procedimento nei confronti di MAZZARELLA Luciano e altri, n. 36019/10 RGNR, n. 26156/11 R.GIP, January 7, 2014 [arrest warrant].

T47   Tribunale di Napoli, Ufficio GIP, Sezione XI, Sentenza nei confronti di ACCARDO Antonio + 52, June 18, 2014 [sentence].

T48   Tribunale di Napoli, Sezione GIP, Ufficio XLIV, Ordinanza applicativa di misure cautelari e di sequestro preventive nei confronti di Giacinto Basilicata + 30 (Elivra), n. 1787/14 RGNR, n. 4823/14 R.GIP, January 7, 2015 [arrest warrant].

T49   Tribunale di Napoli, Sezione GIP, Ufficio XXIV, Ordinanza di applicazione di misure cautelari personali e reali nei confronti di Amato Carmine + 11, n. 7630/2015 RGNR, n. 8774/2015 R.GIP., n. 461/15 R.OCC, March 30, 2015 [arrest warrant].

T50   Tribunale di Napoli, Sezione GIP, Ufficio XXVI, procedimento nei confronti di Ambra Beniamino +76, n. 17358/14 RGNR, n. 3297/15 R.GIP, n. 227/15 R.OCC, May 8, 2015) [arrest warrant].

T51   Tribunale di Napoli, Sezione GIP, Ufficio II, procedimento nei confronti di Caso Annunziata + 2, n. 23287/15 RGNR, n. 23577/15 R.GIP, n. 378/15 R.OCC, August 10, 2015 [arrest warrant].

T52   Tribunale di Napoli, Ufficio GIP, Sezione XI, procedimento nei confronti di Mariano Marco + 92, August 28, 2015 (Mariano) [arrest warrant].

T53   Tribunale di Napoli, Sezione GIP/GUP, Ufficio III, Ordinanza sulla richiesta di applicazione di misure cautelari nei confronti di Aulitto Ciro + 43, n. 15195/13 RGNR-DDA n. 8564/14, n. /16 R.OCC-DDA, 2016 [arrest warrant].

T54   Tribunale di Napoli, Ufficio GIP, Ufficio VIII, procedimento nei confronti di Marianna Abbagnara + 107, procedimento n. 42578/13 RGNR, n. 223 R.OCC, May 5, 2016 [arrest warrant].

T55	Tribunale di Napoli, Sezione GIP, Ufficio X, Ordinanza di applicazione e rigetto di misura cautelare personale nei confronti di Ciro Acanfora + 213, procedimento penale n. 1718/11 RGNR, n. 1718/2011 RGNR, n. 37959/2015 R.GIP, n. 296/2019 R.OCC, December 7, 2016 [arrest warrant].
T56	Tribunale di Napoli, Sezione GIP, Ufficio XIX, giudizio abbreviato, Sentenza nei confronti di Marianna Abbagnara + 73, n. 33168/16 RGNR, n. 28780/16 R.GIP, October 20, 2017 [sentence].
T57	Tribunale per i minorenni di Napoli, Sentenza contro Abbagnara Mariano + 3, n. 58/15, n. 679/16, 200/17, June 8, 2017 [sentence].
T58	Tribunale di Napoli, Sezione GIP, Ufficio XL, procedimento penale nei confronti di Terracciano Anna., n. 30318/2017 RGNR, n. 21310/2017 R.GIP, 460/17 R.OCC, November 6, 2017 [arrest warrant].
T59	Tribunale di Napoli, Ufficio GIP, Sezione XXIII, Ordinanza sulla richiesta di emissione di misure cautelari personali nei confronti di Giuliano Paola + 4, n. 13200/14 RGNR, December 12, 2017 [arrest warrant].
T60	Tribunale di Napoli, Sezione GIP, Ufficio XIX, Ordinanza di applicazione di misure cautelari nei confronti di Giulio Ceglie + 9, procedimento n. 31294/17 RGPM, n. 254451/17 R.GIP, n. 126/18 R.OCC, March 13, 2018 [arrest warrant].
T61	Tribunale di Napoli, Sezione GIP, Ufficio XI, Sentenza all'esito di giudizio abbreviato nei confronti di Maria D'Amico + 5, n. 33011/16 RGNR, n. 15051/17 R.GIP, April 12, 2018 [sentence].
T62	Tribunale di Napoli, Sezione GIP, Sezione XXVIII, Sentenza nei confronti di Giuliano Paola + 4, n. 4156/18, 8172/18 e 1196/18 RGNR, 7.2018 [sentence].
T63	Tribunale di Napoli, Ufficio GIP, Sezione XXXIX, Sentenza contro Aulitto Ciro + 27, R.sent. n. 1190/2018, Reg.Gen. 18588/12 Mod., n. 19531/17 RGNR, September 19, 2018 [sentence].
T64	Tribunale di Napoli, Sezione GIP, Ufficio VII, Sentenza nei confronti di Terracciano Anna, n. 1542/18 R.sent., n. 30318/17 RGNR, n. 21310/17 R.GIP, November 5, 2018 [sentence].
T65	Tribunale di Napoli, Ufficio GIP, Ordinanza di misura cautelare personale nei confronti di Antonio De Martino, n. 18798/2017 RGNR, n. 30214/2018 R.GIP, n. 445/19 R.OCC, December 6, 2018. D'Amico [arrest warrant].
T66	Tribunale di Napoli, Ufficio GIP, Sezione XXXIX, Ordinanza di applicazione di misure coercitive nei confronti di Albano Ciro + 24., n. 8406/17 RGNR (stralcio dal n. 30016/16) RGNR, n. 3525/18 R.GIP, 500/19 R.Mis.caut, October 16, 2019 [arrest warrant].
T67	Tribunale di Napoli, Sezione GIP, Ordinanza applicativa di misura cautelare nel procedimento nei confronti di ARPAIA Mirko + 57, n. 42656/2014 R.G.N.R, n. 31557/15 R.GIP, November 18, 2019 [arrest warrant].
T68	Tribunale di Napoli, Ufficio GIP, Sezione XXI, Sentenza nei confronti di Giulio Ceglie + 7., R.sent n. 1419/19, R.GIP 25445/17, December 5, 2019 [sentence].
T69	Tribunale di Napoli, VII Sezione penale, Sentenza contro Andreotti Andrea + 37, n. 1851/6/98 R.Trib, n. 17476/94 RGPM, February 22, 2000 [sentence].

T70   Tribunale di Napoli, Sezione del GIP, Ufficio XXX, Sentenza nei
                   confronti di Mazzarella Vincenzo, n. 39244/00 RGNR, n. 16539/00
                   R.GIP, n. 2593/00 R.sent., July 8, 2000 [sentence].

Tribunale di Santa Maria Capua Vetere, Tribunal of Santa Maria Capua Vetere (SMCV)

SMCV1   Tribunale di S. Maria Capua Vetere, Sezione Misure di Prevenzione,
                   Ordinanza di applicazione di misure di prevenzione nei confronti
                   di Angela Barra, n. 96/2002–2/03 RGMP, October 23, 2003
                   [preventative measures: non conviction-based asset forfeiture].
SMCV2   Tribunale di Santa Maria Capua Vetere, Ordinanza di applicazione
                   di misure di prevenzione nei confronti di D'Agostino Assunta,
                   procedimento n. 1/09 RGMP, n. 42/2008–1/09 RGMP, May 4, 2009
                   [non-conviction-based asset forfeiture].
SMCV3   Tribunale di Santa Maria Capua Vetere, Sentenza contro Pasquale
                   Aveta + 16, n. 19477/08, 2122/08, 1868/10 R.sent. November 29,
                   2010 (Belforte) [sentence].

Investigations

Italian Trial Transcriptions

Tr1   Trascrizione integrale della conversazione fra Busiello Gennaro
                   e Sodano Anno, avvenuta il 24.01.98 preso la circondariale di
                   Poggioreale dale ore 9.50–10.50 am in attuazione del Decreto 55/98
                   del January 20, 1998, Pro pen 3056/9/99.
Tr2   Anna Carrino—testimonies—n. 304532/2007 mod. 45, p. p.
                   _____ mod. 21, November 2007–8.
Tr2-1   November 30, 2007
Tr2–2   March 14,2008
Tr2–3   May 2, 2008.
Tr2–4   November 23, 2007.
Tr3   Corte D'Assise di Napoli, Va Sezione Assise, veberale di udienza
                   redatto in forma steonotipica, Proc. Penale 02/11 a carico di Roberti
                   Giuseppe + 1, udienza July 5, 2011.
Tr4   Tribunale di Napoli, Procedimento penale n. 18566/09, udienza del
                   March 4, 2010: Giuseppe Roberti.

Legione Carabinieri Campania, Carabinieri (C)

C1   Rapporto Giudiziario relative alla denuncia a carico di Gionta
                   Valentino, prot. n. 228/1, Torre Annunziata, July 21, 1984 [notice of
                   crime].
C2   Legione Carabinieri. Napoli, Gruppo Napoli Primo, Nucleo
                   operativo, prot. n. 530/39. Rapporto Giudiziario relativo alla
                   denuncia di Ammaturo Umberto + 1, June 18, 1992 [notice of
                   crime].
C3   Legione Carabinieri Napoli, Gruppo Napoli Primo, n. 530/39 di
                   prot. Rapporto Giudiziario, relativo alla denuncia di Umberto
                   Ammaturo + 1, Napoli, May 18, 1982 [notice of crime].

C4   Regione Carabinieri "Campania," Comando Provinciale di Napoli,
        Reparto Operativo—Nucleo Operativo, n. di prot. 447/51, n.
        2000/02 giugno 2005, Indagine Michele, Comunicazione di
        notizia di reato ex art. 347 del C.P.P. inerente alla denuncia in
        stato di libertà delle sottoelencate persone tutte appartenenti
        all'organizzazione camorristica denominata Clan Sarno operante
        nel quartiere di Napoli Ponticelli, June 2005 [notice of crime].
C5   Regione Carabinieri Campania, Compagnia di Torre Annunziata,
        Nucleo operativo e radiomobile, n. 1586/1, Oggetto: Comunicazione
        di notizia di reato circa la denuncia in stato di indagato libero di
        Donnarumma Gemma, October 1, 2003 [notice of crime].
C6   Raggruppamento Operativo Speciale Carabinieri, Sezione
        Anticrimine di Napoli, n. dio prot. 113/5–26. Indagine "World,"
        informativa di reato, ex art. 347 c.p.p., nei confronti di ALESSI
        Ugo + 27, February 28, 2006 [notice of crime].

Polizia di Stato, Questura di Napoli/Naples Police

Q1.1   Questura di Napoli, *Rubrica delle Persone ricercate*, edizione 1956,
        elenco I e II [list of wanted criminals].
Q1   Questura di Napoli, Squadra di Polizia Giudiziaria, Castellamare
        di Stabia, Rapporto preliminare di denuncia a seguito di indagini
        a carico di Mercurio Pasquale + 4, n. M1/1981, February 27, 1981
        [notice of crime].
Q2   Questura di Napoli, Decreto di applicazione misura prevenzione nei
        confronti di Zaza Michele, Liguori Giuseppe e Smirgalia Vincenzo,
        January 18, 1985 [police order of preventative measure].
Q3   Questura di Napoli, Squadra Mobile, *Indagini relative alle
        organizzazioni camorristiche denominate clan MAZZARELLA, clan
        FORMICOLA, clan RINALDI, clan REALE, clan ALTAMURA, gruppo
        D'AMICO, operanti nella zona di S. Giovanni a Teduccio della città
        di Napoli,* n. 0236026 Sq.Mob.Sez.1, Prot. 2615 U./2000, Napoli,
        March 7, 2000, vol. 1 [police investigation for public prosecutor's
        office].
Q4   Questura di Napoli, Squadra Mobile, *Indagini relative alle
        organizzazioni camorristiche denominate clan MAZZARELLA,
        clan FORMICOLA, clan RINALDI, clan REALE, clan ALTAMURA,
        gruppo D'AMICO, operanti nella zona di S. Giovanni a Teduccio
        della città di Napoli,* n. 0236026 Sq.Mob.Sez.1, Prot. 2615 U./2000,
        Napoli, March 7, 2000, vol. 2 [investigation].
Q5   Questura di Napoli, Squadra Mobile, Oggetto: Informativa di
        reato ex art. 347. C.p.p a carico di Salvatore Terracciano + 13,
        N._____/2006/U/Sq.Mob.Sez.6ª/Napoli, March 31, 2006 [notice
        of crime].
Q6   Questura di Napoli, Squadra Mobile, 3^ Sezione, n. 0226681/II/
        Sq.Mob.Sez.3^ Prot. 9516/U/06, Oggetto: procedimento penale n.
        66184/04. Indagini relative all'esistenza di un'associazione di stampo
        camorristico facente capo a MAZZARELLA Gennaro, attiva nel
        quartiere cittadino Mercato—Pendino, dedita alla commissione
        di una pluralità di delitti, volti ad assumere ed a mantenere, in via
        esclusiva, il controllo del territorio di interesse al fine di gestirne

ogni attività economica, Napoli, September 27, 2006 [police report to the public prosecutor].

Q7   Questura di Napoli, Squadra Mobile, 3∧ Sezione, Oggetto: P. P. 19964/05/21—Indagini sull'associazione a delinquere di stampo camorristica denominata gli Scissionisti, operativa in Napoli nel quartiere Scampia e nei comuni di Melito, Mugnano e Casavatore, Prot. Nr._____/U/3ª/2007, Napoli, March 26, 2007 [police report to the public prosecutor].

Q8   Squadra Mobile, 7∧ Sezione, Indagine mirata a comprovare la responsabilità di Pagano Rosaria + altri, in relazione ai reati di cui agli art. 416-bis, 629 CP, 73 e 74 DPR 309/90 [police report to the public prosecutor].

Q9   Questura di Napoli, Informativa riassuntiva complessa circa le indagini effettuate sull'organizzazione camorrista denominata dei "Casalesi" nell'ambito del procedimento penale 3615/R/93, 125/NA/ H3/19/6∧ di prot.828 Napoli, November 9, 1994 [police report to the public prosecutor].

Polizia di Stato, Questura di Roma, Rome Police (QR)

QR1   Questura di Roma, Squadra Narcotici (Drug Squad, Roma). Rapporto Giudiziario di denuncia a carico di Bono Giuseppe + 159 ritenutiresponsabili di assocazione per delinquere di tipo mafioso e finalizzata al traffico delle sostanze stupefacenti, vol. 1–2 del February 7, 1983, Roma [notice of crime].

Tribunal de Grande Instance de Marseille (Marseille Tribunal)

TGIM1   Réquisitoire de Renvoi devant le Tribunal Correctionnel et de non lieu Partiel contre Sanoukian Marius + 50, March 11, 1991.

Ministry of the Interior

MI1   Ministero dell'Interno, Dipartimento della Pubblica Sicurezza, Direzione Centrale della Polizia Criminale, Servizio Interpol, Oggetto: Commissione Rogatoria Internazionale n. 50/90 del 5.11.1991 emessa dal Sig. Sampieri, Giudice Istruttore di Marsiglia/ Francia nei confronti di Giuseppe Liguori ed altri accusati di violazione alla legaislazione sugli stupefacenti ed altro, Roma December 10, 1991.

MI2   Ministero dell'Interno, Dipartimento della Pubblica Sicurezza, Ufficio Coordinamento e Pianificazione Forze di Polizia, Osservatorio Permanente Sulla Criminalità, Rapporto Annuale Sul Fenomeno Della Criminalità Organizzata per il 1995, "La donna nella criminalità organizzata, 1–87, ['Women in Italian Mafias'], May 1996.

MI3   Ministero dell'Interno, Dipartimento della Pubblica Sicurezza, Ufficio Coordinamento e Pianificazione Forze di Polizia, Osservatorio Permanente Sulla Criminalità, Parte IV, Argomento di Particolare Interesse, 273–343.

Secondary Sources

Ackerly, Brooke, and Jacqui True. *Doing Feminist Research in Political and Social Science*. London: Palgrave Macmillan, 2010.

Aldridge, Judith, and Juan Medina-Ariza. *Youth Gangs in an English City: Social Exclusion, Drugs, and Violence: Full Research Report ESRC End of Award Report*, RES-000-23-0615. Swindon: ESRC, 2007.

Allum, Felia. "Becoming a Camorrista: Criminal Culture and Life Choices in Naples." *Journal of Modern Italian Studies* 6, no. 3 (2001): 324–347.

Allum, Felia. *Camorristi, Politicians, and Businessmen: The Transformation of Organized Crime in Post-War Naples*. London: Routledge, 2006.

Allum, Felia. "Doing It for Themselves or Standing in for Their Men? Women in the Neapolitan Camorra (1950–2003)." In *Women and the Mafia*, edited by Giovanni *Fiandaca*. Amsterdam: Springer, 2007, 9–17.

Allum, Felia. *The Invisible Camorra: Neapolitan Crime Families across Europe*. Ithaca: Cornell University Press, 2016.

Allum, Felia. "Married to the Mob: What the Lives of Two Camorra Women Tell Us about How to Challenge the Power of the Mafia." *The Conversation*, December 18, 2022, https://theconversation.com/married-to-the-mob-what-the-lives-of-two-camorra-women-tell-us-about-how-to-challenge-the-power-of-the-mafia-193924.

Allum, Felia, and Irene Marchi. "Analyzing the Role of Women in Italian Mafias: The Case of the Neapolitan Camorra." *Qualitative Sociology* 41, no. 3 (2018): 361–380.

Allum, Felia, Isabella Clough Marinaro, and Rocco Sciarrone, eds. *Italian Mafias Today: Territory, Business, and Politics*. Chelmsford, UK: Edward Elgar, 2019.

Allum, Felia, and Anna Mitchel. *Graphic Narratives of Organised Crime, Gender, and Power in Europe: Discarded Footnotes*. London: Routledge, 2022.

Allum, Felia, and Luca Palermo. "Street Art: Young Italians Shake Camorra's Hold on Public Space." *The Conversation*, November 15, 2017, https://theconversation.com/street-art-young-italians-shake-camorras-hold-on-public-space-87267.

Allum, P. A. *Politics and Society in Post-War Naples*. Cambridge: Cambridge University Press, 1973.

Allum, P. A., ed. *Giuseppe Galasso, Intervista sulla storia di Napoli*. Bari: Laterza, 1978.

Ardituro, Antonello. *Lo Stato non ha vinto: la Camorra oltre I Casalesi*. Rome: Gius. Laterza & Figli, 2015.

Armao, Fabio. "Why Is Organized Crime So Successful." In *Organised Crime and the Challenge to Democracy*, edited by Felia Allum and Renata Siebert. Abingdon: Routledge, 2003, 27–38.

Arsovska, Jana, and Felia Allum, eds. "Women and Transnational Organized Crime." Special Issue, *Trends in Organized Crime* 17, no. 1 (2014): 1–15.

Badolati, Arcangelo. *Le 'Ndrangheta dell'Est, Profili Internazionali della Mafia Calabrese*. Coesenza: Luigi Pellegrini Editore, 2017.

Bakkali, Yusef. *Life on Road: Symbolic Struggle and the Munpain*. PhD diss., Sussex University, 2017, https://core.ac.uk/reader/151171210.

Bates, Laura. *Men Who Hate Women: From Incels to Pickup Artists, The Truth about Extreme Misogyny and How It Affects Us All*. Naperville, IL: Sourcebooks, 2021.

Beard, Mary. *Women and Power: A Manifesto Updated*. London: Profile Books, 2018.

Beare, Margaret E. *Women and Organized Crime*. Ottawa: Public Safety Canada, 2010.

Beatrice, Filippo. "Uno Stile Tipicamente Aziendale (Il Modello Impresa e la Criminalità Camorristica)." In *Questione giustizia*, Bimestrale promosso dalla Magistratura Democratica, Fascicolo 3. Milano: Franco Angeli, 2005, 1–11.

Behan, Tom. *The Camorra*. London: Routledge, 1996.

Behan, Tom. *See Naples and Die: The Camorra and Organised Crime*. London: I. B. Taurius, 2002.

Belknap, Joanna. *The Invisible Woman: Gender, Crime, and Justice*. Belmont, CA: Wadsworth, 2001.

Belmonte, Thomas. *The Broken Fountain*. New York: Columbia University Press, 2005.

Bruce, Berg, Qualitative Research Methods for the Social Sciences. 6th ed. Boston: Pearson Education, 2007

Bianchini, Roger-Louis. *Mafia Argent et Politique: Enquête sur des Liaisons Dangereuses dans le Midi*. Paris: Editions des Seuils, 1995.

Bodrero, Lorenzo. 2019. "The Rise and Fall of Mafia Women." Organized Crime and Corruption Reporting Project. https://www.occrp.org/en/blog/9642-the-rise-and-fall-of-mafia-women.

Bosisio, Antonio, Giovanni Nicolazzo, and Michele Ricciardi. "I Cambi di Proprietà delle Aziende Italiane durante l'Emergenza Covid-19: Trend e Fattori di Rischio." *Transcrime*, 2021, https://www.transcrime.it/wp-content/uploads/2021/05/Ownership-changes-report-1.pdf.

Bourdieu, Pierre. "The Forms of Capital." In *Handbook of Theory and Research for the Sociology of Education*, edited by John G. Richardson. Westport, CT: Greenwood, 1985, 241–258.

Brancaccio, Luciano. *I Clan di Camorra. Genesi e Storia*. Rome: Donzelli, 2017.

Brancaccio, Luciano. "Violent Contexts and Camorra Clans." In *Mafia Violence: Political, Symbolic, and Economic Forms of Violence in Camorra Clans,* edited by Monica Massari and Vittorio Martone. Abingdon, UK: Routledge, 2019, 135–153.

Brancaccio, Luciano, and Vittorio Martone. "The Camorras in Naples and Campania: Business, Groups and Families." In *Italy Mafias Today*, edited by Felia Allum, Isabella Clough Marinaro, and Rocco Sciarrone. Cheltenham, UK: Edward Elgar, 2019, 30–46.

Bright, David, Johan Koskinen, and Aili Malm. "Illicit Network Dynamics: The Formation and Evolution of a Drug Trafficking Network." *Journal of Quantitative Criminology* 35, no. 2 (2019): 237–258.

Camera di Commercio di Napoli. *Profilo economico della provincia di Napoli,* 2018, https://www.na.camcom.gov.it/index.php/crescita-dell-impresa/informazioni-statistiche-ed-economiche/profilo-economico-della-provincia-di-napoli.

Camera dei Deputati. XVI Legislatura, *Relazione sui programmi di protezione, sulla loro efficacia, e sulle modalita generali di applicazione per coloro che collaborano con la Giustizia* (Secondo Semester 2018), Doc XCI, 1, trasmessa il 13 agosto 2019, Rome.

Campana, Paolo, and Federico Varese. "Studying Organized Crime Networks: Data Sources, Boundaries, and the Limits of Structural Measures." *Social Networks*, 2020, file:///Users/mlsfsa/Downloads/Campana-and-Varese_2020_Studying_organized_crime_networks__-3.pdf.

Campbell, Anne. *The Girls in the Gangs*. 2nd ed. London: Blackwell, 1984.

Carabellese, Felice, Alan R. Felthous, Domenico Montalbò, Donatella La Tegola, Fulvio Carabellese, and Roberto Catanesi. "The Psychopathic Dimension in Women of Mafia." *International Journal of Law and Psychiatry* 74 (2021), https://doi.org/10.1016/j.ijlp.2020.101600.

Casini, Annalisa. "Glass Ceiling and Glass Elevator." In *The Wiley Blackwell Encyclopaedia of Gender and Sexuality Studies*, 5 vols, edited by Nancy Naples,

Renee Hoogland, C. Wickramasinghe, Wong Maithree, and Angela Wai Ching. Oxford: Blackwell, 2016, 1–2.

Catino, Maurizio. *Mafia Organizations: The Visible Hand of Criminal Enterprise.* Cambridge: Cambridge University Press, 2019.

Chesney-Lind, Meda. "Jailing "Bad" Girls." *Fighting for Girls: Critical Perspectives on Gender and Violence.* Albany: State University of New York Press, 2010, 57–79.

Chesney-Lind, Meda, and Lisa Pasko. *The Female Offender: Girls, Women, and Crime.* Thousand Oaks, CA: Sage, 2004.

Ciconte, Enzo. *Riti Criminali: I Codici di Affiliazione alla 'Ndrangheta.* Soveria Mannelli: Rubbettino Editore, 2015.

Cirrincione, Dario. *Figli dei Boss.* Milano: San Paolo, 2019.

Cockshott, Paul. *How the World Works: The Story of Human Labor from Prehistory to the Modern Day.* New York: Monthly Review Press, 2019.

Colletti, Alessandro. *Il Welfare e il Suo Doppio: Percorsi Etnografici nelle Camorre del Casertano.* Milan: Ledizioni, 2016.

Connell, Raewyn. "Introduction." *Gender.* 2nd ed. Cambridge: Polity Press, 2009.

Cottino, Antonio. "Sicilian Cultures of Violence: The Interconnections between Organized Crime and Local Society." *Crime, Law, and Social Change* 32, no. 2 (1999): 103–113.

Coward, Rosalind. *Patriarchal Precedents: Sexuality and Social Relations.* London: Routledge, 1983.

Criado Perez, Caroline. *Invisible Women: Exposing Data Bias in a World Designed for Men.* London: Vintage Books, 2019.

Daly, Kathleen, and Meda Chesney-Lind. "Feminism and Criminology." *Justice Quarterly* 5, no. 4 (1988): 497–538.

De Gregorio, Sergio. *I Nemici di Cutolo.* Napoli: Pironti, 1983.

Deuchar, Ross, Simon Harding, Robert McLean, and James A. Densley. "Deficit or Credit? A Comparative, Qualitative Study of Gender Agency and Female Gang Membership in Los Angeles and Glasgow." *Crime and Delinquency* 66, no. 8 (2020): 1087–1114.

Dino, Alessandra. "Women and Transnational Organised Crime: The Ambiguous Case of the Italian Mafias." In *The Routledge Handbook of Transational Organized Crime*, edited by Felia Allum and Stan Gilmour, 2nd ed. Abingdon, UK: Routledge, 2022, 354–370.

Dodge, Mary. "Women and White-Collar Crime." In *Oxford Research Encyclopaedia of Criminology and Criminal Justice, A Community of Scholars*, edited by Henry N. Pontell. Oxford: Oxford University Press, 2019.

Enzensberger, Hans Magnus. "Pupetta o la fine della Nuova Camorra." In *Politica e Crimine, Nove saggi.* Rome: Bollati Boringhieri, 1998.

Feinman, Clarice. *Women in the Criminal Justice System.* Santa Barbara, CA: ABC-CLIO, 1986.

Ferrell, Jeff. "Ghost Method." In *Ghost Criminology: The Afterlife of Crime and Punishment*, edited by Michael Fiddler, Theo Kindynis, and Travis Linnemann. New York: New York University Press, 2022, 67–87.

Fleetwood, Jennifer, and Gary R. Potter. "Ethnographic Research on Crime and Control: Editors' Introduction." *Methodological Innovations* 10, no. 1 (2017): 1–4.

Fleisher, Mark S. *Dead End Kids, Gang Girls, and the Boys They Know.* Madison: University of Wisconsin Press, 2000.

Figurato, Marisa, and Francesco Marolda. *Storia di Contrabbando: Napoli 1945–1981*, Napoli: Tullio Pironti Editore, 1981.

Gallhier, John F., and James A. Cain. "Citation Support for the Mafia Myth in Criminology Textbooks." *American Sociologist*, 9, no. 2 (1974): 68–74.

Gambetta, Diego. *The Sicilian Mafia: The Business of Private Protection*. Princeton: Princeton University Press, 1993.

Gambetta, Diego. *Codes of the Underworld*. Princeton: Princeton University Press, 2011.

Garofalo, Sabrina, and Giovanna Vingelli. "Masculinity in Crisis? Men's Accounts of Masculinity, Power, and Gendered Relations in Contemporary Cosenza." In *Reimagining Masculinities: Beyond Masculinist Epistemology*, edited by Frank G. Karioris and Cassandra Loeser. Oxford: Inter-Disciplinary Press, 2014, 141–163.

Goddard, Victoria. *Gender, Family, and Work in Naples*. London: Berg, 1996.

Ghodsee, Kristen. *From Notes to Narrative, Writing Ethnographies that Everyone Can Read*. Chicago: Chicago University of Press, 2016.

Giddens, Anthony. *The Constitution of Society: Outline of the Theory of Structuration*. Cambridge: Polity Press, 1986.

Giuliano, Nunzio. *Dario di una Coscienza*, edited by Maria Rosaria Riviecco and Roberto Marrone. Napoli: Tullio Pironti, 2006.

Grace, Sharon, Maggie O'Neill, Tammi Walker, Hannah King, Lucy Baldwin, Alison Jobe, Orla Lynch, Fiona Measham, Kate O'Brien, and Vicky Seaman. *Criminal Women: Gender Matters*. Bristol, UK: Bristol University Press, 2022.

Gribaudi, Gabriella. *Donne, Uomini, Famiglie: Napoli nel Novecento*. Vol. 1. Napoli: L'Ancora del Mediterraneo, 1999.

Gribaudi, Gabriella. "Donne di Camorra e Identità di Genere." In *Donne di Mafia*, edited by Gabriella Gribaudi and Marcello Marmo. Meridiana Rivista di Storia e Scienze Sociali, 67. Roma: Viella, 2010, 145–154.

Gribaudi, Gabriella. "The Use of Violence and Gender Dynamics within Camorra Clans." In *Mafia Violence*, edited by Monica Massari and Vittorio Martone. Abingdon, UK: Routledge, 2019, 236–249.

Gribaudi, Gabriella, and Marcella Marmo, eds. *Donne di Mafia,* Meridiana Rivista di Storia e Scienze Sociali, 67, Roma: Viella, 2010.

Griffiths, Neil. *Betrayal in Naples*. London: Penguin, 2005.

Gutierrez Rivera, Lirio, and Luisa Delgado Mejia. "Agency in Contexts of Violence and Crime: Coping Strategies of Women Community Leaders vis-à-vis Criminal Groups in Medellín, Colombia." *Journal of Illicit Economies and Development* 4, no. 3 (2022): 282–295, https://jied.lse.ac.uk/articles/10.31389/jied.130/.

Haynes, Natalie. *Pandora's Jar: Women in the Greek Myths*. London: Picador.

Heyl, Barbara Sherman. "Ethnographic Interviewing." In *Handbook of Ethnography*, edited by Paul Atkinson, Sara Delamont, Amanda Coffey, John Lofland, and Lyn Lofland. London: Sage, 2001, 369–383.

Heywood, Andrew. *Key Concepts in Politics*. Basingstoke: Palgrave, 2000.

Hobbs, Dick. *Lush Life: Constructing Organised Crime in the UK*. Oxford: Oxford University Press, 2013.

Hofstede, Geert, and Willem A. Arrindell. *Masculinity and Femininity: The Taboo Dimension of National Cultures*. London: Sage, 1998.

Hume, Mo, and Polly Wilding. "Beyond Agency and Passivity: Situating a Gendered Articulation of Urban Violence in Brazil and El Salvador." *Urban Studies* 57, no. 2 (2020): 249–266, https://doi. org/10.1177/0042098019829391.

Ingrascì, Ombretta. "Women in the 'Ndrangheta: The Serraino-Di Giovine Case." In *Women and the Mafia*, edited by Giovanni *Fiandaca*. New York: Springer, 2007, 47–52.

Ingrascì, Ombretta. "Donne, 'Ndrangheta, 'ndrine. Gli spazi Femminili nelle Fonti Giudiziarie." In *Donne di Mafia,* Meridiana Rivista di Storia e Scienze Sociali, 67 edited by Gabriella Gribaudi and Marcella Marmo. Roma: Viella, 2010, 35–54.

Ingrascì, Ombretta. *Gender and Organized Crime in Italy: Women's Agency in Italian Mafias.* London: Bloomsbury Academic, 2021.

Istat. "Il Censimento permanente della populazione in Campania." 2019, https://www.istat.it/it/archivio/253433.

Istat. "Comunicato Stampa, Autori e Vittime di Omicidio." 2021, https://www.istat.it/it/archivio/253296.

Jacquemet, Marco. "Namechasers." *American Ethnologist* 19, no. 4 (1992): 733–748.

Jacquemet, Marco. *Credibility in Court: Communicative Practices in the Camorra Trial.* Cambridge: Cambridge University Press, 1996.

Jamieson, Alison. *The Antimafia: Italy's Fight against Organized Crime.* New York: Macmillan Press, 2000.

Jones, Nikki. "Working 'the Code': On Girls, Gender, and Inner-City Violence." *Australia and New Zealand Journal of Criminology* 4, no. 1 (2008): 63–83.

Jones, Nikki. *Between Good and Ghetto: African America Girls and Inter-City Violence.* London: Rutgers University Press, 2010.

Kandiyoti, Deniz. "Bargaining with Patriarchy." *Gender and Society*, Special Issue to Honour Jessie Bernard, 2, no. 3 (1988): 274–290.

Kara, Helen. *Creative Research Methods in the Social Sciences: A Practical Guide.* Bristol: Policy Press, 2015.

Kincheloe, Joe L. "On to the Next Level: Continuing the Conceptualization of the Bricolage." In *Key Works in Critical Pedagogy.* Leiden: Brill, 2011, 253–277.

Kintrea, Keith, Jon Bannister, Jon Pickering, Maggie Reid, and Naofumi Suzuki. *Young People and Territoriality in British Cities.* York, UK: Joseph Rowntree Foundation 6, 2008, https://herd.typepad.com/files/2278-young-people-territoriality.pdf.

Kimmel, Michael S. *The Gendered Society.* New York: Oxford University Press, 2000.

Khan, Milka, and Anne Véron. *Women of Honor: Madonnas, Godmothers, and Informers in the Italian Mafia.* Oxford: Oxford University Press, 2017.

Latza Nadeau, Barbie. *The Godmother: Murder, Vengeance, and the Bloody Struggle of Mafia Women.* London: Penguin, 2022.

Ledeen, Michael A. *Virgil's Golden Egg and Other Neapolitan Miracles: An Investigation into the Sources of Creativity.* Abingdon: Routledge, 2017.

Lenz Kothe, E. "Inquiry while Being in Relation: Flâneurial Walking as a Creative Research Method." In *The Flâneur and Education Research: A Metaphor for Knowing, Being Ethical, and New Data Production,* edited by Alexandra Lasczik Cutcher and Rita Irwin. London: Palgrave Studies in Movement across Education, the Arts and the Social Sciences. Palgrave Pivot, Cham, 2018, 29–57.

Levi, Michael, Hans Nelen, and Francien Lankhorst. "Lawyers as Crime Facilitators in Europe: An Introduction and Overview." *Crime Law and Social Change* 42 (2005): 117–121.

Longrigg, Clare. *Mafia Women.* London: Vintage, 1997.

Luci, Nita. "Endangering Masculinity in Kosovo: Can Albanian Qomen Say No?" *Anthropology of East Europe Review* 20, no. 2 (2002): 71–79, file:///Users/mlsfsa/Downloads/458-Article%20Text-2033-1-10-20100420-1.pdf.

Marsh, Brendan. *The Logic of Violence: An Ethnography of Dublin's Illegal Drug Trade.* Abingdon: Routledge, 2019.

Mazerolle, Paul. "The Poverty of a Gender-Neutral Criminology: Introduction to the Special Issue on Current Approaches to Understanding Female Offenders." *Australian and New Zealand Journal of Criminology* 41, no. 1 (2008): 1–8.

Melillo, Giovanni. "Organizzazioni criminali, modelli di impresa e mercati." In *Organizzazioni criminali. Strategie e modelli di business nell'economia legale*, edited by Stefano Consiglio, Paolo Canonico, Ernesto De Nito, and Gianluigi Mangia. Rome: Donzelli Editore, 2019, 3–21.

Messerschmidt, James W. "On Gang Girls, Gender, and a Structured Action Theory: A Reply to Miller." *Theoretical Criminology* 6, no. 4 (2002): 461–475.

Mies, Maria. *Patriarchy and Accumulation on a World Scale: Women in the International Division of Labour*. London: Bloomsbury, 2022.

Miller, Jody. *One of the Guys, Girls, Gags, and Gender*. Oxford: Oxford University Press, 2001.

Monnier, Marc. *La Camorra, Saggio Introduttivo*, edited by Felia Allum and Alessandro Colletti. Perugia: Edizioni di Storia e Studi Sociali, 2014 (1863).

Moran, Michael. *Politics and Governance in the UK*. Basingstoke, UK: Palgrave Macmillan, 2005.

Morselli, Carlo, ed. *Inside Criminal Networks*. Vol. 8. New York: Springer, 2009.

Morselli, Carlo, ed. *Crime and Networks*. Abingdon: Routledge, 2013.

Mottola, Giorgio. *Camorra Nostra*. Roma: Sperling & Kupfer, 2017.

Naffine, Nagaire. *Female Crime: The Construction of Crime*. London: Allen & Unwin, 1987.

National Crime Agency. *High End Money Laundering, Strategy and Action Plan*. 2014, https://www.nationalcrimeagency.gov.uk/who-we-are/publications/16-high-end-money-laundering-strategy/file.

National Crime Agency. *National Strategic Assessment of Serious and Organised Crime*. 2018, https://www.nationalcrimeagency.gov.uk/who-we-are/publications/173-national-strategic-assessment-of-serious-and-organised-crime-2018/file.

Nicaso, Antonio, and Marcel Danesi. *Made Men: Mafia Culture and the Power of Symbols, Rituals, and Myth*. Lanham, MD: Rowman & Littlefield, 2013.

Nicaso, Antonio, and Marcel Danesi. *Organized Crime: A Cultural Introduction*. Abingdon, UK: Routledge, 2021.

Nussbaum, Martha C. *Creating Capabilities: The Human Development Approach*. Cambridge, MA: The Belknap Press of Harvard University Press, 2011.

Orum, Anthony M., Joe R. Feagin, and Gideon Sjoberg. "Introduction: The Nature of the Case Study." In *A Case for the Case Study*, edited by Joe R. Feagin, Anthony M. Orum, and Gideon Sjoberg. Chapel Hill: University of North Carolina Press, 1991, 1–26.

Palaganas, Erlinda C., Marian C. Sanchez, Visitacion P. Molintas, and Ruel D. Caricativo. "Reflexivity in Qualitative Research: A Journey of Learning." *Qualitative Report* 22, no. 2 (2017): 246–438.

Palinkas, L. A., S. M. Horwitz, C. A. Green, J. P. Wisdom, N. Duan, and K. Hoagwood. "Purposeful Sampling for Qualitative Data Collection and Analysis in Mixed Method Implementation Research." *Adm Policy Mental Health* 42, no. 5 (2015): 533–544.

Parsons, Anne. *Belief, Magic, and Anomie: Essays in Psychosocial Anthropology*. New York: Free Press, 1969.

Peacock, James L., and Dorothy C. Holland. "The Narrated Self: Life Stories in Process." *Ethos* 21, no. 4 (1993): 367–383.

Pickering-Iazzi, Robin. *The Mafia in Italian Lives and Literature, Life Sentences and Their Geographies*. Toronto: University of Toronto Press, 2015.

Pine, Jason. *The Art of Making Do in Naples*. Minneapolis: University of Minnesota Press, 2012.

Pitts, John. *Reluctant Gangsters: Youth Gangs in Waltham Forest*. Luton, UK: University of Bedfordshire, 2007, 1–107, https://www.wfcw.org/docs/reluctant-gangsters.pdf.

Pizzini-Gambetta, Valeria. "Women and the Mafia: A Methodology Minefield." *Global Crime* 9, no. 4 (2008): 348–353.

Pizzini-Gambetta, Valeria. "Women in Gomorrah." *Global Crime* 10, no. 3 (2009): 267–271.

Pizzini-Gambetta, Valeria. "Organized Crime: The Gender Constraints of Illegal Markets." In *The Oxford Handbook of Gender, Sex, and Crime*, edited by Rosemary Gartner and Bill McCarthy. Oxford: Oxford University Press, 2014, 448–467.

Principato, Teresa, and Alessandra Dino. *Mafia donna: le vestali del sacro e dell'onore*. Vol. 20. Palermo: Flaccovio Editore, 1997.

Rahman, Mohammed, Robert McLean, Robert Deuchar, and James Densley. "Who Are the Enforcers? The Motives and Methods of Muscle for Hire in West Scotland and the West Midlands." *Trends in Organized Crime* 25, no. 2 (2020): 1–22.

Rawlinson, Patricia. "Mafia, Methodology, and Alien Culture." In *Doing Research on Crime and Justice*, edited by Roy E. King and Emma Wincup. Oxford: Oxford University Press, 2000, 351–362.

Rawlinson, Patricia. 'Look Who's Talking: Interviewing Russian Criminals." *Trends in Organized Crime* 11, no. 1 (2008): 12–20.

Reuter, Peter, and Letizia Paoli. "How Similar Are Modern Criminal Syndicates to Traditional Mafias?" *Crime and Justice* 49, no. 1 (2020): 223–287.

Richardson, Laurel. *Fields of Play: Constructing an Academic Life*. New Brunswick, NJ: Rutgers University Press, 1997.

Ruggiero, Vincenzo. *Organized and Corporate Crime in Europe: Offers That Can't Be Refused*. Aldershot, UK: Dartmouth, 1996.

Ruggiero, Vincenzo. "Introduction: Fuzzy Criminal Actors." *Crime, Law, and Social Change* 37, no. 3 (2002): 177–190.

Saar, Maarja, and Hannes Palang. "The Dimensions of Place Meanings." *Living Reviews in Landscape Research* 3, no. 3 (2009): 5–24, http://lrlr.landscapeonline.de/Articles/lrlr-2009-3/download/lrlr-2009-3Color.pdf.

Sales, Isaia. *La Camorra e le Camorre*. Roma: Editori Riuniti, 1988.

Sales, Isaia. *Le Strade della Violenza: Malviventi e bande di camorra a Napoli*. Napoli: L'Ancora del Mediterraneo, 2006.

Saviano, Roberto. *Gomorrah: Italy's Other Mafia*. London: Macmillan, 2007.

Saviano, Roberto, *La Paranza dei bambini*. Roma: Feltrinelli, 2016.

Sciarrone, Rocco, ed. *Alleanza nell'Ombra: Mafie ed economie locali in Sicilia e nel Mezzogiorno*. Roma, Donzelli Editore, 2011.

Sciarrone, Rocco. "Mafie, relazioni e affari nell'area grigia." In *Alleanza nell'Ombra: Mafie ed economie locali in Sicilia e nel Mezzogiorno*, edited by Rocco Sciarrone. Roma: Donzelli Editore, 2011, 3–43.

Scott, Joan Wallach. *Gender and the Politics of History*. Rev. ed. New York: Colombia University Press, 1999.

Schneider, Jane, and Peter Schneider. "Mafia, Antimafia, and the Plural Cultures of Sicily." *Current Anthropology* 46, no. 4 (2005): 501–520.

Selmini, Rossella. "Women in Organized Crime." *Crime and Justice* 49, no. 1 (2020): 339–383.

Shen, Anqi. "Women Who Participate in Illegal Pyramid Selling: Voices from Female Rural Migrant Offenders in China." *Asian Journal of Criminology* 15 (2020): 91–107.

Siani, Giancarlo. *Giancarlo Siani: Il Corraggio della Cronaca*, edited by Amato Lamberti. Salerno: Metafora Edizioni, 1991.

Siebert, Renata. *Secrets of Life and Death: Women and the Mafia*. London: Verso, 1996.

Siegel, Dina. "Conversations with Russian Mafiosi." *Trends in Organized Crime* 11, no. 1 (2008): 21–29.

Siegel, Dina. "Women in Transnational Organized Crime." *Trends in Organized Crime* 17, no. 1–2 (2014): 52–65.

Siegel, Dina, and S. de Blank. "Women Who Traffic Women: The Role of Women in Human Trafficking Networks—Dutch Cases." *Global Crime* 11 (2010): 436–447.

Smith, Chris M. *Syndicate Women: Gender and Networks in Chicago Organized Crime*. Berkeley: University of California Press, 2019.

Tavory, Iddo. "Interviews and Inference: Making Sense of Interview Data in Qualitative Research." *Qualitative Sociology* 43, no. 4 (2020): 449–465.

Tewksbury, Richard. "Qualitative versus Quantitative Methods: Understanding Why Qualitative Methods Are Superior for Criminology and Criminal Justice." *Journal of Theoretical and Philosophical Criminology* 1, no. 1 (2009), 38–58.

Thompson, Paul A. "Pioneering the Life Story Method." *International Journal of Social Research Methodology* 7, no. 1 (2004): 81–84.

Van Dijk, Meintje, Veronni Eichelsheim, Edwards Kleemans, Melvin Soudijn, and Steve Van de Weijer. "Intergenerational Continuity of Crime among Children of Organizational Crime Offenders in the Netherlands." *Crime, Law, and Social Change* 77, no. 2 (2021): 207–227.

Van Maanen, John. *Tales of the Field: On Writing Ethnography*. 2nd ed. Chicago: Chicago University Press, 2011.

Varese, Federico. *The Russian Mafia: Private Protection in a New Market Economy*. Oxford: Oxford University Press, 2001.

Varese, Federico, eds. *Organized Crime*. London: Routledge, 2010.

Varese, Federico. *Mafia Life: Love, Death, and Money at Heart of Organised Crime*. London: Profile Books, 2017.

Venkatesh, Sudhir. *Gang Leader for a Day: A Rogue Sociologist Takes to the Streets*. London: Penguin, 2008.

Venkatesh, Sudhir. *Floating City: A Rogue Sociologist Lost and Found in New York's Underground Economy*. New York: Penguin, 2013.

Von Lampe, Klaus. "Introduction to the Special Issue on Interviewing 'Organized Criminals.'" *Trends in Organized Crime* 11 (2008): 1–4.

Whyte, William F. *Street Corner Society: The Social Structure of an Italian Slum*. Chicago: University of Chicago Press, 2012.

Windle, James, and Andrew Silke. "Is Drawing from the State 'State of the Art'? A Review of Organised Crime Research Data Collection and Analysis, 2004–2018." *Trends in Organized Crime* 22, no. 4 (2019): 394–413.

Wolf, Naomi. *The Beauty Myth*. London: Vintage Books, 1991.

Zaccaria, Anna Maria. "Donne di camorra." In *Traffici criminali: Camorra, mafie e reti internazionali dell' illegalità*, edited by Gabriella Gribaudi. Turin: Bollati Boringhieri, 2009, 280–309.

Zaccaria, Anna Maria. "L'emergenza rosa: dati e suggestioni sulle donne di camorra" In *Donne di Mafia*, edited by Gabriella Gribaudi and Marcella Marmo. Meridiana Rivista di Storia e Scienze Sociali 67, Roma: Viella, 2010, 155–173.

Zaccaria, Anna Maria. "Donne Fuori Luogo. Camorra e profili femminili." *Fuori Luogo. Journal of Sociology of Territory, Tourism, Technology* 1, no. 1 (2017): 81–99.

Zhang, Sheldon X., Ko-Lin Chin, and Jody Miller. "Women's Participation in Chinese Transnational Human Smuggling: A Gendered Market Perspective." *Criminology* 45, no. 3 (2007): 699–733.

Films/documentaries

Belve. Writer and director, Francesca Fagnani. Rai 2, https://www.raiplay.it/video/2022/06/Anna-Carrino---Belve-04062021-ea3dfecd-1d02-4077-a59e-0542103e3e17.html. May 29, 2021.

ES17. Written by Diana Ligorio and Conchita Sannino; editor, Emiliano Bechi Gabrielli; idea of Roberto Saviano, https://www.emisevenmedia.com/project/es17-baby-gans-in-naples/. 2018.

Gomorrah. Director, Matteo Garrone. Rai Cinema, Rome. 2008.

Il Prezzo, Le donne della mafia. Writer and director, Francesca Fagnani. Rai 3, https://www.raiplay.it/video/2018/09/Il-Prezzo-5391739d-6164-4258-b056-4963dad0c428.html. September 19, 2018.

Robinù, I veri ragazzi della Gomorra. Director, Michele Santoro. 2016.

La Sfida. Director, Francesco Rosi. 1958.

Index

active agents of history, 191
active participation, 74, 189
affiliation ritual, 17, 63, 88
Afragola, 47, 49, 173, 176
agency xii, xiv, xv, 2–9, 107, 177, 184–190
  agencyless, 74, 166
  criminal, 33, 37, 49, 62, 64, 70–72, 107, 145
  female, 18, 26–28, 71–72, 163–166, 167–170, 192–193
  foot soldiers, 119, 121, 130
  Ingrasci, Ombretta, 6, 184
  leaders, 145–146, 148, 153
  Longo, Rita, 187
  managers, 135–136, 139, 144
  Maresca, Assunta/Pupetta, 50–53, 55
Alfieri, Carmine, 93
Alfieri Confederation, 15, 93, 195, 211n60
alliances, 2, 15, 93–94, 106, 133, 161
alternative voices, 197
Amato-Pagano clan, 1, 66, 99, 110, 188
Ammaturo, Umberto, 54–55
ambassador, 133
antimafia associations, 21
antimafia National prosecutor, 16, 145
antimafia prosecutors, 5, 8, 12, 18, 32, 36, 152, 207n68
army
  of drug pushers/dealers, 127–128
  foot soldiers, 119–131
  of minors, 99
  reserve, 3, 132
  street, 119
  of subordinates, 44
  of women, 45, 58, 116, 120
  of workers, 131
Arrivoli, Giovanna, 103, 217n97
associates, 35, 49, 70, 80, 69, 138–139
  Camorra space, 8, 16, 72–74, 113, 160
  criminal, 49–54, 117
  Esposito, Antonio, 50–51, 54
  familial, 72, 75, 77, 82
  gray zone, 16, 72, 73, 74–75, 77, 81
  Licciardi, Maria, 113–114
  See also foot soldiers
autonomous, 2, 71, 138, 145–146, 159, 170

autonomy, 62, 64, 127, 128, 135, 137, 152
Avellino, 9, 18, 31, 32

baby gangs, 99, 182
Bakkali, Yusuf, 20
Bardellino, Antonio, 56, 59
bargaining with patriarchy, 28, 192
bassi (ground floor flats), 48, 119, 127, 138
Bates, Laura, 166
Beatrice, Filippo, xix, 2, 201n11, 203n65, 208n68
Belmonte, Thomas, 3, 91–2
betrayal, 91, 101, 148, 173
  by women, 159
black economy, 12, 120, 131
blood, 90, 198, 117, 142
  family, 16, 72, 93–94, 99, 106, 136, 149
  relatives, 17, 94, 100, 132
  ties, 15–18, 27, 52, 63, 72, 77, 78, 85, 91, 94, 98, 106, 115, 121, 125, 142, 148, 172
Bologna, 38
Bourdieu, Pierre, 27
Brancaccio, Luciano, 13, 89, 94
British National Crime Agency (NCA), 76
businesswoman, 86, 142, 153

Calabria, 1–2
Caldarelli clan, 122, 124
Campbell, Anne, 33–34
Camorra (Neapolitan)
  definitions of, 1, 3, 9, 13–17
  family, 67, 94–95, 101, 107, 122, 148–149
  foot soldiers, 119–124
  ideology, 88
  leaders, 151
  masculine, 111, 165, 173
  managers, 134
  membership, 17, 36, 39
  mother figures, 94–95, 99, 182
  recruitment, 71, 119
  women, 18, 29
  values, 43, 66–67, 90, 94–95, 101, 149, 161, 181
  wives, 3, 5, 7, 18, 59, 65–67, 69, 82, 86, 90, 94–104, 110, 115, 119, 124, 133, 137, 141, 150, 155, 176, 181, 186, 188–189

www.ingramcontent.com/pod-product-compliance
Lightning Source LLC
Chambersburg PA
CBHW051728260326
41914CB00040B/2023/J